Hidden Facts Behind British India's Freedom

Hidden Facts Behind British India's Freedom:

A Scholarly Look into Allama Mashraqi and Quaid-e-Azam's Political Conflict

By grandson of Allama Mashraqi:
Nasim Yousaf

Table of Contents

Acknowledgements   11
Important Notes   13
About the Author   15
Introduction   19
Background   21

Chapter 1   27
Allama Mashraqi's Life of Struggle

Chapter 2   41
The Khaksar Tehreek & Uprise of the Nation for Freedom

Chapter 3   55
The Muslim League's Efforts to Exploit the Khaksar Tehreek's Power

Chapter 4   71
The British & Muslim League's Attempts to Wipe Out the Khaksar Tehreek

Chapter 5   109
Mashraqi Released - Efforts for United Front for Freedom

Chapter 6   149
Mashraqi's Efforts for Jinnah-Gandhi Meeting

Chapter 7   183
Mashraqi's Endeavors After Failure of Jinnah-Gandhi Talks

Chapter 8   203
Another Attempt to Eliminate the Khaksar Tehreek -
1945-46 Elections & Khaksar Constitution

Chapter 9   227
Towards Freedom

Chapter 10   241
Break-up of British India

Chapter 11   271
Consequences of Partition

Chapter 12   283
Conclusion: All India Muslim League's Thirst for Power

Epilogue   303

Photographs   305

Appendices

Appendix I   353
Bogus Attack on Quaid-e-Azam by a Muslim Leaguer

Appendix II   371
Muslim League as Seen in Late Thirties & Forties

Appendix III   385

Appendix IV   387

Appendix V   391
Mashraqi's Address: Where Leaders Fail
A Dispassionate Dissection of Indian Politics from a Non-Party Point of View

Appendix VI   401
Outline of the Agreed Khaksar Constitution
Other Features of the Constitution
Members

Appendix VII   411
1937 Elections

Bibiography, Glossary & Index

Works Cited & Bibliography   415
Glossary   421
Index   423

This book is dedicated to my
beloved father and mother

Mohammad Yousaf Khan and Masuda Yousaf

Acknowledgements

I would like to thank my wife, Ambereen, for her encouragement and support and my children, Mehreen, Zain and Myra for their help. I especially owe a greater gratitude to my daughter, Mehreen, without whose help this extensive assignment would not have materialized.

Important Notes

This book MUST be read in its entirety to clearly understand how the Indian sub-continent's history has been distorted.

The following are spelled in several different ways including:

Mashraqi; Mashriqi; Mashraqui; Mashriqui
Al-Mashriqi; El-Mashriqi
Khaksar; Khaksaar
Tehreek; Tehrik; Tehrique
The Khaksar Tehreek is also known as the Khaksar Movement.

About the Author

The author, Nasim Yousaf, was born in Pakistan. He started his career as a Pilot Officer in the Pakistan Air Force. However, within a few years, he resigned and established his export business in Pakistan. As a result of his hard work and dedication toward his profession, he achieved success at a very young age. At age thirty three, he became a member of the Board of Directors of a public limited company, The Pakistan Commercial Exporters of Towels Association (PCETA). He also held other important positions with the said Association. He gained valuable experience as he traveled the world in connection with his business. In the late 1980s, Mr. Yousaf decided to close down his flourishing business and moved to the USA.

For the past decade, the author has devoted a significant portion of his time to conducting research on Pakistan and India's freedom movement. In pursuit of his quest to find the truth behind the creation of Pakistan and India, he has visited various world-renowned research and academic libraries in the USA, Canada and the U.K. As a result of his study, he has been able to produce a number of articles and books for academia and the mainstream.

Mr. Yousaf possesses in-depth knowledge and insight into the events that led to the independence of British India. In his academic and scholarly works, he has incorporated knowledge from his extensive research on British India's freedom as well as from being a part of a political family. The author's works focus on Allama Mashraqi and the Khaksar Tehreek (Movement)'s role in the independence of British India. These works are ready-reference resources for historians, authors, journalists, political analysts, educationists or any person interested in the history of the Indian sub-continent.

The author is indeed different from many other writers. He brings to the table a varied set of experiences and has written books in two entirely different categories: academic and scholarly, as mentioned, and business resource, specifically import and export.

Mr. Yousaf's books on import and export are a result of his knowledge on international business, which he acquired through his association with trade, as well as his extensive travel around the world. His works are reference resources, particularly helpful for people who are new to the import/export business. These books are not generic guides on starting an import or export business, but rather aim to help individuals get started right away in a specific line of business. This differentiates Mr. Yousaf's books from other such resources.

Mr. Yousaf's works include the following:

Academic & Scholarly Books:

❖ *Allama Mashriqi & Dr. Akhtar Hameed Khan: Two Legends of Pakistan*
❖ *Pakistan's Freedom and Allama Mashriqi: Statements, Letters, Chronology of Khaksar Tehrik (Movement), Period: Mashriqi's Birth to 1947*
❖ *Pakistan's Birth & Allama Mashraqi: Chronology & Statements, Period: 1947- 1963*

Import & Export Books:

❖ *Import & Export of Apparel & Textiles; Part I: Export to USA, Part II: Import from Pakistan*
❖ *Import & Export of Hand Knotted Oriental Rugs: Part I: Export to USA, Part II Import from Pakistan*
❖ *Export Housewares, Gifts and Decorative Accessories to the United States of America*
❖ *Importing Gifts, Housewares & Decorative Accessories from Hong Kong*

Articles & Research Papers:

❖ "Pakistan Resolution and the Massacre of the Khaksars"
❖ "41st Death Anniversary In Memory of Allama Mashriqi"
❖ "7th Death Anniversary a Tribute to Dr. Akhter Hameed Khan"
❖ "Allama Mashraqi and the Unity of Mankind"
❖ "Freedom of British India through the Lens of the Khaskar Movement"

Forthcoming Books, Articles & Research Papers:

The author is currently working on additional books and articles:

❖ Tentative title: *Government of British India & Allama Mashraqi's Khaksar Tehreek (Movement)*
❖ Tentative title: *Import from Pakistan*
❖ Tentative title: "All-India Muslim League—A Tool in British Hands"

For updates on the author's works, visit the following web sites:

- ❖ http://www.nasimyousaf.info
- ❖ http://www.nasimyousaf.8m.com

The author's works are also listed on these web sites dedicated to Allama Mashraqi and Dr. Akhtar Hameed Khan:

Web sites on Allama Mashraqi:

- ❖ http://www.allamamashraqi.com
- ❖ http://www.allamamashriqi.info

Web site on Dr. Akhtar Hameed Khan:

- ❖ http://www.akhtar-hameed-khan.8m.com

Introduction

For a long time, I have been pondering over the idea of writing about the relationship between the Khaksar Tehreek and the All India Muslim League (AIML) in the context of the Indian subcontinent's freedom movement. This is an extremely sensitive subject as in the process of discussion, criticism on respected Quaid-e-Azam Muhammad Ali Jinnah (founder of Pakistan) is bound to occur. In my biography of Allama Mashraqi, *Allama Mashriqi & Dr. Akhtar Hameed Khan: Two Legends of Pakistan*, I refrained from discussing this subject because I was conscious of the fact that people would not be able to digest criticism on the high command of AIML, particularly on Quaid-e-Azam. Based on this apprehension, it took me a long time to decide whether to write on this delicate subject.

From a historical point of view, it is extremely important to unearth many hidden realities of British India's independence movement. I feel that I will fail in my duty towards my brethren in both countries (Pakistan and India), if I do not apprise them of many buried facts of British India's freedom that I am aware of. Furthermore, Pakistan is currently undergoing a very critical stage, and unless it mends its ways, it is heading toward further disintegration. Under the circumstances, it is even more important for people to know the unknown facts of their history so that they can learn from the mistakes of the past. Therefore, though confounded, I finally decided to write on this topic.

My knowledge on British India's independence movement comes not only from being part of a political family but through the extensive research I have been conducting for nearly a decade. It is further validated by what I have learned from Khaksars and my analysis of political events (before and after partition). This work primarily sheds light on the relationship between the Khaksar Tehreek and AIML. In doing so, it also enlightens the reader about Allama Mashraqi's efforts towards the unity he sought between Muslims and non-Muslims, so that the designs of rulers would not materialize. In addition, this work informs people on how imperialists met their agenda of weakening the Muslims. From the War of Independence in 1857 in India, to the dissolution of the Ottoman Empire to the division of British India, only time will tell how far this will go.

Before I proceed any further, I would like to categorically state that the intent of this work is not to disparage, condemn or demean anyone, including the respected Quaid-e-Azam, who is, after all, the father of the nation. And after reading this book, some people might think I am anti-Pakistan or anti-Quaid-e-Azam Muhammad Ali Jinnah. I emphatically and zealously proclaim to be neither anti-Pakistan nor anti-Quaid-e-Azam.

This book presents the view of the nationalists of British India. Since the topic of this book is sensitive, it cannot be written without highlighting some negatives of the All India Muslim League (AIML). This book will, indeed, open the reader's eyes to the reality of British India's independence movement. I ask people to put aside their feelings and read this work from an academic and unbiased perspective, and I ask that they examine, with an open mind, the history surrounding the sub-continent's freedom movement, so that they can learn from past mistakes and brighten the future of the people in the region.

This work is purely for the purpose of academic study. If, in its discussion, I hurt anyone's feelings, which is possible, I ask for forgiveness from the deepest core of my heart.

Background

Most Pakistanis seem to subscribe to the theory that the AIML is the sole creator of Pakistan; this is quite untrue. In fact, the independence movement was not carried out alone by the AIML. The Khaksar Tehreek (Khaksar Movement) played a vital role towards freedom and dominated the politics of the Muslims in India for an extended period of time. Furthermore, as this book will show, the Muslim League actually played in the hands of the British.

In order to fully understand the events detailed in the book, one first needs to study a bit of history of the sub-continent. It is also important to learn more regarding the early beginnings of the Muslim League. Thus, the following is a brief synopsis of the early history of India. It should provide greater context for the events that took place later and is essential to the understanding of this book.

*****

If we study the history of the sub-continent from the fall of the Mughal Empire onwards, we realize that Muslims were reduced from a nation of heroes to a nation of subordinates and slaves, in a mental sense. They regressed from having a superiority complex to suffering from an acute inferiority complex. How did this happen?

After the fall of the Mughal Empire, the British took over. They attempted to weaken the Muslims, who had ruled India for almost 1,000 years. Meanwhile the Muslims in India continued to live in fools' paradise. They were too enamored by their glorious past to wake up and face reality. They refrained from seeking basic education and from moving towards the learning of sciences or trade.

The affluent Muslim class lived on the wealth that they had inherited during the Mughal era, including land, jewels and gold. Many of their properties were sold to Hindus at low prices. As a result, the Muslims lost such means of subsistence by sitting idle. By and large, Muslims avoided being part of the Indian administration because they were egoistic and hated to be servants or slaves of the British. The Hindus filled those positions and were obviously encouraged by the British to do so. Whatever the reasons were, Muslims kept themselves aloof and remained ignorant but proud of their rich culture, heritage and civilization.

Hatred toward British rule led to the War of Independence in 1857. This was a revolt against the British and was fought by Muslims and Hindus together. The failure of the 1857 War of Independence left behind consequences, particularly for the Muslims who were held responsible for the war. Thus, repressive and discriminatory policies were adopted against the Muslims. Freedom fighters were closely watched, and their properties, even of those remotely associated with the struggle, were confiscated. The idea was to completely crush the freedom fighters and strengthen British rule in India.

After the war, the British sought to avoid any repetition of this kind. As such, Indians, and particularly Muslims, were to be brought under the influence of British culture and values. Thus Muslims were encouraged to take education in tune with the British education system. To accomplish this, jobs were kept open to those who knew the language. Those who acquired an English education were given positions in the administration. Many of them were given admission to the Universities in England to expand British influence in India. In other words, they would travel to the West and then bring that influence back to India with them. Those who studied in Britain were given important positions upon return to India. Indians who served the British properly were awarded Knighthood (title of *Sir)* and *jagirs.* This is the same practice, though the rewards have changed, which we observe in the world today. Further, it was propagated that the safety of the Muslims lay in acquiring Western education and knowledge. The British would not have allowed Sir Syed Ahmed Khan (Founder of Aligarh Muslim University) to start English education, unless this was in line with their agenda.

To the Indians, all of this sounded correct and very well in line with the demand of the time. However, behind this, there was a hidden agenda to assert Western influence over India. This worked and the strategy was and has been enormously beneficial for the West.

Further, the education system[1] in British India was not one to create scholars or thinkers. The British did not allow a system to exist that would create brains

---

[1] The repercussions of that system can even be seen in Pakistan today. The level and system of education remains very poor in Pakistan, even after 59 years of independence. Many people lack independent thinking and most people can only think to a limit. With apology, I go to the extent of saying that most people lack vision, and stereotypical thinking prevails, while new ideas are generally rejected right away. The education system discourages analysis and initiative.

The poor level of education is evident from the following example. Over the years, I have asked many well-educated men what leadership is all about, and I am shocked that they cannot even answer such a basic question. To me, one of the characteristics of a true leader is that s/he has roots in the group or community that s/he represents and lives in the manner that his/her followers live. These people are not to be blamed because that is how they were raised. In Pakistan, reading habits are not developed from childhood and half of the population (women) lives confined to the four walls of her house. Thus, by and large, people lack vision and far-sightedness.

or people with vision. Thus, educational institutions were of poor quality and produced people with the mentality of subordinates who serve their masters. There was no emphasis on extensive research on various topics such as science. Students reproduced what they were taught. Under the circumstances, inquisitive minds, important for growth and development, were suppressed. Another negative result was that people who learned English began to look down upon those who were not well-versed in it. The elite did not touch Urdu books in fear of belonging to the lower class (this somewhat remains today). By giving importance to English, the mother tongue of Urdu suffered tremendously.[2] I am not implying that the English language should have been rejected. What I am stating is that Urdu should not have been ignored or reduced to a secondary language. These factors led Muslims to suffer from complexes, and they drifted from their real values. The education system greatly affected the Indians socially, culturally, economically and politically and led them to stay behind the West. Remember! It is not numbers but brains that rule the world.

*****

If we examine history, by and large, circumstantial evidence proves that the British targeted the Muslims more than any other community. It was important to the British to cripple Muslims who had ruled India, with a non-Muslim majority, for almost 1,000 years. This phobia led the British to create both Muslim-Hindu disunity as well as divisions within the Muslims. In order to accomplish this, the Englishmen applied intelligent techniques based on the occasion and time.

Hindus were preferred by the rulers in all walks of life, and the British bureaucracy created circumstances to widen the gap between the Muslims and the Hindus. Any collaboration or solidarity between these major communities would weaken their rule, thus a rift between the Muslims and Hindus was strategically imperative. It is for this reason the AIML was allowed to be born.

In 1906, the elite class of Muslims founded a party under the title of the All-India Muslim League. The party was founded by Nawab Salimullah Khan at Dhaka (now in Bangladesh), apparently with the goal of safeguarding Muslim interests and political rights. As a matter of fact, the British encouraged this party to come into existence in order to contain the Indian National Congress

---

[2] The effect of learning English carried on and is visible even today. In general, people are enthusiastic and take pride in adopting Western ways of life, while condemning their own culture. For instance, children are more familiar with Mickey Mouse than stories of their own heritage. The permeation of Western brands and chain stores helps to spread Western influence. For example, McDonald's can now be found almost anywhere in the world.

I am not against adopting good values and traditions of the West, and I am not against globalization or anything that unites mankind. However, my point is that the East must not forget and abandon its culture and morals. It must pass its way of life on to the West as well, for example its tradition of hospitality, warmth in relationships and respect for parents and adults. Unity of mankind is possible when different civilizations meet on equal footing.

(INC), thereby laying the foundation for the rift between Muslims and Hindus. For instance, when Gandhi supported the Khilafat Movement, a purely Islamic issue, the British did not appreciate it.

As stated, from the start, the British could not tolerate Muslims and Hindus uniting under any circumstance. Hence, they would use prominent people, in both communities, for their own ends. The rift they created between Muslims and Hindus and the results of this are quite evident from historical events. The following letter explains the mentality of the rulers in India. On September 21, 1922, Lord Reading, Viceroy of India, wrote to the Secretary of State for India:

> "I have sent you a telegram which will show you how near we have been to a complete break between Muslims and Hindus. I have been giving the greatest attention to this possibility, and I have the greatest assistance from Shafi in my council, who is a highly respected Mohammadan."[3]

*****

As far as the club (All India Muslim League) itself was concerned, its elite members tried to benefit from the AIML, and it served as a forum for gaining publicity. The AIML was not considered to be well-organized; consequently, they were unable to work with or for the masses. The elite members were more than happy to accept the supremacy of the British but most were not ready to accommodate each other.

For the next two decades, the AIML and other Indian political leadership (including Muslims and non-Muslims) absolutely failed to deliver anything substantial that would benefit the common people. There was not a single leader among Muslims and non-Muslims who was capable of posing a threat or challenge to the British rule.

The Muslim community's position too was pitiable. They were nothing politically, economically or educationally. Muslims had been living a deplorable life of stagnation since the fall of the Mughal Empire. They were a demoralized, dissatisfied and peeved community suffering from various complexes, which are still visible today.

For the British, their vast empire extended throughout the world; the sun literally never set on their Empire. They were proudly ruling not only over India but in many parts of the world and were using the world's resources to their benefit. It was not possible for anyone to take *punnga* or to meddle with their affairs, in light of their power. The irony is that the British were using Indians, for instance those in the defense forces, to safeguard their rule in India.

---

[3] Khan, Khan Abdul Wali. Chapter 1.

How ridiculous it was that a small population of Englishmen was ruling over 400 million people in India. It would not be wrong to state that if 400 million people exhaled collectively, the British would have been blown away.

*****

It was at this juncture — with the AIML politically ineffective and the Indian masses in dire straights — that Allama Mashraqi emerged onto the Indian political landscape. Mashraqi, who had been observing the failures of the existing leaders, founded the Khaksar Movement to awaken the nation from its deep slumber, build its character and ultimately bring freedom to India. Mashraqi's efforts were critical to achieving independence; however, as this book will detail, his role has been suppressed by pro-Muslim Leaguers and those with vested interests.

Chapter 1

Allama Mashraqi's Life of Struggle

ALLAMA MASHRAQI (Inayatullah Khan) was one of the greatest reformers, leaders and scholars ever born. He was a brilliant thinker, a prolific writer and a powerful orator. He was an incredibly down to earth person, and he spent his life in service to mankind. Mashraqi lived his whole life in the unending quest for self-purification. Mashraqi practiced humility and preached humanism and submission to God. To Mashraqi, the material world and its attractions had little meaning, but he claimed to be no prophet. He first chose to live simply and then asked others to seek simplicity.

Mashraqi believed in the unity and equality of humankind as the former brings strength and the latter inculcates a sense of humility. He demolished the wall that stood between the rich and poor, which speaks of his unsurpassed and unequalled love for people of all classes. He sought no distinction or discrimination against anyone regardless of religion, caste, color or creed. He said "Islam forbids strictly anything but friendly relations with neighbouring nations."[1] He did not look down upon his fellow beings on account of their supposed lack of wealth or social status. His idea of society was to ensure equal opportunity and identical rights for all. He aimed at seeking justice for the human race, whether Muslim, Hindu, Christian, Jew, Parsee, Scheduled caste, colored or white. As stated by some, he was more of a reformer rather than a politician. Mashraqi's struggle was not for power or against any individual, and he sought no public office or personal glorification.

*****

Allama Mashraqi's political thoughts were shaped as a child by his father, Khan Ata Mohammed Khan. Mashraqi's father was not only a very well-known and respected figure but a great literary person. He owned *Vakil*, a weekly paper from Amritsar, India, which was indeed a great source of political awakening. Khan's supervision and guidance provided Mashraqi with

---

[1] *The Eastern Times,* October 04, 1946.

an opportunity to learn not only from his father but also from the learned people who were associated with the weekly. People such as Maulana Abul Kalam Azad also edited the weekly.

Mashraqi was groomed by his parents to alter the world and bring peace and harmony. Since his early adulthood, he took keen interest in national and international politics. Mashraqi joined Christ's College at the University of Cambridge, England in 1907 and completed his education in 1912; his academic achievements were highly praised. While at Christ's College, Mashraqi earnestly started thinking about changing the fate of the Indian people.

While he was in England, Mashraqi was offered Premiership of Princely State of Alwar; however, he did not accept the offer as he preferred to be part of the Education Department in the Government of India. Upon Mashraqi's return to British India in 1913, Sir George Ross-Keppel, Chief Commissioner[2] of North West Frontier Province (NWFP), offered him the position of Vice Principal of the Islamia College in Peshawar, NWFP. He accepted the position and joined it as the youngest Vice Principal of any college in British India. He was only twenty five years old, and he did an outstanding job during his association at the Islamia College.

Mashraqi joined the Education Department to reform the educational curriculum; his purpose was to lift the masses through the education system and finally change the destiny of the people of British India. During his tenure in the Government service, he introduced religious education in NWFP institutions in the teeth of the British Government's opposition.

In 1917, he was made Principal of the same college, and in the same year, Lord Chelmsford (Governor General of India) appointed him Under Secretary (Education Department) in place of Sir George Anderson. This was a position of great significance, and within a few years of his return from England, Mashraqi had attained a place among the elitist class of Indians.

However, as a Government employee, Mashraqi faced mighty resistance from the rulers in changing the educational system and its curriculum. When differences developed with the British, Mashraqi was demoted from the post of Under Secretary and authorities made him headmaster of a Government High School in Peshawar (NWFP) in October 1919.[3] This punishment was given to him for not working in accordance with the British authorities. The rulers thought demotion would bring Mashraqi to his senses, but this did not work. In fact, his firmness and stance increased, and his bold attitude was very well regarded in the general public. The rulers realized Mashraqi's importance and popularity among the public and the respect that he enjoyed for his steadfastness and doctrines.

---

[2] Chief Commissioner was equivalent to Governor at that time.
[3] *Report on Public Instructions...* P. 16.

*****

During the Khilafat Movement[4], there was an outflow of people toward Afghanistan. Owing to his popularity, Mashraqi was thought to be an excellent candidate by the British to prevent the migration of people to Afghanistan. To regain his blessings and support, the British offered him Ambassadorship to Afghanistan in 1920, followed by Knighthood in 1921. Sir Alfred Hamilton Grant, Chief Commissioner[5] of North West Frontier Province, extended these offers. The British thought that like other Indians, Mashraqi would jump at their offers.

Little they knew of Mashraqi. He turned down these offers, as he did not want to be a sell out. For any other person, it would have been very tempting to accept the offers as they were associated with power, wealth, influence and fame. By turning down the offers, Mashraqi sent a clear message to Indians — reject such offers, as these are insignificant and insult your self-respect as Indians; titles bestowed by those who do not seek your well being are a disgrace to you. His message was to those who considered such titles a great honor bestowed upon them by their masters. The recipients of titles ignored the fact that these were conferred upon them as a reward for rendering services and showing loyalty to the British, otherwise why would they honor someone. Indians were expected to accept these honors as a matter of great prestige and tribute conferred upon them by His Majesty. It was very uncommon for such important honors or positions to be turned down by Indians. Mashraqi's rejection of these offers surely brought resentment in the eyes of the rulers, but even as headmaster of a school, Mashraqi was well regarded by the public.

*****

In 1924, Mashraqi completed *Tazkirah*. Mashraqi drew his life's inspiration not only from the Holy Quran but also from the history of Islam. In his book, *Tazkirah*, Mashraqi scientifically examined the Holy Quran so that people would understand the real Islam and not the Islam preached by Maulvis (clerics). After *Tazkirah*, Mashraqi authored other books including *Maulvi Ka Ghalat Mazhab* (The False Religion of the Muslim Priests). According to Mashraqi, Maulvis' interpretation of Islam was wrong and did not fit the fundamental teachings of the religion; real Islam would, indeed, help the conservation of world peace and justice. Mashraqi laid great importance on the study of Islam in the light of science; he believed that the salvation of humanity and the glory of mankind lies in the sensible blending of both spirituality and exploration of the universe through science. *Tazkirah*, which combined science and religion, had become imperative in a world where, by neglecting science, the East had become slave to the West, and by neglecting

---

[4] The Khilafat Movement was started after World War I to protect the Ottoman Empire from dismemberment.
[5] Chief Commissioner was equivalent to Governor at that time.

spirituality and religion, the West had adopted a cruel and supercilious imperialistic approach.

*****

Differences with the British continued to grow and were further heightened after Mashraqi (while in service and against the wishes of the Government authorities) led a delegation to Cairo, Egypt in 1926 and delivered his historic speech, *Khitab-e-Misr*. At Cairo, he apprised the attendees of the imperialists' designs and suggested remedies. During his trip, he met a large number of scholars and dignitaries from various countries and pleaded unity in the Islamic world to revive Muslim eminence that was lost after the collapse of the Ottoman Empire in 1923.[6] He suggested pooling resources and jointly responding to threats and challenges to the Muslim world. His message was one of unity and unified action. He warned them that if this was not done, forces against the Muslims would continue to disintegrate them. He asked them to watch for evil elements in their own ranks that support anti-Islamic forces. Mashraqi was the only leader who at that time understood the machinations of the imperialists, thus, he asked the Muslims to unite. He made recommendations, sought their help in this regard and gave them direction, before going to Europe. His suggestions and proposals were obviously irksome to the British.

At the invitation of Professor Albert Einstein and Adolph Hitler, Mashraqi met with them in Europe. Einstein invited Mashraqi to his house, where as Hitler came over to meet him. Both personalities were highly impressed with Mashraqi's intellect. With keen interest, they discussed Mashraqi's monumental work, *Tazkirah*, which had just been published then. In an article, *The Deccan Times* reported, "Hitler and Einstein expressed their appreciation of the book, when they met Allama Mashriqi in 1926."[7]

Mashraqi returned to India, highly disappointed with the Muslim leadership and the overall state of affairs that prevailed in the Muslim world. From his observations and from the scholars he met during his trip, Mashraqi's sense was confirmed that the Muslim leadership throughout was generally self-serving. These leaders seemed to be interested only in their own well-being, ignoring public interest. They lacked vision and believed in making flowery speeches to satisfy their people, without taking any concrete and practical steps. Unfortunately, much of this still prevails today.

Under the circumstances, Mashraqi was left with no choice but to go to his own people and bring about a revolution through them. Within a few years of his return, Mashraqi resigned from his secure Government job with a lucrative salary and came to the rescue of the Indians. Very few others, with his

---

[6] *The Ottomans.org.*
The Ottoman Empire lasted from the late 13th century to 1923. (*The Ottomans.org*)
[7] *The Deccan Times,* November 18, 1945.

qualifications, would risk their own lives and brilliant career. For Mashraqi, it would have been very simple to become a tout and instrument of the British and to take the important honors and positions they were offering him. The rulers were more than willing to accept his political role, provided Mashraqi was disposed to follow their line of action. As it is common knowledge, leaders in the third world are made by powerful nations; this was no different then. Mashraqi could not serve the British interest and was left with no choice but to launch his own movement.

To obtain his ultimate objective of revival of the people's eminence, he first revolutionized his own life and rejected all luxuries that he could have continued to enjoy. He became a commoner. This in itself is a very difficult decision, particularly when one is accustomed to luxury and comfort. Besides that it requires a lot of courage to abandon a life of ease, particularly when most of his contemporaries were enjoying the luxuries through the blessings of the British. Even Muslim political leaders were maintaining high profile lifestyles, though they claimed to be working for the Muslim cause. But Mashraqi was different, and his conscience would not allow him to maintain a high profile lifestyle, when his fellow countrymen had no food on their plates.

In short, Mashraqi kept the well-being of his people before himself and, with his personal funds, launched the Khaksar Tehreek in 1930. He ignored the fact that his movement would bring tremendous financial losses for him. Allama Mashraqi finally laid the foundation for the Khaksar Tehreek, also known as the Khaksar Movement, in October 1930.

*****

After the creation of the Khaksar Tehreek, Mashraqi led a hectic political life, spending almost eighteen hours a day toward the movement. He worked day and night and mobilized the people, speaking at various places in a single day. He needed no rehearsed or written speeches. Mashraqi was a grassroots leader. His personality and demeanor had an instant impact on his audience. Indeed! His image, uniqueness and persona were extremely impressive, appealing and dominating, and his presence demanded attention and deference.

As the movement attained a lot of success very quickly, amassing millions of followers and supporters, the Government cracked down on Mashraqi and the Khaksars. On March 19, 1940, Mashraqi was arrested in Delhi and was taken far from his home. In jail, he was kept in horrifying conditions and denied basic amenities permitted to political prisoners. His family members and Khaksars were barred from visiting him. Mashraqi's bank accounts were frozen, and his family was brought to the stage of starvation. Barrister Mian Ahmed Shah wrote to the Chief Secretary to the Government of United Provinces (U.P), Sir Francis Mudie, and stated that Mashriqi's family "is nearly starving" without money.[8] Mashraqi's sons were also arrested. His son,

---

[8] Barrister Mian Ahmed Shah's letter, October 17, 1940. IOL L/P&J/8/680.

Ehsanullah Khan Aslam, who was injured from a tear-gas grenade by the police on March 19 and needed funds for proper treatment, died in May 1940 because of lack of funds. The height of cruelty is that Mashraqi was denied attendance to his son's funeral. He could not overcome this grievance for the rest of his life. One can imagine how a father must have felt when he was denied to take a last glimpse of his beloved son prior to burial.

The atrocities did not end there. In jail, Mashraqi was asked to abandon the Khaksar Tehreek or die in prison. He refused to surrender to any pressure. Thus, he remained in prison for a long time without a trial, despite the fact he had been ill in jail. Kazi Abdul Baqi, a Khaksar leader and a prominent attorney of Lucknow, appealed to Jinnah in his letter for the release of Allama Mashraqi, "whose continued detention and 'prolonged illness'…had caused 'deep consternation and irreconcilable irritation in the Khaksar World'…"[9] In addition to their own efforts, the Khaksars and Mashraqi's family looked to the AIML for support. Aside from passing resolutions, the League did nothing to get him released or his restrictions abrogated. Throughout this gloomy period of extreme anxiety and desperation, the League provided nothing but lip service. None of the main leaders ever visited the family to provide any comfort. They did not even visit Mashraqi in jail. In fact, Mashraqi's family and the Khaksars found AIML to be very nervous when he was finally released. According to them, AIML wanted Mashraqi to remain in prison or at least have his movements restricted. Mashraqi later pointed out the conspiracy against the Khaksar Tehreek in a statement; he said:

> "19th [March, 1940] and the 26th July [1943][10] both were 'well-planned attacks' on the Khaksar organisation, the one from the side of the Government and the other from the side of Mr. Jinnah"[11]

Mashraqi was finally released on January 19, 1942 after fasting for 80 days in protest. Throughout his detention, Mashraqi never showed any sign of surrender or giving in to the pressure from the Government to abandon the movement. When he came out of jail, his family members could not recognize him as he had gone pale and extremely weak. Mashraqi's family could not forget the period while Mashraqi was rotting in Vellore Jail under miserable conditions, and later when he was in a restricted area (Madras Presidency) and not permitted to return home. When restrictions on Mashraqi's movements were removed on December 28, 1942, this brought tears of joy not only in the family, but literally in the eyes of many Khaksars and supporters. Though Mashraqi was released, secret and intelligence services of police kept his movements under close watch.

---

[9] Kazi Abdul Baqi's letter to Jinnah.
[10] On July 26, 1943, Jinnah was attacked. The assailant was falsely alleged to be a Khaksar. The attack was later shown to be a conspiracy against the Khaksars.
[11] Hussain, P. 193.

After his release, in spite of poor health owing to the deplorable conditions he was kept under, Mashraqi again continued his rigorous political activities and successfully mobilized the people for independence. As hard as the British tried to crush Mashraqi, they could not succeed and Mashraqi continued to work for independence in the face of strong opposition. By mobilizing and awakening the people to rise for freedom, he, in fact, successfully shook the pillars of colonial rule in British India.

Though *The Deccan Times* was a pro-League newspaper, it could not resist praising Mashraqi and on November 18, 1945 wrote:

> "Born of a well-to-do Pathan family of Amritsar in the year 1888, Inayatullah Khan had an exceptionally brilliant academic career both in India and England. He became the Vice Principal and later on Principal of Islamiah College, Peshawar. But in whatever capacity he served, he showed unflinching enthusiasm in serving his community... *Tazkira*, which gave to the world a new interpretation to the Quranic philosophy. The book won world-wide tributes and in 1925, the Nobel Prize Committee even asked for its translation in one of the Primary European languages. This request, however, was not complied with. Even Hitler and Einstein expressed their appreciation of the book, when they met Allama Mashriqi in 1926. Encouraged by this favourable reception, he published another book *Isharat* through which he issued a call to his nation for action...the aim of the Movement was world-conquest...
>
> The dynamic personality of the leader and the militant character of the organisation soon attracted a large number of Muslim Youths. Within five to six years, the Khaksar Movement spread to all parts of India...
>
> The Khaksar organisation grew from strength to strength...
>
> The happenings in the Punjab[12] [March 19, 1940 Khaksar massacre] and U.P.[13] gave to the Khaksars the rank of martyrs. They commanded the love and respect of every Muslim heart [for their courage, discipline and community service]. The Mussalmans entertained great hopes about him...
>
> The Allama was arrested...After about two years he was released but was not allowed to leave Madras presidency. During the two years the situation in India changed completely. There was a great awakening among the Muslims. They rallied round the Leaguer, which gave to them in Pakistan a goal to fight and die for. Though they still retained their love and respect for the Khaksars..."

*****

After the creation of Pakistan, Mashraqi's life was made difficult in the new country. Mashraqi was harassed by the Criminal Investigation Department (CID) and secret and intelligence services of the police, and he was arrested many times; only some of these arrests have been detailed in this chapter. The

---

[12] See Chapter 4.
[13] See Chapter 3.

police hovered around his house most of his life and harassed his family. Mashraqi founded the Islam League in October 1947; he was arrested on fabricated charges in 1952, in order to prevent him from launching an election campaign for Islam League candidates to contest the forthcoming elections. He was tortured in jail and was forced to remain silent and quit politics or stay in jail. The authorities used every conceivable method to crush him and his political activity. They resorted to incarceration of Mashraqi and thousands of followers; they used methods of torture, repression and more. But Mashraqi stood firm and refused to succumb to any pressure.

Upon his release, Mashraqi lamented on July 23, 1952:

"My arrest on the eve of the Punjab elections and my subsequent systematic victimization for 18 months at the hands of a Muslim Government where perhaps every device was used to torture me for the sake of torture may have caused satisfaction to the few who were responsible for this, but I have no rancor. I am thankful to the Muslims, especially Muslims organizations and the Press who unanimously upheld that my arrest was unjustifiable and this shows that I as well as Islam League belong to no party of the Muslims. The Press is the last hope of an oppressed people and I am grieved to find that it has split up preparatory to death at a time when it should have united with all force at a critical juncture full of external as well as internal difficulties.

Unearned power has always become unbridled and the present Muslim League is no exception to this. A feature of the present situation is that the Muslim League has lost whatever vitalness it had during the five years. The exhortations of its own leaders for its revitalization disclose what is going on in it. Under these circumstances it becomes imperative for me to clear my own position in view of various changes put against me by the few men of the rod at the top who arrested me and who can do worse things if I do not publicly divest myself of these charges.

Khaksar Movement was the first organized attempt among the Muslims during the British rule to make Muslims strong and I devoted the best part of my life to it. I failed to make them so and I disbanded it before the advent of Pakistan because I feared the British had crushed every military quality of the Muslims during their rule and such qualities could not have been revived under slavery. This naturally resulted in the massacre before and after Partition of millions of Masalmans at the hands of Hindus who had no military quality whatever. To charge me, therefore, with having been anti-national in my activities is manifestly wrong. This charge fits more the Muslim Leaguers themselves who were the right hand men of the British Government for generations.

To charge me as having been the cause of assailing Quaid-e-Azam through a Khaksar in 1943 is equally ridiculous as the Bombay High Court judgment said that Mr. Jinnah had not been able to prove that the assailant was a Khaksar and the man himself announced that he was a favorite Muslim Leaguer. My differences with Mr. Jinnah were only on the point that I wanted undivided

Punjab and undivided Bengal with the provinces of U.P. and Bihar to be the least Pakistan of the Muslims. I told him in 1942 that his present Pakistan of the two provinces 1400 miles apart could not last and this would result in the ruin of one crore [10 million] Muslims and the complete decimation of five crore [50 million] Muslims of remaining India.

To charge me with trying to raise a private army to capture power in Pakistan is also manifestly wrong as, if that would have been the case, I would not have disbanded the Khaksar Movement in 1947 when nearly 70,000[14] Khaksars gathered in Delhi at my order under most difficult circumstances and under teeth of British opposition...

To say that the proposed Islam League conference which four lakh people of city of Karachi were to attend with 10,000 Razakars[15] was for the purpose of capturing power and defying law and order was still more absurd as I had it postponed three time when Karachi authorities put ban exclusively on it. The aim of the conference was undoubtedly to tell the people to change the present Muslim League Government by constitutional means."[16]

In 1957, Mashraqi was again arrested so as to stop him from leading a peaceful march of one million people towards India to draw world attention and mobilize public opinion to seek the freedom of Kashmir. Despite Government restrictions to organize the march, Mashraqi did what he thought was right. Owing to stern restrictions, only 300,000 Khaksars were able to come together. *The Times*, London, referring to his struggle, wrote that Allama Mashraqi "opposed British rule in India" and "in 1957 he led 300,000 followers" in order to seek Kashmir's freedom.[17]

In 1958, at the age of 70, Mashraqi was falsely implicated in a murder case of the ex-Chief Minister of West Pakistan (Dr. Khan Sahib). Mashraqi and his son were arrested. The height of barbarity is that the Scholar of the East, a great patriot with an illustrious reputation and a very large following, was handcuffed when taken for court proceedings. In prison, he was kept in miserable conditions and was mentally and physically tortured. No heed was paid to public protests. When he was seriously ill, no proper medical care was arranged, despite the grave concern that was expressed by his family members and the public. When Mashraqi's health deteriorated, he was taken to the hospital, where he remained handcuffed. Various requests, complaints and demonstrations were disregarded, and authorities denied his release. On the other hand, every endeavor was made to prove that he was behind the murder of Dr. Khan Sahib, so that Mashraqi could be taken to the gallows and executed. But God helped him survive; nothing was proven against Mashraqi, and he was honourably acquitted.

---

[14] *Dawn*, Delhi of July 02, 1947 reported 70,000 to 80,000 Khaksars.
[15] Islam League members were known as Razakars.
[16] Hussain, Pp. 247-249.
[17] *The Times*, August 29, 1963.

When Mashraqi came out of prison, he was diagnosed with cancer; within a few years, he passed away in Lahore. Before he took his last breath, he wanted to see Kashmir liberated. From his death bed, he asked "Kashmir ka kia banay ga?" ("What will become of Kashmir?")[18] and gave a message to the nation:

> "Mashriqi said that 'Pakistan's unheeding Western allies are at the moment unable to see things clearly; they would not hesitate even to give up Pakistan to placate India. They are merely giving verbal assurances to Pakistan that military supplies they are making to India would not be used against Pakistan.' He warned Pakistan to be aware of the 'stupid approach' of its socalled Western 'friends' which posed a 'serious threat to Pakistan's security.' He said, 'I appeal to President Ayub even now to…prepare each of his countrymen to lead a soldierly life.'"[19]

Mashraqi departed for the eternal world on August 27, 1963, and with his death, an important chapter in the history of Pakistan and India was closed.

It is extremely important to take note that in his long political struggle, Mashraqi underwent the wrath of the British and Pakistani regimes for a considerable amount of time. He was imprisoned numerous times, before and after partition, for prolonged jail terms; all arrests, in British India and Pakistan, were politically motivated.

*****

Allama Mashraqi's death was widely mourned. After his death, newspapers throughout the country filled with news about Allama Mashraqi and the Khaksar Tehreek. People from all walks of life expressed their heartfelt condolences. It is impossible to include every paper and news item here. However, I am including some of the messages that were published upon his death.

President Muhammad Ayub Khan's message to Mashraqi's family:

> "I am very much grieved to learn that your husband has passed away. He was a great scholar and organiser who had given up a brilliant academic future to serve the people, as he thought right. He was also a man with courage of his conviction. May his soul rest in eternal peace. Please accept my heart-felt sympathy in your bereavement."[20]

---

[18] *Imroze*, August 29, 1963.
[19] Yousaf 2003, Pp. 228-229; see more of Mashraqi's last message in this source.
[20] *The Pakistan Times*, August 29, 1963.

The words of Khawaja Nazimuddin, Former Governor General and Prime Minister of Pakistan and President of the All-Pakistan Muslim League (Councillors):

> "... a very interesting figure who took prominent part in the politics of the Indo-Pakistan sub-continent... I pray to Allah that his soul may rest in peace and grant patience and courage to his children to bear the loss."[21]

Malik Amir Muhammad Khan's, Governor of West Pakistan, message to Mashraqi's wives[22]:

> "I am deeply distressed to hear of the sad demise of your illustrious husband. Please accept and convey to other members of the family, my heartfelt condolences in your irreparable loss. May his soul rest in eternal peace."[23]

The words of Maulana Syed Abul Ala Maududi, Head of Jama'at-i-Islami (one of the oldest and most prominent political parties in Pakistan):

> "With the death of Allama Mashriqi a chapter in the history of the Indo-Pakistan Muslims has come to an end... It is undoubtedly true that Allama Mashriqi displayed at that time great organisational capacity in building up the Khaksar Movement throughout the length and breadth of Indian sub-continent."[24]

> According to *The Pakistan Times*, "Maulana Maududi said at a time Allama Mashriqi's movement had brought into its fold the whole Muslim nation and had greatly aroused the Muslims to fight for their freedom. That he said, was the outcome of his ability as a great organiser. He prayed for the eternal peace of his soul and offered sympathy with the bereaved family."[25]

Various newspapers within and outside Pakistan, such as *Jang*, *Nawai-waqat*, *Tameer*, *Mashriq*, *Kohistan*, and *Dawn*, wrote on Mashraqi's life.

The Eastern Examiner wrote:

> "In the death of Allama Enayatullah Khan Mashriqi, not only an important chapter of the independence movement finally closes, but also comes to an end the career of one in the subcontinents most colourful personalities, a mathemetical genius, an intellectual and a leader of the first rank. Allama Mashriqi... rose to political prominence with the birth of his Khaksar movement..."[26]

---

[21] *The Pakistan Times*, August 29, 1963.
[22] At the time of his death, Mashraqi had two wives, Mohtarma Saeeda Begum and Mohtarma Bisharat Begum.
[23] *The Pakistan Times*, August 29, 1963.
[24] *The Civil and Military Gazette*, August 28, 1963.
[25] *The Pakistan Times*, August 29, 1963.
[26] *The Eastern Examiner*, August 29, 1963.

The Morning News wrote:

> "In the death of Allama Inayatullah, generally known as Allama Mashriqi, the nation has lost a great organiser, an intellectual of a high order and a great lover of Islam. After a brilliant career which manifested itself in more than one field of knowledge both in his own country and England, he chose to serve in the department of education in which he rose to the position of under secretary in the late Government of India. He first came into prominence through his famous book 'Tazkirah'... Perhaps after a long contemplation over the fate and future of Muslims he came to the conclusion that the Muslims had lost grip over the world affairs due to the absence of a disciplined and active life. The Khaksar Movement was an answer to this problem of decay and decline of Muslims... This movement... became very popular in areas where it received the impact of his leadership... Khaksar Movement provides a great lesson... to organise the Muslim people..."[27]

The Times, London of August 29, 1963 wrote:

> "...A brilliant scholar, a graduate of Cambridge, he...was appointed Principal Islamia College... Later he held a post with the rank of Under Secretary...after differences had arisen, left Government employ. He made the transition to politics in 1930, forming the Islam-Orientated Khaksar Movement which grew to a strength of several hundred thousands[28] before he was imprisoned during the Second World War.
>
> Mashriqi, whose parades of spade-carrying followers were a feature of pre-independent India, was also imprisoned after partition...In 1957 he led 300,000 followers near to the border of Pakistan and India to launch what he said would be a fight for liberation of Kashmir...his movement was later disbanded."

*****

Mashraqi became one of the foremost Muslim figures and dominated the political stage of the sub-continent for over three decades (1930-1963). His services to the cause of unity, contributions to freedom and struggle to empower the people shall always be remembered. He was enemy of those leaders who exploited religion and fostered sectarianism or communalism to seek political advantage. As a matter of fact, religion should never be dragged into the domain of politics. He detested those who spread hate for gains. He disliked those who maintained disparity between rich and poor but claimed to be champions of the poor. He was among rare leading personalities at the time, who wanted to eradicate all types of discrimination from the face of the earth. Mashraqi's idea of independence was equal rights, equal opportunity and justice for everyone. He earnestly strived for a new world order based on

---

[27] *Morning News*, Karachi, August 29, 1963. *Morning News*, Dacca, August 31, 1963.
[28] The followers and supporters of the Khaksar Movement were well over four million in number. Various sources confirm such large numbers; see Yousaf 2003, P. 124.

equality, unity, brotherhood, peace and co-existence. His vision was one of high character, discipline, self-reliance and community service. Mashraqi's leadership was not for seeking personal gain or political power but was for serving the people. He was one of the few leaders who turned down the many offers of entry to the corridors of power. Indeed! He was an exceptional personality of the world.

Mashraqi's contemporaries were intimidated by his commanding personality and popularity. Thus, he was kept in jail with or without a trial. Mashraqi was one of the most victimized political leaders in the sub-continent, whose life was made miserable in the land for which he fought.

Chapter 2

The Khaksar Tehreek &
Uprise of the Nation for Freedom

> "Long Live The Ideals of the Khaksars...Peace, Amity Brotherhood,
> Service—Irrespective of Caste or Creed, One God, One Humanity,
> One Practical Religion, — Yes, One Religion, which means
> Goodness In Action."[1]

After the British took over India, the Muslims lived under depression. The effects of a long period of British domination lurked amongst them, and they were under-confident and weak in many respects. Mashraqi was saddened by the state of the common people in India. Under the circumstances, he could not sit idle and decided to draw them out of this sad and grim condition.

Mashraqi wanted to awaken the nation. In his eyes, this mission could not be accomplished unless people were rejuvenated and strengthened and possessed a sense of discipline, unity and high character. He believed that in order for the nation to emerge as a ruling power, it had to develop the important characteristics that it lacked. Hence, he formed the Khaksar Tehreek in 1930 in order to lift the masses and revive the nation to its glory.

*****

The Khaksar Tehreek's ideology was initially defined by 24 principles. A 14 point decree, which further elaborated on the ideology, was later announced on October 15, 1937.[2] Together, the 24 principles and the 14 points clearly explain the philosophy and objectives of the movement.

---

[1] *The Radiance*, February 06, 1943.
[2] For the 24 principles and 14 fourteen points, see Yousaf 2003, Pp. 111-114.

The Khaksar Tehreek sought inspiration from true Islam, and this was reflected in all of its tenets. One of the Tehreek's 14 points states:

> "The true Islam is the practice of the 'Quran-i-Awwal' (i.e. the earliest period in Islamic history). The Khaksar does not recognize anything as true Islam other than the practice of the Prophet."[3]

Islam is a religion of peace and kindness. Hence, the Khaksar Tehreek stood for love, brotherhood and unity. Mashraqi wanted to liberate mankind from communalism and sectarianism, which seek and spread hatred and nothing else. The Khaksar Tehreek welcomed men and women from all backgrounds, regardless of religion, caste, color, creed or wealth. They were to respect all and expect the same in return. All were to be held accountable for their own mistakes, and justice and equality were to be ensured for all. All this was emphasized in some of the Tehreek's points:

> "We, Khaksars, stand for the establishment of an order that will be equal, non-communal and tolerant, yet non-subservient, by the crushing of all communal sentiment and religious prejudices of mankind by our good and serviceful conduct; an order which will afford proper treatment and protection to all communities and will be founded on eternal justice, goodness and goodwill."[4]

> "The Khaksar stands for (a) regard for the religious and social sentiments of all communities, Hindu, Muslim, Sikh, Parsi, Christian, Jew, and Untouchable etc., (b) maintenance of their particular culture and customs and (c) general tolerance; and believes this policy to be the secret of Muslim rule in India for a thousand years."[5]

To revive the nation, Mashraqi also placed special emphasis on character building, focusing on honesty, integrity, accountability and a deep sense of high morals and values. The Tehreek endorsed humility and simplicity and expected Khaksars to be self-reliant, selfless and to work for the greater good. The Tehreek stressed avoiding gossip, and it placed great importance on punctuality, reliability, obeying seniors and keeping away from sloppiness.

The Khaksars were to seek self purification. Special emphasis was laid on prayer, as this would not only connect people with the Divine but would refresh their souls and energize their bodies. It would provide an opportunity for everyone, from the Head of the State to an ordinary laborer, to stand in the same line to acknowledge that God is eternal and that we are all humble souls. The Khaksars were to fear no one except God.

The Tehreek's creed was also to make community service an integral part of every Khaksar's lifestyle. Every Khaksar would be required to perform community service for Muslims as well as non-Muslims, without accepting

---

[3] Yousaf 2003, Pp. 112-113.
[4] Yousaf 2003, P. 112.
[5] Yousaf 2003, P. 113.

remuneration in return. Activities were to include helping the poor, elderly, sick and needy, keeping respective neighborhoods clean, and rendering services in the event of a national calamity or disaster. Social service would generate the spirit of brotherhood and nation building and set an example for others to follow.

The Khaksar Tehreek aimed to instill both mental and physical discipline in its members. Mental discipline through the characteristics already discussed and physical discipline through physical fitness. The Tehreek called on Khaksars to engage in daily parades and drills. These activities would remove lethargy and sloppiness and promote physical fitness, discipline and a state of readiness. They would provide order and infuse self confidence. They would prepare Khaksars not only for freedom but for any type of emergency that could befall the nation. A soldiery aspect to the movement was necessary in order to convert Indians into a strong and disciplined nation. Mashraqi's address (*Khitab-e-Lahore* May 28, 1950) reflected why a military structure was part of the Khaksar Movement and what advantages soldierly qualities in a nation could bring. He said,

> "Militarisation of the nation will breed in it sense of duty, discipline, organisation, struggle, thriftiness, equality, solidarity, self respect, magnanimity, valiance and desire for victory, which are essential for the general advancement of the nation." (translated from Urdu)[6]

Under the Tehreek's ideology, the Khaksars were to wear a Khaki military type uniform, which would instill in them a sense of belonging to a group, equality and pride. Wearing uniform would immediately put one in the mind set that one is part of a force with a clear objective. Wearing uniform would also show unity, regardless of wealth and religion, and bring self esteem. Saluting each other was also required in order to exhibit discipline and respect for one other. The spade was made part of the uniform to represent the dignity of honest labor, humility and leveling of society. The spade would put one in the mind set of carrying an arm, which makes one feel strong. Further, a spade's usefulness was multifold, as it could be used as a cooking pot, a food dish, a weapon for protection or in fight (a weapon of Prophet Muhammad, peace be upon him, in the battle of Uhud), and a pillow for rest or sleep. Mashraqi stressed all of these features as he knew that, without them, sleeping Indians could not obtain sovereignty.

Finally, Mashraqi's Tehreek was to instill a spirit of *do or die* in the Khaksars, as Mashraqi firmly believed in action, not mere talk.

*****

Through all of this, the Khaksar Tehreek was to mobilize the people to rise from their miserable state and to bring prosperity to the nation. Ultimately, it

---

[6] Hussain, P. 282.

would seek the freedom of India from the British. It is important to highlight that Mashraqi *did not want power for himself*; he wanted to see his fellow countrymen empowered. One of the Tehreek's 14 points states:

> "We, Khaksars, are sworn enemies of and shall take severe revenge even at extreme personal sacrifice upon treacherous and dishonest leaders who have harmed the national cause and are exploiting the masses upon the mercenaries of hostile nations, upon anti-national editors and journalists, upon misleading propagandists, upon betrayers of the country's interests, and upon miscreants, to whatever community they may belong, who have stirred up sectarian animosities among the various communities of India or among the various sections or groups of Muslims."[7]

The Tehreek also had a global vision and aimed to bring prosperity and peace to the world. Mashraqi wanted to put an end to discrimination and conflict based on religion. The Tehreek's creed was to ensure protection of rights for all, thereby empowering people to progress politically, materially and spiritually.

> "The Khaksar believes that he can win over every community and every individual in the world by his goodness and integrity alone. These moral virtues form common property of more or less all religious scriptures."[8]

> "The aim of the Khaksar is to establish sovereignty over the whole world to secure social and political supremacy through their fine conduct."[9]

Those who think that it was not possible to gain power through fine conduct probably forget that Islam spread, not through violence, but through the exemplary conduct of the Prophet Muhammad (peace be upon him). Mashraqi was an apostle of non-violence and peace. Later on, the Khaksar Tehreek was wrongly projected by anti-Khaksar elements as a violent movement. Those allegations were ludicrous! The Khaksars sought love and liberation of all mankind. The Khaksar creed was to stay away from violence; if attacked they would ask the attacker to refrain, but if continued to be attacked, they would strike back hard.

Indeed! The Khaksar Tehreek was a complete institution with a well-formulated ideology for the revival of the nation's eminence.

*****

With this ideology set, Mashraqi set out to spread his message. He had more faith in the common man than in the rich. Thus, he went to individuals of

---

[7] Yousaf 2003, P. 114.
[8] Ibid.
[9] Yousaf 2003, P. 113.

lower and middle classes to ask them to become part of his Khaksar Movement. He would reach out to ordinary people, such as cobblers, tailors, laborers, office clerks/workers and shopkeepers. These were the people who were to be organized and would be ready to pay any price for the cause of freedom.

Mashraqi did not approach the titled gentry, Nawabs or big landlords, as they were very different from the common people. The titled gentry would conduct drawing room politics, with no change for the masses. They only sought social status, leisure and entertainment, as well as influence, wealth and power. Further, the elite tended to be individualists and absolutely lacked audacity and concept of collective action. Mashraqi knew that, under these circumstances, they would never fight against their sponsors' interests. He had no faith in them because they had no will, desire or ability to resist or to bring about a revolution. So there was no point asking them to follow his ideas. Besides, if Mashraqi did ask them to pick up the spade and parade, they would have considered this a crazy idea and would have rejected it right away, as they had no knowledge of how mass movements were to be organized. Remember! It is the common man who brings a revolution.

Mashraqi used no other technique except for canvassing, in order to spread his message and mobilize people. He would sit with people, while maintaining no distinction, and explain what his ideas were of reviving the Muslim glory and how results could be achieved. Muhammad Saeed explains,

> "His movement [Mashraqi's Khaksar Movement] was not the result of a landslide. It was constructed painstakingly. Each entrant had to be persuaded...
> ...Clad in khaki kameez and pyjama, with a long, graceful beard and protuberant kameez pockets stuffed with papers and other articles, he would sit at any shop and try to persuade the people around to join his movement... His method was straight canvassing.
> Sitting at a tailor's shop on the ground-floor of a building on Fleming Road [Lahore], I saw the Allama approaching. He came and took his seat on the protruding wooden plank. The tailor did not care much. After running the whole length of the cloth in the machine he lifted his head rather casually and said: 'Allama Sahib, I have pondered over your suggestion. I don't feel persuaded to march up and down the streets with a spade on the shoulder. The whole thing looks bizarre'.
> The Allama listened to the remark with utmost calm and said a few words emphasising the need for discipline amongst the Muslims. Then rounding off his talk with a little show of animation, he said: 'Look, I have been coming to you for the past five days. I am aware of your feeling and the sense of shyness. They are indeed hard to overcome. Nevertheless, I have not despaired. I know you will, one day, hold the spade. You know I would not go to the Governor even if he called me five times. It is you whose cooperation I ask.'
> The tailor kept silent. The words had visibly sunk. The Allama had gone. The next evening the tailor was seen in the midst of

a little Khaksar battalion, thumping the dusty road of the locality with his over-enthusiastic but clumsy feet."[10]

Mashraqi's convincing methods were awe-inspiring and appealing. People understood, agreed with, and followed him. People found him to be genuine and sincere. The beauty of his character was that he himself first did what he expected his followers to do. Wearing a Khaki and simple dress, he picked up the *belcha* (a tool of a laborer), and then asked them to carry out a military drill and parade with him.

In uniform with belchas on their shoulders, the first batch of Khaksars, led by Mashraqi in Khaki dress and with belcha on his shoulder, proudly paraded in the village of Pandoki near Lahore. This was the moment Mashraqi was desperately waiting for — to revive the nation and ultimately bring downfall of British rule in India. Hence, the Scholar of the East rejected all discrimination and distinction and paraded with commoners.

People who agreed with Mashraqi's ideology began to organize public gatherings where Mashraqi would deliver speeches and motivate them to join his movement. The word started to spread and Mashraqi began traveling from place to place to deliver his message. Khaksars also traveled to various places using different modes of travel, including bicycles, to organize Khaksars in various cities. Pamphlets carrying Mashraqi's message were published and distributed.

The Khaksar Tehreek started to spread fast. Soon, Khaksar community leaders (Salars) were established in every mohalla (locality) and at regional levels all across India. Khaksar leaders' conventions were held in various cities to provide guidelines. Local leaders were entrusted with responsibilities in the areas under their command. This gave structure and organization to the Tehreek. Another advantage of delegating authority was that it built leadership qualities among those who had little or no opportunity to utilize their abilities. As a result, leaders were produced at local levels.

These leaders began to organize activities based on Khaksar ideology or instructions they would receive from the Khaksar headquarters. Daily activities included community service, drills and parades, and collective prayers. Encouraging people to enroll in the Khaksar Tehreek and delivery of the Tehreek's message continued. The local leaders and Khaksars under their command were also assigned to guide and motivate people based on Khaksar ideology. To accomplish this, local leaders organized lectures and speeches. These lectures emphasized the Tehreek's ideology including the importance of honesty, respect for all religions, unity, brotherhood, social service and fear of no one except God. The lectures also promoted certainty in action and removal of lethargy, the wearing of the Khaksar badge of brotherhood on the shoulder (Khaksar flag represents brotherhood) and passing on the Khaksar message to

[10] Saeed, Pp. 157-158.

every soul. This brought desirable results, and Khaksars followed these messages conscientiously, energetically and, most importantly, voluntarily.

The publication of *Al-Islah* (a Khaksar weekly) was initiated in 1934 to further spread Khaksar ideas and accelerate the process of expansion. It carried Mashraqi's speeches, messages from the Khaksar headquarters for the Khaksars, answers to people's questions on the movement and so on. The Khaksars provided copies of *Al-Islah* to their neighbors, relatives and friends so that they could read Mashraqi's speeches and messages. This was a great source of motivating people and delivering messages all across India. Copies of *Al-Islah* were also sent to foreign Muslim countries. The Khaksar Tehreek's numbers began to grow by leaps and bounds and its members followed the philosophy of the Tehreek religiously.

With such growth, Khaksar camps were organized to achieve the Tehreek's ultimate aim of freedom. Such camps were to obtain the following objectives:

❖ Deliver the Tehreek's message
❖ Provide training and generate disciplinary qualities
❖ Develop organizational skills and leadership qualities
❖ Unite people
❖ Train attendees to prepare them for the cause
❖ Encourage onlookers to watch Khaksar activities
❖ Enroll interested people

Mashraqi attended the Khaksar camps and delivered speeches. At the camps, his stay was like any other Khaksar, and he paraded with his followers. People constantly visited him at these camps to listen to his ideas. Mashraqi's powerful writings and speeches motivated and captivated people's minds. Further, they would witness Mashraqi's lifestyle as one of simplicity and without frills. As opposed to his contemporaries, he was very accessible and people could easily talk to him. For a common man, it was unbelievable to see a world-renowned mathematician and scholar amongst them, who made no distinction between himself and everyone else. All of this gave confidence and strength to the public. As a result, people grew to love Mashraqi and he started to live in their hearts; their devotion grew to such an extent that they would do anything for him at a wink of an eye.

The camps became a great success and were held regularly, for a few days at a time. Mock wars were also held from time to time to train Khaksars on war tactics. Khaksars, including Mashraqi, participated in activities at their own expense, leaving behind their businesses, work and families. They also contributed to the expenses of these camps, for instance, people donated tents etc. This was obviously a burden on their domestic budgets, as many Khaksars were from the lower or middle class, but they voluntarily and enthusiastically participated in these activities. Apart from Khaksars, thousands of people from all walks of life would come to the camps and observe Khaksar activities with tremendous interest. They had never seen this type of movement before. Therefore, Khaksar camps were not only used to motivate and impart training to constituents, but they became a great source of enrolling new members. Those who could not become members became its supporters. The camps brought together people from different walks of life on a common platform and instilled understanding, unity and focus.

In their own localities, Khaksars also spent time engaging in daily drills and parades. This instilled in them the Tehreek's ideas of discipline, self confidence and physical fitness. For Khaksars, military type activities were a completely new phenomenon, but they took keen interest in all activities and every one of them put in their best. These activities were important, as in their absence, no nation can rise to seek independence and defend its sovereignty. The street parades, in military uniform with shining spades, boosted the morale of the public and brought a sense of self-assurance not only among the Khaksars but among the masses too. Witnessing these activities, a large number of people continued to became part of the movement.

In their daily lives, the Khaksars also spent considerable time doing community service and offering prayers. Their social service included keeping their localities clean, digging wells to ensure adequate water supplies, maintaining sewer lines and so on. They also provided assistance to orphans, widows, elderly and sick people, and during catastrophes, such as earthquakes and fires. Community service brought a lot of respect for the Khaksars from people from all walks of life and all communities. It generated love, harmony and brotherhood, as well as a sense of self-reliance.

Mashraqi put forth rigorous efforts and the movement grew at an unbelievable pace. Mashraqi's powerful message and hectic efforts as well as the Khaksars' devotion and activities inspired and awakened people[11]; soon the movement spread all over India and established branches in other countries.

*****

By 1939, India was practically under the grip of the Khaksar Tehreek. In a short span of time (from 1930 to late 1930s), the Tehreek had raised four million Khaksars and millions of supporters.

---

[11] "It is a movement of men, lions, soldiers and belligerents... When nations are in the throes of death and decline" and "everybody is helpless" to grasp where the actual problem is; at that point it is of utmost importance to awaken the nation from the deep slumber and "once the individuals of a nation are infused with courage, power, energy, aspiration, will, and action is instilled in their limbs and action in hands, feet, body, soul" and if "determination... action and only action" are infused, "then nothing on earth can stop that nation from its onward march." The Khaksar Tehreek was doing exactly this to regain their freedom from the clutches of the foreign power by "instilling" the "lesson" of "glory, power and determination." (All quotes in this paragraph are Mashraqi's words as quoted in Muhammad, Pp. 5-6.)

"He [Mashraqi] asserted that 40 lakh [four million] persons had joined his movement and they carried the red badge on their shoulders."[12]

"...Khaksar movement spread with such 'accelerated speed' that by 1938 it was able to mount two-thousand strong counter-demonstrations against the State Congress."[13]

The Tehreek's members came from the masses from all over India and represented many different religions, though its main strength was based on Muslims. Importantly, the Tehreek comprised of members from the lower and middle classes. Its membership was not reserved for Muslims only but was all-inclusive, irrespective of religion, nationality, color, caste or creed. The movement's activities attracted non-Muslims, such as Hindus, Sikhs, Christians and others, and they joined the Tehreek in sizeable numbers.

The Tehreek's followers comprised of laborers, businessmen, politicians, professors, judges, engineers, lawyers, doctors, landlords, technocrats, personnel of defense forces, Government servants and members of legislative assemblies. Talpurs, Pirs, Sayeds, Bhurgaries and Kazis from Sind, Khans, Arbabs and Mians from NWFP, and Nawabs from Deccan, Kunjpura, Oudh and Ferozepur also became followers of the movement. From the common man to the Nawab, all were put on equal footing under the authority of the Salars, who were mainly from the lower and middle classes.

Many Khaksars, though highly educated and some of them prominent and wealthy individuals, participated in Khaksar activities. Those, who were unable to be active, provided support however they could. Many donated money and material that were needed to organize sham battles and/or Khaksar camps. They realized that the Khaksar Tehreek and its leadership and followers were selfless people and had no personal agenda in mind. They had witnessed the amount of respect and dedication Mashraqi enjoyed from his followers. No one else, at least among Muslim leaders, had the honor of such unflinching dedication from his/her followers. Many of them admitted that the Khaksar Movement was the only party that was capable of bringing uprise and change to the destiny of the nation.

It is important to note that Mashraqi had created such a large organization, without any academy and without any membership fee. Its members had been trained in open yards, playing fields or on the streets of British India and without subscriptions or fundraising. All Khaksars, including Mashraqi, were to use their own money for participating in Khaksar activities.[14] Politicians think that scarcity of funds cannot run a movement or party, but Mashraqi proved to the world that it could be done. The movement had spread

---

[12] *The Eastern Times*, November 01, 1942.
[13] Copland, P. 807.
[14] Mashraqi gave direction to leaders not to use party funds (generated from the public) for personal expenses, such as travel, even though they may be related to the party's activities.

unostentatiously and quietly, without seeking any publicity. Not a single Muslim leader, political party or group in British India had achieved the rapid growth that the Tehreek had achieved within a few years of its formation.

*****

Indeed, the Khaksar Tehreek was a movement of a large number of *disciplined* people, trained like an army, yet without association with a regular military or armed forces academy; this was an unprecedented achievement! No party in any community was even comparable to its discipline, dedication and unity. By the late 1930's, *it was the only major Muslim party that had such a large following at the grassroots level.*

The Khaksar Tehreek had become incredibly powerful with its unmatchable discipline, unity, dedication and self-sacrificing outlook. The secret of its growth was its overall ideology, Mashraqi's altruistic service for the cause, without any agenda of personal glorification, and the Khaksars' devotion. No doubt Mashraqi had emerged as a powerful leader with a very bold and resilient following in the masses. In short, Mashraqi's ideology brought tremendous results and spoke of his exceptional organizational skills, political wisdom, clear vision and foresight. Within a few years of founding the Khaksar Tehreek, he was in the forefront of the Indian politics.

Mashraqi's organizational skills were well-acclaimed, and *The Deccan Times*, Madras wrote,

> "As an organiser he [Allama Mashraqi] was first rate; his supremacy was supreme there. He created militant spirit in an otherwise dull youth. He preached the message of action in the world that thought only in terms of idealism. Muslim India stood by him and promised him all support."[15]

Foreign newspapers acknowledged Mashraqi's strength and the role that the Khaksar Tehreek was capable of playing. *The Christian Science Monitor* (an American newspaper) and *The Scotsman* of Edinburgh (a newspaper from Scotland) described Mashraqi and the Khaksar Tehreek in these words:

On July 17, 1938, *The Christian Science Monitor* (Boston, USA) wrote:

> "Its [Khaksar Tehreek] founder, Alama Inayatullah Mashraki [Mashraqi]...a typical example of India's contented...Moslem gentry, gave up a [US] $700 a month...graduated from England...after a remarkable career as a student. As a result of his academic distinctions he was appointed Under-Secretary to the Government of India in the Educational Department... The founder [Mashraqi]...controls the 'Army of Spades' [Khaksar Tehreek]... An efficient force [Khaksar Tehreek] of this size, however, is bound to

[15] *The Deccan Times*, October 28, 1945.

play an important part some day in India where discipline is a much needed quality." [16]

The Scotsman of Edinburgh wrote on August 15, 1938 (or 1939, exact date is not legible in the source):

> "The Khaksars...are well-built young men who bear spades on their shoulders instead of rifles. Highly disciplined, they pay implicit obedience to the founder and leader, Allama Mashriqi, or 'Sage of the East.'" [17]

The Deccan Times wrote in the later years:

> "Based on the Quranic ideals and militant action, his [Allama Mashraqi] organisation spread like wild fire, commanding awe in the government ranks and admiration among Indians. He inspired old and young alike. The Khaksar ideals were so attractive that they drafted into their fold some of the best brains in the country. KAZI ABDUL BAQI of U.P. renounced his lucrative practice at the bar and rallied round the banner of the ALLAMA [Mashraqi]. The late NAWAB BAHADUR YAR JUNG was the Khaksar Chief of Hyderabad. The Movement gathered momentum day by day; branches shot up in every district and it grew up to be one of the most powerful organisations in the country." [18]

The Khaksar Tehreek gave new shape and structure to Indian politics. In view of its tremendous popularity, on November 28, 1939, Mashraqi announced a goal of enrolling another 2.5 million people within the next six months and printing of an additional 25,000 copies of *Al-Islah* per week in the near future. [19] These targets were easily attainable.

*****

The Khaksar Tehreek's muscles were first revealed during the clash with the Government of U.P. in 1939, when the Khaksars brought down the Congress Ministry (this is discussed in more detail in Chapter 3). Within a few months of this clash, in February 1940, a ban on Khaksar activities was imposed by Sir Sikandar Hayat Khan, Premier of Punjab and a member of the Working Committee of the All India Muslim League (AIML). Mashraqi tried his best to get the prohibition removed. Meanwhile, on March 19, 1940, 313 Khaksars came out on the streets of Lahore (Punjab) in peaceful protest and paraded in military formation. The police resisted their march and opened fire. Many Khaksars were killed on the spot and a large number were seriously injured. According to unofficial reports, well over 200 people were butchered by the police firing. Some of the injured later passed away. On the same evening

---

[16] IOL L/I/1/629. P. 62.
[17] IOL L/I/1/629. P. 60.
[18] *The Deccan Times*, October 28, 1945.
[19] Hussain, P. 153.

(March 19, 1940), police with entire armor and steel raided Khaksar headquarters. Mashraqi's son (Ehsanullah Khan Aslam) protested, and he was hit by the police with a tear-gas grenade; he was seriously hurt, and a few months later, he succumbed to the injury and died on May 31, 1940.[20] On the evening of March 19, Mashraqi was also arrested in Delhi, where he was staying in connection with negotiations with Muslim leaders as well as the Government to get the ban on the Tehreek removed.

With their actions, the Khaksars proved to the world the spirit of *do or die*. The Khaksars' dedication, boldness and challenge to the Government were proven during the aforementioned conflicts with the Government of United Provinces (U.P) in 1939 and the Government of Punjab in 1940. They proved that they were not cowards and were determined to win freedom. The Khaksars who were arrested never showed signs of surrender.

There is no doubt that the Khaksars developed enough strength to bring the rulers to their knees. When India was groaning under repression, injustice and destitution, the nation's hearts were filled with bitterness. Under these circumstances, the Khaksars could not rest. The Khaksars' dedication and strict discipline had the authorities scared stiff and petrified of the Khaksars and their final objectives; the authorities and anti-Khaksar elements applied full force to completely wipe out the movement.[21] Meanwhile, the Muslim

---

[20] Yousaf 2003, P. 178.

[21] Under rigorous measures and restrictions by the Government, many Khaksars went underground while others remained on the surface. The dilemma for the Government was they could never figure out the total strength of the Khaksars in the entire India. The Government grossly underestimated the actual following of the Khaksar Tehreek, and the figurers in the intelligence reports were far from the actual numbers. In fact, it was not even possible for the Government to assess these figures accurately; the Khaksars had their roots in the masses and it would have been costly, cumbersome and perhaps impossible to investigate each locality in the entire India to ascertain the exact strength of the Khaksars. Such an expense would have been avoided especially in light of the costly World War II in the 40s.

The authorities thought that their strict measures had brought the Khaksars under control. They were vastly mistaken. In fact, the atrocities committed against the Khaksars in the years following March 19, 1940 made the Khaksars even more determined and strengthened their

League first attempted to exploit the Tehreek for its own benefit, but ultimately supported the anti-Khaksar elements in undermining the movement. Yet the Tehreek remained intact, inspired others and focused on its goal of ending foreign rule in India.

conviction for liberty. Never did they forgot their objective and adopted all methods to continue mobilizing the nation to rise for freedom and, at the same time, maintained their demands.

Chapter 3

The Muslim League's Efforts to Exploit the Khaksar Tehreek's Power

Around March or April of 1939, Shia-Sunni riots erupted in Lucknow in which "20,000"[1] Muslims were imprisoned, "hundreds were wounded...and thousands...starved."[2] Mashraqi believed that the Congress Ministry of the Government of United Provinces (U.P.) was behind these riots deliberately and for vested reasons. Based on Khaksar ideology to eradicate sectarianism and seek peace for all, Mashraqi asked the Congress Ministry to stop the Shia-Sunni riots immediately or he would have no choice but to come to Lucknow and stop them himself. He even threatened to bring down the Congress Ministry if they failed to achieve peace between the two Muslim sects. The Congress Ministry failed miserably, whether on purpose or for other reasons, in stopping the riots, and Mashraqi sent a call asking Khaksars to arrive in Lucknow.

On Mashraqi's directive, thousands of Khaksars rushed to Lucknow. They traveled at their own expense and came in batches from various provinces, mainly from the Punjab and NWFP. They arrived in military type khaki uniforms with sparkling spades on their shoulders. They came to Lucknow with the mindset to stop the Shia-Sunni ongoing riots and ensure unity — the essence of the Khaksar Tehreek!

Mashraqi himself arrived in Lucknow toward the end of August 1939. Leading members of Shias and Sunnis met him to sort out the matter successfully. Due to Mashraqi and the Khaksars' sincere efforts and intentions, both sects came to an agreement and the severe riots, that had been ongoing for months, were stopped. This was no small achievement on the part of Mashraqi and the Khaksars. Their success established that the Khaksar Movement was in fact capable of putting into practice its ideology of bringing unity and removing sectarianism.

---

[1] Khan Bahadur Shaikh Fazl-i-Haq Piracha's speech, September 23, 1942, Pp. 460-486.
[2] Ibid.

The Khaksars' discipline, dedication, unity and spirit were witnessed and were commendable. Their arrival upon Mashraqi's order showed their sense of loyalty to their leader. The fact that they came together in batches displayed their unity. The spirit with which they brought an end to these riots showed their genuineness toward the noble cause of bringing harmony and eradicating sectarianism. All of this was a completely unique phenomenon that was witnessed in India.

*****

The Congress Ministry gave no credit to Mashraqi and the Khaksars. In fact, they were upset at the method adopted by the Khaksars, and they considered this an interference in provincial matters. However, these positive results raised the prestige of the Khaksars in the eyes of the public. The Congress Ministry lay helpless in the matter and felt embarrassed in front of everyone. In reaction, the Congress Ministry arrested many Khaksars on the plea that Khaksars were disturbing the peace. Mashraqi was arrested on September 01, 1939 and then released the next day under heavy resentment shown by the public in favor of Mashraqi. Since the Shia-Sunni matter was now under control, Mashraqi left Lucknow along with many of the Khaksars. A sea of people came to the railway station to bid farewell to Mashraqi and thanked him for resolving the issue.

As stated, the Congress Ministry was highly embarrassed by the way Mashraqi was able to intervene and settle the issue. After Mashraqi left, the Congress Ministry, in order to save face, made a false proclamation that he was released only after submitting a written undertaking and promising not to return to Lucknow for one year or send any Khaksars. Mashraqi was disgusted with this fake apology with his forged signature and this false proclamation, as such Mashraqi returned on September 13, 1939. At Malihabad Railway Station (near Lucknow), he was warned not to enter Lucknow or he would be arrested. He disregarded the warning and was taken into custody into Lucknow jail; he was tried in court and sentenced for one month imprisonment. News of Mashraqi's arrest spread like wild fire and thousands of Khaksars from all over the country, abandoning their work and leaving their families behind for an indefinite period, rushed to Lucknow to seek his release. Thousands of Khaksars, from Peshawar to Calcutta, arrived at their own expense; such dedication speaks for itself that Mashraqi lived in the hearts of his followers!

*****

Meanwhile, the All India Muslim League (AIML) had been unable to take any concrete action in resolving the Shia-Sunni riots. This is evident from Sir Harry Graham Haig's (Governor of U.P.) secret letter to Lord Linlithgow (Viceroy of India), dated May 09, 1939. Haig mentioned the 1939 Shia-Sunni riots in Lucknow and the Muslim League's inability to settle the issue. He also mentioned that the Muslim League was

> "so nervous about their own organisation being disrupted by this controversy that they would take no line at all, and I [Haig] was told even that Jinnah had threatened ex-communication to any Muslim Leaguer who should try to intervene. I [Haig] have read in the paper today that Jinnah suggests that the Muslim League may find some solution [to the riots], but I am disposed to doubt whether this means anything."[3]

In a meeting on August 12, 1939, the League decided not to interfere in the Shia-Sunni conflict despite "numerous representations from Moslems of both sects requesting intervention by Mr. M.A. Jinnah."[4] If the League had been an influential party among the Muslims, as it claimed to be, it would have taken initiative to keep the two sects of Muslims from fighting or at least called a meeting between them. To stay away from the issue was the easiest decision.

Yet the League, along with everyone else, was watching the events in Lucknow very closely. The strength, popularity and vigor of the Khaksar Tehreek could not go unnoticed. Hence, the Muslim League tried to seek the goodwill of the Khaksar Tehreek in order to gain political advantage from the Khaksar-Congress Ministry conflict. The AIML had no standing anywhere in India at that time; this was evident from their miserable failure in the elections of 1937.[5] With this poor position, the AIML wanted to somehow use the Khaksar strength for its own political motives. The Khaksar-Congress Ministry conflict provided an excellent and ideal opportunity to do so.

Thus, on October 04, 1939, Quaid-e-Azam Muhammad Ali Jinnah (President of the AIML) sent a messenger to Mashraqi in jail, with a message asking Mashraqi to provide authority to Quaid-e-Azam to discuss the question of the Khaksar conflict with Linlithgow, Viceroy of India. The messenger insisted that Mashraqi provide this authority immediately, however Mashraqi provided no such response. Jinnah was to meet Linlithgow the next day and wanted to show him that he had influence on Mashraqi; this is why, prior to his meeting

---

[3] IOL MSS EUR F125/102. P. 184.

[4] *The Statesman*, August 14, 1939.

[5] "It [Congress] won 711 out of total number of 1,585, the rest being divided among fifteen other groups including the Moslem League. The Moslems were entitled to 482 of these 1,585 seats but the League won only 108, less than one fourth of the Moslems electorate and less than one fifteenth of the total Indian electorate. It did not get a majority in a single province, not even in the predominantly Moslem northern provinces of North West Frontier (95 per cent Moslem), Sind, Punjab and Bengal, the first two of which elected Congress governments and the latter two, coalition ministries." Congress swept eight of the eleven provinces. (Kane, P. 68.) Also see Appendix VII.

with Linlithgow, Quaid-e-Azam was seeking an immediate confirmation from Mashraqi.

At the same time, Jinnah also offered his services of mediation to Nehru, in order to settle the conflict between the Congress Ministry and the Khaksars. Quaid-e-Azam asked Nehru to ask Rafi Ahmed Kidwai, Acting Premier of Congress Ministry[6], to send papers about the Khaksar dispute to Jinnah. Jinnah's request was complied with. Jinnah also spoke to Kidwai in this regard.

On October 05, the Khaksar deputation also had a meeting with Rafi Ahmed Kidwai. Both sides expressed their point of views. The deputation later also met Mashraqi in jail.[7] The Tribune of October 06, 1939 also reported that the deputation would meet Kidwai again.

On the same day (October 05, 1939), Quaid-e-Azam met with the Viceroy and right after with Sikandar Hayat (Punjab Premier).[8] According to the Khaksar circle, Quaid-e-Azam discussed the Khaksar issue at these meetings, however, no details of the meetings were released to the press. This Khaksar version can hardly be refuted because the Khaksar-Congress Ministry conflict was constantly being reported in the press; there was no way that the Jinnah-Linlithgow meeting could have ignored the hot topic in which the Khaksars had challenged the Congress Ministry. This conflict was enough for the British to sense that challenge to the Central Government was not far ahead. Anyhow, the matter was kept secret for certain reasons that created suspicion in the Khaksar circle.

Quaid-e-Azam again wrote to Mashraqi on October 06, 1939. The next day, on October 07, 1939, Jinnah had a telephone conversation with Rafi Ahmed Kidwai regarding the Khaksar issue.[9] It is important to note that Quaid-e-Azam had not paid much attention to the Khaksars in the past, and this extra keenness and advances from his side would raise questions in anyone's mind. Hence, skepticism and disbelief in Mashraqi's mind were quite natural. Mashraqi had no choice but to stay quiet and wait until he was released. This was the right thing to do.

Meanwhile, the Congress Ministry of U.P., which was already under extreme pressure and was facing humiliation, was attempting to resolve the issue with the Khaksars amongst themselves. On October 08, 1939[10], the U.P. Premier sent Mashraqi his proposals for ending the Congress Ministry-Khaksar conflict. No agreement came out of the message and the conflict persisted.

---

[6] Pandit Govind Vallabh Pant was the Premier of U.P.
[7] The Tribune, October 06, 1939.
[8] Ibid.
[9] The Tribune, October 09, 1939.
[10] See Mashraqi's letter on October 25, 1939.

The Muslim League continued to interfere in the matter. At its October 08, 1939 meeting, the U.P. Muslim League Council discussed the Khaksar Tehreek. *The Tribune*, Lahore of October 10, 1939 reported on this meeting:

> "Discussion appears to have taken place at...[the] meeting of the U.P. Muslim League Council over the question of attitude to be adopted by the Muslim League towards the Khaksar movement. It was emphasised that in so far as the Khaksar movement had proved a source of strength to the Muslim community it was the duty of the Muslim League to stand by them and prevent their effacement...Prominent leaders among those who spoke were Sir Raza Ali (who was the sponsor of the resolution), Ch. Khaluquz Zaman, Mr. Z.A. Lari and other prominent Muslim U.P. legislators."

It is important to note that, at this time, the Muslim League had no ministry in any province and the League did not have any power to enable it to protect the Khaksars. The Khaksar Movement on the other hand was at its peak and had millions of followers across India. Hence, such statements were issued by the League to send a message to the Muslims that the League was trying to support the Khaksar Tehreek. In this manner, the League hoped to gain public support and build up its own following. According to the Khaksar circle, the Muslim League was interfering in the Khaksar-Congress Ministry conflict without any request from Mashraqi thus far. The Muslim League was getting involved for its ulterior motives of seeking benefits in the public and in Government circles. Hence, all these steps by the Muslim League were nothing but political opportunism. The following Governor of U.P.'s letter endorses this.

On October 08, 1939, Sir Harry Graham Haig (Governor of U.P.) wrote a secret letter to Lord Linlithgow (Viceroy of India). He mentioned the Government's concern that the Muslim League may support the Khaksars. Haig stated,

> "...there were threats that the Muslim League might support the cause of the Khaksars before long. This is simply political opportunism, the utilization of a convenient weapon for attacking the Ministry..."[11]

Dr. Sir Zia ud Din (Vice Chancellor Aligarh University and a supporter of the Muslim League and of the Khaksar Tehreek) was considered to be close to Mashraqi. Thus, the AIML tried to use his services to get a favorable answer from Mashraqi. On October 08, Dr. Sir Zia ud Din, visited Mashraqi in Lucknow jail after seeing the Premier of U.P. He talked about Quaid-e-Azam's strong desire to see Mashraqi. Additionally, Nawab Ismail Khan, President of the U.P. Provincial Muslim League, insisted on interviewing Mashraqi in jail to discuss the Khaksar-Congress Ministry of U.P. settlement. Nawab Ismail Khan along with Begum Habibullah and Mubashar Hussain

---

[11] IOL MSS EUR F125/102. P. 339.

Kidwai, Secretary of the U.P. Muslim League, went to meet Mashraqi on the same day (October 08). They brought Jinnah's message and desperately attempted to persuade Mashraqi to accept Jinnah's offer of resolving the problem. It is important to note that Mubashar Hussain Kidwai admitted to Mashraqi in Lucknow jail that the Khaksars' conflict with the Congress Ministry had put new life into the Muslim League in U.P. This again shows that the Muslim League's continued interest in the Khaksar-Congress Ministry issue was for vested motives. Under these circumstances, Mashraqi was bound to become skeptical of the League's intentions, however, Mashraqi agreed to discuss the matter face to face with Quaid-e-Azam, after his release.

On the same day (October 08), Nawab Ismail Khan briefed Quaid-e-Azam over the phone[12] about the meeting with Mashraqi and said that Mashraqi was willing to meet Jinnah after his release. On the same day, Quaid-e-Azam spoke to Rafi Ahmed Kidwai, Minister in U.P., and suggested the release of Allama Mashraqi on parole, so that Mashriqi could meet Quaid-e-Azam.[13] Allama Mashraqi did not agree to be released on parole or to conduct a phone conversation with Quaid-e-Azam. To my understanding, Mashraqi did not want to accept any favors. Mashraqi decided to wait until his release (set for October 14, 1939), after which he was willing to meet with Quaid-e-Azam. Refusal of release on parole or phone conversation was again a correct decision, as Mashraqi in jail could not know what the actual motives of such aggressive initiatives were.

On October 08, 1939, the U.P. Muslim League passed a resolution that if the Congress Ministry did not settle with the Khaksars by October 20, then from October 22, the League would start a civil disobedience.[14] Again, the League was trying to send a message to the Muslims that they were working in the interest of the Khaksars. In actuality, the intent of the League was to use the Khaksars to weaken the Congress Ministry. (Despite this resolution, the League did not start the civil disobedience movement because they could not do it without the Khaksars' help).

On October 09, 1939, Nawab Ismail Khan met with the Viceroy and discussed the Khaksar issue. Nawab Ismail Khan also met Quaid-e-Azam and explained various developments regarding the Khaksar Tehreek issue with the Congress Ministry. All these efforts kept the Muslim League in the public eye and limelight of publicity. While these activities by AIML were in full swing, the Congress Ministry and Khaksar deliberations also continued.

Three days prior to Mashraqi's release, on October 11, 1939, Quaid-e-Azam (from New Delhi) sent a written invitation to ensure that Mashraqi would not change his mind and still meet him. Obviously this meeting was meant to send a signal to all concerned that there was a strong possibility of the Muslim

---

[12] *The Tribune*, October 09, 1939.
[13] *The Hindustan Times*, October 09, 1939.
[14] *The Tribune*, October 09, 1939.

League and the Khaksar Tehreek uniting or working together. But the advantage was not to go to the Khaksar Tehreek.

Quaid-e-Azam wrote:

"Dear Allama Mashriqi,
This is just to inform you that at my request the acting Prime Minister of U.P. sent me all the papers relating to the conflict between the Government and the Khaksars from the Government point of view with his covering letter dated the 5th of October.
Thereafter at my suggestion he agreed to release you without imposing any condition so that you may come to Delhi and meet me, and if there was any hitch in your agreeing to this suggestion you should be enabled to speak to me on the phone from Lucknow jail.
Hon'ble Mr. Rafi Ahmad Kidwai informed me that you were not willing to do either. I, therefore, apprehending some misunderstanding, got in touch with Nawab Ismail Khan, who was in Lucknow, on phone to communicate to you personally my suggestion. He had an interview with you on the 8th [October 1939] at the Lucknow jail and on his arrival at Delhi on the 9th [October 1939] he informed me that you told him that you would only come after your present term of imprisonment expires about the 15th [14th] of October [1939].
Since then Dr. Sir Ziauddin Ahmad met me today and explained to me the situation further. You know that I am anxious to do all I can to help the Khaksars in the matter, and I once more request you to come to Delhi without delay. I would have come to Lucknow but just at this moment it is not possible for me to do so and Dr Sir Ziauddin will explain to you why at this critical moment I can't leave Delhi.
I do hope that you will in these circumstances come to Delhi, so that we could handle the matter at once as any delay may complicate the situation.
I shall be obliged if you will send me an immediate reply.
Yours sincerely,
Sd. M.A. Jinnah"[15]

On October 11, 1939, Dr. Sir Zia ud Din met with Quaid-e-Azam to discuss the Khaksar-Congress Ministry issue. While these deliberations were on, public support for the Khaksars continued. On October 14, 1939, in order to show their support, over 10,000 people gathered at Jamia Mosque Aligarh and passed a resolution condemning the actions of the Congress Ministry of U.P. against the Khaksars.

After completing his sentence, Mashraqi was released on October 14, 1939. The Khaksar discord with the Congress Ministry was yet to be settled. Upon Mashraqi's release, Dr. Sir Zia ud Din came to Lucknow, again with Quaid-e-Azam's request for Mashraqi to meet Jinnah. Quaid-e-Azam wanted this

[15] Yousaf 2004, P. 80.

meeting at all costs. Under these circumstances, it was impossible for Mashraqi to not meet him. Hence, Mashraqi and Dr. Sir Zia ud Din traveled together to Delhi. During their travel, they discussed various issues including the Khaksar issue with the Congress Ministry of U.P. and Quaid-e-Azam's involvement in the issue. From the conversation, Mashraqi gathered that Quaid-e-Azam had been implying that the Congress Ministry of U.P. was listening to Mashraqi on Quaid-e-Azam's behest. Mashraqi also gathered that political ends were desired. From Mashraqi's letter (as follows), it seems that Mashraqi also got the impression that Quaid-e-Azam was siding with the Congress on the Khaksar issue, for some political advantage. All of these factors brought a bad taste to Mashraqi's mouth. Thus, prior to the meeting with Quaid-e-Azam, Mashraqi wrote a letter (on October 14, 1939), explaining his position on the matter and at the same time seeking clarification from Quaid-e-Azam. This letter somewhat reflects Mashraqi's annoyance.

"My dear Jinnah,
Your letter sent through Dr. Sir Ziauddin Ahmad asking me to have a talk with you concerning the struggle between Idara-i-Aliyyah and the U.P. Govt.
The U.P. Government have given me in writing that they desire peace. It was on account of this undertaking that I came over to have a friendly talk with you, but in view of the most shameful demonstration of force and heartless cruelty displayed by the U.P. Government to-day at 9 a.m. at the very moment when I was released from jail and more especially when they gave me an undertaking of desire of peace, I find that it will be impossible for me to begin any talk of peace with you until U.P. Govt. stop at once all exhibition of force, e.g., lathi charge and firing. One Khaksar is reported to have been so very seriously injured that he must have died by now.
Till negotiations go on Government should stop all force. I shall then arrange to have the matter discussed with you.
Please let me know the intentions of the Govt. through Sir Ziauddin Ahmad. I shall remain in Delhi tomorrow Sunday and if necessary Monday also.
I appreciate the trouble you are taking in the matter.
Yours Sincerely,
Inayatullah Khan"[16]

On October 15, Jinnah replied and wrote the following letter to Mashraqi:

"Dear Inayatullah Khan,
I am in receipt of your letter. I am afraid you have not understood my position in this matter and I did not think that I shall have to carry on any correspondence with you. I do not represent the U.P. Government and I am sorry to find that you are treating me as if I were the agent of the U.P. Government.
I was moved entirely in the interest of Muslim India as many letters and telegrams were sent to me and also several influential Musalmans [Muslims] saw me and urged me to do

---

[16] Yousaf 2004, P. 82.

something with regard to the unfortunate conflict that was created between the U.P. Government and the Khaksars and hence I wanted to know all the facts correctly.

In the course of my conversations with Pandit Jawaharlal he offered to ask the U.P. Government to send me all the facts from the point of view of the Government. When I received the papers from Mr. Kidwai, the acting Prime Minister of U.P., it naturally struck me that I should know first hand from you the version of the Khaksars and hence my suggestion to Mr. Kidwai that you should be released without any condition being imposed upon you to come and meet me so that I may know exactly all the facts and then see what I can do in the matter in the interest of the Musalmans.

I regret deeply the loss of life and serious injuries to the Khaksars that have been caused.

I am sorry you are imposing conditions upon me before you can come and talk to me as if I was acting on behalf of the U.P. Government. I am not asking you to 'begin any talk of peace with me' but U.P. Government in the best interests of Musalmans.

I don't know what undertaking the U.P. Government has given to you. There are no negotiations going on between the U.P. Government and myself except that at my suggestion you were released for the purpose indicated above...
Yours sincerely,
M.A. Jinnah"[17]

It is important to note that Mashraqi was not released on Quaid-e-Azam's request. He was freed after completing the one month term of his sentence.

*****

Owing to the continued insistence of the Muslim Leaguers as well as Quaid-e-Azam's desire that had been conveyed to Mashraqi, Mashraqi met with Jinnah on October 15, 1939 at Nawabzada Liaquat Ali Khan's house.[18] It was important to hear from Quaid-e-Azam himself as to what he had to say. The deliberations did not end in the first encounter.

On October 16, 1939, Quaid-e-Azam and Liaquat Ali Khan visited Mashraqi at the Khaksar camp in Karol Bagh (Delhi). In line with the Khaksar ideal of simplicity, no frills, red carpets, or anything ostentatious (which Leaguers were used to) was arranged for this meeting. Everyone sat on ordinary and inexpensive chairs, instead of luxury sofas. However, a military style Guard of Honor was accorded to Quaid-e-Azam.[19] The two leaders met in a modest atmosphere. Barrister Mian Ahmed Shah and Dr. Sir Zia ud Din were also present. Mashraqi and Quaid-e-Azam again discussed various issues including the Khaksar-Congress Ministry of U.P. conflict, the overall political situation,

---

[17] Yousaf 2004, Pp. 82-83.
[18] Yousaf 2004, P. 83.
[19] Ibid.

the well-being of the masses, etc. During these meetings, Jinnah convinced Mashraqi that he could bring about a settlement in the Khaksar-U.P. issue.

At these meetings, Quaid-e-Azam also stated that he desired to bring the Khaksars under the Muslim League flag. Mashraqi discussed representation of commoners in the Muslim League as well as the well-being of the masses. Quaid-e-Azam was vague about representation of commoners in the League, and he had nothing on his plate to help the masses. Mashraqi was highly disappointed and hurt to note that Quaid-e-Azam was only interested in seeking political benefit for the Muslim League by using the Khaksars. Mashraqi was already well-versed in the aims of top leadership of the Muslim League but these meetings further convinced him that the Muslim League's objectives were completely different from those of the Khaksar Tehreek. In fact, these meetings gave a signal that the two organizations were poles apart in their goals and these meetings laid the foundation for their rift. However, in spite of disillusionment, Mashraqi did not close this door.

After this meeting, Mashraqi left for Lahore and correspondence between Mashraqi and Quaid-e-Azam regarding the Congress Ministry-Khaksar conflict continued. On October 19, 1939, Mashraqi sent a telegram to Quaid-e-Azam:

> "Wire next move demand viewing Government hostility free to-day"[20]

On the same day, Quaid-e-Azam replied to Mashraqi's telegram regarding the ongoing negotiations with the Congress Ministry of U.P.:

> "Discussed matter fully with Dr. Katju [a minister in Congress Ministry] he informed me that he will let me know from Lucknow on his return the Government answer to your proposals."[21]

In the meantime nothing happened, and in desperation owing to lack of results, Mashraqi sent three telegrams between October 17 and October 24 and a letter on October 25[22] to Quaid-e-Azam.

*****

Meanwhile, the Congress Ministry of U.P. remained on its toes. On October 18, 1939, the Governor of U.P. (Sir Harry Graham Haig) sent a letter to the Governor of Punjab (Sir Henry Duffield Craik). Haig wrote,

---

[20] Hussain, P. 118.
[21] Yousaf 2004, P. 85.
According to Jinnah's press statement on October 26, 1939, he met with Dr. Katju on October 18, 1939 in Delhi.
[22] Hussain, P. 117.

"These large jathas [groups of Khaksars] arrived in the Meerut Division usually without any notice and caused us the gravest anxiety...This Khaksar movement, with its military formations and its formidable weapons, masquerading as merely a civil resistance movement, presents a new problem in India..."[23]

A copy of this letter was also sent to the Viceroy of India. The letter itself indicates the Government's nervousness and apprehensions, particularly of the Khaksar Tehreek's militant ability. The militant ability of the movement had two sides to it; first, to convert the indolent people into a robust nation, an extremely important feature for any community to demand freedom. Second, it sent a clear-cut message to the British that their rule was challenged and an uprise had begun. Both sides of the movement were obviously a source of serious worry for the ruler; this was no small achievement for the Khaksar Tehreek.

*****

On October 25, 1939, Mashraqi returned to Delhi to attend a Khaksar camp. Since his meeting with Jinnah on October 16, Quaid-e-Azam had not achieved anything. In spite of the assurances made at the Mashraqi-Jinnah meeting, nothing had changed. Mashraqi was frustrated. Hence, upon his arrival, he wrote (on October 25, 1939), out of disappointment, to Quaid-e-Azam from the Khaksar Camp at Karol Bagh, Delhi:

"My dear Mr. Jinnah,
I have just come over from Lahore. Twelve precious days have been wasted and I understand from [Barrister] M. Ahmad Shah that nothing particular has come about except what Government already agreed to on October, 8. I am sure I would have moved mountains in these twelve days. It is a shame if Government has ignored your presence in the peace discussions.
I want a quick and final reply now. If Government declines to accept the terms in toto and most especially the compensation that we demand per Khaksar as well as a guarantee for the protection of Muslim rights, I fear I shall have to do something very drastic in order to bring the present Ministry down to reason and I am sure that I shall succeed. You know we are pledged to bring the Ministry down if they do not accede to our demands, and you will see in the next few days that we shall have that done at all costs provided they do not resign of their own accord. Of course, I shall be ready to listen if you can make the Ministry see the seriousness of the situation.
Yours Sincerely,
Inayatullah
P.S. I have already sent you three telegrams in this connection."[24]

---

[23] IOL MSS EUR F125/102. P. 359.
[24] Yousaf 2004, Pp. 86-87.

On October 26, 1939, Quaid-e-Azam issued a press statement:

> "Dr. Katju saw me in Delhi on October 18 [1939] on behalf of the
> United Provinces Government in connexion with the situation created
> with regard to the Khaksars and I placed before him the proposals of
> the Khaksars. After a full discussion he told me that he would go
> back to Lucknow and confer with his colleagues and let me know
> finally on or before October 25 how far the United Provinces
> Government is prepared to meet the demands formulated by the
> Khaksars.
>   I received from him last night the proposals on behalf of
> the Government showing how far it is prepared to meet the Khaksars'
> demands. I have forwarded the Government's proposals in answer to
> the Khaksars' demands to Allama Mashraqi (their leader) to-day for
> him to consider and deal with them in such manner as he may be
> advised."[25]

Instead of talking to Mashraqi, Quaid-e-Azam issued a press statement, which
was unnecessary. Political analysts would certainly endorse that such
statements are made to gain political benefits. The intent was nothing but to
gain public support. The statement sent a message to the public that the
Muslim League was sincere to the Khaksars and was doing its best to help
another Muslim organization.

Jinnah also sent a reply on October 26, 1939 to Mashraqi's letter of October
25, 1930. Quaid-e-Azam explained his position and the actions he had taken to
resolve the issue. He also enclosed the Congress Ministry's proposals with this
letter. These proposals offered nothing that could have brought a settlement,
and Quaid-e-Azam had no influence either on Mashraqi or on the Congress
Ministry. In fact, Jinnah knew that his interference was not bringing desired
results and the proposals would not end the conflict, that is why he withdrew
from the mediation and stated in his letter:

> "You [Mashraqi] know that from the very commencement neither
> you nor the U.P. Government [Congress Ministry] were willing to
> submit to my arbitration or abide by my advice and that is why I
> express no opinion at present with regard to your demand and the
> Government also. It is now for you to adopt such course as you may
> fit proper."[26]

This was the end of the Muslim League's attempt to use the Khaksar-Congress
Ministry conflict to promote itself for political reasons. Their attempt to use
the Khaksars and bring them under their fold by gaining their sympathies
could not materialize. However, they did manage to get publicity.

On October 26, 1939, Mashraqi rejected the Congress Ministry's proposal.
(Mashraqi and the Khaksars had demanded the protection of Muslim rights,

---

[25] *The Statesman*, October 28, 1939.
[26] Hussain, P. 119.

compensation for the Khaksars killed in Bulundshahr (U.P.) on October 08, 1939, the release of arrested Khaksars, and the payment of fares to return home for all Khaksars who had arrived in U.P. from various cities of India.)

On October 27, Rafi Ahmed Kidwai (U.P. Government) sent Chaman Lal to persuade Barrister Mian Ahmed Shah (a Khaksar leader) to meet Rafi Ahmed Kidwai for a truce. On October 29, 1939, Barrister Mian Ahmed Shah met Rafi Ahmed Kidwai and discussed Khaksar demands.

Meanwhile, the tension between the Congress Ministry and the Khaksars continued. It is important to note that Quaid-e-Azam could not bring satisfactory results, and it continued to be viewed that the Muslim League was involving itself only to get prominence and benefit itself; this was also evident in the news from that time. *The Tribune*, Lahore of October 31, 1939 reported that in reply to a question regarding the Khaksars at the U.P. Assembly on October 30, 1939,

> "Mr. Rafi Ahmed Kidwai, Minister [U.P.]...suggested that the Muslim League had lost their influence in the U.P. and were, therefore, trying to regain it through the Khaksar organisation."

*****

The Khaksar-Congress Ministry conflict was yet to be resolved. The Government of India was undeniably shaken up at the Khaksar-Congress Ministry conflict; phone calls and secret letters were immediately exchanged between the Governor of U.P. (Sir Harry Graham Haig), Viceroy of India (Lord Linlithgow) and the Governor of Punjab (Sir Henry Duffield Craik) about the Khaksars. Governments in various provinces were closely watching the situation. The nervousness of the British Government in India was visible from their correspondence about the Khaksars during this period and after. The Khaksars Tehreek's strength had created a new and significant issue for the British Government, particularly at the time, as World War II had just begun on September 01, 1939. At this juncture, the British did not want to open another front in India with the Khaksars. For the Indians it was the right time to send a warning sign to the colonial power that their rule in India had been challenged. The Khaksar Tehreek's challenge was evident from the correspondence of the high ups in the British circle from 1939 onwards.

The Congress Ministry of United Provinces itself was thunderstruck by the power, discipline and unity of the Khaksar Tehreek, which it had witnessed during the Shia-Sunni conflict and after the arrest of Mashraqi. The Congress Ministry found itself completely helpless and powerless. It appeared that the Khaksars were in greater control of the situation in Lucknow than the Government itself. On October 30, 1939, within a few days of Mashraqi rejecting the proposal sent through Jinnah (on October 26, 1939), the Premier of U.P., Pandit Govind Vallabh Pant, met the Governor of U.P. to submit the Congress Ministry's resignation. The mishandling of the Khaksar issue was the main reason that the Congress Ministry had to resign. However, they put up their resignation which was accepted by the Governor on November 03, 1939, on the same day, when "the Congress Ministries throughout India quitted [resigned] on 3rd November as a protest against Britain declaring war against Hitler without taking the Indians into confidence or as a measure of blackmail."[27] Resignation on this same day allowed the Congress Ministry to save face.

The Ministers resigned and agreement between Khaksars and the U.P. Governor was finalized on November 04, 1939[28]. The Government released the arrested Khaksars, agreed to pay their fares back and provided compensation for the dead. It is important to note that this serious matter was resolved on Khaskar terms, and the credit taken by the Khaksars for the downfall of the Congress Ministry does indeed hold merit; this is evident from the Governor's letter dated November 08, 1939. The Governor of U.P.'s exact wording is produced here for clear understanding. On November 08, 1939, the Governor of U.P. in his letter to the Viceroy wrote:

> "I said good-bye to Pant [Pandit Govind Vallabh Pant, Premier of U.P., on October 30]... The Khaksar problem was also a great embarrassment. It was clearly desirable to show considerable forbearance in Lucknow... I telegraphed to you on November 2nd that the situation involved embarrassments and that I proposed to accept the resignation of the Ministers next morning. After sending that telegram I had a letter from Kidwai complaining in rather petulant terms about the difficulties of the situation, particularly in connection with the Khaksars, and saying that the Ministers felt their position and authority were being jeopardised and questioned. I discussed the position with him...and made it clear that while I recognized their difficulties, the situation from my point of view also was far from easy... On the 3rd November, having heard from Your Excellency [Viceroy], I wrote to Kidwai saying that I had decided regretfully to accept the resignation of the Ministers...
>
> We also agreed to pay the fares of the men [Khaksars who had come to Lucknow from other provinces] back to their homes. I should have preferred to omit both these terms, but it was clear that if we wanted an immediate settlement we would have to accept something on these lines and I felt it was better to settle at once than to run the risk of long discussions with a possibly doubtful issue..."[29]

*****

Hence, the Khaksars were able to settle the issue with the U.P. on their own and without the Muslim League. Prior to this settlement, Mashraqi had written to Quaid-e-Azam that if the Congress Ministry of U.P. failed to listen to the Khaksars' demands, then as a last resort, Mashraqi would have to take dire

---

[27] Hussain, P. 119.
[28] Governor of U.P.'s letter, November 08, 1939. IOL MSS EUR F125/102. Pp. 380-385.
[29] IOL MSS EUR F125/102. Pp. 380-381.

measures to bring about results. This was conveyed in Mashraqi's letter to Jinnah which he had written on October 25, 1939:

> "I [Mashraqi] fear I shall have to do something very drastic in order to bring the present Ministry down... if they do not accede to our demands, and you will see in the next few days that we shall have that done at all costs..."[30]

Mashraqi, a man of great credibility and strong conviction, proved to the world what he had stated in his letter to Quaid-e-Azam. It can be well-imagined how commanding and authoritative the Khaksar Tehreek had become. It was no small success for a movement to dictate its terms and force the Government to submit. So, the Khaksar Tehreek's claim of bringing down the Congress Ministry is well-founded.

Anti-Khaksar forces were dumbfounded at the power of the Khaksar Tehreek and submission of the Government to Khaksar demands, including agreeing to pay the fare for Khaksars to return to their homes. The Khaksars returned home and received outstanding ovation for their campaign, successful handling of the Shia-Sunni issue, triumphant agreement with the Government of U.P. and bringing down of the Congress Ministry.

As a result, Khaksar popularity grew phenomenally and a very large number of people became attracted to the movement and joined the Khaksar Tehreek. Public support for the Khaksars grew multi-fold. The Khaksar challenge to the Government brought tremendous results. This conflict opened the eyes of all communities in India and made them aware that British rule could be brought to an end; the demand for an independent India picked up tremendous momentum from this incident onwards.

On November 28, 1939, Mashraqi announced a goal of enrolling another 2.5 million people within the next six months and printing of an additional 25,000 copies of *Al-Islah* per week in the near future.[31]

Mashraqi now began to move aggressively toward launching the Khaksar Tehreek's ideology and finally leading the Indians toward freedom.

*****

Until this point, there was no comparison between the Khaksar Tehreek and the Muslim League with regard to their strength, reputation and esteem in the masses; the Tehreek clearly outpaced the AIML in every respect. As stated previously, the advances by the Muslim League to settle the issue between the Khaksars and the U.P. Government were politically motivated. The League wanted to fulfill its agenda, enhance its prestige in the public and Government

---

[30] Yousaf 2004, P. 86.
[31] Hussain, P. 153.

circles, and somehow impress Mashraqi (who was well respected and powerful) to bring the Khaksar Tehreek under the flag of the Muslim League. The idea was to use the strength of the Khaksar Tehreek to benefit the Muslim League.

Mashraqi was willing to join hands with the Muslim League, despite the power he had already attained. He was keen on giving full assistance to the Muslim League as long as it benefited the common man. However, there were differences in ideology between the two parties. Mashraqi was in favor of lifting the masses, whereas the Muslim League leadership was interested in using the Khaksars for their gain; in fact, the League had been lifting the upper classes. The Khaksar Tehreek was representing the common man where as the Muslim League was representing a Westernized galaxy of Knights, Khan Bahadurs, Nawabzadas and big landlords. Mashraqi was working towards the freedom of India, whereas the Muslim League had no concrete plan except using the Muslim community for their vested interests. The Khaksar Tehreek wanted to eliminate communalism; the Muslim League adopted the policy of communalism.

Under the circumstances, compromise between the Muslim League and the Khaksars was not possible. They were a world apart in their aims and ideology and lifestyles and demeanor; thus agreement between Mashraqi and Quaid-e-Azam could not be reached; the Muslim League resented Mashraqi and the Khaksar Tehreek's popularity, and it started thinking of ways to undermine the Khaksar Tehreek.

Chapter 4

The British & Muslim League's Attempts to Wipe Out the Khaksar Tehreek

The Khaksar Tehreek's muscles were revealed during the conflict with the Congress Ministry in U.P. in 1939. The incredible unity, discipline, dedication and authority with which they brought the Congress Ministry down and influenced the U.P. Government to accept their terms sent shock waves not only to the British but throughout the anti-Khaksar circles in the Congress and the All India Muslim League (AIML). The victory over the U.P. Government sent a clear signal to the Indians, that they could resist the rulers and end British rule. This event unquestionably enhanced the standing of the Khaksars in the eyes of the public. Within almost a decade of its creation in 1930, the Khaksar Tehreek's prestige had reached its peak and the Khaksars were well praised for their activities.

Mashraqi's offer of 50,000 Khaksars for the defense of India at the beginning of World War II, further displayed the Khaksars' strength; this offer was sent from Mashraqi on October 04, 1939 from Lucknow Jail to the Viceroy of India.[1] This also shook the anti-Khaksar elements. Sir Sikandar Hayat Khan, Premier of Punjab, did not like Mashraqi's offer. He viewed it from a different perspective. First, someone else had emerged very powerful in his province who could offer such a large number of trained people for the defense of India. Second, the Premier was not in a position to even offer one person to the British for the said cause. This was an insult for him, particularly because he looked impotent in front of the British, who were seeking Indian help in World War II. Most importantly, the Premier saw the Khaksar Tehreek as a great threat to his political career in the Punjab.

As stated, the Khaksar Tehreek had sent serious alarm and generated fear amongst the anti-Khaksar forces. This led them to take necessary steps to crush the movement. Therefore the anti-Khaksar forces in the Muslim League, the Indian National Congress (also known as Congress Party or Congress) and

---

[1] Yousaf 2004, Pp. 73-74.

the British started working against the Khaksars and decided to eliminate the movement. Sir Sikandar Hayat Khan (Premier of Punjab and member of the Working Committee of the All India Muslim League) took on the task of getting rid of the Khaksar Movement. After the Lucknow event, Sikandar Hayat launched his propaganda against the Khaksars. The media was encouraged to write against the Khaksar Tehreek. Hindus were told to ask questions in the Punjab Assembly regarding Khaksar activities, all in order to create a sense of fear about the Khaksars.

It is important to note that initially the Muslim League attempted to benefit from the Khaksar's power. When the Mashraqi-Jinnah meetings took place from October 15-16, 1939 in Delhi, Jinnah tried to bring the Khaksars under its flag. But these meetings did not bring any desired results and the Muslim League considered the Khaksar Tehreek to be a rival party. When the Leaguers realized that they could not gain benefit from the Tehreek, they moved to crush the movement.

Hence, a treacherous game to wipe out Khaksar Tehreek had begun! As history tells us, Muslims have suffered because of intrigues amongst themselves. The Khaksar Tehreek suffered because certain powerful elements in the All India Muslim League supported the British. Further, Sir Sikandar Hayat Khan, member of the Working Committee of the Muslim League and Premier of Punjab, clamped down on the Khaksar Tehreek and imposed restrictions on its activities. Mashraqi and thousands of Khaksars ended up in jail and other members and supporters suffered tremendously.

The following is a story of how anti-Khaksar elements worked to eliminate the Tehreek.

*****

On December 04, 1939, in the Punjab Legislative Assembly, Sir Sikandar Hayat Khan declared the Khaksar Tehreek to be a *communal movement*.[2] In fact, the Tehreek was the opposite as evident from its ideology and the fact that there were Muslims, Hindus, Sikhs and people from various religions and backgrounds in the movement. Mashraqi was not in favor of communalism as it brings hate and violence. The Khaksar Tehreek sought unity among all communities regardless of religion, caste, color or creed. In fact, the Tehreek was to frustrate the designs of those who used communalism for their own political advantage. The Khaksars were peace loving as demonstrated from their activities since 1930. Even on occasions when they were attacked, they only protected themselves. There was no history of them indulging in any violent activities. Despite all this, Sikandar declared the Tehreek to be a *communal movement* for his own political ends. By declaring Khaksars to be communal, he was preparing grounds to impose the ban in Punjab. In addition, the media was encouraged to write against the Khaksars.

---

[2] *The Tribune*, December 05, 1939.

On December 24, 1939, Sir Sikandar Hayat Khan met with Jinnah in Bombay for three hours. According to the Khaksar circle, the Khaksar Tehreek was discussed at this meeting, although no such discussion was made public. Sir Sikandar Hayat Khan began to build support for what he was planning.

From February 03-06, 1940, the Muslim League held a meeting of its Working Committee in New Delhi. The meeting was attended by members, including Quaid-e-Azam and Sikandar Hayat Khan. The Khaksar Tehreek was discussed. Within days of this meeting, Sir Sikandar Hayat Khan, with the blessings of anti-Khaksar elements — among the British, the All India Muslim League and non-Muslim leaders in the Punjab Legislative Assembly — ordered a raid on the Mohammadi Press in Lahore, which printed the Khaksar weekly, *Al-Islah*. On February 22, 1940, the raid on Mohammadi Press was held and copies of *Al-Islah* and Khaksar materials were confiscated.

Sikandar continued his efforts against the Khaksars. Steps that were taken included the following: the media was used rigorously to propagate and write against the Khaksar Tehreek; non-Muslim support was obtained by Sikandar to raise voices in the Punjab Legislative Assembly questioning the Khaksar Tehreek's activities; and the Khaksar Tehreek was falsely propagated to have links with the German Nazis. The fact that Mashraqi had offered 50,000 Khaksars to defend India from any aggression was ignored.

Mashraqi arrived in Delhi on February 27 and met Quaid-e-Azam and other leaders, asking them to use their influence to stop Sikandar from taking such actions. Mashraqi was confident that Jinnah, in the interest of Muslim unity, would use his influence on Sikandar, who had recently been elected (on January 12, 1940) unanimously as President of the Parliamentary Party of the Muslim League. But Quaid-e-Azam politely declined by saying "I wish Sikandar could be my man. If it had been so I would have ordered him."[3] Quaid-e-Azam's reply was not appreciated in the Khaksar circle and it was understood that he was leaning toward the side of Sikandar in his actions against the Khaksars. It was firmly believed by the Khaksars that if proper pressure was applied, Sikandar, being an important member of the Muslim League, would have succumbed. Also, none of the prominent Muslim Leaguers, including Quaid-e-Azam, issued any statements to counter anti-Khaksar propaganda. Mashraqi was highly disappointed at Quaid-e-Azam's indifferent attitude.

On February 27, 1940, Mashraqi sent a telegram to the Viceroy of India:

> "Premier of Punjab attempting serious clash Khaksars on ground having published pamphlet...request immediate interview otherwise terrible disaster critical time war reaching Delhi tomorrow"[4]

---

[3] Yousaf 2003, P. 127.
[4] IOL L/P&J/8/680.

Within a few days of the raid at Mohammadi Press, on February 28, 1940, Sikandar placed a ban on Khaksar activities in Punjab, including parading, wearing of uniform, and so on. Sikandar had already declared the Khaksar Tehreek, which was a non-communal party, to be communal; thus implying that it spread hate. The other argument that Sikandar gave to defend the ban was that he could not allow any para-military force to operate in Punjab, as it would be difficult to maintain peace and would encourage other political groups/parties to follow suit. Sikandar produced no evidence that the Khaksars had ever disturbed the peace in his province (since the movement's creation in 1930). In fact, he ignored that such parties were needed to end British rule. The Khaksar Tehreek had set the ball rolling and brought an uprise; other communities had already begun to copy the Tehreek and started their own volunteer movements, as this was needed to end foreign rule. The Khaksars had not resorted to any violence thus far; according to the Khaksar circle, even if the Khaksars had to depend on violence as a last resort to free British India, Sikandar should have turned a blind eye and let such forces rise to remove foreign rule. But Sikandar was a right-hand man of the British, and he had to prove his loyalty to his superiors. Here was a man prepared to support the British against the Khaksars.

Mashraqi wanted to avoid confrontation, therefore, on March 03, 1940, he sent the following telegram to A.K. Fazl-ul-Haq (a prominent Muslim Leaguer from Bengal), seeking his intervention to resolve the Khaksar issue with Sikandar:

> "Pb. [Punjab] Premier bent on crushing Khaksar Movement. Terrible clash inevitable. Intervene effectively."[5]

However, nothing came out of this telegram.

On March 06, 1940, Jinnah arrived in Aligarh. The Khaksars presented him with a military style Guard of Honor. On March 08, the Khaksars again welcomed Quaid-e-Azam upon his arrival in Bareilly from Aligarh and presented him with a Guard of Honor. The Khaksars overlooked Quaid-e-Azam's lack of interest in the restrictions on the Tehreek's activities. Primarily, these gestures were to show unity towards the League.

On March 12, 1940, Mashraqi issued a statement to let the public know that propaganda against the Tehreek's activities was false and Sikandar's decision to impose a ban on the Khaksars' peaceful activities was unjustified. The statement said:

> "We have been doing social service openly and collectively for the last ten years and no Government has taken exception to this. We now consider it our right and are prepared to give a physical fight, without transgressing any law, to any power which would want to

[5] Yousaf 2004, P. 97.

snatch this right of ours...It is ridiculous that a jamaat [party] which has offered services of 50,000 of its members for the defence of India should be proceeded against under the Defence of India Rules. I am filing a case in the court of law and would try to obtain a stay order till its final disposal."[6]

The ban on the Khaksars was in discussion amongst the Muslim, non-Muslim and British circles. Jinnah's meeting with the Viceroy on March 13, 1940 was of significance. People expected Quaid-e-Azam to do his best to get the ban removed. If, as per his statement, he had no influence on Sikandar Hayat, then he would at least ask the Viceroy not to ban the Khaksar Tehreek. Yet, after the meeting, nothing was said regarding the Khaksar issue. If Quaid-e-Azam did not discuss the ban, why was this important issue not raised? This was obviously disappointing, not only for the Khaksars, but for the people who supported the Khaksars. The Muslim Leaguers were giving the Khaksars the cold shoulder, and it was obvious that they were not serious about the removal of the restrictions.

Despite Mashraqi's desperate efforts, Sikandar maintained the ban, obviously with the consent of the British. The Khaksars were brought to the point of resistance. On March 19, 1940, Khaksars protested against the ban and came out on the streets of Lahore. Their march was completely peaceful yet the police opened fire and killed many innocent Khaksars indiscriminately. According to K.L. Gauba (Member of the Punjab Legislative Assembly), 200 Khaksars were killed, however the Government admitted only 32; an outrageous number. This was the most brutal massacre in the 20th century in India, after the Jallianwala Bagh massacre in Amritsar by Brigadier-General Reginald Dyer on April 13, 1919. After the massacre, on the same evening, Allama Mashraqi was arrested in Delhi.[7] The police also raided the Khaksar headquarters in Lahore (adjacent to Mashraqi's house) and arrested Allama Mashraqi's two sons.[8] His third son, Ehsanullah Khan Aslam, was seriously injured by the police. He was wounded by a tear gas grenade and later died (on May 31, 1940). An extremely tense situation existed within the public in light of the Khaksar massacre, injury to Mashraqi's son and the arrests of Mashraqi, his sons and the Khaksars. This tragedy sent shockwaves throughout the entire India. The Muslims were even more shocked because this happened in a province where the Premier was a Muslim and member of the Working Committee of the AIML, a party that was supposed to protect Muslims and their interests and not crush them. After the massacre, persecution of the Khaksars started and a large number of Khaksars were thrown in jails.

Quaid-e-Azam avoided condemning Sikandar, and, sensing the delicacy of the situation, he issued diplomatic statements. Quaid-e-Azam wanted to kill two

---

[6] Yousaf 2004, P. 99.
[7] During his stay in Delhi, Mashraqi had sought assistance from Quaid-e-Azam, Sir Shah Sulaiman, Dr. Sir Zia ud Din, Sir Zafarullah Khan, Nawab Bahadur Yar Jang and others for the removal of the restrictions on Khaksar activities.
[8] *Dawn*, June 07, 1942.

birds with one stone, that is, to satisfy Muslims and tell them that he supported the Khaksars and also to not condemn Sikandar because he needed Sikandar's support to promote the AIML in Punjab. On March 20, 1940, in Delhi, Jinnah issued two statements. He stated:

> "...I...appeal to the citizens of Lahore particularly to maintain peace and order and to prove to the world that we are capable of adjusting controversial matters justly and fairly. At this critical moment the prestige and honour of the All-India Muslim League is in the hands of the Mussalmans of the Punjab. I feel confident that they will fully respond to my appeal and will conduct the deliberations of the session of the League in a manner which will do credit to Islam."[9]

On the same day, Quaid-e-Azam issued another statement to the press regarding the police firing on March 19, 1940:

> "I am deeply grieved to hear the tragic account of the incident in Lahore last evening regarding the clash between the police and the Khaksars, resulting in terrible loss of life and injury on both the sides. I hope the Khaksars will carry out the instructions issued by their leader, Mr. Innayatullah Mashraqi, published in the newspapers of this morning. As one who has always been so kindly treated by the Khaksars, I appeal to them most earnestly to keep the peace and not precipitate matters by defying law and order. It is difficult to say anything till I am in possession of full facts of the situation." Jinnah also stated that the upcoming Muslim League Session would still be held in Lahore as planned.[10]

Quaid-e-Azam's statements were carefully worded and did not express any disapproval toward Sikandar or the Punjab Governor. These statements implied nothing but appeals to remain calm, with some sympathetic words for the Khaksars. Quaid-e-Azam also indirectly touched the inner sense and egos of the Muslims. He said, "prove to the world that we [Muslims] are capable of adjusting controversial matters." In other words, if the Muslims did not stay calm and instead resorted to protests, they would fall under the category of being deficient, in a sense. He also stated, "prestige and honour of the All-India Muslim League is in the hands of the Mussalmans." Again he appealed to the emotions of the Muslims to not let his request down. Then Jinnah stated "conduct the deliberations of the session of the League in a manner which will do credit to Islam." He was thus again attempting to utilize the people's emotions toward Islam for the benefit of the AIML.

In his second statement, issued on the same day, Jinnah sympathized with the Khaksars. This was to please and earn the goodwill of the Khaksars and their supporters. These statements also sought goodwill from Sikandar and the British, as he did not make any statement against them. Quaid-e-Azam showed sympathy to the policemen to earn amity of the British. He requested that the

---

[9] *The Hindustan Times*, March 21, 1940.
[10] Ibid. *The Statesman*, March 21, 1940.

Khaksars maintain peace and gave them hope that he would deal with the problem. In asking the Khaksars to stay calm, Quaid-e-Azam was actually helping Sikandar and the Government, by removing difficulties that were anticipated as a result of the massacre. Quaid-e-Azam could not afford Sikandar's resentment, because Sikandar, as Premier of the Punjab, had a standing in Punjab and was very popular with the British. Sikandar was in a position to help the Muslim League gain strength in the Punjab. On the other hand, Quaid-e-Azam was not hoping to get much from the Khaksar Tehreek at this juncture. Thus, it was politically beneficial for him to support Sikandar and not annoy the British. It is interesting to note that Quaid-e-Azam, at no occasion, condemned the British Governor of Punjab or even the police's action. Quaid-e-Azam avoided criticism of Sikandar, the Government and even the massacre itself.

*****

In spite of the great tragedy of March 19, 1940 when a large number of innocent Khaksars were killed and the fact that a ban on public gatherings under Section 144 was in place, the Muslim League decided not to postpone its session scheduled for March 22-24, 1940 in Lahore. The ban was suspiciously removed to hold the historic session of the All India Muslim League. This raised eyebrows and suspicion amongst the public. The Khaksars sensed a conspiracy against their movement.

If one studies the history prior to and after the March 19 massacre, this leads one to believe that there was in fact an intrigue against the Khaksar Movement. What political motives were behind the Khaksar massacre? Who was behind the ban on the Khaksar Tehreek? Why did Sikandar remove Section 144 to allow the League session to be held? Why did the Governor not keep the Premier from removing Section 144? Why did the Muslim League not launch rigorous efforts for the release of Mashraqi and removal of the ban on the Khaksar Tehreek? There are many other questions that need to be answered and require a discussion at length. Will historians discuss these topics, however, or will they avoid debates on purpose so that they do not implicate important personalities? The souls of those Khaksars who died on March 19, 1940 will always ask these questions.

Here I address one question. Why did the Muslim League refuse to cancel the session despite the extraordinary tragedy in Lahore? Circumstantial evidence proves that the Muslim Leaguers would gain some benefits from holding the session on schedule. These benefits included the following: (and all of these calculations turned out to be correct)

- ❖ The massacre was bound to attract a large crowd to the city, and this would benefit the League's meeting
- ❖ The ban on the most powerful Muslim party, the Khaksar Tehreek, in India would allow the Muslim League to gain prominence

78 | Nasim Yousaf

- ❖ The massacre would politically finish the Premier Sikandar Hayat's[11] hold in the Punjab; this would obviously benefit the Muslim League, which up until that point, had no standing in the Punjab province. The Muslim League would emerge as a strong party in the presence of Sikandar's loss of grip in Punjab politics

*****

On March 20, 1940, Quaid-e-Azam left Delhi by train to attend the historic session in Lahore. At railway stations along the way, Jinnah encountered people protesting against the Government's action and brutal murder. They also demanded the release of Mashraqi and the Khaksars as well as the removal of the ban on the Khaksar Tehreek. They raised slogans in support of Mashraqi and the Khaksars.

On March 21, 1940, the Viceroy of India wrote to the Secretary of State for India (Lord Zetland). In his letter, he stated, that the clash on March 19 showed "how great a potential danger the Khaksar Movement has become."[12]

On the same day (March 21), Quaid-e-Azam arrived in Lahore. Sikandar Hayat Khan (Premier of Punjab) received him at the railway station and later had a long discussion with him. Sikandar apprised him of the situation regarding the police firing on March 19, 1940.

Quaid-e-Azam witnessed the concern of the people everywhere — en route to and upon arrival in Lahore. In view of the public's restlessness and sympathy with the Khaksars, he feared that there could be an outbreak. He also realized that the Muslim League session could be in jeopardy and could turn into a chaotic situation, if at that critical moment people's heightened emotions (as a result of the grave tragedy) were not solaced. Sensing the emotions of the public, Jinnah, at his host Nawab Sir Shah Nawaz Mamdot's residence (Mamdot Villa), made a statement to the press:

> "The unfortunate tragic events that have taken place during the last three days resulting in loss of life and injury must not lead you to lose your balance. You must deal with the situation calmly and dispassionately and I feel confident that you shall find a solution of the situation."[13]

Through his statement, Quaid-e-Azam pacified the people and requested that they remain calm. At the same time, he gave them hope for a solution. Again, Quaid-e-Azam did not condemn the Punjab Government's actions. Based on the serious and grave situation that prevailed in Lahore, he could clearly see people losing balance which would disturb the Muslim League session. Very

---

[11] Sikandar Hayat belonged to the Unionist Party of Punjab. The Muslim League's collaboration with him was a political move.
[12] IOL MSS EUR F125/9. Pp. 179-80.
[13] *The Tribune*, March 22, 1940. *The Hindustan Times*, March 22, 1940.

tactfully, he controlled their mindset so that no untoward incident would take place at the start of the League's session that could be embarrassing for him, Sikandar or the Punjab Government. Quaid-e-Azam selected his words with extreme care.

Indeed! Lahore's public was fully charged and could have blown away the Muslim League session. They monitored Quaid-e-Azam's activities and expected him to visit the wounded Khaksars in the hospital. Soon after his arrival in Lahore, Jinnah, accompanied by Sir Raza Ali and Mian Abdul Haye (Education Minister), visited the injured policemen and the Khaksars in the hospital. He first visited the police officers, D. Gainsford (Senior Superintendent of Police) and Beaty (Deputy Superintendent of Police). He then also made a short visit to the injured Khaksars who asked Quaid-e-Azam to see their injuries. Obviously, Muslims did not appreciate that Quaid-e-Azam first visited and sympathized with the police officers, who were responsible for the mass killing, and later paid a very quick visit to the Khaksars.

After visiting the Khaksars in the hospital, Quaid-e-Azam arrived at Minto Park in the afternoon (on March 21, 1940) to unfurl the Muslim League flag. People had already gathered at Minto Park in hopes that Quaid-e-Azam would speak about the Khaksars. Slogans in favor of Khaksars and against Sir Sikandar and the Punjab Government were raised.[14] Again the crowd conveyed to Quaid-e-Azam that they were sympathetic to Mashraqi and the Khaksars. When people heard that Quaid-e-Azam had visited the Khaksars in the hospital prior to coming to Minto Park, they raised slogans in favor of Quaid-e-Azam. In history books, these slogans have been attributed to the Muslim League's popularity and their support for the League's session. In light of the Khaksar tragedy, people's emotions were at their peak. Quaid-e-Azam calmed the emotions of the general public and made the following speech:

> "You have today given me the privelege... of unfurling the flag of the All-India Muslim League... Before I say anything more, I want to tell you what is uppermost in my mind as I have just returned from the Mayo Hospital. I'm sure that we all deeply grieve the unfortunate tragedy which has resulted in a large number of lives being lost and injured. I think every man and every woman must sympathise with the families and the dependents of those who have died and those who have been injured. The session of the All-India Muslim League is going to open on the eve of this most unfortunate situation that has been created in Lahore.
>   Let me put to you what is the acid test of a great nation and of a great people. The answer is the greater the difficulties, the more we should keep ourselves calm and cool.

---

[14] These slogans, condemning Sikandar and showing support for the Khaksars, are a historical fact but have been eliminated from history on purpose. We do not read about them in books or in supplements that are published on March 23 every year in Pakistan. However, they are clearly mentioned in newspapers of the time.

The Muslim League, I am sure will not fail to rise to the occasion, irrespective of the parties concerned, to handle this question in a manner which is just and fair. You must, therefore, rely that this is the one and the only organization of the Muslims of India. We must, therefore, stand as one man with one voice under this flag which you have honoured by asking me to unfurl. I have no doubt. I have full confidence in my people, and we shall face any and every difficulty in a manner which will be worthy of this great Muslim nation. I, therefore, earnestly appeal to you—let us not have any kind of doubt or suspicion with regard to the decisions of the Muslim League and let us take a right decis'n and stand by it."[15]

At the ceremony, people's sympathy with the Khaksars was worth witnessing. They rose slogans in support of the Khaksars such as, "Allama Mashriqi Zindabad," "Khaksar-e-Azam Zindabad," and "Khaksar Shuhdha Zindabad." Once again, Jinnah consoled people and gave them hope when he stated, "The Muslim League, I am sure will not fail to rise to the occasion."

When Quaid-e-Azam showed his support for the Khaksars, the crowd chanted "Quaid-e-Azam Zindabad." If people had not been raising slogans in support of the Khaksars, Jinnah would have had no reason to make the said speech. One cannot remain silent about the skill that Quaid-e-Azam applied and how tactfully he handled one of the gravest situations of his life by using appropriate words such as "stand as one man with one voice under this flag which you have honoured by asking me to unfurl." In his speech, he gave hope to resolve the Khaksar issue, comforting people on the tragedy and asking them to support the Muslim League.

At a Muslim League Council meeting that evening, Z.H. Lari (M.L.A. Deputy Leader of the Muslim League in the U.P. Assembly) wanted to move a resolution regarding the tragic killing of the Khaksars. Jinnah disallowed this on the technical ground that a resolution could only be moved with 15 days prior notice. However, Z.H. Lari responded that it would have been impossible to provide 15 days notice when the incident took place only days ago. Thus, it was finally agreed that the resolution would be moved in the meeting of the Subjects Committee. Again, Quaid-e-Azam was doing his best to help Sikandar. He shifted the speech to be made at the Subjects Committee's meeting. *The Tribune* of March 23, 1940 reported that:

"The Press was excluded from the meeting of the Council of the Muslim League…this was done…for the first time because previously the Press was always allowed to watch the proceedings of the Council."

It was quite obvious why the Muslim League was taking these steps.

*****

[15] *The Hindustan Times*, March 22, 1940.

On March 22, 1940, the 27th Session of the All-India Muslim League commenced in Lahore. People again rushed to the venue of the Muslim League session in anticipation to see the Khaksar issue resolved. Restlessness prevailed and many tears were shed. Slogans were raised in support of the Khaksars and against Sir Sikandar. People's support for the Khaksars was praise worthy. They repetitively demanded withdrawal of the ban on the Khaksar Movement and immediate release of Mashraqi and the Khaksars. There was a demonstration against Sikandar Hayat Khan at the session and Sikandar was provided with an extra guard force.

The Tribune wrote:

> "Shouts of 'Sikander Hyat Murdabad' [death to Sikander] were raised by…the audience in the 'pandal' when the name of the Punjab Premier was mentioned by the Chairman of the Reception Committee…The demonstration created a sensation in the 'pandal.'
>
> Immediately after Mr. Jinnah finished his speech a Muslim woman got up on the platform and referred to the happenings[16] at Lahore [the massacre on March 19, 1940].
>
> A crowd held demonstrations against the Punjab Ministers as they left the 'pandal' in their cars."[17]

According to another source:

> "On the eve of the Muslim League session at Lahore… Banners proclaiming 'Sikander murdabad' [death to Sikander] were hoisted near the entrance to the hall where the session was to be held. Sikander was indebted to Jinnah for shelving discussion of the issue at the open session of the League: Jinnah thus…safeguarded the position of the Punjab ministry, but also maintained the unity of the League in a very difficult situation, and increased his influence over Leaguers in the Punjab."[18]

The public was frustrated as to why, up to this point, Quaid-e-Azam had not openly condemned the actions of the Government against the Khaksars. People who were protesting were whisked away or moved out by the Muslim League guards. However, they continued raising slogans in favor of Mashraqi and the Khaksar Tehreek but against Sikandar and the Punjab Government. While the League session was in progress, the police in Lahore tear-gassed the peacefully demonstrating Khaksars and arrested many. The situation was tense, and there was resentment against the behavior of the Muslim League and its delaying tactics of not demanding action against the Punjab Government.

---

[16] The media was under censorship, hence it could not directly refer to the March 19, 1940 tragedy. Instead this newspaper used "happenings" to refer to the said event.
[17] *The Tribune*, March 23, 1940.
[18] Singh, P. 60.

The Subjects Committee of the All-India Muslim League met that night behind closed doors. The press was once again excluded from this meeting.

*****

On March 23, 1940, at Minto Park, Lahore, the second open sitting of the All-India Muslim League began at 3:30 pm, an hour later than the time announced. Another demonstration against Sikandar Hayat Khan was held at the session. A big crowd surrounded the pandal. Great resentment prevailed; the crowd was restless and demanded that a resolution on the Khaksars be taken up immediately. The public was getting enraged as thus far no action had been announced by the Muslim League. People again shouted "Sikandar Hayat Muradabad" and "Turn out Sikandar Hayat from the League." National Guards and volunteers were rushed in to control the situation. The Muslim Leaguers tried to calm the people down but nothing worked. The people demanded that Jinnah speak to them. News of this demonstration was also reported in *The Tribune*, Lahore of March 24, 1940; it reported:

> "Mr. Jinnah on coming out of the *pandal*, acceded to the demand of the crowd to speak to them...He addressed the crowd and appealed to them to have patience and remain quiet and orderly.
> Referring to the demand of the crowd [that a resolution on the Khaksars be taken up immediately], Mr. Jinnah said that the matter would be thoroughly examined by the Subjects Committee and they would not be influenced by anybody. The issue, he said, would be taken up tonight by the Subjects Committee and they would rise only after coming to some final decision."

Restlessness in favor of the Khaksars continued amongst the people. Slogans in favor of Khaksars and against Sir Sikandar were raised continuously. People were uneasy and wanted to hear of the Muslim League's action against Sir Sikandar. Quaid-e-Azam had to appeal to the jittery and angered crowd to remain patient. He again gave hope to the crowd.

On March 23, 1940, the Subjects Committee met once again and discussed the Khaksar Resolution. Sir Sikandar Hayat Khan was present at the meeting and made a statement to explain his position. Sikandar gave a very emotional speech to cover up what had happened on March 19 with the Khaksars. He obviously justified his position. Many Muslim Leaguers severely criticized and blamed Sir Sikandar for the tragedy that occurred on March 19, 1940. Protests were made during the Subjects Committee meeting. Finally, the Subjects Committee approved a resolution on the Khaksar issue, which would be moved the next day by Quaid-e-Azam.

Sir Henry Duffield Craik (Governor of Punjab), who was constantly receiving updates on the Muslim League's reaction to the Khaksar issue, wrote a secret and personal letter to Lord Linlithgow (Viceroy of India) on March 24, 1940. Craik wrote about Sikandar's account of the Subjects Committee from the previous evening. In the meeting, "Six differently-worded [Khaksar] resolutions"[19] were considered by the Muslim League regarding the Khaksar incident on March 19, 1940. After this, Sikandar made a speech and mentioned that "malign influences were at work."[20] Then "Jinnah...announced that no further discussion would be necessary."[21] It was then agreed to present a resolution in the open session of the next day (March 24, 1940). In the letter, Craik stated that he thought that this resolution would sympathize with the people and would also announce "an independent and impartial committee of enquiry which will command the confidence of the people."[22] Craik added that Sikandar told Jinnah that the "resolution should be put from the Chair"[23] meaning "passed without discussion."[24] Jinnah responded that "this would be difficult, as people might insist on speaking."[25] Craik thought that the idea was that Jinnah would announce that the Subjects Committee was unanimous in regards to the resolution.

This letter reveals the proceedings of the Subjects Committee's meeting. This meeting was extremely important, as the Khaksar Resolution had to be announced the next day. It is evident from the letter that different versions of the Khaksar Resolution were presented and one was picked strategically to serve a purpose. Soon after these resolutions, Sikandar was asked to speak on the subject. He made a very emotional speech and tried to earn sympathy. After Sikandar's speech, people wanted to make speeches but right at that moment, when Sikandar had earned some sympathy, Quaid-e-Azam intervened and did not allow anyone else to speak on the subject. The timing was perfect to prevent aggravation of the situation and save Sikandar. Another tactical move, which was pre-determined, was that Quaid-e-Azam would move the Khaksar Resolution. Prior to announcing the Khaksar Resolution, he would state that it had been unanimously accepted. Therefore, there would be no need to discuss it any further. The Governor of Punjab's letter is self-explanatory as shows how everything had been pre-planned.

*****

On March 24, 1940, the public continued to be highly restless and demanded that the Khaksar issue be addressed. The Muslim League held an open session in the morning. Nawabzada Liaquat Ali Khan[26] informed the people (amidst cheers) that the Khaksar issue would be taken up at the night session of the Muslim League. Knowing that the people were extremely supportive of

---

[19] IOL MSS EUR F125/89. Pp. 53-55.
[20] Ibid.
[21] Ibid.
[22] Ibid.
[23] Ibid.
[24] Ibid.
[25] Ibid.
[26] Nawabzada Liaquat Ali Khan was a prominent Muslim Leaguer and later became the first Prime Minister of Pakistan.

Allama Mashraqi and the Khaksars, Liaquat Ali informed a restless and uneasy crowd that the Khaksar issue would be dealt with.

Meanwhile, the Khaksars demonstrated in Lahore and a large crowd gathered to watch. Shops in the area were closed and traffic was suspended. Police arrived on the scene and called in a tear-gas squad. Prominent Muslims, including K.L. Gauba (Member Punjab Legislative Assembly) and Mian Amir ud Din, assured the Khaksars that the Khaksar massacre was on everyone's mind and could not be avoided as a topic of discussion in the Muslim League Session. Upon hearing this assurance, the Khaksars agreed to stop the demonstration. The Khaksars then proceeded to the Muslim League Session with the Muslim leaders. Meanwhile, other Khaksars held a demonstration in another part of Lahore and in Anarkali, where a large crowd gathered. To stop these demonstrations, Nawab Bahadur Yar Jang, a leader of the Khaksars in Hyderabad (Deccan) and a supporter of the Muslim League, met with the Naib Salar-i-Azam of the Khaksar Tehreek, Punjab, who was in jail. Nawab Yar Jang requested the Naib Salar of Punjab to authorize him to stop the ongoing demonstrations by the Khaksars. Nawab Yar Jang assured the Naib Salar that the question of the removal of the ban on the Khaksar Tehreek had been taken up by the Muslim League. Upon this assurance, the Naib Salar authorized Nawab Bahadur Yar Jang to instruct the Khaksars in Lahore to suspend their demonstrations.

Influx of Khaksars from other cities continued and they joined the ongoing demonstrations in Lahore. At a demonstration at Golden Mosque in Dabbi Bazaar, the Khaksars addressed the large crowd that had gathered. The City Magistrate asked the Khaksars to surrender, but the Khaksars refused. At this point, Nawab Bahadur Yar Jang arrived and informed the Khaksars that negotiations for a compromise regarding the Khaksar issue were in progress between Quaid-e-Azam and the Government. He also informed them that the imprisoned Naib Salar-i-Azam of the Khaksar Tehreek, Punjab had authorized him to stop the demonstrations. He thus appealed to the Khaksars to surrender their belchas and uniforms and suspend their *satyagraha*. The Khaksars acceded to Nawab Jang's appeal. The fact, that the Khaksars turned down the request of the City Magistrate, but accepted the orders of the imprisoned Naib Salar-i-Azam, spoke of the discipline and obedience of the Khaksars toward their own superiors.

On March 24, 1940, Maulana Shahid Fakhri (President of the City Congress Committee, Allahabad and U.P.) said in a statement:

> "The statement that Mr. Jinnah issued to the Press, after the firing in Lahore [on March 19, 1940], and in which Mr. Jinnah advised the Khaksars to maintain peace but did not utter a word against the action taken by the Punjab Government was surprising. It appears that the

personalities of Mr. Jinnah and Sir Sikandar Hayat Khan have been considered above human criticism."[27]

People resented the fact that Quaid-e-Azam was using diplomatic language and was not openly criticizing Sikandar or the Punjab Government.

On March 24, 1940, before the night session of the Muslim League, Sikandar Hayat Khan threw a party. Quaid-e-Azam was the guest of honor at the party. The party was also attended by Sir Henry Duffield Craik (Governor of Punjab), besides other higher-ups in the Government. At the party, Quaid-e-Azam's discussion about Mashraqi and the Khaksar Tehreek with the Governor of Punjab was exceptionally important. The discussion was reported to the Viceroy by the Governor of the Punjab in a secret letter (dated March 25, 1940):

> Craik wrote, "Jinnah handled a difficult situation with very great skill. His primary objective was, of course, to preserve unity in the League."
>
> Further, the Governor wrote about his talk with Jinnah. He said that Jinnah's attitude was friendly toward him, however "ascendency... has slightly gone to his head." The Governor pointed out to Jinnah that there seemed to be "malign influences working in the background" of this Khaksar incident. Jinnah talked about his meeting with Mashraqi in Delhi and said "that he [Mashraqi] was hardly sane, extremely difficult to reason with and dangerously fanatical." Jinnah also "spoke of the Khaksars as being an organization with 'several lakhs' of members...he cited... evidence of his estimate... He then went on to say that he hoped to be able to find sober and responsible men, of whom he said there were many among the members of the organization, to assume direction and control over it and to devote its energies into more useful channels, such as village uplift...'social service'... actually I [Craik] fancy he visualizes the Khaksars as a potentially powerful propaganda agency on behalf of the Muslim League. He [Jinnah] expressed the hope that if he was able to accomplish what he had in mind, my Ministry would agree to rescind their order declaring the Khaksars an unlawful association... He admitted...military side of the Khaksars'...was a menace to the public peace and could not be permitted." Jinnah also suggested that there should be a judge from outside of Punjab, so as not to imply that the committee was biased; Sikandar was of the same view.
>
> In his letter, Craik said that the Khaksar incident had done damage to the Ministry, however he was hopeful that this would not be permanent. He also said that the press had been well-handled by the government's officers. The Governor thought that Mashraqi would not be able to resume his leadership and "for a long time to come he [Mashraqi] must not be allowed his liberty." The Governor further wrote that he (Governor) and Sikandar were both thankful to Linlithgow for his support on the matter and for arresting Mashraqi.

---

[27] *The Hindustan Times*, March 27, 1940.

Sikandar was visiting Craik daily and following his advice and assured him that he should not worry about anything. Craik stated that the "fate of his [Sikandar's] own Ministry was in the balance and his own political future at stake" and Craik admired Sikandar's courage.[28]

The Governor also sent Linlithgow copies of newspapers that talked about more demonstrations. The Governor appreciated the role of Nawab Bahadur Yar Jang.

When one reads Quaid-e-Azam's language (as above) about Mashraqi and his suggestions, one is amazed how a very respectable person like Quaid-e-Azam could talk against Mashraqi to add scare in the Governor's mind regarding Mashraqi and achieve his own objective. Quaid-e-Azam appeared to be on the side of the Government. He wanted to use the Khaksars (as is evident from the Governor's letter) for the benefit of Muslim League. Quaid-e-Azam used offensive and critical words to describe Mashraqi in order to convince the Governor that Mashraqi was a very difficult person to work with and that the Government would not be able to deal with him. Thus, Quaid-e-Azam was suggesting to the Governor that Mashraqi must be removed from the Khaksar Tehreek's leadership. Quaid-e-Azam clearly told the Governor that he was going to replace Mashraqi whereas to the outside world, he appeared to be a well-wisher of the Khaksars (through his statements). Further, Quaid-e-Azam never demanded that Mashraqi be released and ban on the Khaksar Tehreek be removed. Otherwise, the Governor would have definitely talked about this in his letter.

In the public eye, Quaid-e-Azam's position toward the Khaksars was completely different. He appeared as if he was a well-wisher of the Khaksars and sincerely helping them in their time of difficulty. In reality, this was not true. Quaid-e-Azam's sole purpose was to bring the Khaksars under the Muslim League. It is a fact that Muslim Leaguers never tolerated any other Muslim party. They were anti- Khaksars, Unionists, Red Shirts, Ahrars, Jamiat Ulamah-e-Hind, etc. However, they feared Mashraqi the most as his party was the most powerful and had spread all over India with branches overseas; they feared Mashraqi's popularity and dedicated followers.

It is unbelievable to note how Quaid-e-Azam allowed himself to be used for the cause of the British. Didn't he know that the Khaksars were against British rule and that finishing the Khaksars meant helping the British? Quaid-e-Azam misled people about the Khaksar Tehreek. If he spoke well of the Khaksars to show his sincerity toward them, this was meant for public consumption only; otherwise people would have become anti-Quaid-e-Azam.

---

[28] IOL MSS EUR F125/89. Pp. 55-59.

People should know that what is said behind closed doors could be completely different from what the world is told. So one should not have blind faith in political leaders, and one should question and analyze their moves.

*****

Returning to Sikandar's party in honor of Jinnah on March 24, 1940, others present at the party were Sir Douglas Young (Chief Justice of the Lahore High Court), other Judges of the High Court, A.K. Fazl-ul-Haq (Premier of Bengal), heads of various Government departments, prominent citizens, ministers and leading Muslim Leaguers. The presence of Sir Henry Duffield Craik (Governor of Punjab) at Sikandar's party for Jinnah was viewed with suspicion in the Khaksar circle. It was evident that the British were supporting Quaid-e-Azam for their own ends. The Muslim League at its own could not seek the division of India. If the Government was against the Muslim League Session, then the Governor would not have attended this party, which was held only a few hours before the Pakistan Resolution was adopted.

It is also to be noted that Sikandar was part of this scheme; this is why Sikandar gave Jinnah a very warm welcome upon arrival. As a member of the Government, the Premier could not have done this, if the Muslim League session did not have approval of the British. So the question is, did the Muslim League session have the consent of the British to demand division?

At the Azad Muslim Conference in front of a large number of Muslims and Hindus, Khan Akhbar Khan of the Frontier said:

> "The idea of Pakistan is of foreign origin and has been imported from outside the borders of India...its mischief and its very harmful..."[29]

Maulana Mazhar Ali Azhar (Member Legislative Assembly) addressing a conference said:

> "No one has been able to understand the meaning of Pakistan. The average Muslim using the term hardly understands its import..." According to the newspaper, "He warned the Muslims not to be lured away by the cry of Pakistan."[30]

It is important to highlight that Quaid-e-Azam and Sikandar's relationship was, at the least, a political friendship. Jinnah enjoyed some degree of influence over Sikandar yet Jinnah had said to Mashraqi (at their Delhi meeting on March 27, 1940), "I wish Sikandar could be my man. If it had been so I would have ordered him."[31] Sikandar definitely came under *greater* influence of Quaid-e-Azam after the March 19th tragedy. *The Hindustan Times* wrote on July 08, 1940:

[29] *The Tribune*, June 07, 1941.
[30] *The Tribune*, September 03, 1941.
[31] Yousaf 2003, P. 127.

"Sir Sikandar had sought telegraphic permission from Mr. Jinnah to see Maulana Abul Kalam Azad... Mr Jinnah replied Sir Sikandar saying that he could meet the Congress President as Premier, but not as a member of the Working Committee of the [Muslim] League."

This is substantial proof that Jinnah had control over Sikandar. In the Khaksar circle, it was felt that the Muslim League, if it desired, did have the influence to secure Mashraqi's release and removal of restrictions on the Khaksar Tehreek.

*****

The night session of the Muslim League was held on March 24, 1940, and it opened around 9 p.m. Sikandar was highly embarrassed because of the ongoing protests, thus he did not attend the session on purpose.

The press reported:

"When the open session met at 8.50 p.m. on Sunday [24 March], the atmosphere in the *pandal* was surcharged with excitement in expectation of the Khaksar resolution being taken up. From the very start the proceedings were interrupted with shouts of 'Khaksars Zindabad' and 'Sikandar Ko League Se Nikal Do (expel Sikandar from the [Muslim] League).'" "An atmosphere of subdued excitement created by the prospect of the resolution on the Khaksar question" prevailed.[32]

A huge crowd was present to hear the outcome of the proceedings on the Khaksar issue. Nawabzada Liaqat Ali Khan again had to assure the restless congregation that the Khaksar Resolution was forthcoming and the session would not end without it. He begged the audience to remain calm and assured them that the session would not end without the resolution. He had to make requests to the people "to be peaceful and calm."[33] The crowd was highly impatient and such assurance was needed to keep the people's emotions from getting out of hand.

Since the day of the massacre and the arrest of Allama Mashraqi, everyone including Quaid-e-Azam had been witnessing the increasing support of the public in favor of Mashraqi and the Khaksars. The public outcry was well observed throughout the Muslim League session and wailing and crying by the Khaksars and the general masses was worth seeing. The large attendance at the Muslim League Session, due to the grave tragedy of March 19, showed that the Muslims wanted to see a resolution in respect to the Khaksar Tehreek. People remained restless throughout the session. The public shouted slogans in

[32] *The Hindustan Times*, March 25, 1940.
[33] Ibid.

support of Mashraqi and the Khaksars and vehemently denounced the Punjab Government and Sikandar. The crowd's demands included:

* To hold Sikandar responsible for the massacre of the innocent Khaksars in Lahore on March 19, 1940
* To openly condemn Sikandar and take serious action against him, including expelling him from the Muslim League
* To provide compensation to the families of the Khaksar martyrs
* To release Allama Mashraqi and other Khaksars from jail
* To remove the ban on the Khaksar Tehreek

Finally, when Quaid-e-Azam moved the Khaksar Resolution, thunderous and resounding cheers were heard. Keeping in view the sympathies of the Muslim public, the Muslim League unanimously passed the Khaksar Resolution. The Pakistan Resolution (moved by Fazl-ul-Haq) was passed first, which promised the Muslim community salvation from a totally imagined Hindu domination in Muslim majority provinces. The resolution on the Khaksars was unanimously passed third. The Khaksar Resolution stated:

> "This Session of the All India Muslim League places on record its deep sense of sorrow at the unfortunate and tragic occurrence on the 19th March, 1940, owing to a clash between the Khaksars and the Police resulting in the loss of a large number of lives and injuries to many more and sincerely sympathizes with those who have suffered and with their families and dependents.
>
> This Session calls upon the Government to forthwith appoint an independent and impartial committee of inquiry, the personnel of which would command perfect confidence of the people with instructions to them to make full and complete investigation and inquiry in the whole affairs and make their report as soon as possible.
>
> This Session authorizes the Working Committee to take such actions in the matter as they may consider proper immediately after the publication of the report of the Committee.
>
> This Session urges upon the various governments that the order declaring the Khaksar organisation unlawful should be removed as soon as possible."[34]

At the close of the session, Quaid-e-Azam was very happy that he handled the critical situation and was able to pacify the public outcry. He managed the situation very smartly and tactfully. Further, in a secret and personal letter to the Viceroy, dated March 25, 1940, the Governor of the Punjab showed satisfaction over the Khaksar Resolution and his Ministry coming out of an "extremely critical" problem at the Muslim League session.[35]

---

[34] Yousaf 2004, P. 123.
[35] IOL MSS EUR F125/89. Pp. 55-59.

The day after the session (March 25, 1940), Quaid-e-Azam summed up his impression of the Muslim League Session and acknowledged that the Khaksar tragedy brought all Muslims together. He stated:

> "The first thing that has emerged from the session of the All-India Muslim League is that in the face of the unfortunate occurrence on March 19 resulting in the loss of a large number of Muslims, which shook the Muslims of India and, particularly of the Punjab and Lahore, the Subjects Committee, after many hours of deliberations, came to a unanimous decision and a still more remarkable fact is that the entire body of delegates in the open session and the vast public accepted the [Khaksar] resolution moved by the chair also unanimously. This has shown beyond doubt that the Muslims are capable of standing and going through an ordeal and trial worthy of any great political organization. In my opinion, therefore, this session was far more successful than it would have been otherwise..."[36]

On March 26, 1940, *The Civil & Military Gazette* (Lahore) wrote:

> "The three-day session commenced under the heavy shadow of the Khaksar disturbance, but the use of hard words with reference to it was carefully avoided throughout the proceedings in distinct contrast to the League's methods of approach to other problems...The wording of the resolution was cautious, attempting to avoid embarrassment to the Punjab Government and at the same time satisfying all sections of opinion...Thus the League has taken on a position which in substance confirms the attitude taken by the Punjab Government...As regards the part [of Khaksar Resolution] which urges the removal of the ban declaring the Khaksar organisation an unlawful body, the words 'as soon as possible' in the [Khaksar] resolution are significant and place the onus on the Khaksars themselves."

On March 26, 1940, *The Civil & Military Gazette* (Lahore) wrote in its editorial:

> "As for the resolution touching on the Khaksar incident in Lahore, its only admirable feature was the diplomatic manoeuvre of its presentation...By the stratagem of putting the resolution from the chair and by couching the resolution in language as unexceptionable as it was colourless, Mr. Jinnah cleverly avoided a debate which would most certainly have been acrimonious and might easily have resulted in schism not easily healed. The by no means silent section which condemned Sir Sikandar Hyat Khan and his government for the ban which precipitated the clash between police and Khaksars in Lahore might have adopted methods which would have forced the Punjab Premier to withdraw altogether from his association with the League. Fortunately for Mr. Jinnah and the League (so far as the Punjab is concerned) this was avoided."

---

[36] *The Hindustan Times*, March 26, 1940. *The Tribune*, March 26, 1940.

The Khaksars were unhappy with the Muslim League's behavior and resolution. They saw the resolution as nothing but an inconsequential piece of paper. The contents of the Khaksar Resolution failed to condemn Sikandar or the British Government, and the resolution was passed merely under massive public pressure, otherwise it had no value or significance. In the resolution, there was no demand for the immediate release of Mashraqi or the Khaksars or *immediate withdrawal* of the ban on the Khaksar Tehreek. They knew that the Muslim League willfully delayed the passing of the Khaksar Resolution to the last date. It is intriguing to think about why the Khaksar Resolution was put off to the last session. According to the Khaksars, some of the reasons that it was delayed were as follows:

* The Khaksar tragedy was drawing a large crowd, increasingly so until the last session. People were coming to the session everyday to hear the Muslim League's decision regarding the Khaksars; hence it was in the interest of the League to hold off the resolution until the end, so as to attract a continuous stream of people to the session
* Quaid-e-Azam avoided talking of the Khaksar issue until the last session, as discussing it any earlier would excite the public and jeopardize the Muslim League's own session
* It was best for the League to pass the Khaksar Resolution at the end and move it from the Chair, so as not to allow speeches which would enhance Khaksar popularity and condemn Sikandar and the British

Regarding the large crowd during the three day session, the Muslim League claimed that the gathering at its session was the result of its own strength; this was completely untrue. Historical facts provide evidence of the reality that the Muslim League had no strength in the Punjab at that time. In fact, many people who came to the three day session had no idea what the session was about. The Pakistan scheme represented at the session was ambiguous and people (even Muslim Leaguers) did not understand it, so there was no reason for them to be excited about it. The fact of the matter is that the majority of the crowd came to the session to seek the Muslim League's intervention to redress their grievances regarding the massacre, release of Mashraqi and the Khaksars, and removal of the ban on the Khaksars. The public could not sit idle at one of the most brutal massacres of innocent people of 20th century. According to political circles, Sikandar wanted to postpone the Muslim League session, so that he would discourage a big gathering and avoid embarrassment.

The film clips that are shown of this session on Pakistani holidays of August 14 or March 23 have been edited and do not show the slogans that were raised in favor of the Khaksars and against Sikandar and the Punjab Government. It is highly deplorable that this important event, a turning point in the history of Pakistan, has been completely misrepresented and the Khaksars' role in the resistance movement afterwards has been completely disregarded. The public outcry at and after the session and the resistance of the Khaksars thereafter are missing from Pakistan's history.

*****

After the Muslim League session, on March 26, 1940, in front of a packed visitor's gallery at the Punjab Assembly, K.L. Gauba (M.L.A. in the Punjab Assembly) moved an adjournment motion at 4:30 pm regarding the March 19th incident. Miss Fatima Jinnah (Quaid-e-Azam's sister), Nawab Bahadur Yar Jang, Nawab Mohammad Ismail Khan, Raja and Rani of Mandi, Nawabzada and Begum Liaquat Ali Khan and other Muslim League leaders were among those present at the proceedings. Gauba stated that the Government should issue a list of all those who were injured or killed on March 19, 1940. He also narrated the story of the incident, saying that he saw pools of the Khaksars' blood on the streets. He further added, "The act of shooting was no less than cold-blooded murder."[37] Gauba stated that the number of Khaksars who lost their lives in this incident was grossly understated in the Government's announcements. He later wrote in his book that 200[38] Khaksars had lost their lives.

Supporting K.L. Gauba, Dr. Gopichand Bharghava (Leader of the Opposition) stated that the firing was not just to disperse the Khaksars and was done in a vindictive spirit. K.L. Gauba asked the Premier (Sikandar) to provide a full explanation of the incident. While replying to the adjournment motion in the Punjab Assembly, Sikandar attempted to justify the police firing. He also sympathized with the British Police officers (and their families) who were injured during the clash. *The Tribune*, Lahore of March 27, 1940 wrote, "The Premier paid a handsome tribute to the sense of duty and gallantry displayed by Mr. Gainsford and Mr. Beaty." The mover (Gauba) was never given a chance to reply to Sir Sikandar's statements. Mian Abdul Aziz and D. Chaman Lal protested, "We have never heard of the movers not being given the right to reply."[39] As time ran out, a vote was called, and K.L. Gauba's adjournment motion was defeated.

Meanwhile, on March 26, 1940,[40] Nawab Bahadur Yar Jang called a meeting of the Khaksars to be held on March 28, 1940 at Nawab Ismail Khan's (a Muslim Leaguer) house in Meerut. The purpose of the meeting was to choose a successor to Allama Mashraqi (who was in jail). Neither Nawab Bahadur Yar Jang nor any Muslim Leaguer consulted Mashraqi in this regard. At the meeting, it was proposed that Nawab Bahadur Yar Jang replace Mashraqi as leader of the Khaksars. The Khaksar leaders refused to accept new leadership and stated that any move to replace Mashraqi would be vehemently crushed. Nawab Bahadur Yar Jang also stated that he was conducting negotiations with the Punjab Government in order to remove the ban on the Khaksar Tehreek. He appealed to the Khaksars not to send volunteers to Punjab until a successor to Allama Mashraqi had been chosen.

---

[37] *The Tribune*, March 27, 1940.
[38] Gauba, P. 204.
[39] *The Tribune*, March 27, 1940.
[40] Ibid. *The Hindustan Times*, March 27, 1940.

On the evening of March 26, 1940, Quaid-e-Azam, Fatima Jinnah, Nawabzada Liaquat Ali Khan and Begum Nawabzada Liaquat Ali Khan left Lahore for Delhi. Nawab Bahadur Yar Jang also left on the same train. Quaid-e-Azam arrived in Delhi from Lahore. Khaksars and their public supporters were hoping that Quaid-e-Azam would not leave Lahore until he had settled the issue with Sikandar, and his departure from Lahore brought disappointment.

On April 09, 1940, the Governor of North West Frontier Province, Sir George Cunningham, wrote in his report to the Viceroy of India:

> "The connection between the League and Khaksars has, I think, in the past been closer here than in other Provinces, and the more responsible leaders see the danger of a split as a result of the outburst in Lahore. None of them [Muslim Leaguers] offer any defence for what the Khaksars did, and they are attempting to bring the organisation more under the discipline of the League..."[41]

On April 19, 1940, in a meeting with Barrister Mian Ahmed Shah, Quaid-e-Azam asked him to forget about Allama Mashraqi (when Mashraqi was in jail) and amalgamate the Khaksar Tehreek with the Muslim League.

After Quaid-e-Azam left Lahore, he did nothing concrete for the release of Mashraqi and removal of the ban. Khaksars met him but they came back with the impression that Quaid-e-Azam was least interested in the release of Mashraqi. However, he was keen on bringing the Khaksar Tehreek under the Muslim League. This state of affairs was highly disturbing for the Khaksars. Even the public was noticing Quaid-e-Azam's indifferent behavior. To remind him of his responsibility, the public, from various parts of the country, sent messages and letters to Quaid-e-Azam telling him not to sleep over the Khaksar issue. Hence, on May 08, 1940, Quaid-e-Azam issued the following press statement:

> "I have received numerous telegrams from influential persons from various parts of India and in particular from the Punjab during the last few days urging me to go to Lahore at once and negotiate with the Punjab Government a settlement regarding the Khaksar trouble.
>
> I wish to inform the public and the Muslim Leaguers specially that I have no authority or power given to me by the Khaksar organisation or those who are the leaders now and guiding the movement. I have spoken to many of them, who came to see me, but none can speak with authority or give me the authority to bring about a just and honourable settlement with the Government.
>
> The Muslim League at Lahore had to deal with the situation purely from the point of view and on the basis that Khaksars being a mainly Muslim organisation it was incumbent upon us to see that full justice was done to them and that the Punjab Government dealt with them fairly and justly. But the organisation has not so far cared to

---

[41] IOL MSS EUR F125/75. P. 29.

take the fullest advantage of our services, as they have acted and are acting independently of the Muslim League.

In order to refresh the public memory as to what the exact position was before the sessions of the Muslim League at Lahore, may I point out shortly that there were four questions raised:-

    (1) The ban on Khaksar activities of a military and semi-military character which was already imposed upon them by the Punjab Government.

    (2) The defiance of this ban, which was going on.

    (3) The unfortunate clash between the Khaksars and the police culminating in the firing upon them, which resulted in a terrible loss of life and injuries on March 19, 1940.

    (4) Order declaring the Khaksar organisation unlawful.

The Muslim League session by its resolution urged upon the Government to appoint an impartial and independent tribunal to enquire into the firing and the cause which led to the clash, which resulted in terrible blood shed. That enquiry is going on. The Muslim League also called upon the Government to withdraw the order by which the Khaksar organisation was declared unlawful as soon as possible. In the meantime it was expected that the Khaksars would cease the defiance of the ban and observe peace to enable us to examine the terms of the ban, which was directed against their alleged military or semi-military activities.

According to the declared creed of the Khaksars it was urged and pointed out, their aims and objects were religious and social service and hence any misunderstanding or apprehension on the part of the Government should be removed. But after the Lahore resolution was passed, it was difficult to find anyone on behalf of the Khaksars, who could either control or guide their members and give me the requisite authority and power to negotiate with the Government. On the contrary, the defiance of law and order continued and this has led to the situation getting from bad to worse.

I must point out that the Khaksar organisation is entirely independent of the Muslim League and it has no connection with it. The Muslim League cannot do anything in the matter as we have no control or supervision over the activities of the organisation nor have we got any authority or power to speak on their behalf and come to a settlement which would be implemented or fully carried out and adhered to.

In these circumstances with all my sympathies for the Khaksar organisation I feel helpless in the matter."[42]

This was a most disappointing statement for the Khaksars. It sent shockwaves to the Khaksars and their supporters. Quaid-e-Azam practically abandoned the Khaksars when he stated "I must point out that the Khaksar organisation is entirely independent of the Muslim League and it has no connection with it." The Khaksars felt highly let down, and they realized that Quaid-e-Azam was trying to avoid providing assistance to them on the pretext that he had not been given legal authority to intervene. The Khaksars felt that Quaid-e-Azam could

---

[42] *The Star of India*, May 10, 1940.

have helped them if he had really wanted to, and that he did not require any authority for helping out the Khaksars.

After the historic session at Lahore, despite promises, the Muslim League provided only lip service to the Khaksars and did nothing to get the ban removed or Mashraqi and the Khaksars released. Instead, they put forth efforts to replace Mashraqi and to bring the Khaksars under their flag. Further, the resolution on the Khaksars brought no results; the inquiry committee, headed by Sir Douglas Young (Chief Justice of the Lahore High Court), was appointed by the Government on March 28, 1940 and did not include anyone from the public. The inquiry ended on May 15, 1940, but its report was never published.

In place of helping and strengthening the Tehreek, in a meeting on June 15, 1940, the League adopted a resolution[43] to organize the Muslim League National Guards and Volunteer Corps. This organization was nothing but a copy of the Khaksar Tehreek.

*****

Meanwhile, the Government of India was keeping the authorities in London informed on the happenings in India. On May 24, 1940, the Viceroy wrote to L.S. Amery, Secretary of State for India (in London):

> "Meanwhile the Khaksars have formally renewed their offer to me of 50,000 men to help in the War ... (But there is the) formal statement by Jinnah that he accepts no responsibility for Khaksars or the present attitude of the Khaksars in the Punjab it would not be advisable for me to enter into any correspondence with them or their leaders, and I propose accordingly to leave, the telegram (offering help) unanswered."[44]

It is clear from the Viceroy's words, that despite the Khaksars' strength in the masses, the Viceroy decided to ignore the Khaksar Tehreek altogether. In effect, the Viceroy had accepted Jinnah as the leader of the Muslims, as he found Quaid-e-Azam to be fit to follow British policy. The AIML was given a green signal to fight against all forces that were against the British.

The Viceroy now decided to use every possible avenue to crush the Khaksar Movement. He fully used the Punjab Government and Sikandar in this effort. The Viceroy called a meeting of important persons on May 26, 1940 at Simla; the following were present:

- ❖ Governor General/Viceroy of India
- ❖ Commander-in-Chief

---

[43] See Resolution # 4 adopted in a meeting on June 15, 1940 in Bombay in Yousaf 2004, Pp. 183-185. Also see *The Hindustan Times*, June 18, 1940.

[44] Khan, Khan Abdul Wali. Chapter 5. IOL MSS EUR F125/9. P. 251.

❖ Sir Maurice Garnier Hallett, Governor of the United Provinces (U.P.)
❖ Sir Henry Duffield Craik, Governor of Punjab
❖ Sir Reginald Maxwell (Home Member)
❖ H.S.Stephenson, Secretary to the Governor of the United Provinces (U.P.)
❖ Sir John Gilbert Laithwaite, Private Secretary to the Viceroy of India

In the course of the meeting, the Governor of Punjab brought to the attention of attendees:

> "Sir Sikander Hyat Khan felt strongly that the time had come to ban this movement throughout India. It would, Sir Sikander thought, have to be done sooner or later; and he suspected that there was behind it some sinister influence, possibly foreign…His deduction was that influence was Nazi: that could not as yet be proved."[45]

At the meeting,

> "The Viceroy observed that one point was certain, namely that it would be entirely wrong and mistaken to tolerate Khaksars in the hope that they might serve as a counter to Congress action."[46]

It was concluded that the Government of India should consider the following on urgent basis:

❖ Instructions to all Provinces to arrest local Khaksar leaders
❖ The arrest of six or seven professors at Aligarh University
❖ United Provinces to watch Khaksar entry into Punjab
❖ Effective and close liaison between Provinces

Sikandar, without any proof, had declared the Khaksars to be Fifth Columnists, implying that they had connections with the Nazis. He did this on purpose to create panic in the minds of the British and all other forces that were anti-Nazi. He had injected this idea in the mind of the Governor of Punjab; the Governor brought it to the attention of the Viceroy and other important people who had attended this extremely important meeting.

Sikandar completely supported the Viceroy's effort in crushing the Khaksar Movement and enhanced his own strategy in this regard. It was very important to gain public opinion in their favor, hence on June 11, 1940, Sikandar issued a press statement:

> "Government are satisfied that there are definite indications of real connexions between the Khaksar movement and enemies of this country…
>   It is unfortunately not possible for the Government at least not at present to divulge information which they possess about certain

---

[45] IOL L/P&J/8/680.
[46] Ibid.

organizations receiving inspiration and instruction from abroad, because Government cannot afford to disclose their sources and contacts."[47]

Sikandar's statement, that the Khaksars had connections with the enemies of India, had no basis. These accusations were made only to grant legitimacy to the actions of the Government against the Khaksar Tehreek. Now one can imagine the evil and sinister move of Sikandar against the Khaksar Tehreek. He had established in the minds of the Viceroy, Governors and the public that the Khaksar Tehreek was helping the enemy of the British.

*****

It is important to discuss the allegation against the Khaksars. Some people claim(ed) that Mashraqi was influenced by Hitler. This is completely untrue. In fact, Hitler was the one who wanted to meet the Scholar of the East who had a brilliant academic record and wrote *Tazkirah* which scientifically interpreted the Holy Quran. It was as per Hitler's desire that the meeting between him and Mashraqi took place in Germany in 1926. Hitler had read Mashraqi's monumental work, *Tazkirah*, and discussed religion and the concept of Jihad in his meeting with Mashraqi. Mashraqi was not party to Hitler's designs nor did he have any links with the Nazis. Mashraqi simply met Hitler, as per the latter's request. If the anti-Mashraqi elements or authorities had found even a remote connection, as they desperately tried to do so, they would have sentenced Mashraqi to life imprisonment or capital punishment.

Mashraqi had formed the Khaksar Tehreek with the belcha as part of its uniform "much before the emergence of Hitler in Nazi Germany."[48] He stated:

> "I [Mashraqi] was astounded when he [Hitler] told me that he knew about my Tazkirah. The news flabbergasted me... He discussed Islamic Jihad with me in detail. In 1930 I sent him my Isharat concerning the Khaksar Movement with a picture of a spade-bearer Khaksar at the end of that book. In 1933 he [Hitler] started his Spade Movement."[49]

Dr. Sir Zia ud Din said in the Central Legislative Assembly on September 23, 1942 that he was an old friend of Mashraqi's. He further stated that:

> "Hitler at that time was not heard of and he did not at that time draw up any scheme of Nazi organization. In case there is any similarity [between Khaksars and Nazis], it is a pure accident. If anyone copied the other, it must be Hitler who copied Allama Mashriqi as the constitution of the Khaksars was drawn up long before anyone heard of Nazi movement."[50]

---

[47] *The Statesman*, June 14, 1940.
[48] Muhammad, P. 152.
[49] Baljon, P. 12.
[50] ORCLAD, Pp. 460-486.

Sir Muhammad Yamin Khan commented in the Central Legislative Assembly on September 23, 1942 that a "lot of prejudice has been created"[51] against the Khaksars, and spades have been referred to as symbols of "Hitlerism."[52] He added, "I would like to say this that long before Hitler's name was even heard of Allama Mashriqi had started the *Belcha* and the uniform."[53]

After his final release, Mashraqi addressed people at Lahore and rejected that the Khaksar Tehreek had any links with Hitler, as was being propagated while he was under arrest. *The Tribune*, Lahore of January 04, 1943 referring to Mashraqi's address wrote:

> "He [Mashraqi] contradicted the allegation that he had anything to do with Hitlerism or Nazi movement. He characterised this allegation as baseless and without any foundation."

The Viceroy on June 15, 1940 sent a telegram to the Secretary of State referring to Sikandar's statement of June 11, 1940. The Viceroy wrote,

> "Jawahar Lal Nehru in Lahore on 12th apparently referring to this statement is reported as saying it was not fair of Punjab Govt. to describe Khaksars as Fifth Columnists."[54]

*****

In response to Sikandar's false and baseless propaganda, Barrister Mian Ahmed Shah sent a telegram that also appeared in the press. *The Star of India*, Calcutta published this telegram (on June 18, 1940) from Barrister Mian Ahmed Shah to Khawaja Sir Nazimuddin, A.K. Fazl-ul-Haq and Maulana Akram Khan Saheb, who were attending the Working Committee meeting of the Muslim League in Bombay. Mian Ahmed Shah's telegram stated:

> "Strongly challenge Sir Sikander Hayat Khan's mis-statement regarding 'Fifth Column,' and lame excuse for justifying his action. Kindly see Working Committee is not misled. - Mian Ahmed Shah."

Mian Ahmed Shah conveyed his concern and reminded the attendees of the Working Committee not to forget the Khaksars, to do something about the ban and to not be misled by Sikandar. Quaid-e-Azam and Sikandar Hayat Khan were also present at the meeting. This telegram was also a test from the Khaksars to see if any of the prominent Leaguers would step forward to prevent the Khaksars from being crushed. None of the Leaguers even made a statement that the Khaksars were not Fifth Columnists and that false propaganda must be stopped. This clearly implies that the Leaguers were supporting the efforts to crush the Khaksar Movement.

---

[51] ORCLAD, Pp. 460-486.
[52] Ibid.
[53] Ibid.
[54] IOL L/P&J/8/680.

A few days after the Working Committee's meeting, Jinnah met the Viceroy on June 27, 1940. They discussed the Khaksar issue[55], however, when Jinnah spoke to the press after the meeting, he did not disclose whether he had discussed the Khaksar issue with the Viceroy, and if so what the details of that discussion had been. *The Tribune*, Lahore reported (on June 28, 1940) under the heading, "Mr. Jinnah Meets Viceroy: Complete Secrecy Maintained." If Jinnah had pressured the Viceroy to remove the ban and release Mashraqi and the Khaksars, he would have definitely stated this to the press and there would not have been the need for such secrecy. His lack of statement automatically tells us that that Quaid-e-Azam did not make any attempt in this regard.

Suspicion in the Khaksar circle gained strength when Quaid-e-Azam did practically nothing to help the Khaksars. The Muslim Leaguers remained unconcerned, but the public was extremely upset with the League and even with Quaid-e-Azam's attitude. The public maintained their pressure which Jinnah admitted in a press statement on June 28, 1940. Quaid-e-Azam said:

> "I have received a number of letters and was personally pressed by the Muslim public on my way to Simla from Bombay to intervene in the Punjab Government-Khaksar trouble. There is also an impression among the Muslim public and the rank and file of the Khaksars that the All-India Muslim League is not doing anything in the matter. I may reiterate that it is the declared policy of the All-India Muslim League to do all it can to help the Muslims wherever they may be and see that justice is done to them. I personally have not concealed my sympathy with the Khaksars generally and I would like to repeat that if the Khaksar leaders put their heads together and enable me with authority to serve them and follow my advice I shall be prepared to do all I can to find an honourable solution of the present impasse."[56]

Yet again, Jinnah merely issued a press statement clarifying his position and reiterated that he had no authority to take any action on behalf of the Khaksars. In the eyes of the Khaksars and their sympathizers, Quaid-e-Azam's words were seen as nothing more than sugar coated pills to satisfy and calm the pressure from the Muslim community. Although Quaid-e-Azam sympathized with the Khaksars in his statement, thus far he had taken no real and practical action to help the Khaksars.

Even though the Khaksars did not think that Quaid-e-Azam needed their permission to bring about a settlement regarding the Khaksar issue, they still decided to send him a telegram officially granting him authority to resolve their issue with the Government. Thus, following Quaid-e-Azam's statement, Dr. Mohammad Ismail Nami[57] sent a telegram to Jinnah (on July 03, 1940):

---

[55] It is clear from the text of Quaid-e-Azam's letter to the Viceroy, Linlithgow, dated August 02, 1940 that they did discuss the Khaksar issue on June 27, 1940. This letter is available later in the chapter.

[56] *The Hindustan Times*, June 29, 1940.

[57] While Mashraqi was in jail, Dr. Nami was acting as leader of the Khaksar Tehreek.

"Regarding your recent statement I, the present Head of the Khaksar Movement, delegate authority to you for honourable peace with the Punjab Ministry including removal of ban of February 28, release of Allama Mashriqi and others, compensation to the survivors of those killed, refund of fine and return of property confiscated by the Government."[58]

On July 06, 1940, Jinnah replied to Dr. Mohammad Ismail Nami's telegram of July 03, 1940:

"Your telegram. My advice suspend defiance pending negotiations. If your instructions obeyed by rank and file your authority cannot be doubted. Willing help find solution."[59]

The next day (July 07, 1940), Dr. Nami sent the following telegram to Quaid-e-Azam:

"Advice accepted. Orders issued for suspending defiance of law till July 27 [1940]. Instruct Sir Sikandar Hyat Khan also to suspend arresting Khaksars."[60]

As per Quaid-e-Azam's demand, Khaksar demonstrations were suspended. After four days (on July 11, 1940), Quaid-e-Azam responded to Dr. Nami:

"I received your telegram of the 6th July suspending defiance of law by the Khaksars in Punjab till 27th July. I will communicate with you in the matter as soon as possible."[61]

On July 16, 1940, Jinnah wrote to the Viceroy of India:

"Dear Lord Linlithgow,
    With reference to our talk regarding the Khaksar situation in the Punjab, I have made one more attempt to find a satisfactory solution and I am enclosing here with a copy of the statement that I issued from Simla and the subsequent development that is shown by the correspondence that has passed between me and Dr. Mohammad Ismail Nami of Calcutta.
    I am inclined to think from what information is available to me that he is next to the Mashraqi in the Khaksar organisation.
    He has accepted my advice and has suspended defiance till 27th July, but if necessary I will be able to persuade him for continuing this suspension pending our being able to find a satisfactory solution. I think we ought not to miss this opportunity at this juncture to bring the Khaksars round as the matter has now gone beyond the Khaksar organisation and there is a universal feeling among the Mussalmans all over India and particularly in the Punjab

[58] Yousaf 2004, P. 195.
[59] Yousaf 2004, P. 196.
[60] Ibid.
[61] Yousaf 2004, P. 198.

that they are being crushed by the Punjab Government at the bidding of Sir Sikander Hyat Khan.

        If you are inclined to take up the matter as I thought you were inclined, during the course of our conversation, I shall be glad to do all I can do to see that a reasonable solution is accepted by the Khaksars.

Yours sincerely,

M.A. Jinnah"[62]

Quaid-e-Azam also enclosed the following: copies of correspondence between him and Dr. Muhammad Ismail Nami, text of his press statement made on May 19, 1940 and text of his press statement made on June 29, 1940.

This letter exerted no pressure for the release of Mashraqi or the Khaksars or for the removal of the ban. The letter told the Viceroy that Jinnah had influence and control over the Khaksars and in fact implied that he was more inclined toward helping the British than the Khaksar Tehreek ("I will be able to persuade him for continuing this suspension pending our being able to find a satisfactory solution. I think we ought not to miss this opportunity at this juncture to bring the Khaksars round"). The other point of writing this letter was to indicate to Khaksar supporters that Quaid-e-Azam was helping Khaksars. This letter provided face saving to the Muslim League so as to avoid public criticism, and nothing else.

With apology, I state that Quaid-e-Azam's actions, including his statements, Khaksar Resolutions, and letters, were all politically motivated and were not sincerely meant to help the Khaksars. Letters to the Viceroy or any resolution in favor of the Khaksars were also meant to send a signal to the British that if they did not listen to the Muslim League, the League would support the Khaksar Tehreek. The Muslim League's attitude toward the Khaksars was evident even from Government reports,

> "In May [1940] Jinnah was approached by Khaksars in Bombay for his support, which he refused...and he undertook to do anything which the Punjab Premier thought suitable."[63]

On July 24, 1940, the Viceroy, Lord Linlithgow, wrote to Quaid-e-Azam:

> "...I do not see how I can intervene in this matter, which is primarily one for the Punjab Government. I now understand that Sir Sikander Hyat Khan has published the conditions on which he would be prepared to revoke the order which makes the Khaksar movement an unlawful association."[64]

Linlithgow put the responsibility on Sikandar's shoulders. The Viceroy did not want to ease the Khaksar situation as this could have potentially led to a

---

[62] Yousaf 2004, P. 199. Also see Ahmad, Pp. 40-46.

[63] IOL MSS EUR F125/143. Pp. 10-11.

[64] Yousaf 2004, P. 201. Also see Ahmad, P. 105.

Mashraqi-Jinnah alliance. If Jinnah was successful in getting the ban removed and obtaining Mashraqi's release, obviously this would have resulted in their alliance. The British wanted to see the end of the Khaksar Tehreek. On the other hand, Quaid-e-Azam was also satisfied with the Viceroy's lack of action, as Quaid-e-Azam had already been recognized as a leader of the Muslims. It was against his interest to seek Mashraqi's release and removal of the ban.

Still the Khaksars hoped that Quaid-e-Azam, under public pressure, would bring results. Therefore, they waited and extended suspension of peaceful demonstrations. On July 26, 1940, Dr. Nami extended his order of suspending demonstrations until August 10, 1940.

Owing to the failure of Quaid-e-Azam to obtain desired results, a committee was formed on July 29, 1940 to impress upon the Punjab Government to remove the ban and release Mashraqi and Khaksars. The committee was headed by Barrister Mian Ahmed Shah. Other members included Barrister Whaeedud Din, Dr. Sir Zia ud Din, Nawab Abdullah Khan Kusmandi and Nawab Bahadur Yar Jang.[65] Nawab Bahadur Yar Jang's inclusion was essential as he was a Muslim Leaguer and had influence over Sikandar and Jinnah. Nothing came out this effort.

On August 02, 1940, Quaid-e-Azam wrote a letter to the Viceroy:

> "Dear Lord Linlithgow,
> I am in receipt of your letter about the Khaksar movement, dated the 24th July 1940.
> I moved in the matter firstly, because Your Excellency showed concern about the Khaksar situation in the Punjab in the course of our conversation on the 27th June; and secondly, that in the earlier stages Sir Sikander Hyat Khan, in the course of our correspondence, indicated in the following words: 'It may be necessary to consult the Government of India also, and consequently it will take some time before final decision can be taken.' Lastly, I can cite more than one instance that the Viceroy and the Governor General have found a way to intervene when it was considered necessary.
> However, I am sorry if Your Excellency considers that in this case you do not see your way to intervene.
> I am glad that Your Excellency informs me that Sir Sikander Hyat Khan has published the conditions on which he would be prepared to revoke the order which declares the Khaksars an unlawful association. I am not aware of those conditions, but I have requested Dr. Nami to obtain a copy of those conditions and get in direct touch with Sir Sikander Hyat Khan.
> Yours sincerely,
> M.A. Jinnah"[66]

---

[65] Zaman 1987, P. 71.
[66] Yousaf 2004, P. 203. Also see Ahmad, Pp. 50-51.

A few important things are noticeable in this letter. Its language was apologetic and accepted the Viceroy's non-intervention. The language implied no direct or indirect pressure regarding the Khaksar issue. The fact that Quaid-e-Azam was unaware of the published conditions mentioned in the letter showed that the issue was not on his agenda and he was not discussing it with Sikandar; this illustrated his overall lack of interest in the matter. Further, the letter mentioned that Jinnah had told Dr. Nami to deal with Sikandar himself, hence Quaid-e-Azam again relieved himself of the problem.

This was the end of Jinnah's efforts toward the Khaksar issue. Jinnah's political position was improving due to the Khaksar resistance, but he became indifferent toward the Khaksar issue. According to the Khaksar circle, Quaid-e-Azam conveniently shifted the responsibility onto the Punjab Premier's shoulders. Jinnah disappointed the Khaksars and earned resentment as they felt betrayed and cheated. Disillusioned with Quaid-e-Azam, the Khaksars continued to put forth efforts on their own. On August 07, 1940, Barrister Mian Ahmed Shah met Sir Francis Mudie, Chief Secretary of the Government of United Provinces (U.P.) in the same connection.

These letters to Linlithgow were meant to keep pressure on Sikandar Hayat Khan to support the League in the Punjab, or else the League would support the Khaksars (obviously Sikandar would have highly resented this). While Jinnah was not helping the Khaksars, he was also trying to undermine Sikandar's position. This was substantiated by Government reports:

> "The recent change in Jinnah's attitude is suspected by the Punjab Premier [Sir Sikandar Hayat Khan] to be deliberately intended to create mischief...Jinnah's recent behavior in regard to the Khaksar agitation is designed to embarrass the Punjab Government, and may be not unfairly attributed to pique on account of the Punjab Premier's intolerance of Jinnah's autocracy in the League."[67]

*****

Quaid-e-Azam was not at all interested in settling the Khaksar issue. The League was only interested in power, which is quite evident from events of the time. The Leaguers were willing to do anything as long as they were in power. According to *Facts are Sacred* by Khan Abdul Wali Khan, Jinnah had asked the Viceroy:

> "Muslim League should be taken into full and equal partnership with H. M-Government in the ruling of this country and the authority shared with them."[68]

This clearly shows the League's efforts for entering the corridors of power.

---

[67] SQS, Pp. 10, 11, 20.
[68] Khan, Khan Abdul Wali. Chapter 6.

While Jinnah was busy consolidating his position, Barrister Mian Ahmed Shah was struggling to seek Mashraqi's release; he met Sikandar on August 27, 1940, but Sikandar refused to release Mashraqi.[69]

On September 02, 1940, as a result of the Khaksars' ongoing demonstrations, the ban on the Tehreek in the Punjab was removed and *some* Khaksars were released. However, the Government still refused to release Mashraqi and many other Khaksars, including those sentenced to life imprisonment.

On September 24, 1940, Quaid-e-Azam met with the Viceroy and Sir Sikandar Hayat Khan in Simla but nothing was said on the Khaksar issue.[70]

During the next many months, desperate efforts continued for the release of Mashraqi and the remaining Khaksars. These included protests, Khaksar fasts, and the observance of "Mashraqi Day" (on May 02, 1941).[71] The Khaksars took every possible measure to liberate their beloved leader; when his release didn't come through, they decided to undertake a massive resistance, from the North West Frontier Province to Bengal. Intelligence agencies, which were monitoring Khaksar moves closely, informed the Government of British India of the Khaksars' plan. This time (June 06, 1941), the *Central Government banned the Khaksar Tehreek in the entire India.*

The Government was nervous that the ban on the Khaksar Tehreek would be used by anti-British elements within and outside the country (including Germany that was in war) to criticize British actions against the Khaksars. To counter public reaction following the ban, the Secretary of State for India sent a telegram from London to the Home Department in India. In the telegram, he proposed to urgently secure public statements from prominent Muslims in support of the ban.[72]

Under the influence of the Government and other anti-Khaksar elements, the media wrote against the Khaksars. Despite the Government's best efforts to the contrary, the Khaksars were determined to keep the Tehreek and its objectives alive. The efforts for the release of Mashraqi continued, but the Government refused to free Mashraqi and other convicted Khaksars.

*****

On June 21, 1941, Quaid-e-Azam replied to Zauqi's (Muslim Leaguer) letter of June 03, 1941. He said,

> "...I certainly agree with you that... the Khaksars should work as members of the Muslim League under one flag and one platform."[73]

---

[69] Zaman 1987, P. 73.
[70] Yousaf 2004, P. 211.
[71] *The Star of India*, May 03, 1941.
[72] IOL L/P&J/8/680.
[73] Mujahid, P. 90.

On October 25, 1941, Sikandar Hayat Khan met with Quaid-e-Azam. Nothing came out of this meeting. It is not known if they discussed the Khaksar problem.

On October 28, 1941, Qazi Mohammad Ahmad Kazmi presented a resolution in the Central Assembly regarding the release of the ban on the Khaksar Tehreek. Quaid-e-Azam and Liaquat Ali Khan did not attend this session of the Central Assembly, even though their participation was badly needed to put pressure on the Government to release Mashraqi.[74]

Meanwhile, in jail, Mashraqi had reached the brink of death, as he had started fasting on October 16, 1941 to demand his as well as other Khaksars' release; yet none of the Muslim Leaguers even paid a courtesy call to him. The Leaguers, again, did not even bother to take a procession to pressure the Government to release him. As stated, they wanted him and the Khaksars to stay in jail as it was benefiting them; they were using this as a pressure card on the British. There is no denying the reality that they resented the Khaksar Tehreek; this is also evident from what happened in the Assembly on December 17, 1941. Hassan wrote to Jinnah on December 18, 1941:

> "Yesterday in the Assembly when Fazlul Huq [A.K. Fazl-ul-Haq] said that he was at heart 'Khaksar', there were shouts from the Muslim League benches: 'No, you are a traitor; you are a quisling.' Again, when he went on to say that he expected such a demonstration, there were cries from our benches: 'Guilty conscience', the man was absolutely non-plussed. The great joke came when he addressed us and said: 'Rely on me to do the best', there was such jeering and derisive laughter from our benches that the hideous fox was completely dumbfounded."[75]

This letter indicated nothing but intolerant behavior on the part of the Muslim Leaguers towards the Khaksars.

*****

In the Khaksar circle, it was viewed that in reality many anti-Khaksar Muslim Leaguers wanted the ban on the Khaksar Tehreek to remain in place so that they could take full advantage of the situation. An unbiased mind would understand that the Muslim League was not helping the Khaksars at all; in fact Sikandar was used by the British and the Muslim Leaguers to eliminate the movement and to keep the field open for the Muslim League. The Muslim League, after the prohibition, made no serious and genuine effort to obtain Mashraqi and the Khaksars' release or the removal of the ban. In fact, soon after the Muslim League session in March they tried to bring the Khaksar Movement under the Muslim League flag, but they failed.

---

[74] ORCLAD.
[75] Zaidi, P. 230.

The Khaksars equally blamed Quaid-e-Azam for neither helping them nor using his influence over Sikandar. Jinnah's influence over Sikandar is evident from the statement Sikandar issued about a month before he died. According to the newspaper, Sikandar

> "declared that he accepted Mr. Jinnah as the leader of the Mussalmans of India and even though he might express his difference of opinion with him on certain occasions, yet he will never disobey him."[76]

Time wore on, but the Muslim League did nothing concrete. To everyone's disappointment, Mashraqi continued to suffer in jail in extremely disgusting conditions and the chase and imprisonment of the Khaksars continued. None of the Leaguers had visited Mashraqi in jail since his arrest. The Khaksars came to the understanding that the Muslim Leaguers did not want Mashraqi to be released. With Mashraqi behind bars, the political field was open for the Leaguers to flourish. Without the Khaksar Tehreek, the League could claim to be the sole spokesman of the Muslims, which they had always wanted. It was also in the interest of Sikandar Hayat Khan not to lift the ban in order to safeguard his political career in the Punjab, where the Khaksar Tehreek had become very strong with its headquarters in Lahore. Thus the ban was not only inline with the British, it was also in the interest of other opponents including anti-Khaksar Muslim Leaguers. The Khaksars understood that a conspiracy had been hatched. Under the circumstances, the split between the Muslim League and the Khaksars became evident.

There is no denying the fact that the Muslim League gained strength at the expense of Mashraqi and the Khaksar Tehreek. While Allama Mashraqi and the Khaksars rotted in jail and suffered mentally, financially and physically, the Muslim Leaguers arrived in beautiful cars, like royalty, and conducted negotiations with the rulers. The Muslim Leaguers used Mashraqi and the Khaksar sufferings and threat (to the British) to their own benefit, without a word of acknowledgement for them. This was again done on purpose to eliminate Khaksars from the public eye and to avoid any credit to the Khaksar Tehreek.

The atrocities on Khaksars and the March 19 tragedy, though a turning point of Pakistan history, have been completely ignored and the Khaksars' role in the resistance movement for the sake of freedom has been completely disregarded. The Khaksars' resistance to the imperialists in the freedom struggle was the longest, toughest, and most unparalleled fight since the Khilafat Movement. Freedom is not achieved without personal sacrifices and resistance; and the Khaksars provided all of these for the freedom of Indo-Pakistan. All of this is missing from history books and supplements that are published on March 23 or August 14 every year. These events are not discussed in any public form, including discussions on radio and television on

---

[76] *The Tribune*, November 18, 1942.

Pakistan movement. According to the Khaksar circle, film flashes that are shown about the session on the Pakistan Resolution have been edited and public outcry and slogans in favor of Khaksars have been ejected.

History is witness to the fact that the Khaksar massacre brought the Muslims of India together under the flag of the Muslim League and led to the creation of Pakistan. Unfortunately, these facts have been purposely twisted in history books for vested reasons. One day, history shall be corrected and people will realize the reality and the sufferings of Mashraqi and the Khaksars toward freedom.

Chapter 5

Mashraqi Released -
Efforts for United Front for Freedom

After his arrest on March 19, 1940, Mashraqi remained in Vellore Jail for almost 22 months. The authorities could not bring any charges against him, yet Mashraqi remained in jail without a trial. In protest for his unlawful detention, Mashraqi fasted for 80 days in jail. Mashriqi wrote a letter from jail to Dr. Rafiq Ahmed Khan of Aligarh Muslim University informing him:

> "My last days are nearing. It will be alright if I receive a reply and I am released. Otherwise I am going to die...I am not going to change my decision nor do I repent for it. I am happy because I am going to lay down my life..." At the conclusion of his letter, he stated, "Again gird up your loins. Do not let my face be blackened. Save the honour of Islam..." [1]

Mashraqi was finally released from prison on January 19, 1942, but he remained under detention (interned)[2]. He was not allowed to leave Madras Presidency[3] and many restrictions were placed on his actions and movements.

> "...though out of jail, his movements were still restricted. He was not allowed to make a public statement or to speak a word publicly. The movement was still unlawful."[4]

Technically, to the world, Mashraqi had been released, however in reality he remained in confinement and the authorities made his life extremely difficult. He was constantly monitored by the intelligence agencies. Even contact with his family was made an ordeal. Yet Mashraqi would not rest and he had the drive and the influence to convey his message to the public.

---

[1] Muhammad, P. 85. Also see Yousaf 2003, P. 193.
[2] The total period of Mashraqi's imprisonment and confinement to Madras Presidency was almost three years.
[3] Under British rule, most of south India was integrated into a region called the Madras Presidency. In 1956, the Madras Presidency was disbanded and Tamil Nadu was established.
[4] *The Radiance*, February 06, 1943. P. 23.

After his release from jail, Mashraqi issued a statement explaining his position and the reasons for his fast. This statement was published in *Dawn* on January 25, 1942:

> "I started fasting from October 16, 1941 in defence of the religious Islamic principles of active brotherhood, Godly actions, amity with all, prayers, bodily health, social service, etc., on which the Khaksar organisation is based, also for the release of the remaining Khaksar prisoners. Government of India has already before this released several hundred prisoners in May and June last and had also intimated to me the full and unconditional release of my personal money amounting to several lakhs, also had asked me to apply for the release of my invalid pension amounting to several thousands. On the 51st day of my suffering the Government of India informed that only circumstances in which my permanent release would be considered, would be if I were to issue a public pronouncement to the effect that the movement was to be abandoned and the entire Khaksar organization wound up and if I were at the same time to order my followers to act accordingly. This position was impossible and I continued suffering...
>
> On the expiry of the eightieth day, viz., January 4, 1942, after the Government became amenable I discontinued my fast with the extremest gratitude to the almighty Lord that I have passed through the ordeal successfully"[5]

In another statement, he further explained the circumstances surrounding his fast:

> "In the 32nd day started my serious afflictions. Telegrams were arranged from many persons asking me to give up fast. On the fiftieth day I was taken on stretcher from the Vallore Jail to a damp dingy cell in Madras. The purpose was to frighten me either to give up fast or die. For the first time I received a communication from the Government on the 51st day, that is on December 05, 1941, asking me to disband the Khaksar Movement and that there was no other way of release ...I sent back the reply that Khaksar Movement was not my property that I could do with it whatever I liked, nor can it be discontinued. I sent a detailed letter to the Government on 19th December asking the Government to accept the offer after which I would discontinue fast. The Government accepted the offer but spent another fifteen days in debating it and then decided on January 16 to release me. However my movements were restricted to the Madras Presidency"[6]

Despite restrictions, Mashraqi began working toward his goal of ending British rule. He asked his followers to further increase their efforts toward mobilizing people to demand the complete independence of India. In light of

---

[5] Also see Yousaf 2003, Pp. 195-96.
[6] Hussain, P. 152. Yousaf 2003, P. 196.

World War II and the situation that the British were already facing; this was the right time to put pressure on the British to leave India.

After approximately two months of Mashraqi's release, Sir Stafford Cripps (a Minister in the cabinet of Prime Minister Winston Churchill) arrived in India (on March 23, 1942) to discuss the future of the country; this visit is famously known as Cripps' Mission. The Cripps proposal called for:

> "the creation of a new Indian Union which shall constitute a Dominion, associated with the United Kingdom and other Dominions by a common allegiance to the Crown, but equal to them in every respect."[7]

This mission was sent after the fall of Singapore (on February 15, 1942) and Rangoon (on March 08, 1942) to the Japanese. In the face of this critical situation, the British tried to make friendly gestures to win over India's support. The Cripps Mission was nothing but an attempt to somehow seek cooperation of the Indians to deal with World War II.

Mashraqi wanted no proposals from the British other than to quit India. On March 23, 1942, Mashraqi sent a telegram to Sir Stafford Cripps:

> "The British Government have sent you to rectify the wrongs and to reconciliate and secure the co-operation of India at this late hour. I put before you the unparalleled tyranny of the Government on the Khaksars and ask redemption. I committed the crime of offering to the Viceroy on October 6, 1939, when every political party was irreconcilably hostile, 50,000 Khaksars unconditionally for the defence of India to the last drop of their blood and of also publishing a pamphlet exhorting everybody to help the British to the utmost. The result was that the pamphlet was confiscated, I was jailed, the organisation was banned, 2,000 Khaksars were arrested, forty Khaksars were murdered in cold blood, my house where women inmates observed purdah [conservative way of life for women, consisting of dress covering full body and no interaction with men outside immediate family], was thrice raided, my eldest son aged sixteen years was jailed, my women and children were thus thrown to winds, my other son aged thirteen years was murdered, my entire money amounting to several lakhs of rupees was confiscated, my family of twelve persons was starved, my daughter was refused dowry, I was forced to pay Rs. 1,000 towards personal expenses in jail, I was threatened with lashes and was locked, tortured and kicked by the Superintendent and was solitarily confined, even smoking was disallowed, my servants were removed during the fast, my invalid pension of Rs. 300 a month which was in arrears and amounted to Rs. 12,000 was confiscated, my wife, children, brother and friends were not allowed to interview me—until after twenty-two months' detention without trial I secured my release on death-bed after fasting

[7] *Government of Pakistan's official web site.* (1).

for 80 days, and I am still ordered to remain in Madras till a settlement.

Can you hope to reconciliate India or secure her co-operation when your men commit such wrongs on persons of my position? I have now offered the Government most accommodating terms of a settlement, as prearranged, but I am getting evasive reprimands in reply. My case is explained chronologically in the following communications:—April 1, 1940 (ten pages), May 18, 1940 (two pages with enclosures), May 24 (Telegram to the Viceroy), June 23 (three pages), August 23 (to the Viceroy, three pages), December 7 (to the Viceroy, six pages), May 14, 1941 (five pages), July 22 (nineteen pages), February 12, 1942 (three pages), March 16 (four pages).

Immediate lifting of the ban and release of the prisoners is essential to removal of extreme bitterness throughout India, as also adequate recognition of the political importance of the Khaksars in any future constitution. Considering the terrible price paid for showing unconditional practical loyalty, I now join the Muslim League, the Congress and the Mahasabha in most emphatically demanding *complete* independence for India."[8]

This was an extremely important telegram and the announcement (demanding *complete* independence of India) that Mashraqi made after his release; the Khaksar Tehreek openly declared to the British to leave India. There was no ambiguity in Mashraqi's message to British authorities. This telegraphic message was published by the media and was read all across India and London. Mashraqi categorically stated that nothing short of complete independence would be acceptable.

The message was bound to stir up the British circle. Such a strong announcement, from a leader of Mashraqi's stature, unquestionably sent a clear signal to the authorities in India and at 10-Downing Street, London that British rule in India was heading toward its end.

Through this telegram, Mashraqi also injected the idea of complete independence in other leaders' minds; the Congress Quit India Movement was inspired by this and was launched within a few months.

On March 26, 1942, S.S.M. Bahmany, Secretary Communal Unity Committee and Hakim-i-Aala, Madras also vocalized Mashraqi's demand for complete independence and appealed to the Indian leaders. This was published in *The Radiance*:

"An Appeal to Mahatma Gandhi, Moulana Abul Kalam Azad, Qaid-e-Azam Jinnah, V.D. Savarkar and Pandit Jawaharlal Nehru.

Now that Allama Mashriqi has been the first to declare that he joins the Congress, the Muslim League and the Hindu Mahasabha in emphatically demanding complete independence for India, the

[8] *Dawn*, March 29, 1942. *The Radiance*, February 06, 1943. Yousaf 2003, Pp. 200-202.

pressing need of the hour is that this united demand be formally put before Sir Stafford Cripps at this critical juncture for the purpose not only of creating unanimity and providing ground for common action of parties, but also to tell the world what India wants, also that she is united on this demand. The British Government up till now, have only led the world to believe that there is nothing in India but chaos of differences and dissensions and that therefore nothing can be given to India, nor are they fit to have anything.

This unanimity of demand will indeed bring to lime-light the false propaganda of the British. Everybody knows what Sir Stafford Cripps has got up his sleeve, which he has not revealed yet. It cannot possibly be much more warming to imagination than the well-known phrases of the 'Offer of Eighth August' or the so called 'Dominion Status'. The utmost that he could have done, is to have evolved a sort of formula out of the political legerdemain of these phrases, and now when Japan is advancing rapidly and hundreds of thousands of helpless civilians are fleeing in panic from wherever he goes and the Government are unable to send these hordes of helpless men, women, and children to places of safety at their Railway expenses in order to provide facilities for their forces to withdr[aw] easily, this formula cannot be more than a m[ere] play-thing at the utmost. Giving concessions [to] India at this juncture, when the enemy is kno[cking] at our door is, to my mind, meaningless.

What Sir Stafford Cripps, I take it, ought [to] have done at this moment, was to ask the Congress, the League, the Mahasabha and the Khaks[ars] urgently to offer at least one million men...for saving India somehow or other from [the] clutches of the enemy so that these four mill[ion] men, even if they had served as mere fodder [in the face of] ...Japanese guns, would have shed the last drop [of] their blood, and we Indians would at least h[ave] had the satisfaction of having resisted the ene[my] to the utmost, as in China. God alone kno[ws] why Sir Stafford Cripps does not ask for...help, also why he insists on bestowing those concessions of 'Dominions Status' on 'India-...danger', so much that he has taken the trouble [of] coming over here at great personal risk to say [to] us 'Do accept these concessions, but we do [not] need your help in defence; we ourselves will defe[nd] this house, which is presently going to beco[me] yours, alone and shall hand it over to you intact.'

These facts serve to show that all this propaganda has been maintained in order to please [the] world and most especially to rouse America that, that lethargic monster who has not wok[en] up even after four months of war, may at le[ast] nominally send some few soldiers for the defen[ce] of India. I, therefore, most strongly appeal [to] Mahatma Gandhi, Moulana Abul Kalam Azad, Qaid-e-Azam M.A. Jinnah, Veer D.Savar[kar] not to be lured with this propaganda, but to present the demand for the complete independence of India unitedly, and thereafter to concentr[ate] their sole attention jointly to save the defence [of] civilian population, which is apt to get massacred [in] millions in this war most innocently, from [the] ravages of the British and the Japanese bom[b]. It will be easier for the British to fight...Japanese when the civil population is remo[ved] and this will also constitute a real service to [the] Indian Government. If all these parties rend[er] this real service in an organized and united manner for the defence of our country, we would have on the one hand, saved millions of innocent lives in this conflict, which even the British Government thinks is not ours, and, on the other hand, we would have by our concerted action acquired in the end enough power to force the British Government to agree to our demands of complete independence.

I maintain that independence is obtained by united action and not by begging and receiving offers.

Dated the 26th March, 1942   S.S.M. Bahmany"[9]

After five days of Mashraqi's message to Cripps, Mashraqi wrote to Quaid-e-Azam on March 28, 1942:

"Dear Mr. Jinnah,

I understand that a copy of my telegram to Sir Stafford Cripps has been sent to you. I can see what he has to offer, but he can very well utilize our communal differences to his own account.

If you can at this moment manage, at least, to present the united demand of complete independence, I have already declared that I am with the Muslim League, the Congress and the Hindu Mahasabha, and shall do whatever you ask me to do unitedly.

I have written to this effect to Messers Azad [Maulana Abul Kalam] and Savarkar [V. D. Savarkar, Chief of Hindu Mahasabha] also."[10]

Mashraqi also communicated his program to major party leaders. Obviously these letters were creating concern in the British circle. The British intelligence agencies monitored Mashraqi's activities. They knew that Mashraqi had sent these letters to Jinnah and others. Intelligence agencies sent reports on political matter to the Governor, which would in turn reach the Viceroy of India, the Secretary of State, and/or other relevant agencies.

Returning to Cripps' visit, on March 29, 1942, Cripps disclosed the contents of his declaration at a press conference. The Khaksar Tehreek found his proposal ridiculous and absurd. Thus, on April 03, 1942, the Khaksar Tehreek officially rejected the Cripps proposal; this was proclaimed publicly and reported in the press. *The Radiance*, Aligarh, reported:

"The Khaksar organisation, led by Allama Mashriqi, have today, the 3rd April, rejected the proposals of Sir Stafford Cripps in their entirety.

Interviewed, Allama Mashriqi, the chief of the Khaksars, remarked '...Any promise of what is to be given after the war is mischievously fictitious, and it looks like a joke from the British not to let us defend a country new to the last drop of our blood, which the British promise to hand over to us wholesale after the war. I see nothing but subterfuge and perhaps self-deception in the whole

---

[9] *The Radiance*, February 06, 1943. Pp. 10-11.
The text within brackets represents my assumption, as it was not legible in the source.
[10] Yousaf 2004, P. 235. Hussain, P. 155.

conspiracy of simulated friendship. I, therefore, reject the proposals in entirety unless of course every party in the land is freely allowed to defend their own country now, and an Indian Defence Minister, with full powers, who can galvanize India at once is immediately appointed.'"[11]

On the same day, Mashraqi sent the following telegram to Quaid-e-Azam, Maulana Abul Kalam Azad, Mahatma Gandhi, Pundit Jawaharlal Nehru, Dr. Pattabhi Sitaramiyya, and Veer D. Savarkar:

"Khaksar organization rejects Cripps' proposals in entirety, considers them meaningless, unreal, while enemy actually India's door, unless every party is unhesitatingly fully armed in order to defend India utmost, also unless an Indian Defence Minister, capable of galvanising India utmost; is immediately appointed."[12]

The Tehreek was the first party to announce its disapproval and also the foremost to press for the appointment of a Defense Minister. Mashraqi wanted no proposals except British to relinquish India. He demanded immediate appointment of an Indian Defense Minister as this would give India control over its territory and would also reveal the sincerity of British intentions. To the Khaksar Tehreek, the Cripps proposal was nothing but an attempt to look for Indian support to use them in the British's war effort and to somehow ensure continued British rule over India.

The All India Muslim League (AIML) and Indian National Congress (INC) later followed suit and rejected the proposal on April 10, 1942.[13] After all the major parties had rejected Cripps' proposal, Cripps announced withdrawal of his offer in a press conference on April 11, 1942. Cripps stated:

"I have had most regretfully to advise His Majesty's Government that there is not such a measure of acceptance of their proposals as to justify their making a declaration in the form of the draft. The draft, therefore, has been withdrawn and we revert to the position as it was before I came out here."[14]

On the same day (April 11, 1942), Mashraqi congratulated all the parties of their decision in his telegram to their presidents. He stated:

"Your rejection of the Cripps proposals is the happiest augury to a united and peaceful India. Accept heartiest congratulations. I fully undertake the responsibility of securing by negotiation complete independence for India from the British Government within six months, provided the Congress, the League and the Mahasabha unitedly demand independence now, and of also non-communally

---

[11] *The Radiance*, February 06, 1943. P. 11.
[12] Ibid.
[13] *The Radiance*, February 06, 1943. *The Tribune*, April 11, 1942. Hussain, P. 156.
[14] *The Tribune*, April 12, 1942.

organising for the safety of civil population everywhere. I offer immediately half a million Khaksars for service, irrespective of caste or creed. I have wired similarly to other presidents. Deliberate profoundly. Do not miss this critical opportunity."[15]

This telegram was another important message that Mashraqi sent. Mashraqi did not want any concession except for immediate independence. Mashraqi proclaimed to obtain India's independence within six months; he sent no secret messages and openly announced his intentions. An offer of half a million Khaksars was a huge force for protecting Indian lives and to force the British to leave India or face rebellion. If needed, millions[16] of remaining Khaksars could have been deployed. He had no intention of allowing the British to prolong their rule even for a day. He mentioned that this was a "critical opportunity" to avail. All Mashraqi wanted from the AIML and Congress was their support in this regard. The undoubtedly disciplined and militarily trained Khaksars would have easily overpowered the small population of British in India. With World War II underway, the British had no capacity to open another front in India.

This was another opportunity for the AIML and Congress to avail. Congress leaders were inclined to work with Mashraqi; however, the AIML, which should have immediately come forward to form a united front to seek freedom, avoided supporting Mashraqi. In fact, the Muslim League leadership was upset at Mashraqi's re-entrance into the field of politics after his release from jail.

The League, instead, continued with its efforts of seeking the division of India; its main thrust for seeking partition was based on communalism and Islam. Mashraqi was opposed to using communalism and religion in politics. Mashraqi's anti-communalism thoughts were well-explained in a decree Mashraqi had issued on October 15, 1937.[17] The Khaksar Tehreek, in name, philosophy and logic, was non-communal. The AIML, on the other hand, was the only political party that was seeking independence on the basis of communalism and was using Islam to meet its political objective. This was highly condemned by the Muslims and non-Muslims and was reported in the media. Many learned people issued press statements in this regard and declared the League's method un-Islamic. Islam preaches peace and love. The

---

[15] Yousaf 2004, P. 236. *Dawn*, April 19, 1942. *The Radiance*, February 06, 1943. P. 12.

[16] "He [Mashraqi] asserted that 40 lakh [four million] persons had joined his movement." (*The Eastern Times*, November 01, 1942. Yousaf 2003, P. 124.)

[17] Of the fourteen points of decree, two points listed below explain the Khaksar Tehreek's non-communal philosophy:

❖ "We, Khaksars, stand for the establishment of an order that will be equal, non-communal and tolerant, yet non-subservient, by the crushing of all communal sentiment and religious prejudices of mankind by our good and serviceful conduct; an order which will afford proper treatment and protection to all communities and will be founded on eternal justice, goodness and goodwill." (Yousaf 2003, P. 112).

❖ "The Khaksar stands for (a) regard for the religious and social sentiments of all communities, Hindu, Muslim, Sikh, Parsi, Christian, Jew, and Untouchable etc., (b) maintenance of their particular culture and customs and (c) general tolerance..." (Yousaf 2003, P. 113.)

For all fourteen points, see Yousaf 2003, Pp. 112-114.

League's methods were to spread hate, fear for Islam in danger and fear of Hinduism. In fact, it was the League's political agenda that was in danger and so they wanted to protect it by spreading fear. To a nationalist, the Leaguers had ulterior motives and they were using these channels for their own purpose. Gandhi said: "Those who are instilling this poison into Muslim mind are rendering the greatest disservice to Islam."[18]

*****

The Congress leaders were anti-division too, and they shared Mashraqi's point of view. Chakravarti Rajagopalachariar[19], also known as Rajaji, had discussed issues of freedom with Mashraqi in Vellore Jail. The British authorities that prepared a *Note on the Khaksar Movement* on February 27, 1941 wrote, "Some sort of negotiations had taken place between Inayatullah and Rajagopalchari in the Vellore Jail."[20]

Mashraqi's main message was that the Congress must work with the League to seek freedom and must not ignore what the League had to say. This is the best advice that Mashraqi could have given, as he knew that any rift would be exploited by the rulers. The British were using the Muslim League to confront the Khaksars and the Congress. Given the circumstances, it was in the interest of India for all its parties to come together, or else, the British would take advantage of the situation and use the League to achieve their own ends. Based on Mashraqi's influence, Rajagopalachariar came up with his proposal, the C.R. formula.[21]

Based on Mashraqi's deep influence on the political arena, Rajagopalachariar desired to visit Mashraqi on April 21, 1942 to discuss this matter. However, owing to the tense situation in the country, deadlock between Congress and AIML and to avoid other political implications, he could not come. On April 21, 1942, Rajagopalachariar sent his regret through Saeed Ahmed to Allama Mashraqi. Rajagopalachariar wrote:

"Dear ALLAMA SAHIB,
I had intended to call on you to-day at 9 a.m. and make inquiries about your health and Saeed Ahmed Sahib was kind enough to inform you about it.
On subsequent thought I have come to the conclusion that in the present tense state of affairs I may be embarrassing many others and giving rise to speculations and misunderstandings if I meet you at this juncture. You will therefore accept this letter as a token of my regards and not expect me to call on you as arranged by Mr. Saeed Ahmad.

[18] Wolpert, P. 195.
[19] A leader of the Congress, Prime Minister of his home state of Madras (now Tamil Nadu) from 1937 to 1939 (*Encyclopedia Britannica Online.)* After independence he succeeded Lord Mountbatten as Governor General of India.
[20] IOL L/P&J/8/680. Also see Zaman 1988, P. 238.
[21] Zaman 1988, P. 238. See reference note later in this chapter as well as Chapter 6 for more details.

Yours Sincerely,
C. Rajagopalachariar"[22]

With this letter, Rajagopalachariar also gave a message to Saeed Ahmed to convey to Mashraqi; Rajagopalachariar suggested that Mashraqi mediate and help resolve the issues between the AIML and the Congress.

In reply to Rajagopalachariar's message, Mashraqi sent a message, also through Saeed Ahmed, on April 22, 1942:

> "Mr. Saeed Ahmed told me...you desired to discuss the present deadlock and a way out of it by my mediation, if possible.
> If you can let me know the details of your proposals, I shall be able to let you know exactly what I can do in the matter. I am also very keen that the present deadlock be resolved as early as possible."[23]

On the same day, Rajagopalachariar sent the following message back to Mashraqi:

> "I am very grateful for what you have said. My opinion is that Allama Sahib should have a long talk with Maulana Abul Kalam Azad in person. Also that Allama Sahib should use his influence with Mr. Jinnah, make him shed his fear of a National Government in India, postpone all questions of the future and make a united demand for immediate National Government for India. This will lead to complete independence and unity.
> If nothing else can be done, Mr. Jinnah may be induced at least to say definitely on what conditions he can agree to join the Congress in forming the National Government at once.
> This can easily be done by Allama Sahib."[24]

On April 22, 1942, K. Srinivasan (editor of the daily newspaper *Hindu* from Madras) also sought Mashraqi's mediation. He "requested Allama Sahib to mediate in the present deadlock between Muslim League and Congress."[25] Owing to Mashraqi's strength and influence, his services were sought by the Congress and Hindu political leaders in this regard.

*****

---

[22] *The Radiance*, February 06, 1943. P. 12.
[23] Hussain, P. 157. *The Radiance*, February 06, 1943. P. 12.
[24] Ibid.
[25] *The Radiance*, February 06, 1943. P. 12.

The AIML immediately made an attempt to not allow the Congress to gain Khaksar support and offered Mashraqi to become part of the Working Committee of the All-India Muslim League. On April 26, 1942, Mashraqi called a Khaksar meeting to discuss the League's proposal that stated:

> "Upon Allama Sahib agreeing to join the All-India Muslim League and declaring to that effect and requesting his followers to join the Muslim League, which is the only authoritative and representative political organisation of the Musalmans in India, the President of the League will be glad to have the prominent Khaksars associated with the executives of the Provincial Leagues and Allama Mashriqi will be welcomed to join the Working Committee of the All-India Muslim League."[26]

This conditional proposal was nothing but an attempt to end any Khaksar-Congress collaboration. This offer was also meant to remove the Khaksar Tehreek from politics and bring the entire strength of the Khaksar Tehreek under the League's command. The proposal implied that the AIML represented the entire Muslim community in British India. To mention this in a proposal was absurd on AIML's part as it automatically closed the door to an agreement. Some efforts were made to reach an agreement, but Mashraqi and Jinnah were poles apart in their goals. Quaid-e-Azam wanted nothing but to use the Khaksars. Thus agreement could not be materialized.

As discussed in previous chapters, the Khaksar Tehreek was different from the AIML; its philosophy and objectives were opposed to those of the AIML, for example:

❖ Khaksars sought a united India, as division would not resolve problems of the *entire* Muslim community as was propagated by the League.
❖ Khaksars sought love, fraternity and unity; the League was spreading hate and disunity.
❖ Khaksars were to lift masses; the League was to lift classes.
❖ Khaksars sought non-discrimination and non-sectarianism; the League worked for the spread of communalism.
❖ Khaksars sought simplicity; Leaguers sought luxury.
❖ Khaksar leadership sought no power; League leadership wanted power.
❖ Khaksars wanted commoners to be powerful; the League was against this.
❖ Khaksars believed in service to the masses; the League believed in ruling the masses.

Under different principles and philosophies, it was not possible for Mashraqi to accept the League's offer. Besides, the AIML's overall structure was undemocratic, in the sense that it did not include the masses. All powers basically rested with Jinnah. No one could challenge Jinnah unless the British chose to replace his leadership. The League's undemocratic attitude can be

---

[26] Yousaf 2004, P. 237. Muhammad, P. 128.

observed from A.K. Fazl-ul-Haq's statement, who resigned from the Muslim League in protest against the power structure of the Muslim League. According to the newspaper,

> "Huq stated…principles of democracy and autonomy in the All-India Muslim League were being subordinated 'to the arbitrary wishes of a single individual [Quaid-e-Azam], who seeks to rule as an omnipotent authority even over the destiny of thirty-three millions of Muslims in the province of Bengal, who occupy the key position in Indian Muslim politics.'"[27]

This statement came from the person who moved the Pakistan Resolution. There are many other examples that can be given for the overall autocratic attitude of Quaid-e-Azam.

The Muslim League was not ready to entertain any of the Tehreek's agenda and was not willing to adopt democratic lines and accept commoners in the Working Committee of the Muslim League. The titled gentry and Nawabs of the League did not want commoners sitting side by side with them deciding the destiny of India. Mashraqi did not want to be part of an organization whose ideology was poles apart from that of the Khaksar Tehreek. Under these circumstances, an alliance could not be formed and Mashraqi could not accept their offer. Yet Mashraqi tried to help the League however he could. For example, the Khaksars were allowed to be part of the AIML and Mashraqi did not try to undermine Jinnah's leadership.

*****

Returning to Mashraqi's efforts to form a united front to overthrow the British Government, Mashraqi sent telegrams to Maulana Abul Kalam Azad and Quaid-e-Azam on April 28, 1942:

Telegram to Azad:

> "Ex-Premier Rajagopalachariar, in his message of 22nd, suggests my long talk with yourself, also my urging Mr. Jinnah to put united demand for National Government. Editor Srinivasan also suggests my mediation between Congress and Muslim League. Prepared making effort. Can you meet?"[28]

Telegram to Quaid-e-Azam:

> "Ex-Premier Rajagopalachariar also Editor [K.] Srinivasan [*Hindu* newspaper from Madras] suggest, in their messages of 22nd [April, 1942], my mediation between League and Congress concerning

[27] *The Tribune*, September 11, 1941.
[28] *The Radiance*, February 06, 1943. P. 13.

united demand National Government. Moment critical, Unity essential. Do you agree mediation?"[29]

Meanwhile, Mashraqi continued to impress upon Rajagopalachariar that the Congress must reach an agreement with Jinnah. Thus, on May 02, 1942, in its resolution, the All-India Congress Committee necessitated that the Congress agree to hold consultations with the League to come to an agreement on the formation of a National Government. The All-India Congress Committee did not agree to plans which would split India by giving freedom to any territory to secede from it.

Mashraqi was in the midst of carrying on crucial negotiations with various important political leaders (Muslim and non-Muslim) and great possibilities were building. Time was of the essence, and Jinnah was expected to immediately seize these opportunities and come to the negotiating table. However, Quaid-e-Azam was least interested in a united demand, and he did not want Mashraqi to play any role in politics, so he kept quiet and did not send a reply to Mashraqi's telegram of April 28, 1942. Jinnah's approach was obviously frustrating for all those who were immediately seeking unity to demand complete independence. Mashraqi knew very well the purpose for which Jinnah remained tacit. Under the circumstances, the only alternative left was to mount pressure on him and not allow him to fall prey in the hands of those seeking to divide the Indian people. Hence, on May 05, 1942, Allama Mashraqi sent another telegram to Quaid-e-Azam as a reminder:

> "My telegram dated 28th April unreplied. Can you state minimum conditions for united demand for National Government? Do you approve active cooperation of Khaksars with Rajagopalachariar."[30]

In this telegram, Mashraqi asked Jinnah to present his demands so that dialogue could be initiated. Mashraqi was attempting to convince Quaid-e-Azam to go for united demand for a National Government because he knew that partition would divide India and Muslims into three parts; a Pakistan with two wings would not last and division would ruin Muslims.[31] On the other

---

[29] Yousaf 2004, P. 237. *The Radiance*, February 06, 1943. P. 13.

[30] Yousaf 2004, P. 238.

[31] Mashraqi had made the prediction more than once that a Pakistan with two wings would not last. This came true and East Pakistan was lost in 1971.

Before partition, in 1942, Mashraqi made this prediction to Jinnah. "I [Mashraqi] told him [Jinnah] in 1942 that his present Pakistan of the two provinces 1400 miles apart could not last and this would result in the ruin of one crore Muslims and the complete decimation of five crore Muslims of remaining India." (Mashraqi's statement on July 23, 1952 in Hussain, P. 248)

After the creation of Pakistan, in 1956, at a public address in Minto Park, Lahore, Mashraqi predicted losing East Pakistan. He stated:

"Ye Muslims! Today from this platform I sound you a warning. Listen carefully and ponder. Sometime in the future, probably in 1970, you will be confronted with a perilous situation. In 1970—I see it clearly—the nation will be stormed from all sides. The internal situation would have deteriorated gravely. A panic of widespread bloodshed will sweep the nation. The frenzy of racial and provincial prejudices will grip the whole country. *Zindabad* and *murdabad* will deafen your ears. Plans will be initiated to dismember the country. Take it from me that in 1970, Pakistan

hand, Quaid-e-Azam, for his own reasons, did not visualize that two wings of a country with 1,400 miles in between was an impractical idea, and he continued with the demand for division. However, Jinnah noticed that Mashraqi's influence was working on the political stage, and he saw the Khaksar Tehreek's importance in these negotiations. Thus, again Jinnah tried to use the Khaksars and asked Mashraqi to bring the Khaksars under the Muslim League. Quaid-e-Azam's telegram dated May 11, 1942 to Mashraqi stated:

> "Your telegram 5th May [1942]. My appeal to Khaksars is to join and support wholeheartedly League policy at this critical juncture. Not possible discuss terms united demand as requested by means correspondence."[32]

In his telegram, Jinnah completely avoided commenting on Mashraqi's efforts to arrange a Jinnah-Congress leaders meeting and refused to hold discussion on a united front. Instead he made a plea to Mashraqi to bring the Khaksars under the AIML. Mere appeals would not convince people to join the AIML; people had to be convinced that the idea of Pakistan was a better option.[33] Quaid-e-Azam was not interested in a National Government or united India. His appeal to Khaksars to join the AIML was nothing but an attempt to use Khaksars to strengthen his political position in front of the Congress and the British. It is important to note that Jinnah did not comment on Mashraqi's message of "Do you agree mediation?" or "active cooperation of Khaksars with Rajagopalachariar"; this obviously meant that Quaid-e-Azam did not want Khaksar mediation. He even ignored the reality that the Khaksar following of millions of people was substantial to seek independence of one India, and instead solicited to strengthen his own party. If Quaid-e-Azam had wanted to strengthen the Muslims, he should have sent an open offer of bringing AIML under the Khaksar flag. It was the time that AIML should have

---

will be plagued with a grave threat to its sovereignty. You might actually lose it if the reigns of the country were not in the hands of courageous and unrelenting leadership.

India will, in that grave situation, try to take advantage of your internal turmoil and devour you. Or, the governance of the country will fall in the hands of spineless self-seekers or self-centred opportunists who might on their own accord push you into the Indian lap. I warn you about 1970. I warn you to prepare from now to face the situation which will emerge in that year. In 1947, you had a refuge to protect yourself but in the coming days of 1970—I can clearly visualise—you will have river Attock on one side and the Chinese border on the other, and you will have no place to go..." (Hussain, Pp. 256-257).

[32] Hussain, Pp. 158-159. *The Star of India*, May 14, 1942. *The Radiance*, February 06, 1943. P. 14.

[33] The Pakistan scheme would not appeal to the nationalist for a number of reasons; at the least, the scheme would not be able to secure the entire Muslim community in British India. It did not make any sense to divide the provinces where Muslims were already in majority with Muslim Governments.

Even two years after the adoption of the Pakistan Resolution, people did not know what the Pakistan scheme was all about. Nothing had been put in writing on the Pakistan scheme for the public to review and then decide whether they were agreed with it or not. The Pakistan scheme was merely promoted through slogans that incited communal feelings and gave hope to the poor people for a better future. The illiterate poor masses did not understand the real implications of the Pakistan slogan. The Pakistan scheme remained a mystery until partition; this was done on purpose, because if it had been revealed, it would not have gotten any support.

supported a disciplined force like Khaksars and listened to Mashraqi for creating a united front to end British rule.

Never did Quaid-e-Azam offer to bring AIML under the Khaksar Tehreek, which illustrates that he sought to strengthen AIML. There are a number of examples, including historical documents, which confirm that Quaid-e-Azam wanted to lead the political arena and did not want Mashraqi to be in politics at all; I have included such examples in this work.

Despite Jinnah's indifferent stance, Mashraqi sent another telegram to Quaid-e-Azam on May 12, 1942:

> "Your telegram 11th May [1942]. Assure you Khaksars unflinching support every endeavour Muslim League for India's complete independence, Muslim-Hindu unity, united demands, united private protection of evacuees. Fix date discussion terms united demand New Delhi."[34]

Mashraqi was again supportive of Quaid-e-Azam and provided him full assurance of his unwavering and staunch support. Mashraqi conveyed to Jinnah that he sought Muslim-Hindu unity and asked Jinnah to convey what terms would be agreeable to him to seek united demand for a National Government. Mashraqi realized that the correspondence with Quaid-e-Azam was not bringing desired results, hence in his telegram, he asked Jinnah to fix a date for a face-to-face meeting. However, Quaid-e-Azam avoided such a meeting for political reasons. First, Mashraqi's objective of an undivided India was not in line with Jinnah's. Second, Jinnah did not want to jeopardize his relations with the British, who wanted no unity between the Khaksars and AIML. Further, Quaid-e-Azam had no solid Pakistan scheme that would convince Mashraqi or any nationalist, hence he kept avoiding a face-to-face meeting.

It is important to note from the telegram that Mashraqi was non-prejudiced and non-communal. He was very close to Islam, which prohibits spreading hatred. How noble Mashraqi's stance had been that he sought no communalism, which is destructive for humanity. Pleading for Muslim-Hindu unity, which the AIML used against him, also speaks of Mashraqi's vision. Mashraqi knew if Pakistan was obtained on a communal basis, this would lay the foundation for everlasting hatred in the region. It is important to read what Mashraqi had decreed on October 15, 1937 to understand his perspective of forming a united front. The points reflect his Islamic perspective and call for cordial relations with non-Muslims.[35]

---

[34] Hussain, P. 159. *The Radiance*, February 06, 1943. P. 14.

[35] Two of the points that Mashraqi had decreed on October 15, 1937 were:

❖ "The true Islam is the practice of the 'Quran-i-Awwal' (i.e. the earliest period in Islamic history). The Khaksar does not recognize anything as true Islam other than the practice of the Prophet." (Yousaf 2003, Pp. 112-113.)

Mashraqi did not see partition as a remedy to resolve issues of either community, Muslims or non-Muslims. So he, in his message, insisted on "united demand for National Government." He could not go against the decree he had issued in 1937. He wanted a united India to avoid devastation of people regardless of religion, caste, color or creed. Thus, it was against the Khaksar Tehreek's agenda to seek division. The League's agenda was not in line with the Khaksar Tehreek. Instead of joining hands with the Khaksars and other parties, the Muslim Leaguers were bent on division; it was considered by the nationalists that they were following the agenda of the colonial power. If the AIML had amalgamated with the Khaksars or extended the cooperation that Mashraqi was seeking, matters could have been sorted out.

*****

While these messages were being exchanged with Jinnah, Mashraqi was also talking to other Muslim and non-Muslim leaders, either through emissaries or via other means of correspondence. These leaders included Mahatama Gandhi, Jawaharlal Nehru, Maulana Abul Kalam Azad (leader of Indian National Congress) and Subhas Chandra Bose.

On May 12, 1942, Allama Mashraqi sent the following telegram to Maulana Abul Kalam Azad:

> "...Viewing Quaid-e-Azam's yesterday's reply prepared discussing Jinnah verbally terms united demand provided you give minimum amenable fundamental conditions. Your proposal of selecting five representatives both sides unwieldy, unhelpful."[36]

While he was asking Jinnah to come out with his terms, Mashraqi also asked the same from Azad so that all issues could be put on the table. He also reminded Azad to be flexible and accommodating and to not pre-fix conditions. So Mashraqi was very intelligently and wisely creating an amicable atmosphere so that a fruitful outcome could be obtained.

Azad replied on May 13, 1942 and informed Mashraqi of his basis of an agreement. Azad wrote:

> "Your telegram 12th May [1942]. Please refer to my Allahabad statement. There can be no other method in such matters."[37]

❖ "The Khaksar considers it the first duty of his organization to secure of every community its proper civic rights and to guard its internal and external interests. In order to maintain cordial relations amongst the various communities, the Khaksar is prepared to recognize each community as its ally and comrade, and invites them to be so." (Yousaf 2003, P. 113.)
For all fourteen points, see Yousaf 2003, Pp. 112-114.
[36] Hussain, P. 159. *The Radiance*, February 06, 1943. P. 14.
[37] Yousaf 2004, P. 238. *The Radiance*, February 06, 1943. P. 14.

Via telegram, Mashraqi informed Azad on May 16, 1942:

> "Your telegram 13th May [1942]. Allahabad statement cannot fructify without fundamental personal understanding. Yours and Jawaharlal's proposal reaching Madras opportune. Endeavouring Jinnah come. Wire date arrival together."[38]

In the above telegram, Mashraqi conveyed to Azad to be flexible.

Mashraqi was also informed that both Azad and Nehru were willing to discuss the matter at Madras and Mashraqi's presence in the meeting with Quaid-e-Azam was essential. Upon receipt of a positive signal from these leaders that a meeting could take place, Mashraqi, hopeful of resolving the issue, sent another telegram to Quaid-e-Azam on May 16, 1942 and asked Jinnah to fix the date for this meeting:

> "Reference my telegram twelfth May [1942]. Abulkalamazad [Abul Kalam Azad], Jawaharlal [Nehru] reaching Madras. Can you accept my humble invitation? Fix near date."[39]

Again Quaid-e-Azam remained unspoken. It was frustrating for Mashraqi to see that the Congress leaders were cooperating and stating what their conditions were, but Quaid-e-Azam was neither making any conditions for settlement nor confirming the date for the proposed meeting. Still, Mashraqi felt that the doors of negotiation must not be closed and the British's ulterior motive of weakening Indian unity must be nullified at all costs; thus, he continued his efforts.

Meanwhile, around this time, various Provincial and District Conferences were being held in Nagpur, Chittoor, Madanapalle and other places. Mashraqi was invited to attend these conferences.[40]

---

[38] Yousaf 2004, P. 238. *The Radiance*, February 06, 1943. P. 14.

[39] Hussain, P. 159. *The Radiance*, February 06, 1943. P. 14.

[40] On May 16 and 21, 1942, Mashraqi sent messages to these conferences. He stated:
"After a few fifty years the mastery of India is again in dispute. The struggle is for obtaining our mastery because we are weak, disrupted. No power that is going to win would make us united and strong, therefore our only hope is that we ourselves become united if we are to have no more masters.
    We are not allowed, in fact, we are unable to take up arms against the aggressor. The old as well as the new aggressor are equally against us and we do not matter anywhere. We can only look on to see the old aggressor confirmed or at worst or best a change of masters. In order to gain power in such evil circumstances and in this state of 'nothing-to-do', I have devised the sure remedy:—
1. This is the only occasion during the past one hundred years when 'political' or 'political gains' do not matter, because no body knows who is going to hold India. **Therefore all Parties can unite.**
2. Again, the **only** thing we can do usefully is to save ourselves from the destruction of both aggressors. **Therefore all Parties can unite to do social service irrespective of caste or creed,** because bombs and guns know no caste nor creed.
    This unique opportunity which will never come again will, as if by magic, bring about first: realisation of common danger, then successively: spirit of cooperation, human brotherhood,

"These Conferences expressed their appreciation of the Khaksar
Leader in the following words:- 'Your latest correspondence with Mr.
Jinnah for forming the National Government reveals your political
fore-sightedness and draws deep appreciation from all progressive
quarters.'"[41]

Going back to Mashraqi's correspondence, as per Mashraqi's suggestion,
Azad agreed on a single representative. In response to his confirmation on
May 27, 1942, Allama Mashraqi sent a telegram to Maulana Abul Kalam
Azad:

"...Extremely pleased your agreeing single representative both sides
in your letter of 23rd May to Abdurrahman Sahib. Shall ask
Quaideazam to reach Madras provided you personally discuss
settlement. Remember my undertaking solemnly given in my
telegram of 11th April [1942]. Think seriously. Time precious."[42]

Mashraqi again wired to Jinnah on May 27, 1942:

"My telegrams twelfth and sixteenth May unreplied. Abul Kalam
Azad agrees to appointment single representative both sides,
complains your silence concerning his Allahabad proposal.
Remember my solemn undertaking of securing for India complete
independence within six months in my telegram of 11th April. Agree
meeting Madras. Time precious, critical."[43]

In his telegram, Mashraqi used the words "solemn undertaking," which
displayed the strength of his unyielding and firm conviction that he could
attain the freedom of India within six months, provided Quaid-e-Azam did not
help the British in their divide and rule policy. Owing to Mashraqi's efforts, a
more conducive atmosphere for negotiations was developing, and Mashraqi
reminded Jinnah of his responsibility to come to the negotiating table and
resolve matters.

Mashraqi was an extremely practical person and believed in action, so his
words could not be taken lightly. If Mashraqi, with such strong conviction,
wrote six months, he meant six months. Jinnah knew Mashraqi's abilities, as

realisation of true religion; in the third stage: obedience to superiors and discipline, courage to
face danger, soldiery prowess, military qualities; and finally; patriotism power and FREEDOM.
    For a people so utterly devoid of the qualities of free nations, I cannot think of a more useful
and workable programme than the above at this eventful moment." (*The Radiance*, February 06,
1943. P. 15.)
    Here people might not realize what a philosophy irrespective of caste or creed or program of
community service could do. This brings unity, and unity is strength. Such an environment was
needed to achieve freedom. Those who do not understand the idea behind social service and a non-
biased policy may be deficient in the wisdom behind this philosophy. Mashraqi's non-communal
outlook shows far-sightedness; those who criticize him of promoting Muslim-nonMuslim unity
lack perception and vision.
[41] *The Radiance*, February 06, 1943. P. 15.
[42] Hussain, P. 162. *The Radiance*, February 06, 1943. P. 16.
[43] Yousaf 2004, P. 239. *The Radiance*, February 06, 1943. P. 16.

Mashraqi had proven his worth in any field he had entered — from academia to organizing the most disciplined movement in the history of India.[44] With these characteristics, the British were not naïve to get after Khaksars. Mashraqi's pledge of securing India's freedom within six months frightened the AIML and anti-Khaksar elements. Jinnah saw his political career at stake; this was another big reason Jinnah was abstaining from replying and wanted Mashraqi out of politics. Thus, Quaid-e-Azam avoided joining hands with Mashraqi for multiple pressures and reasons.

On the same day (May 27, 1942), Mashraqi sent the following telegram to Gandhi and Nehru:

> "Appealing at this eventful juncture to your foresightedness to reflect over advantage of Congress League settlement. Maulana Abulkalam Azad agrees to single representative both sides. Should meet Quaideazam Madras personally. Remember my telegram 11th April also repeated warnings given to you in 1928 which went unheeded. Time precious. Make Maulana agree."[45]

In the above telegram, Mashraqi again reminded Gandhi and Nehru (whom he had sent warnings to in 1928), who had great weight on the workings of the Congress, to use their influence and ensure a settlement between the Congress and League. He understood that if either party became unyielding, a united front could not be created; the British would use this communal division to their benefit and the freedom of India would be in jeopardy.

Quaid-e-Azam was in a tight spot. If he joined hands with Mashraqi and reached an agreement with Congress, this would irk the British. Mashraqi fully understood Jinnah's reluctance to come forward, but Mashraqi did not lose his patience and carried on his endeavors. On June 10, 1942, Allama Mashraqi sent another telegram to Jinnah:

> "Implore your immediate attention League-Congress settlement. Pray agree Abul Kalam Azad's proposal single representative. Fix personnel, time, place. Myself responsible utmost satisfaction."[46]

These telegrams put a lot of pressure on Quaid-e-Azam. It was becoming difficult for him to justify his silence. In the political circles, people started viewing him with suspicion of conspiring with or acting as an agent of the colonial power. Thus, a change in Jinnah's stance was felt.

---

[44] Mashraqi had created an institution (Khaksar Tehreek) and a highly disciplined force of four million. Khaksars suffered in jail and laid their lives because of Mashraqi's conviction; they striked and fasted unto death for Mashraqi's conviction. His strength not only lay in Khaksar Tehreek but in public as well as in political and army circles. He was not only leader of the Khaksar Tehreek but he lived in the hearts of the people. They prayed for his long life and the removal of restrictions on his movements.

[45] Hussain, P. 162. *The Radiance*, February 06, 1943. P. 16.

[46] Hussain, P. 162.

Mashraqi heard from his sources that Jinnah would probably agree to a single representative meeting. Mashraqi immediately seized the opportunity and telegraphically contacted Maulana Abul Kalam Azad, Mahatma Gandhi and Jawaharlal Nehru on June 10, 1942:

> "Corresponding Quaideazam further. Probability his agreeing single representative near. Please name Congress representative immediately."[47]

Meanwhile to maintain pressure on all leaders,

> "On the 10th June [1942]...the following appeal was issued by Mr. S.S.M. Bahmany, Secretary, Communal Unity Committee, Madras, to 'Everyone in India' and was broadcast by the Khaksars all over India in many languages in hundreds of thousands. It is estimated that the appeal went to over a million intelligent people and as a consequence more than 25000 people wrote or telegraphed individually to the various political leaders to unite at this juncture.

FURTHER APPEAL TO EVERYONE IN INDIA

> The above telegrams [published in the The Radiance (Aligarh), February 06, 1943] were sent by Allama Mashriqi on the 27th May to the most responsible political leaders of the country. To-day is the 10th of June. This means that two priceless weeks have passed and still both Congress and Muslim League are keeping mum. When precious time is being most relently wasted and the enemy, with a lightening speed, has rushed to the very door step of India, — (Burma had fallen by that time), — the only way to solve the tangle that has been created by our...political leaders is that every son of India, to whom this appeal goes, be he a Congressite, Muslim Leaguer or Mahasabhaite or a non-party man, should not only wire or write in the strongest terms to his chosen leader making it clear to him that an immediate understanding between the political parties is imperative on the pain of [these] parties losing the sympathies of their followers, but should make others write to the same effect.
>
> Every Khaksar throughout the length and breadth of India whom this appeal reaches, should publish it locally in hundreds and thousands and should manage to have hundreds and thousands of such letters and telegrams sent, until these proud leaders bow down before the...of public opinion and the gloomy picture of unfortunate India brightens up once again.
>
> I appeal to everybody not to lose even a moment. Lord Almighty sees our actions."[48]

The appeal was to pressure both sides, AIML and Congress, to shed their differences. These public appeals were not only meant for Indian leaders but were to also send warning signs to the rulers that Khaksars would not rest until

---

[47] Hussain, P. 162.
[48] The Radiance, February 06, 1943. P. 16.

freedom was achieved. These appeals of Khaksar Tehreek and public responses were well noticed by all, including the Government of British India.

All parties, that were taking a nationalistic approach, were getting frustrated at Jinnah's lack of response. On June 12, 1942, Abul Kalam Azad complained to Mashraqi:

CAMP WARDHA

"My dear Inayatullah,
There seem to be no reason why the League should not have responded to my offer, if she was desirous of any settlement.
My offer is still there. The number of representative is of little importance, it may be five, three, or even one only. If the League be prepared to hold talks in response to my offer, she should say so. No sooner than she expresses her willingness to do so, I would call the working committee and get the representatives or representative nominated...
Yours sincerely,
A.K.Azad"[49]

In the above letter, Azad clearly removed the precondition on the number of representatives. Azad's letter above clearly explained that he was willing to move aggressively on a united front, but it showed his frustration on the Muslim League's silence. The Muslim League's silent approach had not only frustrated Mashraqi but Azad and Nehru too. Jawaharlal Nehru contacted Mashraqi and expressed his views on the Muslim League in a complaining tone. Nehru also agreed that the number of representatives did not matter. Nehru wrote from Wardha on June 12, 1942:

"Dear Mr. Inayatullah Khan,
Thank you for your telegram which I have received today... As you know we shall gladly do everything in our power to bring about a friendly settlement between the Congress and the Muslim League, as well as other organizations. The obvious way to bring this about is for representatives to discuss the matter. That is why the Congress President, Maulana Abul Kalam Azad, suggested some time ago that such representatives might be appointed on behalf of the Congress and the League. The number of the representatives is immaterial, though probably it will be better if there were several on each side. Before the Congress can take definite steps in the matter, it should know whether the Muslim League is agreeable to the suggestion made. From creation speeches made by the Muslim League leaders, it would appear that they are not agreeable... it is difficult for any step to be taken till we have more definite and direct knowledge of the Muslim League attitude.
Your sincerely,
Jawaharlal Nehru"[50]

---

[49] Yousaf 2004, P. 240.
[50] Yousaf 2004, Pp. 240-241.

*****

Jinnah's positive response was not forthcoming. Under this state of affairs, Mashraqi could see where the AIML's attitude would ultimately lead Indians — to massive killing and hate. In the interest of his people, Mashraqi appointed Dr. Hajee Aslam Chishti (a Khaksar leader) to meet Jinnah and inquire why he was staying quiet and avoiding coming to the table.

On June 12, 1942, Dr. Hajee Aslam Chishti met Jinnah in Bombay at 1:30 p.m.[51] Quaid-e-Azam gave the following message to Dr. Chishti:

> "I received Allama Mashraqi's telegram to-day. My clear reply is that until the Congress tentatively withdraws the 'Allahabad Resolution' how can attention be given to these proposals. If the Congress withdraws the resolution, I am prepared to negotiate."[52]

Finally, Quaid-e-Azam showed some flexibility on Mashraqi's persistence. But the reason for his obstinate behavior was by now fairly apparent to political circles. They understood that Quaid-e-Azam could not have adopted this behavior unless somebody (i.e. the British) from behind was giving directions.

Based on the information received through Dr. Chishti, Mashraqi sent the following telegram to Maulana Abul Kalam Azad and Nehru on June 18, 1942:

> "Your letter twefth. Quaideazam prepared to negotiate after withdrawal Allahabad Resolution. Technically reasonable. Please arrange expeditiously."[53]

It is to be noted that Mashraqi suggested to Azad and Nehru to consider Jinnah's point of view. He had already received favorable replies from Azad and Nehru on June 12, 1942, and it had been conveyed to him that Congress leaders were willing to cooperate. Mashraqi was trying his level best to promote goodwill on both sides.

On June 19, 1942, Mashraqi communicated with Jinnah via telegram:

> "Abulkalamazad and Jawaharlalnehru both write expressing unequivocal immediate friendly settlement. Prepared calling working committee meeting for selection representative after your agreeability. Your insistence in message through Haji Aslam Chisti withdrawal Allahabad Resolution mere technicality. Unnecessary. Yourself responsible delay. Beseech immediate agreement."[54]

---

[51] *The Radiance*, February 06, 1943. P. 17.
[52] Ibid.
[53] Ibid.
[54] Pirzada, P. 221. *The Radiance*, February 06, 1943. P. 17.

Mashraqi told Quaid-e-Azam not to be adamant and cease his intransigent attitude on the Allahabad Resolution. Mashraqi requested Jinnah to come to the table to reach an agreement. It is to be noted that Mashraqi had successfully brought the circumstances to where differences could be sorted out and agreement between the different parties was possible.

Many Congress leaders were upset with Jinnah's attitude and his pre-condition for a meeting. Thus, on June 23, 1942, Jawaharlal Nehru sent the following letter to Mashraqi from Allahabad:

> "Dear Mr. Inayatullah Khan,
> I have received your telegram in which you say that Mr. Jinnah desires the withdrawal of the Allahabad resolution before he can negotiate. Presumably this refers to the recent resolution of the All-India Congress Committee relating to the unity of India. That resolution merely confirmed the position for which the Congress has stood for 57 years now. Anyway nobody can withdraw it except the All-India Committee. Personally I would be against any change in that resolution as I think the Congress position relating the unity of India is sound. Mr. Jinnah's suggestion that this resolution should be withdrawn is on a par with a suggestion I might make that the Muslim League resolution about Pakistan should be withdrawn. Such suggestions do not help either way. If people are prepared to talk over matters, they do not put forward conditions which in themselves are tentamount to decisions. The suggestion I made in Bombay and elsewhere was that people holding different views on this subject should, while adhering to their views, agree to cooperate on the basis of achieving independence of India and the transfer of full political power to the representatives of the Indian people. Further, they can cooperate then in the defence of a free India. After that they can consider the other questions that divide them and come to an understanding. This course of action does not commit anyone or compel him to give up his own particular point of view.
> Yours sincerely,
> Jawaharlal Nehru"[55]

One can see the anxiety among leaders about Jinnah's attitude. Quaid-e-Azam felt under-confident meeting all these leaders face-to-face because of the weakness of his Pakistan demand.

However, Mashraqi's pressure could not be avoided and Jinnah finally agreed to meet Rajagopalachariar.[56] On purpose, Quaid-e-Azam did not invite

---

[55] Hussain, Pp. 165-166. *The Radiance*, February 06, 1943. P. 18.

[56] Rajagopalachariar resigned from the Congress Working Committee on April 30, 1942 (*The Tribune*, May 01, 1942). The All-India Congress Committee, in its meeting held on May 02, 1942, rejected Rajagopalachariar's formula (also known as the C.R. formula) by heavy vote (*The Tribune*, May 03, 1942). According to political circles, the C.R. formula conceded to the Muslim League's demand of Pakistan. The C.R. formula basically acknowledged the Muslim League's claim for separation. This may have been the reason Jinnah agreed to meet him.
   Mashraqi's prime methodology was Muslim-Hindu harmony and consensus. Mashraqi's influences on Rajagopalachariar had brought C.R. formula. However, Mashraqi's idea

Mashraqi for this meeting; though for the sake of courtesy and unity, he should have, particularly when Mashraqi had been involving Jinnah and was not creating any obstruction to Jinnah's leadership. But Mashraqi did not care as long as a compromise could be reached, and he sent an encouraging telegram to Quaid-e-Azam on June 25, 1942:

> "Congratulations Jinnah Rajagopalacharia Meeting. Fervently urge tangible results."[57]

Nothing came out of the Quaid-e-Azam-Rajagopalachariar meeting. Jinnah could have sought Mashraqi's help, who was mediating between the Hindus and the Muslims, but he did not. It was very disturbing for Khaksars to see that Mashraqi had put in considerable effort in bringing unity, yet Jinnah did not, even as a courtesy, ask Mashraqi to join the meeting. It created suspicion in the Khaksar circle that Quaid-e-Azam, for some reason, kept Mashraqi out of the meeting. Further, Rajagopalachariar did not disclose the details of the meeting to Mashraqi. He had already been in communication with Mashraqi, hence it is likely that he did not disclose this information because of pressure from Jinnah.

Everyone, Muslims and Hindus, were eager to settle the issues, as evident from the correspondence, but Jinnah continued to maintain his stance; in a press interview on July 02, 1942, he reiterated the demand for a separate homeland. Quaid-e-Azam stated:

> "The only way for Britain to do justice is to hand over the Muslim homelands to the Mussalmans and the Hindu homelands to Hindus. It is a practical proposition and will cause the least amount of trouble and privation...
> ...I am confident that, if Britain will take courage in both hands and give their decision in favour of partition, the Hindus will reconsile themselves after a few months, as obviously it is not unfavourable to them, for they will have the government of three-fourths of India in their hands, while the Mussalmans will have only one-fourth of India...
> ...We are a nation with our own distinctive culture and civilisation, language and literature, art and architecture, names and nomenclature, sense of value and proportion, legal laws and moral codes, customs and calendar, history and traditions, aptitudes and ambitions; in short, we have our own distinctive outlook on life and of life. By all cannons of international law we are a nation."[58]

To Mashraqi, division meant abandoning the right of Muslims over India and creating a country insignificant in comparison to India in world politics. The

---

of Pakistan was not what Jinnah had proposed. Mashraqi's idea was complete independence of a united India, for which AIML cooperation was necessary.

See Chapter 6 for more details on the C.R. formula.

[57] Pirzada, P. 221. *The Radiance*, February 06, 1943. P. 18.

[58] *The Tribune*, July 04, 1942.

British must have breathed a sigh of relief on Jinnah's press interview in which he categorically maintained the demand for Pakistan. Quaid-e-Azam was not seeking any agreement with Khaksars or the Congress. To a nationalist, Quaid-e-Azam had to maintain this stance to maintain his leadership, or the British would recognize someone else to be the leader representing Muslims. If Jinnah had agreed with Khaksars and Congress, this would have sent a death warrant for British rule in India.

*****

Among the Muslims, Mashraqi and Quaid-e-Azam were the leading political personalities. Neither of these two leaders could be ignored based on their strength and importance. Hindu leaders were hoping that Mashraqi could use his influence on Quaid-e-Azam. In continuation of Hindu leaders' efforts to reach a settlement with AIML, on July 02, 1942, Dr. Pattabhi Sitaramiyya (a prominent Congressman) met Allama Mashraqi. *The Radiance* (Aligarh), wrote on February 06, 1943:

> "Dr. Pattabhi Sitaramiyya, a prominent Congressman, interviewed Allama Mashriqi at his residence in Madras and they discussed the question of Hindu-Muslim unity for nearly two hours. Dr. Pattabhi agreed with the Khaksar leader that at the present critical juncture, when the fate of India is not known, 'politics' and 'political gains' by parties do not matter, and that the only useful and politically powerful programme at this moment is irrespective of caste or creed in order to create a spirit of communal unity and that these bodies should become total volunteer organisations under their respective leaders. Dr. Pattabhi, however, disagreed with Allama Mashriqi on the point stressed by him that political concessions or gains, for the reason that they have become imaginary on account of the uncertain outcome of war, should be conceded on both sides in order to achieve Hindu Muslim unity. The doctor said that he would try his utmost to mould the opinion of the Congress at the ensuing meeting of the Congress Committee at Wardha in so far as he agreed with the Khaksar point of view in politics."[59]

Further, Sitaramiyya pleaded with Mashraqi to somehow influence Jinnah to come to the negotiating table. Mashraqi made clear his plan of ending British rule within six months provided that the Hindus did not ignore the AIML, because any party alone could not seek independence. Mashraqi's endeavor was to bring about a settlement, so that the process of independence could move forward swiftly. Mashraqi pointed out to Dr. Sitaramiyya the difficulties and the forces that were at work behind the scenes and suggested that the Congress must consider Quaid-e-Azam's demand regarding withdrawal of the Allahabad Resolution.

---

[59] *The Radiance*, February 06, 1943. P. 18.

Mashraqi conveyed the same to Nehru in Wardha, where he was attending a Congress Working Committee meeting, in a telegram dated July 06, 1942:

> "Your letter twentythird June received. Allahabad Resolution cannot be considered as reiteration of the Congress creed, it is more a provocateur antidote to Rajagopalachariar's resolution on Pakistan. Please remove last obstacle put by Jinnah. Also think deeply and practically over plan of Indian independence devised by me and communicated to [Dr.] Pattabhisitaramiyya [Pattabhi Sitaramiyya]."[60]

Mashraqi was in a difficult spot; while he was attempting to build unity to seek freedom of India, he did not want any party to exploit the situation. He attempted to create a balance, and he did not want the Congress to ignore the AIML. Besides, Jinnah could not be ignored because the British would only work with Jinnah from the Muslim side. To a nationalist, what Quaid-e-Azam was stating publicly was not what was being discussed in meetings with the British. Jinnah could not leave the Pakistan demand, otherwise his political career would come to an end. Mashraqi was aware of the Jinnah-British relationship. Based on these difficulties, Mashraqi informed Nehru to be adaptable, as rigidity would be unwise. The Congress had to seek Quaid-e-Azam's support to undo British designs.

Unlike Quaid-e-Azam, Mashraqi was not looking to the British for help. In fact, he had his own strength and plan in place for the removal of the British regime. It is important to note that by bringing all parties on a common platform, Mashraqi was giving a new turn to politics thereby ensuring quick removal of British rule. At that time, the British were in a tight spot; they were in disarray and panic due to World War II and resisting the Khaksar Tehreek would not have been possible. They were scared and worried of Khaksar power.

On July 08, 1942, in response to Mashriqi's telegram of July 06, 1942, Nehru sent the following letter (from Wardha) to Mashraqi (in Madras):

> "Dear Mr. Inayatullah Khan,
> I have received your telegram. I think I have already made our position clear to you. The Congress ever since its inception has been based on the national unity of India. Without that idea of unity, the Congress fails in its purpose and might as well be wound up. The resolution passed by the All-India Congress Committee in Allahabad in effect stated that the Congress should not agree to the break-up of that unity. This resolution may or may not have been necessary, but in effect it merely confirmed the old Congress position. To annul that resolution is to state to the world that the Congress is prepared to consider the division of India into two parts. That would be against the fundamental Congress position.
> Apart from this, however, the Congress has stated that while it stands by the unity of India and considers any division fatal

[60] Hussain, P. 167. *The Radiance*, February 06, 1943. Pp. 18-19.

for all concerned, still it cannot think in terms of compelling any territorial unit to remain in an Indian union against its declared emphatic will.

I have already told you that constitutionally speaking it is beyond my power to upset a resolution passed by the A.I.C.C. only the A.I.C.C. or the full Congress can do that.

I think the position is quite clear. What I suggested to you previously was that the Congress and the Muslim League, as well as others, need not give up their particular positions or objectives but may still cooperate together for the independence and defence of India. What they must all decide is that they will not look up to British Government for help in furthering their particular claims as this is derogatory to the dignity of any Indian or any group in India. It is for us to settle these matters among ourselves without invoking foreign authority.

Yours sincerely,
Jawaharlal Nehru"[61]

In his letter, Nehru tried to explain his position, so as to remove any ambiguity that Mashraqi might have had about the Allahabad Resolution. Nehru echoed Mashraqi's thoughts and clearly stated that it is "derogatory" and undignified to seek British help in resolving matters belonging to the Indians. The British would not help the matter and would create problems. The AIML was not realizing the importance of settling the issues amongst themselves; they were instead running to the British for help.

In the Congress too, agents of imperialism were active who would not allow Muslim-Hindu unity. Rajagopalachariar, who wanted this unity and agreed with Mashraqi's philosophy, had resigned from Congress. Mashraqi, who was desperately seeking Muslim-Hindu unity in order to seek freedom and was anti-communalism politics — may it be from AIML or anyone else —, had immediately congratulated Rajagopalachariar. But Mashraqi was upset as Rajagopalachariar had not conveyed the conversation that took place between him and Quaid-e-Azam. Mashraqi never liked maneuvering or underhanded machinations, whether they came from a Muslim or a non-Muslim. Mashraqi sent a letter to Rajagopalachariar:

"Thousand Lights, Madras
the 11th July, 1942

Dear EX-PREMIER,
Your resignation from the Congress is a clear proof that you will have Hindu-Muslim unity at any cost. I congratulate you on this rare courage in upholding your convictions.

I sent Mr. Allah Bukhsh Syed the other day to find out from you the details of your tour. I did not see your point in not telling him what transpired between you and Qaideazam Jinnah. I have already got, and hope to get something more tangible from both sides but it requires more application. Unless you have something up

[61] Yousaf 2004, Pp. 244-245. *The Radiance*, February 06, 1943. P. 19.

your sleeve which if disclosed to me would prejudice the Hindu-Muslim cause. I trust you will help me to the utmost.
I hope you are well.
Yours sincerely,
Inayatullah Khan
P.S. In case you agree to communicate to me anything I shall send a messenger to get the message dictated by you, or we may meet if that suits you anywhere."[62]

Again the letter shows that Mashraqi remained neutral, open and very straight forward.

Upon receipt of Mashraqi's letter, Rajagopalachariar replied on July 14, 1942 "giving reasons for not disclosing the conversation between him and Mr. Jinnah, also saying that that letter of his was 'not meant for publication.'"[63] Rajagopalachariar also admitted publicly that his talks with Jinnah failed. The question is why Rajagopalachariar pleaded not to make the letter public.

On July 26, 1942, Gandhi wrote in *Harijan*:

> "If the Quaid-e-Azam really wants a settlement, I am more than willing and so is the Congress... If he wants one [a settlement], why not accept the Congress President's offer that Congress and League representatives should put their heads together and never part until they have reached a settlement. Is there any flaw or want of sincerity in this offer?
> ...to-day there is neither Pakistan nor Hindustan. It is Englistan. So I say to all India let us first convert it to the original Hindustan and then adjust all rival claims. This is surely clear. After the restoration of India to the nation there will be no Central Government. The representatives will have to construct it. It may be one Hindustan or many Pakistans."[64]

This statement further endorses that Jinnah's survival was based on conflict. The question is, was division the only solution? India belonged to Muslims and the Muslim nationhood could still be maintained; then why were Muslims or Islam in danger, particularly in Muslim majority provinces?

*****

In the absence of agreement, the Congress Working Committee passed a resolution on July 14, 1942 to launch Civil Disobedience (Quit India Movement).[65] (The Congress actually started the Quit India Movement later on August 08, 1942.[66]

---

[62] *The Radiance*, February 06, 1943. P. 19.
[63] *The Radiance*, February 06, 1943. P. 20.
The actual letter from Rajagopalachariar could not be found.
[64] *The Star of India*, July 27, 1942.
[65] *Gandhi-Manibhavan.org.*
[66] *The Tribune*, August 08, 1942. *Quit India Movement* web site.

The Khaksar Tehreek was called to join the Quit India Movement. Mashraqi was apprehensive of its outcome and did not agree with the Congress Working Committee's resolution and on July 28, 1942, Allama Mashraqi sent the following telegram to Maulana Abul Kalam Azad, Khan Abdul Ghaffar Khan, Mahatma Gandhi, Rajagopalachariar, Jawaharlal Nehru, Rajendra Prasad and Dr. Pattabhi Sitaramiyya. He also sent a copy to Sambamurty (former Speaker of the Madras Assembly). The telegram was published in the press, and it stated:

> "I am in receipt of Pandit Jawaharlal Nehru's letter of July 8th. My honest opinion is that Civil Disobedience Movement is a little premature. The Congress should first concede openheartedly and with handshake to Muslim League the theoretical Pakistan, and thereafter all parties unitedly make demand of Quit India. If the British refuse, start total disobedience. Think profoundly judging consequences. Country emasculated in the midst of war, also unprepared. Real dynamic and vitalising incentive necessary for successful termination of the struggle."[67]

The following telegram was sent to Quaid-e-Azam and Sardar Vallabhbhai Patel, Bombay on July 28, 1942:

> "Mahatma Gandhi and other Congress leaders telegraphed as follows: Received Jawaharlal's letter eighth July. My honest opinion is civil disobedience little pre-mature. First concede Muslim League openheartedly and with handshake theoretical Pakistan. Thereafter unitedly demand Quit India. If refused start total disobedience. Think profoundly. Country emasculated, in midst of war, unprepared. Real vitalising incentive necessary successful termination struggle. Inayatullah Khan."[68]

One can see from the telegrams that Mashraqi was impartial and was not siding with the Congress. He wanted unity and justice and in no way wanted the Muslim League to be ignored. In his telegram, Mashraqi highlighted all points that were needed to make the Quit India Movement successful. Yet, the Congress leaders did not learn any lesson from his vision and did not postpone the Quit India Movement, although some discussion did take place to postpone it, based on Mashraqi's suggestion. The Congress party was probably over-confident that the movement would bring desired results and the British would pack up and leave India in the hands of the Congress.

On the other hand, the AIML wanted the conflict to continue, thus they were very happy when the Khaksar Tehreek did not support the Congress on the Quit India Movement. Mashraqi could not send his acceptance of the Congress' proposal, because he could not see Congress succeeding by going alone. Without unity in the ranks and without preparing the nation, as pointed out by Mashraqi in his telegram, this was a futile effort. It is important to note

---

[67] *The Radiance*, February 06, 1943. Pp. 20-21. Hussain, P. 170.
[68] *The Radiance*, February 06, 1943. P. 21.

that before launching the Quit India Movement, the AIML had to be of the same opinion to stand against the British and openly declare hostility towards them. But AIML would obviously not come out in the open and declare its hostility towards the British. They could not face bullets or even imprisonment.

The British were now basically surviving on the discord among Indians, and Mashraqi was trying to unite the Indians to invalidate the British strategy. The British and AIML, however, were extremely jubilant over Congress' inability to obtain Khaksar support. *The Radiance* wrote about AIML's excitement:

> "This telegram was published in the papers on the 29th July [1942] and was also broadcasted among the Khaksars everywhere. It was hailed by the Muslim Leaguers by a shower of telegrams to Allama Mashriqi, appreciating the timely advocacy of the Pakistan issue and more especially valuing the safe warning given to the Congress for starting a lonely struggle."[69]

Soon the Congress realized its mistake of failing to secure Khaksar and AIML support. Almost immediately they came to realize that Mashraqi was right and meeting between Hindu leaders and Jinnah was thought to be extremely essential.

After Mashraqi's telegram of July 28, Sambamurty interviewed Mashraqi[70] and sought his views on the political situation. Mashraqi reiterated his views and categorically informed him that the Congress should not ignore the AIML and must reach a settlement with Jinnah. Mashraqi also told Sambamurty that Gandhi must meet Jinnah immediately to settle the issues and form a joint front; differences between Muslims and Hindus were providing the British with the opportunity to prolong their stay. During the interview,

> "Sambamurty...told him [Mashraqi] that the telegram was discussed at Wardha between Mr. Gandhi, Mr. Rajagopalachariar and others for a long time and that the results were bound to be good... At any rate the net result of the telegram was that an open talk started in Bombay concerning the desirability of Mahatma Gandhi meeting Mr. Jinnah at once, and steps were actually taken to that effect on the 4th and 5th August."[71]

Sambamurty confirmed that now there was an inclination towards a Jinnah-Gandhi meeting. Mashraqi again reiterated his pledge of obtaining freedom within six months, provided that they followed his course of action. This pledge was meant for every leader in India who was willing to throw out the British without dividing India. Sambamurty asked Mashraqi "prospects of

---

[69] *The Radiance*, February 06, 1943. P. 21.
[70] Ibid.
[71] Ibid.

success" on the Quit India Movement, to which "Allama promptly replied that the movement, being alone and being led as it was, was bound to fail."[72]

In the meantime, owing to its over-confidence, the Congress continued its efforts to launch the Quit India Movement. According to the Khaksar circle, Mashraqi's plan of removal of the British regime was well in place. World War II had weakened the British and their hold on India could come to an end very fast, provided all Indians were united on one platform. Under the prevailing circumstances, the British were incapable of opening a domestic front, thus it was an opportune time, and freedom could be achieved quickly.

*****

"On the 5th of August at 8.50 p.m. Allama Mashriqi, having been delivered a telephonic message from Bombay by a Khaksar that influences were working strongly seducing Mahatma Gandhi from making a contact with Mr. Jinnah and also getting the good news from the papers as well as from the telephonic message that the [Civil] disobedience movement was definitely to be postponed for two weeks and that Mahatma Gandhi was to stay on for some more days in Bombay instead of the original programme that he was to leave the day next to August 7, sent the following last telegram in complete hurry, disregarding all consequences of his illness, also of his detention under the orders of the Government"[73]

Mashraqi sent this telegram (on August 05, 1942) to Quaid-e-Azam Muhammad Ali Jinnah, Abul Kalam Azad, Mahatma Gandhi and Jawaharlal Nehru:

"Beseech God's Sake Mahatma Gandhi settle Quaideazam Jinnah before launching civil disobdience movement. Reaching despite illness and detention. Wait."[74]

It is important to note that while this correspondence was going on, Mashraqi's movements were still restricted to Madras Presidency. On top of this, he was seriously ill. Yet he was willing to ignore restrictions and travel in order to bring these two leaders into agreement, before joining a civil disobedience movement. In his telegram, he made Gandhi realize that the Quit India Movement would not succeed alone, and Gandhi must first settle the political issues with Jinnah.

Mashraqi's telegrams to leaders could not be ignored. They did make a difference, and it was felt in the Congress and AIML circles that Quaid-e-Azam and Gandhi's meeting was indispensable. *The Tribune*'s (of August 08,

---

[72] *The Radiance*, February 06, 1943. P. 21.
[73] Ibid.
[74] Ibid. Yousaf 2004, P. 246.

1942) report confirmed the development of this change in atmosphere; the
newspaper stated:

> "...there have been suggestions that Mr. Jinnah must invite Gandhiji
> for discussion on the Indian political situation.
>
> I [special correspondent] learn from well-informed quarters
> that several members of the Muslim League as also other friends of
> Mr. Jinnah have appealed to Mr. Jinnah to take the initiative and
> write to Mahatma Gandhi or call on Mahatma Gandhi and open
> negotiations with him."
>
> The newspaper further wrote that Quaid-e-Azam must not
> close the doors of negotiation and "there are other equally effective
> ways of protecting the Muslim interest... The present grave situation
> in the country offers Mr. Jinnah once again an opportunity to revert
> to his old role of a true ambassador of Hindu-Muslim unity."

It was indeed frustrating for everyone including Khaksars to observe Quaid-e-
Azam's reluctance for talks, as this was endangering and hampering freedom.
Mashraqi considered it a great wrongdoing that freedom be delayed on
account of the demand for partition. Quaid-e-Azam's actions, for instance not
coming to the table and the Pakistan demand, were understood to have been
pursued on the behest of the British. In the Khaksar circle, Quaid-e-Azam's
speeches and campaign were misleading for the public. In his speeches, he
appeared to be rigorously fighting for the rights of the Muslims and it seemed
that he was not coming to the table as the Congress was not agreeing to terms
based on the Muslim cause. According to the Khaksars, Quaid-e-Azam
sounded extremely sincere to the Muslim cause, but in reality, the public did
not understand that the British were behind him and were creating
circumstances so that he had to maintain a rift among Indians.

Despite some realization in the Congress circle that the Jinnah-Gandhi meeting
had become crucial, the Congress did not wait; in a hurry and on its own, the
Congress launched the Quit India Movement on August 08, 1942.[75] The
Khaksars were again approached to join the Quit India Movement. However,
The Tribune of August 12, 1942 reported:

> "Allama Mashriqi, the Khaksar leader, who is now in Madras [with
> restrictions on his movements] has allowed Agha Ghazanfar Ali Shah
> to release the following statement to the press:— 'The Khaksars are
> strictly prohibited from participating in the Congress movement,
> which is notably premature but is suicidal to the cause of India at this
> juncture.'"

While the Quit India Movement was underway, Mashraqi maintained the
pressure for a Jinnah-Gandhi meeting. Neither Congress nor AIML could
avoid Mashraqi's pressure. While discussion on Jinnah-Gandhi meeting was
going on in the Congress circle, the AIML also called a meeting on August 18,

---

[75] *The Tribune*, August 08, 1942. *Quit India Movement web site.*

1942 to discuss a Gandhi-Jinnah meeting. *The Tribune*, August 19, 1942 reported:

> "It is understood that the Working Committee of the All India Muslim League had for discussion to-day [August 18, 1942] a draft resolution authorising Mr. Jinnah, if he thinks it necessary, to establish contact with Mahatma Gandhi."

Meanwhile, the Quit India Movement did not bring any results and failed. Without the support of all parties in India, the movement was bound to fail. It is also important to note that Jinnah imposed a condition for a meeting that Gandhi should first call off his Quit India Movement.[76] Quaid-e-Azam could not have said this, unless the British wanted him to say this. Under these circumstances, the movement would not be successful. Hence, Mashraqi's prediction came true.[77]

As a result of the Quit India Movement, there was large-scale open rebellion and violence directed at Government properties such as telegraph offices, railway stations, Government buildings, etc. There were widespread acts of sabotage. Crowds looted shops and buses were set on fire. Trains were stoned. Police opened fire at many places.[78] Almost 1,000 people died in four months and property worth almost 1.5 million rupees was destroyed without any result for the effort. The Government held Gandhi responsible for these acts of violence.[79]

The situation in the country was quite grave and unity was yet to be achieved.[80] World War II was on and enemy forces were on the frontiers of India; a united front was badly needed to put pressure on the British to leave India. British authorities were, for the world's sake, demanding an agreed plan from the Indian parties; the British knew this would never materialize as they were the controlling leaders. Mashraqi knew that the British would never allow this agreement, because this would mean that the British would have to leave. Hence, Mashraqi maintained the pressure to make a Jinnah-Gandhi meeting happen.[81]

*****

It is crucial to address why Jinnah remained silent, despite Mashraqi's rigorous attempts.

---

[76] Khan, Khan Abdul Wali. Chapter 8.
[77] It is important to note many of Mashraqi's predictions came true.
See earlier reference note in this chapter.
[78] *The Tribune*, August 10-11, 1942.
[79] *Government of Pakistan information web site.* (1).
[80] See Appendix III.
[81] See more on the Jinnah-Gandhi meeting in Chapter 6.

Quaid-e-Azam's silence was politically motivated. According to the Khaksar circle, Jinnah was doing this for various reasons. First, Jinnah knew that if he had gone to the meeting, not only would the united demand for a National Government have been discussed, but the leaders would have questioned Jinnah's demand for Pakistan. The united demand for a National Government was against the spirit of the Pakistan Resolution. Quaid-e-Azam could not risk his political career because it was the Pakistan Resolution that had greatly enhanced his value. If he supported the united demand, his insistence for an independent state would be sidelined and that could put his political ambition in jeopardy. Further, it is a historical fact that the AIML's plan of Pakistan was totally ambiguous. That is why complete details of Pakistan were not given in the Lahore Muslim League session (March 22-24, 1940) and thereafter. Under the proposed division, there was no way that Jinnah could justify securing 100 million Muslims in Pakistan. Quaid-e-Azam, though adamant on the Pakistan demand, had no answer to convince leaders that his plan was workable. By remaining silent, he was putting pressure on Mashraqi and Congress leaders to come to his terms.

There were other reasons too. During Mashraqi's arrest, the Muslim Leaguers had managed to gain political strength, and they could not risk this by forming an alliance with Mashraqi. The Leaguers were highly concerned and intimidated by Mashraqi's personality, strength and popularity at the grassroots level. Jinnah was willing to accept Khaksars' presence as long as they worked under the Muslim League flag and followed Muslim League's line of action. That is why Jinnah repeatedly tried his best to bring the Khaksars under the League flag. Forthrightly speaking, he could not tolerate Khaksars other than if they were doing social service or serving as a *militia force* of the Muslim League, as this would allow the League to gain political advantage over those who feared Khaksars. Further, the Mashraqi-Quaid-e-Azam alliance was also a threat to some of the leading Muslim Leaguers.

Finally and importantly, the British considered Khaksar Tehreek the most dangerous organization to their rule in India, and for Jinnah, it was not possible to annoy the British and destroy his political career. Quaid-e-Azam feared that if he formed an alliance with the Khaksar Tehreek, the British would replace him with someone else. The British were overbearing, overwhelming and over-present in every sphere of life, so it was very easy for them to pull Jinnah behind and put somebody else in front. If the British were discontented with Jinnah, there was a line-up of others who would have been more than happy to offer their services to the British. The Muslim League representation of Muslims and Quaid-e-Azam's leadership were only acceptable to the British as long as they did not go against British wishes. The British also wanted a rift between various parties to provide them with a reason to continue ruling India. Hence, Jinnah did not want to do anything that would upset the British.

Another question is why could Mashraqi not have changed his stance and supported Jinnah for the division of India? Mashraqi could have easily accepted Quaid-e-Azam's offer of joining the Working Committee of the Muslim League, but Mashraqi knew that the League was being used by the British for its own ends. Mashraqi could not go against his principles and the wishes of the majority of people who were against division and against a Muslim-Hindu rift. He believed in India's oneness and saw it as an indivisible entity. Some of the reasons why Mashraqi was against the division of India are as follows:

- ❖ Partition was overall impractical and unnatural
    - o Large-scale transfer of the population was not possible because of numerous physical and practical difficulties
    - o The Muslim population was scattered all over India; Muslims who would not be able to migrate to Pakistan would become a hopeless minority and would suffer socially, economically and politically in India
    - o The division of assets and liabilities would be another big issue; for instance, the country's natural resources could not be divided. Religious places of worships and Islamic art and architecture could not be transferred
- ❖ Both India and Pakistan would suffer
    - o Communalism and division would bring hatred, rivalry and hostility amongst 400 million people (Muslims, Hindus and others) who had lived together for centuries; it would ruin the foundation of Indian nationalism
- ❖ Many problems would persist for Pakistan
    - o The distance between the Eastern and Western wings of Pakistan would create many problems for Pakistan, including defense and development
    - o Pakistan would have to live under the shadow of India, which would have a larger area and population; Pakistan's global position would be less important than India's and the Muslims would suffer a psychological set back
- ❖ People would lose their heritage
    - o Muslims associated great pride with India as their homeland and the place they had ruled for almost a thousand years; with division, they would lose their highly precious and prestigious heritage. It was difficult for Muslims to forget this and by losing India, their historical pride would be lost
    - o Muslims in India and India itself had played an extremely important and dominant role in the world; division would destroy the dominance of Muslims as well as of India in world politics
    - o By creating Pakistan, the new state would lose all connections with the historical name, India
    - o Overall Muslim interests would suffer in the long run

The nativity of Indian Muslims was associated with India. History is witness to the reality that many wars have been fought and millions of lives have been sacrificed on the basis of holding on to nativity. Mashraqi could not let the nativity of Indian Muslims go. To him, the Two-Nation Theory was conceived for vested reasons. There were many other prominent leaders who agreed with him that India could not be torn apart on the basis of racial, linguistic or religious considerations, as this would destroy the entire national fabric.

If we look around the world, people do live in multi-religious environments. People live with neighbors, who may not be from the same religion, color, caste or creed. Countries co-exist as neighbors with variance in religions. In India, too, Muslims and Hindus lived together for centuries. Hindus served in Muslim courts and vice versa. During the Mughal Empire, Akbar, Jahangir and others took Hindu Rajput princesses as wives and queens. Inter-marriages in all classes of society took place (they take place today in all societies around the world). By and large in India, communal harmony remained the norm and there were hardly any communal clashes. To cut the story short, Muslims and Hindus did co-exist.

"At the Round Table Conference in 1933 the principle of Indian Federation was supported by all the Muslim delegates."[82] Jinnah, in September 1934, said "I am an Indian first and a Muslim afterwards."[83] In February 1935, he again stated:

> "so long as Hindus and Muslims are not united, let me tell you, there is no hope for India and we shall both remain slaves of foreign domination."

In 1936 in its election manifesto, the Muslim League "described as its objective the attainment of full responsible government in India, fostering of the union of Muslims and other communities and replacement of the Act of 1935."[84] Until 1938, as per Nehru's speech, no one thought of any concept other than "national unity."[85]

The success of Congress in the 1937 elections also alarmed the British. It was not in their interest to see the Congress leading in Indian politics. They started considering ways of breaking this monopoly. The Muslim League was a good candidate to create this rift. After its failure in the 1937 elections, the Muslim League took a U-turn and in 1940s utilized Islam and communalism to create a place for itself to get recognition. In August 1939, Quaid-e-Azam declared

[82] *The Tribune*, March 22, 1946.
[83] Merriam, p. 40.
[84] *The Tribune*, March 22, 1946.
[85] Ibid.

India "a vast country with different nationalities."[86] After this, he started talking of communalism.[87]

When World War II broke out in September 1939, the British grew nervous. With Khaksar strength already apparent from the Shia-Sunni dispute and Khaksar resistance after March 19, 1940, the British found their rule to be in danger. This was the time when the British and AIML collaboration became imminent to counter the Khaksar Tehreek[88]. Thus, relations of strategic importance between Jinnah and Linlithgow started building, and the complexion of Muslim League politics in India started to change.

The Muslim League and the British began to bargain with each other. The League passed a resolution to this effect which was considered to be detrimental and was condemned by Nationalist Muslims of Punjab in a resolution:

> "This meeting [Nationalist Muslims' meeting] further opines that the resolution of the Working Committee of the Muslim League passed at its Delhi meeting is detrimental to the national cause and positively harmful to Muslim self-support and honour and undermines the spirit of self-reliance of the Muslims...
>   One of the conditions on the realization of which Working Committee of the Muslim League has promised to give support to the British Government is that the latter should recognize the Muslim League as the only representative body of the Muslims of India."[89]

On October 05, 1939, Jinnah met the Viceroy.[90] Besides other Muslim matters, the Khaksar issue could not have been ignored by them, however nothing was made public about any discussion on the Khaksars. Soon after, Mashraqi came out of jail on October 14, 1939, and activity between Jinnah and the Viceroy increased. All of a sudden, Jinnah started to become important and Linlithgow started talking to him. On October 17, 1939, Linlithgow said that complete weight would be given to the interests of the Muslims. The weight was not to be given through Khaksars but through the AIML. This partnership between the AIML and British became strategically important. All of this is apparent from the Viceroy's letter to Zetland (on November 04, 1939) in which he stated that he had vested interest in Jinnah's position.

---

[86] *The Tribune*, March 22, 1946.

[87] The League planted the seeds of communalism by passing the Pakistan Resolution in March 1940 and used this all along leading them to win the 1946 elections. In the 1946 elections, appeal to the voter on the basis of religion was bound to occur, particularly to the uneducated Muslim masses. The AIML slogan was "Pakistan ka matlab kiya, La ilaha illallah." With a slogan such as this which draws heavily on religion, can any Muslim not vote for AIML? The slogan was nothing but exploitation of religion. It was a mere tactic to attract attention from illiterate Muslims and to gain popularity and strength for the AIML. The concept of a single nationhood had no political or financial benefit for non-nationalists. Thus, political ends were achieved not by a single nationhood but by using communalism.

[88] Read Chapter 4.

[89] *The Tribune*, September 25, 1939.

[90] *The Tribune*, October 06, 1939.

On October 22, 1939, the All India Muslim League passed a resolution appreciating the Viceroy for recognizing AIML as the representative of the Muslims. It stated:

> "…statement of His Excellency the Viceroy, dated October 17, 1939, the Working Committee of the All-India Muslim League appreciate…and note with satisfaction that His Majesty's Government recognize…All-India Muslim League alone truly represent the Mussalmans of India and can speak on their behalf…"[91]

The AIML was encouraged to rigorously bring demand for Muslim rights and communalism and Islam was brought into politics; the British wanted this not because they were sympathetic to Muslims, but because they wanted to create a rift among Indian communities which would allow them to continue to rule India. Soon the Pakistan Resolution was adopted and the British raised no objection to it as it was in their long term vested reasons; it would create a rift between AIML, nationalist Muslims and non-Muslims and suited the British to continue ruling. If the British were opposed to the Pakistan Resolution, the Viceroy, Governor of Punjab and Government officials would have openly and heavily criticized it, particularly when they knew it was an absurd plan. For the British it would not have been difficult to outright reject the partition plan saying that a large chunk of the Muslim population lived in the Muslim minority provinces, as such it would not be workable. If the British did not want it, they did not even have to justify it, as none of the Leaguers had the courage to oppose their decision. The Governor of Punjab's attendance at the party thrown by Sikandar in honor of Muslim delegates, who came to attend the AIML historic session in Lahore where the Pakistan Resolution was adopted on March 24, 1940, was in itself proof that British had practically endorsed the AIML plan.

If we study the historical documents, all these factors are automatically proven. Historical events would endorse that the British bureaucracy, on purpose, recognized AIML as the only authoritative spokesman of the Indian Muslims so that they could manipulate the League to their advantage. The majority of the top AIML leadership was beneficiary of the British. It is historical fact that the Muslim League flourished on the will of the British. Syed Ali Zaheer (President Shia Political Conference) wrote:

> "The British Government, through their officials, both European and Indian, have for far too long a period pampered and nursed the Muslim League."[92]

Based on the facts on the ground, Quaid-e-Azam's special relationship with British high ups cannot be ruled out. If Jinnah openly supported anti-British elements in India, it would have made sense that he was against the British.

[91] *The Tribune*, October 24, 1939.
[92] *The Tribune*, March 22, 1946.

But he opposed all Muslim and non-Muslim organizations that were anti-British. To the world, he was opposing Congress for the fight for Pakistan, but in actuality he was opposing all anti-British elements vehemently, including the Khaksars. Who was benefiting? It was the British.

Accepting the League as the sole representative of Muslims was indeed a significant injustice to a large number of Muslims who supported the Khaksar Tehreek and to other nationalist Muslim organizations. The Viceroy's declaration (dated October 17, 1939) recognizing AIML to represent Muslims was highly criticized by Muslims and non-Muslims, as the AIML had no following in the masses (having lost the 1937 elections even in Muslim majority provinces and having no ministry of its own in any province).

The contention that the League was not supposed to have been accepted to represent Muslims is also proven from the statements of non-Khaksar leaders, for example, on February 26, 1942, Khan Bahadur Allah Buksh (Premier of Sind) said:

> "Mr. Jinnah knows that he reflects the opinion of only a section of the Indian Muslim community. There is unquestionably a larger section of the Mussalman community who do not see eye to eye with Mr. Jinnah and his political organisation..."[93]

Shaikh Mohammad Zahir-ud-Din, President of the Momin party, sent a telegram to Churchill (Prime Minister) and Amery (Secretary of State for India) and repudiated the Muslim League's claim to be the voice of the Indian Muslims.[94] Many other examples are available in the historical documents that reject AIML's claim to represent the entire Muslim community.

On the other hand, British attitude toward the Khaksars remained firm and discriminatory; Mashraqi was under constant watch and Khaksars were not allowed to operate freely. Mashraqi was a hard nut to crack, thus the British avoided him. They had already tested Mashraqi's loyalties when he rejected Ambassadorship and Knighthood (title of *Sir*). So they preferred Jinnah. The Khaksar Tehreek, despite its strong following, was denied to be representative of the Muslims. The British had damaged Muslim interest wherever and whenever they could. The British had a role in demolishing the Ottoman Empire in the 1920's. It is beyond my comprehension how AIML could ignore the fact that the British wanted to sideline the Khaksars to weaken the Muslims. How could AIML not realize that if they did not stand united with Khaksars, the British would again hit the Muslims hard? How could they not realize that by promoting the Two-Nation Theory they were actually weakening and deteriorating the Muslims in the region? How could they not know that British were happy with Two-Nation Theory? The Two-Nation

---

[93] *The Tribune*, February 27, 1942.
[94] *The Tribune*, March 04, 1942.

Theory was a two way street, it helped AIML to grow and on the other hand it helped the British by implementing the policy of divide and rule.

Mashraqi and other nationalists, Muslims and non-Muslims, were highly perturbed that the AIML was misleading people for their vested goals and meeting British agenda. The Leaguers had no scheme and concrete plan or even a history of serving the masses. They had always looked out for their own benefit. It would not be wrong to mention that most of them were merely opportunists. Within AIML, they had been fighting for personal gains. Many of them were *puppets* of the British and ignored the fact that division of India was in the interest of the British. The tragedy is that the Pakistan Resolution was not only dividing Muslims from non-Muslims but also Muslims from other Muslims; a strong conflict to this proposal had come up.

It is clear that such complex political intricacies lay behind the reasons for which Quaid-e-Azam remained silent. Despite Jinnah's apparent unwillingness to resolve differences with the Hindus, Mashraqi continued his efforts to arrange a Jinnah-Gandhi meeting, as is detailed in the next chapter.

Chapter 6

Mashraqi's Efforts for Jinnah-Gandhi Meeting

Though Mashraqi was released from jail on January 19, 1942, his movements remained restricted to the Madras Presidency[1] until the end of 1942. He was finally released from his internment on December 28, 1942. His imprisonment (from March 19, 1940) lasted approximately 22 months, and his movements were restricted for an additional approximately 12 months – altogether totaling almost three years. On December 28, Mashraqi's restrictions were removed and purportedly he was free to move about anywhere in India, but he remained under close watch. His activities were constantly monitored and reported to the Viceroy, Governor and other high officials.

After the restrictions on his movements were removed, Mashraqi immediately increased his activities to mobilize the Tehreek and rally the public to unite and rise against the colonial power. Momentum towards forming a united front, involving all communities, took off. Every Khaksar mobilized people towards unity and a joint front against the British. Mashraqi wanted to oust the British as all the political difficulties within India were due to their presence. Thus, he continued his rigorous efforts to bring the Muslims and Hindus together and pushed both parties to settle their issues.

On January 02, 1943 (while on his way to Delhi and then to Lahore), Mashraqi addressed the Khaksars at Jhansi Railway Station in Utter Pradesh. A considerable number of Khaksars and people from the general public had gathered at the station to pay respect to their leader. *The Hindustan Times* of January 05, 1943 wrote of his speech:

> "Allama Mashriqui...referred to the communal problem...He [Mashriqi] pleaded with the Muslims for religious tolerance, broadmindedness and magnanimity. The Muslims ruled for 1,000

---

[1] Under British rule, most of south India was integrated into a region called the Madras Presidency. In 1956, the Madras Presidency was disbanded and Tamil Nadu was established.

years only because they treated non-Muslims with consideration, loved them and shared their sorrows and troubles, he observed. The Muslim Empire showed signs of decay when Muslim Rulers became intolerant towards non-Muslims and conservatives in their religious outlook. 'I want Khaksars to preach the gospel of Hindu-Muslim unity which is a living force and without which no liberation is possible. Those leaders who preach ratio communalism are not your leaders. You must discard them and throw them overboard.'"

Mashraqi arrived in Delhi on the same day (January 02, 1943), and in his address to a mammoth public gathering at the Delhi Railway Station, he pleaded for unity among different communities. The next day, he left for Lahore.[2] Upon his arrival by Bombay Express at night, he was again given an "enthusiastic reception at the Lahore Railway Station."[3] Addressing the public, Mashraqi thanked God for giving him the opportunity of speaking to the public of the Punjab after 3 years. *The Tribune*, Lahore of January 04, 1943 reported on his address:

> "The Khaksar Movement, he [Mashraqi] said, was not a Muslim movement, but it was a common movement and its membership was open to all communities. The movement was started to serve Hindus, Muslims, Sikhs and other communities alike and to bring about unity among them. India was under bondage to-day because Indians had gone astray from the path of truth and righteousness.
>
> Concluding the Allama said that there was nothing secret about the Khaksar movement, which within a period of 12 years had spread throughout India."

After the removal of restrictions on Mashraqi, thanksgiving prayers were continuously offered in many cities. People were extremely happy and excited at the news of Mashraqi's release and an air of jubilation prevailed. Ignoring the AIML's policy of communalism, Mashraqi again stated publicly and pleaded courageously for Muslim-Hindu unity. He addressed a huge gathering at Badshahi Mosque in Lahore on January 08, 1943. *The Star of India*, Calcutta of January 09, 1943 later reported his public address:

> "The need for communal unity at the present critical times through which India was passing was stressed by Allama Mashriqui, the Khaksar leader, addressing a thanksgiving meeting organised under the auspices of the Anjuman-i-Khaksaran [Khaksar Tehreek] at the Badshahi Mosque this afternoon.
>
> Allama Mashriqui emphasised the non-political and non-communal character of the Khaksar movement which, he said, was primarily designed to promote social service. The need for a band of selfless social workers, he pointed out, was never greater than at the present time when India was threatened with aggression from a ruthless enemy like the Japanese. He however, made it clear that in accordance with the orders of the Government of India the Khaksars

---

[2] *The Hindustan Times*, January 03, 1943.
[3] *The Tribune*, January 04, 1943.

were free to perform social service individually only and not as an organised body.

The Khaksar leader recalled the attempts made by the Congress as well as the Muslim League during the past three years to win over the Khaksars and announced that the separate identity of the movement would be maintained although they were ready and willing to render service to both the organisations.

About half a dozen Hindu and Sikh Khaksars also made speeches repudiating the allegation that the Khaksar movement was intended to crush Hindus and Sikhs."[4]

Mashraqi and the Khaksars' activities were clearly rising; Khaksars in uniform or wearing badges were visible in different parts of India. This created anxiety for the authorities, and they maintained the strictest possible vigilance to ensure that the Khaksars did not become a threat to the British Government in India. On January 12, 1943, within a few days of removal of restrictions on Mashraqi, he was warned by the Punjab Government. Intelligence reports were sent to the various agencies, and the Government of India asked the Punjab Government (on February 19, 1943 in an express letter) to convey to Mashraqi that wearing of any kind of symbol by the Khaksars was not allowed; any defiance, would lead to re-imposition of ban.[5]

An *Addendum to the Note on the Khaksar Movement* was prepared on March 31, 1943 (original note was prepared in 1941) by the Punjab Criminal Investigation Department (C.I.D.). The said note stated that while addressing the Muslims in Badshahi Mosque Lahore on January 08, 1943, Mashraqi said that the Khaksar Tehreek was actuated

"to wake up the sleeping Muslim nation and to serve humanity."[6]

Mashraqi continued his activities. On April 14, 1943, Mashraqi sent a telegram to Nawab Bahadur of Murshidabad, President of Hindu-Muslim Unity Association, saluting the move to bring Muslim-Hindu unity in Bengal. Mashraqi gave him his full help and cooperation.[7] Mashraqi was least concerned that preaching of Muslim-Hindu unity may damage his political career and AIML would use this appeal for political ends and denounce him. Those who opposed unity, including the All India Muslim Leaguers, did exploit the situation. History and current events are full of evidence that leaders use religion, language, communalism and provincialism to spread hate and to gain political advantage. Mashraqi was different! Mashraqi took a bold step and openly pleaded for Muslim-Hindu unity, and he did not support the Two-Nation Theory, which was of course based on communalism. Mashraqi knew that this theory came from the British, as they had a vested interest in it.

---

[4] Also see *The Bombay Chronicle*, January 09, 1943.
[5] Punjab Criminal Investigation Department (C.I.D.), March 31, 1943. Sir Richard Tottenham's letter, May 08, 1943.
[6] IOL L/P&J/8/680.
[7] *The Bombay Chronicle*, April 15, 1943.

The Khaksar organ, *The Radiance* of August 27, 1943, denounced communalism and wrote:

> "Here is no question of Hindu Nation and the Muslim nation. This division cuts across the communal partitions... If this move of dividing, by their favours and punishments, the Indian population into two camps, succeeds, it will be a very sad day indeed. Let no one think that in this way the Hindus and the Muslims will be separated into two nations — a satisfying notion for many... No, this is not the result which I force. On the other hand, there will be a line of cleavage passing through the Hindus as well as the Muslims. The Hindus will be disunited and disintegrated, the Muslims will also be disunited and disintegrated. And in this universal dissension, some people will prosper but the nation as a whole will go under. It will serve nobody. There will be neither unity between the Hindus and the Muslims, nor solidarity among the Muslims nor the Hindus as such.
>
> The duty of the Khaksars is clear. In plain words, not to allow such a state of things to happen. The future of our country, the future of the millat is at stake. Let us not be deluded by the prizes which are being offered. Let us lay aside all pretty quarrels and disputes. This is not the time for them. Lift yourself above personal and party considerations and see whither you are drifting, what game you are unconsciously playing? Can you do anything without unity and solidarity."[8]

The above statement is self explanatory. It is important to note that Muslims were made aware of the political game that was going on in India. This article rightly pointed out that "some people will prosper" and warned the people to wake up and not become trapped by any such game.

*****

As part of his efforts to bring Hindu-Muslim unity, Mashraqi increased his pressure on AIML and Congress leaders to come to the negotiating table. To Mashraqi, agreement between the Muslim League and the Congress was most essential to achieving the purpose. Once he brought this amicable settlement, then it would be worthwhile to apply Khaksar muscles to get rid of foreign rule. However, anti-Khaksar Muslim Leaguers, instead of realizing the sincerity of the effort, used this endeavor against the Khaksar Tehreek and implied the activity of Muslim-Hindu unity to be an anti-Muslim cause. It is important to note that if Mashraqi had ignored others and used only Khaksar muscle to liberate India, then there would have been massive bloodshed, as communalism had been on the rise owing to AIML's policies. Under the circumstances, it was wise on Mashraqi's part to bring Muslims and non-Muslims of India to a mutual understanding and then apply Khaksar strength to seek independence.

---

[8] Muhammad, Pp. 127, 149.

The public also wanted a close collaboration between Allama Mashraqi and Quaid-i-Azam, however, there were forces among the British and within the AIML which prevented this cooperation. On March 01, 1943, *The Star of India*, Calcutta reported:

> "Much interest now centers round Allama Mashriqi as Muslim circles here are of opinion that Allama can no longer sit idle and watch the situation. There is already a move to bring Mr. Jinnah and Allama [Mashraqi] on a common platform or at least make an effective collaboration between them possible. It is also said that Allama does not favour the amalgamation of Khaksar organisation with Muslim League but will support closer co-operation whenever possible."

With regard to Muslim-Hindu unity, Jinnah himself had been stating that he wished to reach a settlement with Gandhi, however reality on the ground does not prove that. But Jinnah was insistent that Gandhi should invite him for a dialogue. Jinnah had said so in his presidential address at the annual session of AIML held in Delhi on April 24, 1943; he had stated:

> "...what is there to prevent Mr. Gandhi from writing direct to me?...Why does he not write to me direct?"[9]

Quaid-e-Azam detested Mashraqi's involvement as a mediator. Here, he clearly asked Gandhi to write to him directly, meaning that he did not want Mashraqi to play that role.

An invitation was very important for Jinnah to hold the meeting with Gandhi. Thus, Mashraqi maintained pressure on the Congress and other Hindu leaders for this meeting. Congress leaders, including Abul Kalam Azad and Gandhi, were in jail (arrested on August 09, 1942 for launching the Quit India Movement) and therefore, Mashraqi had to put pressure on Jinnah and the Government for the meeting. As a result of this long effort, Gandhi finally wrote to Jinnah from jail on May 04, 1943 (the letter was sent through Secretary, Home Department, Government of India, but was never delivered):[10]

> "DEAR QAID-E-AZAM,
> ...I noted your invitation to me to write to you. Hence this letter.
> I welcome your invitation. I suggest our meeting face to face rather than talking through correspondence. But I am in your hands.
> I hope that this letter will be sent to you and, if you agree to my proposal, that the Government will let you visit me.
> One thing I had better mention. There seems to be an " if " about your invitation. Do you say I should write only if I have

[9] *Gandhi Serve Foundation web site.* (1). *The Hindustan Times,* May 27, 1943.
[10] *Gandhi Serve Foundation web site.* (1).

changed my heart? God alone knows men's hearts. I would like you
to take me as I am.

Why should not both you and I approach the great question
of communal unity as men determined on finding a common solution,
and work together to make our solution acceptable to all who are
concerned with it or are interested in it?
Yours sincerely,
M. K. GANDHI"[11]

The Government withheld Gandhi's letter and a communiqué was issued:

"The Government of India have received a request from Mr. Gandhi
to forward a short letter from himself to Mr. Jinnah expressing a wish
to meet him.

In accordance with their known policy in regard to
correspondence or interviews with Mr. Gandhi, the Government of
India have decided that this letter cannot be forwarded and have so
informed Mr. Gandhi and Mr. Jinnah. They are not prepared to give
facilties for political correspondence or contact to a person detained
for promoting an illegal mass movement which he has not disavowed
and thus gravely embarrassing India's war effort at a critical time. It
rests with Mr. Gandhi to satisfy the Government of India that he can
safely be allowed once more to participate in the public affairs of the
country, and until he does so the disabilities from which he suffers
are of his own choice."[12]

Commenting on the Gandhi letter and the Government communiqué, Jinnah
said:

"This letter of Mr. Gandhi can only be construed as a move on his
part to enroll the Muslim League to come into clash with the British
Government solely for the purpose of helping his release... merely
expressing his desire to meet me is not the kind of ephemeral letter
that I suggested in my speech that Mr. Gandhi should write, and
which has been now stopped by the Government. I have received a
communication from the Secretary to the Government of India Home
Department, dated May 24 that Mr. Gandhi's letter merely expresses
a wish to meet me and this letter Government have decided cannot be
forwarded to me... if Mr. Gandhi were to write to me... to come to a
settlement with the Muslim League on the basis of Pakistan, we were
willing to bury the past... I still believe that the Government will not
dare to stop such a letter if it came from Mr. Gandhi."[13]

By refusing to deliver this letter, the hypocrisy of the Government was
revealed and it was evident that the British were not serious in a settlement or
the transfer of power. Jinnah's statement reflected that he worked closely with
the Government and was not willing to fight the British. The Government was
keeping him posted and wanted him to maintain a stand on partition, so that a

[11] *Gandhi Serve Foundation web site.* (1).
[12] *The Hindustan Times,* May 27, 1943.
[13] *The Hindustan Times,* May 29, 1943.

rift continued. Can Quaid-e-Azam's statement bring any good feeling? It seems that Quaid-e-Azam did not want a settlement.

The Government's duplicity and Jinnah's statement were highly condemned by the people who understood British plans. Dr. Shaukatullah Ansari and S.A. Brelvi of the Azad Muslim Conference condemned this in a press statement:

> "The refusal of the Government of India to forward…letter…cannot be too strongly condemned. It shows how Indianization of the Viceroy's Council, without real transfer of power to the representatives of the people, is a snare and a delusion. That individuals calling themselves Indians should deliberately make themselves responsible for hindering an attempt to bring about an inter-communal settlement is a measure of the demoralization which such Indianisation creates. We are, however, not surprised at the decision of the Government which is fully in accord with the policy consistently followed by them of refusing to transfer power to the people and to that end obstructing all genuine attempts at the settlement of the communal problem."[14]

Many Muslims and non-Muslims were upset with Jinnah. Abdur Rehman Mitha (a non-Khaksar) gave a statement that showed his infuriation:

> "The elusive Mr. Jinnah is once again at his best in his time long game of hide and seek…when Gandhiji has responded to his call…Mr. Jinnah has proved himself to be the greatest hoax of the day. He not only shirks the issue, but stoops so low as to attribute motives to Gandhiji's move. What does he expect of the Congress and Gandhiji? Does he want them to apologise, abdicate and surrender the country to his whims?"
>
> Mitha said that since Gandhi has written to Jinnah, this shows his willingness to settle the issue. Mitha further stated that "He [Quaid-e-Azam] is obviously prepared to put up with the present Ordinance Raj and shelve his Pakistan issue indefinitely so long as the Congress does not satisfy his vanity and submit to his whims. If not by choice, potentially Mr. Jinnah is playing the game of imperialism. At least now the people of India know where they stand. How long can he thus eclipse the Muslim masses of his utopia with such tactics?"[15]

Despite frustration shown by people, nothing came out of Gandhi's letter to Jinnah. Based on this, on June 05, 1943, Mashraqi sent the following telegram to Quaid-e-Azam:

> "Gandhiji's letter to you [Jinnah] to meet him is indeed a prelude to the achievement of Pakistan as well as India's independence. Your

---

[14] *The Hindustan Times,* May 28, 1943.
[15] *The Tribune,* May 29, 1943.

attitude towards the matter is extremely perturbing. Request to reconsider the significance of the invitation."[16]

Professor U.N. Ball wrote:

"Even a child may find that the British Imperialists point out communal cleavage as the chief obstacle in the way of India not out of love for India, but to keep up the fight in order that they may enjoy their influence undisturbed."[17]

In their moves of preventing settlement, the Government withheld Gandhi's letter from jail for Jinnah.[18] It was revealed to the public that the British Government was behind this rift and was preventing this meeting so that Jinnah could not arrive at any agreement. Quaid-e-Azam's statements could not be viewed as anything other than in line with British policy. It was not acceptable to Mashraqi that the Government was connivingly preventing a settlement. Thus, Mashraqi issued a directive to Khaksars all over India to send letters, telegrams and the like to put pressure for the Jinnah-Gandhi meeting. This effort was also reported in the press. *The Hindustan Times* June 07, 1943 reported:

"Allama Mashraqi urges upon the Khaksars all over India to strive utmost to create an atmosphere of unity among the Hindus and the Muslims and to send telegrams, letters and resolutions to Mr. Jinnah and the Viceroy to make a Gandhi-Jinnah meeting possible."

According to the newspaper, Mashraqi stated: "Mahatma Gandhi happens to be the only person who can settle with Mr. Jinnah on the very terms on which the British Government desire a settlement as a tentative step to independence. Obstruction put by the Government in this settlement is unreasonable... if the Muslims of India are indeed so keen on Pakistan...they can only get it now after a settlement with the Congress. Mr. Jinnah must find his way now to meet Mahatmaji and keep to his original statement."

There was great response to Mashriqi's directive, and hundreds of thousands of letters, telegrams, memos etc., from all over India, were sent to Jinnah as well as the Viceroy. Most of them were sent between June 15 and July 15, 1943. Regarding these letters, Mashraqi said:

"Two lakh fifteen thousand telegrams, letters, resolutions, petitions, memorials, etc., involving amiable contact of Khaksars with at least 70 lakh intelligent people, have been sent to Quaid-e-Azam Jinnah and His Excellency the Viceroy urging settlement with Mahatma Gandhi on the Pakistan question..."[19]

---

[16] Yousaf 2004, P. 257. *The Hindustan Times*, June 07, 1943.
[17] *The Tribune*, December 01, 1945.
[18] *The Hindustan Times*, May 27, 1943.
[19] Hussain, P. 192. Also see Muhammad, P. 155.

On July 16, 1943, *The Hindustan Times*, Delhi reported that the Khaksars had sent many letters and telegrams to Jinnah urging him to meet with Gandhi. The newspaper further reported that similar letters were sent to the Viceroy. Resolutions were also passed at three Khaksar meetings (one of these was attended by a large number of Hindus).

It was unfortunate that the Muslim Leaguers frowned at Mashraqi's political activities and openly criticized him for his efforts of Muslim-Hindu unity. They looked angrily at these letters from Khaksars. They propagated that Mashraqi was working against the interest of the Muslims. Mashraqi disregarded the criticism and continued pushing Jinnah for the meeting. Mashraqi was mounting the pressure so that as soon the Muslim League and the Congress reached an agreement, he would finally ask British to leave India. If they failed to do so, Mashraqi indicated that they should be ready for the consequences.

The meeting was yet to come despite Gandhi's invitation. Quaid-e-Azam's delaying stance was continuously deplored by nationalists. Muslim Majlis in its manifesto stated:

> "The present all round frustration of our national and economic life points out clearly the interdependence of the Hindu-Muslim problems, which have been made vexatious and almost insurmountable by the political opportunists in India. The attempt to create geographical barrier has been a gigantic political blunder on the part of its propounders...
>
> Mr. Jinnah's leadership of the Muslim League is one of the numerous links of the reactionary chain of the selfish and self-styled leaders. He is, indeed, one of those leaders who have blocked the way to the goal of freedom and national unity. As long as such leaders are allowed to reign supreme, there is no chance of any compromise among the two great communities in India, and there is no chance of attaining freedom of the country. This reactionary leadership is a powerful weapon in the hands of the British Government to resist the aspiration of 400 million people in their struggle for freedom. We must make an end of reactionary leadership to save our community from its baneful effects.
>
> Mr Jinnah is now and then haughtily insisting that all his demands must be accepted verbatim by the Hindus, but he does not like to explain and clarify the issue underlying this absurd and ridiculous demand. Hence the first and most important duty of every well-wisher of the Muslims is to disentangle the Muslim community from the clutches of reactionary leadership, and to lead them on the straight path of freedom"[20]

*****

---

[20] *The Tribune*, July 31, 1943. *The Bombay Chronicle*, August 02, 1943.

While these efforts for a Jinnah-Gandhi meeting were on, other Khaksar activities increased tremendously. Mashraqi's activities continued to be under constant close watch by the intelligence services, despite the fact that restrictions on his movements had been lifted and he was a free person. The intelligence agencies were monitoring the Khaksars too. The Khaksars' activities were highly detested in the British circle and the British were nervous about them.

Sir Richard Tottenham, Additional Secretary to the Government of India, wrote a secret letter on May 08, 1943 to all Provincial Governments and Chief Commissioners (except Panth-Piploda). Tottenham wrote:

> "There have been many indications recently including reports from several Provincial Governments, which suggest that the activities of the Khaksar organisation are tending to an increasing... In fact, there appears to be a wide-spread effort to revive the 'military' side of the organisation."[21]

The Khaksar Tehreek's plan to bring unity and at the same time prepare Khaksars militarily for fight was an excellent strategy. It was the best way to end the British rule within months. If all parties were working in different directions, this would prolong and perhaps permanently maintain British rule, which is exactly what the British desired. Mashraqi's attempts were to build a united and strong front which would undermine British rule.[22]

Linlithgow wrote on May 26, 1943 to all Provincial Governors about the Khaksar Tehreek:

> "I have, as you know, always taken the view that the Khaksars are, potentially, a most dangerous organisation and I have no doubt that the efforts which now appear to be afoot in different parts of India to revive the military character of the movement must be very firmly resisted... But there have been signs...among the Khaksars, of the kind of saber-rattling which I am sure we should do well to suppress at the outset and which will only become more difficult to deal with the longer we leave it alone."[23]

Linlithgow wrote to Amery (Secretary of State for India) on July 05/06, 1943:

> "I am not by any means happy about the Khaksar position...we shall have to deal with these people... It would not, in my opinion, be

---

[21] IOL L/P&J/8/680.

[22] Those who think that Mashraqi could not bring the downfall of the British with spades are highly mistaken. First of all, a spade not only symbolizes labor, but carrying it on one's shoulder while in uniform represents a state of readiness to fight. It is not the spades that matter, as they can be easily replaced. Rather, it is the discipline and spirit that are inculcated in a force that lead to its success. Circumstances around the world today have proven that it is determination, resistance, faith and sacrifice that ultimately win out, even in the face of the most sophisticated weaponry and technology. It is exactly these characteristics that the Khaksar Tehreek embodied.

[23] IOL L/P&J/8/680.

prudent to disregard the possibility that the Muslim League may one day adopt a more bellicose policy towards Government. If, when that time comes, the League finds a powerful instrument, such as the Khaksars, may well become, ready to its hand, we might well be faced with a most dangerous position. I am quite sure that this is a real danger which should be most closely watched."[24]

Mashraqi received threats and warnings to stop his and the Khaksars' activities. The latest warning was received on July 19, 1943[25], according to which, Mashraqi was warned to immediately stop Khaksar activities or the movement would be banned. On July 22, 1943, Allama Mashraqi issued the following statement (he also sent a copy of the statement to Jinnah):

"It appears that the Government of India would not let the Khaksars live or give to them even what is allowed to all others. The ban was raised on December 28 [1942] last after a terrible struggle of three years on clear and definite conditions put in my statement which the Government of India reproduced in their communique of that date, but these conditions were repudiated on January 25.

Since then the Government of India have threatened again and again that I shall be re-arrested and the ban on the Khaksars re-imposed unless the red symbol on the arm of the Khaksars is abolished, the gatherings of the Khaksars forbidden and their social service rendered individually. After the writings of the 3rd March last, I handed over to the Government of India for issue an announcement dated the 9th March to the effect that, being unable to go further, I suspend the Khaksar Organisation throughout India, but this announcement even the Government of India was not pleased to accept.

The latest warning of the 19th July is that, if within a fortnight from that date, the red symbol is not removed from the arm of every Khaksar in India and the display of belchas, drills, marches, also collective service inside camps not abolished, the Government of India will declare the Khaksars to be an unlawful association again. This is called the final warning.

I have always been more in favour of Khaksars being distinguished from non-Khaksars by their useful and noble deeds, their real humility, their sincere social service, their soldierly discipline, alert posture, and Godly qualities than by round or square symbols on their bodies but Government wants to take away from us what it allows to every other organisation in the country and is essential for keeping ordinary discipline. On the other hand, in order to prove my good will, I do not wish to embarrass Government as far as possible. I, therefore, under protest order Khaksars all over India to remove red symbols from their arms at once and without the slightest feelings of ill-will against Government. This will be for the duration of the war only and during that period every Khaksar is required to work so as to get himself distinguished by his noble deeds so that no colour mark is required at all to distinguish him. Every Khaksar,

[24] IOL L/P&J/8/680.
[25] See Sir Richard Tottenham's letter, July 19, 1943. IOL L/P&J/8/680.

henceforth, is also ordered to keep a small copy of his Holy Book (Quran, Geeta, Granth, Bible) always with him for the improvement of his spiritual powers. Khaksars all over India must leave wearing head-dress altogether to show that they are humble and humiliated and cover their heads with ordinary white handkerchiefs when required at the time of prayers.

As regards camps, I order that absolutely no military display of any kind, viz, that of belchas, military uniforms, drills, marches, should henceforth take place even inside camps which must be exclusively reserved for congregational prayers, religious and social lectures and sports. No camps also are to be held anywhere in India for the purpose of doing social service at fairs or melas for the duration of the war.

After August 2, every Khaksar will disobey these orders at his own risk and Government may arrest him. No further orders will be issued to Provincial leaders or centres of the Organisation by the Idara-i-Aliyya but Provincial leaders must issue instructions to their sub-centres and so on at once. I am entirely satisfied with the enormous work done by the Khaksars all over India in connection with Jinnah-Gandhi meeting at my orders and I expect prompt obedience of these orders without a murmur."[26]

In order to avoid a ban on the Khaksar Tehreek, Mashraqi *under protest* suspended the military side of the movement's activities *only* until the end of the war. It was a very wise decision to kill two birds with one stone. Mashraqi did not disband the movement, as was actually desired by the British Government, nor did he abandon his political activity. He was not willing to break the identity and unity of the Khaksars. Thus, he asked the Khaksars to leave the military side of the Khaksar activities, which was a source of great nervousness for the Government, and continue with the rest of the activities. He was not willing to disband congregational prayers, religious and social lectures and sports, and such activities were to continue. Further, he asked Khaksars to use white headdresses during prayers and to keep a copy of the Holy Book of whichever religion they belonged to (Khaksars were Muslims, Hindus, Sikhs, etc.) on themselves. All of this had two purposes; first to have all members seek inspiration from their religions to purify themselves. Second, this would maintain the identity and unity of the Khaksars and would not allow the Khaksar Tehreek to fall apart. It would let the Khaksars continue their activities in various manners, even if they had to disappear underground, and the Khaksars would always be ready at a calls' notice. It is important to note that Mashraqi would not resort to violence, unless he was forced to. Thus, Mashraqi, a bold man, continued with his political activity, which was meant to end British rule. He was determined and focused and nothing could intimidate him. Without a doubt, he was a man of tremendous courage, as were his followers. Mashraqi's statement was not enough for the Government;

---

[26] Yousaf 2004, Pp. 260-61.
News of this statement was also reported in *The Hindustan Times*, July 25, 1943.
Also see IOL L/P&J/8/680.

correspondence between the Home Department and Mashraqi continued, and Mashraqi persisted with his activities.

*****

Mashraqi was moving fast and Khaksar activities had increased tremendously. This bothered Muslim Leaguers as well as the British, despite the fact that political circles and the public considered Mashraqi's presence a necessity.

Then came a bomb shell; just four days after Mashraqi's statement of July 22, Quaid-e-Azam was attacked (on July 26, 1943).[27] According to the book titled *Jinnah Faces an Assassin* written by Jinnah's nephew, the assailant (Rafiq Sabir Mazangavi) was a Muslim Leaguer (Propaganda Secretary in 1939). However, right after the attack and without investigation, he was declared to be a Khaksar. Quaid-e-Azam "sustained minor injuries on his chin and hand"[28] Despite the minor nature of the injury, a case was filed against the assailant. This *bogus and phony* attack was nothing but a conspiracy to eliminate Mashraqi from the political scene.

Mashraqi issued a statement regretting the attack and asking Quaid-e-Azam not to allow this incident to be used for political purposes. Mashraqi's request was ignored. Mashraqi issued a statement on August 26, 1943. The newspaper reported:

> "In a lengthy statement, explaining that the Khaksars are not rivals of the Muslim League, Allama Mashriqi, the Khaksar leader, states that Mr. Jinnah should immediately take steps to solve the political deadlock. He suggests that Mr. Jinnah should immediately meet Gandhiji and write formally to the Viceroy to allow him to see Mahatma Gandhi for the purpose of Hindu-Muslim settlement. In case Mr. Jinnah is refused by the Viceroy an interview with Gandhiji, Mr. Jinnah should ask in another letter 'the name and names of those Hindu gentlemen in India who in the eyes of British Government are best fitted to make Hindu-Muslim settlement which the British Government thinks as essential to the grant of complete independence to India immediately after war.'"[29]

Many political observers were suspicious of the attack on Jinnah and questioned how and why the assailant was named to be a Khaksar without any probes. The *Orient Press* made its own inquiry and reported:

> "It is widely believed that the culprit is not a Khaksar and even assuming him to be such, he is believed to be merely a tool in the hands of a clique for this dirty game."[30]

---

[27] See Appendix I for more details on this attack.
[28] *The Tribune*, July 27, 1943.
[29] *The Tribune*, August 27, 1943.
[30] *The Star of India*, July 28, 1943.

The anti-Khaksar elements' resentment and bashing did not end after declaring Jinnah's assailant to be a Khaksar. The League's *goondas* came to Mashraqi's office in Qarol Bagh (where he was staying) in Delhi in August 1943 and asked the Khaksars to vacate the building and remove the Khaksar Tehreek's flag. The clearing of the building and removal of flag were also reported in *The Tribune*, Lahore September 01, 1943. According to the Khaksar circle, the intent of these rowdy gangsters was to harm Mashraqi and force him to quit politics or face consequences. This type of tactic is still in practice in Pakistan where political opponents are threatened and harassed. Indeed! This is dirty politics and must be condemned.

It seemed that the AIML had been given a green signal by the authorities to use all methods to put to end to the Khaksar Tehreek. A rigorous campaign against the Khaksars had started. It was a shameful act on the AIML's part to attempt to annihilate its own brothers. Khaksars, pro-Khaksar public and Mashraqi were extremely resentful, aggrieved and disgusted at the League's methods to ruin the Khaksar Tehreek's reputation and that the League was ignoring the important issues. Mashraqi's worry was that a rift between Muslims, due to this attack, would be exploited by the rulers and others to damage the Muslim cause. This was not the time for the AIML to make an effort to destroy Khaksar reputation. Further, the public considered Jinnah not meeting Gandhi a national tragedy. In a statement to *Orient Press*, Rajagopalachariar, on Gandhi's letter to Jinnah, said:

> "...if Mr. Jinnah had gone without faith and met Gandhiji I believe that agreement would have issued out of the meeting. Mr. Jinnah played into the hands of the British Government when indeed the occasion could have been made a decisive turning point in the history of India.
>
> ...I shall not say that the Viceroy dare not refuse such a request [meeting with Gandhi] from Mr. Jinnah."[31]

On September 10, 1943, *The Radiance* wrote:

> "How can we let matters drift when the call of the times is so insistent? We know that if a proper move is not made here and now, the question of independence and that of Pakistan along with it will be shelved for another century..." [32]

On September 17, 1943, *The Radiance* again wrote that Mashraqi

> "is now more anxious than ever because the war seems to be drawing to a close in favour of the Allies; our destiny remains in the hands of our old masters, they have laid it down that the Indians must agree between themselves as regards the future status and constitution of their country..."[33]

---

[31] *The Bombay Chronicle*, August 18, 1943.
[32] Muhammad, P. 131.
[33] Ibid.

The League did not care for the critical situation, and heavy press propaganda against the Khaksar Tehreek continued in order to draw political advantage out of the attack on Quaid-e-Azam.

Despite desperate efforts in the court to prove that Jinnah's assailant was a Khaksar, Justice Blagden was not convinced with any evidence that Quaid-e-Azam produced. In his decision on November 04, 1943,[34] Justice Blagden punished the assailant for his act but refused to accept him as a Khaksar. This was a blow to the Muslim Leaguers, and they were highly upset at the Court's decision. However, the League never came out and apologized for their mistake in naming the assailant a Khaksar; instead, soon after Blagden's decision, the Muslim League passed a resolution barring Muslim Leaguers to be part of the Khaksar Tehreek.

The League took these steps on behest of anti-Khaksar forces, within and outside the party, otherwise who would not know that these actions would damage relations with the Khaksar Tehreek and divide Muslims. The attack on Jinnah and the AIML's resolution could not be viewed as anything other than a conspiracy to destroy the Tehreek's goodwill and politically obliterate the Khaksar Movement. The question is who was behind this — the Muslim League itself, the British intelligence or some other party? The involvement of these parties cannot be ruled out as they all felt their position threatened by the Tehreek's power.

To cut it short, enough circumstantial evidence is available to understand that the attack was politically motivated. History is full of conspiracies for meeting political ends; those who think this was not conspiracy against the Khaksar Tehreek likely do not understand what goes on behind the political curtain. According to the Khaksar circle, if political advantage out of the attack was not meant, why was such heavy propaganda launched? So the Tehreek was definitely a victim of a large and well planned conspiracy. Mashraqi was well-aware of the forces against him, but he did not retaliate in order to avoid confrontation with the Muslim League as this would result in division amongst the Muslims; instead, he continued with his activity of creating a united front and kept making efforts for the Jinnah-Gandhi meeting. Mashraqi did not care for the false and concocted propaganda and carried on with his goal.

*****

The attack on Jinnah failed to finish the Khaksar Tehreek, and the Khaksars continued with their activities. Sir Richard Tottenham (Additional Secretary to the Government of India) was not pleased with Khaksars carrying the Quran (as per Mashraqi's statement of July 22, 1943). On November 29, 1943, Tottenham sent copies of the correspondence, that had passed between the Home Department and Mashraqi since September 16 [1943], to all Provincial

---

[34] *The Leader*, November 06, 1943. *The Bombay Chronicle*, November 05, 1943.

Governments and Chief Commissioners, except Panth Piploda. Tottenham also wrote to them:

> "We do not like the practice, which he now seems to be encouraging, of making Khaksars wear a copy of the Koran [Quran] on their persons...object is to make it more difficult to take police action against them. We also have reason to believe that he [Mashraqi] has been issuing secret instructions at complete variance with his promise not to do anything that would cause the least anxiety to Government... 'The Radiance' [Khaksar weekly], continues to stress the military side of the movement...we already have sufficient grounds for taking action against the Allama himself...this course would be preferable to declaring the Khaksars as a whole to be unlawful association.
>
> On the other hand, the whole organisation is now under a cloud in view of its recent condemnation by the Muslim League; and any action by Government at the present moment would give the undesirable impression that we were tied to the apron strings – of that body.
>
> We, therefore, propose to take no further action at present, but we hope all Provincial Governments will keep a careful watch on the Khaksars and their leaders and will not hesitate to suppress any signs of embarrassing activities on their part."[35]

This letter confirms the Government was not ready to accept Khaksar presence in any form. However, the Government did not want the public to get the idea that it was somehow "tied" to the AIML. While Government was doing whatever it could to suppress the Khaksars, Mashraqi continued with his efforts without fear.

On April 28, 1944, Mashraqi addressed the public at Badshahi Mosque, Lahore; he emphasized unity and discussed political matters in his speech.[36]

While Mashraqi was pleading for unity, Gandhi was released on May 06, 1944. Hopes were built up that his release would help the Muslim-Hindu issue. Gandhi was sick and Mashraqi sent him a telegram (on May 09, 1944) wishing him early recovery:

> "Your release delightful. Pray speedy recovery. Requesting Qaid-e-Azam Jinnah to make appointment for meeting you as soon as possible in response to your last year's request. Shall accompany him if necessary. Please wire condition health for possible interview."[37]

---

[35] IOL L/P&J/8/680.
[36] Zaman 1987, P. 162.
[37] Yousaf 2004, P. 273. *The Bombay Chronicle*, May 10, 1944.

On the same day (May 09, 1944), in his communication to Jinnah, Mashraqi stated:

> "Mahatma Gandhi's release has made the situation suddenly most delightful and easy. I implore you with all the humility at my disposal to grasp the opportunity most firmly and start talks with him at once. I have to-day telegraphed to him and await with interest future developments in this direction as well as your friendly gesture to me that you will agree to meet him. As the Mahatma is not in good health, it will be a matter of extreme courtesy to go and see him on his sick bed and no question of prestige can be involved if the step is taken now. In case you ask me to accompany you, I shall be ready to go."[38]

Mashraqi wanted to see a settlement under all circumstances and was willing to do whatever it took. He was even willing to attend the meeting if that could facilitate the settlement. On May 11, 1944, Mashraqi again urged Jinnah to settle his differences with Gandhi, keeping in mind the crucial period that was facing the nation in regards to India's independence. On May 13, 1944, Jinnah acknowledged Mashraqi's communication of May 09, 1944 but did not comment on Mashraqi's request.[39]

On May 15, 1944, Gandhi replied to Mashraqi's telegram. Gandhi thanked Mashraqi and wrote:

> "My last year's request to Qaid-i-Azam Jinnah still stands, and I will be ready to discuss the question of Hindu-Muslim understanding as soon as I get better."[40]

The Bombay Chronicle (of May 17, 1944) reported:

> "Enquiries in informed quarters make it increasingly clear, as forecast exclusively by the Orient Press and now confirmed by Gandhiji himself in his telegram to Allama Mashriqui, that as soon as Gandhiji is restored to health his first task would be to see Mr. Jinnah."

Mashraqi's efforts were working. However, anti-Khaksar elements in the Muslim League were highly perturbed that Gandhi had agreed to a meeting on Mashraqi's suggestion. Nawabzada Liaquat Ali Khan sent a telegram to Mashraqi and stated:

> "Quaid-e-Azam understands politics better than you. Refrain from interfering in Gandhi-Jinnah affairs."[41]

[38] Yousaf 2004, Pp. 273-274.
[39] *Dawn*, May 23, 1944.
[40] Yousaf 2004, P. 274. *The Free Press Journal*, May 17, 1944.
[41] Hussain, P. 200. *Dawn*, May 25, 1944.

Mashraqi paid no heed to this telegram and did not care what Liaquat Ali wrote. Mashraqi continued his efforts and, after Gandhi's positive confirmation, he called a meeting of important Khaksars to discuss how unity and a settlement could be achieved in order to pave the way for independence. On May 16, 1944, *The Bombay Chronicle* reported that Allama Mashraqi summoned prominent Khaksar leaders in order to consult with them on the Jinnah-Gandhi talks. The newspaper also reported that Mashraqi may go to Kashmir to personally request Jinnah to meet with Gandhi.

On May 23, 1944, *The Free Press Journal* published an excerpt from Mashraqi's statement:

> "As regards the letter of the Mahatma, I must confess that his words 'why should not both you and I approach the great question of communal unity with a determination to solve it to both parties satisfaction,' [42] came as a complete surprise to me. The only 'if' with Mr. Jinnah hitherto had been that Mahatma Gandhi did not agree to talk to him as representative of the Hindus and no words than those quoted can express more clearly that 'change of heart' which Mr. Jinnah demanded last year...
>
> Mr. Jinnah has not replied to my letter of 9th instant yet, although he acknowledged the receipt of it on the 13th. I am making a telegraphic request to him to expedite his reply as the Khaksars are determined not only to see that this eventful and momentous meeting between the two political leaders does take place but that the conversations reach a successful issue.
>
> The Mahatma has already telegraphed to me that he is too ill to move about or carry on serious conversation and this renders it imperative that Quaid-e-Azam should see Mahatma at once on his sick bed in order to open up the way to conversation and create an amicable atmosphere. If Churchill can meet healthy Stalin on Russian soil for the good of his people Mr. Jinnah can surely meet Mahatma Gandhi for the sake of Pakistan...
>
> I make another public appeal to Quaid-e-Azam to descend from the heights of Kashmir for deciding the destiny of India without delay as I feel sure that the Mussalman public will get enraged if he shows inaction and despair at this critical moment. Understanding between the Hindus and Muslims must take place at all costs and the Khaksars are determined to see that it is carried on to a successful issue."[43]

Mashraqi's success was making Wavell (Viceroy) nervous. This is obvious from Wavell's private and secret letter to Amery on May 23, 1944:

> "Congress hopes are based on...Allama Mashriqi... It is difficult to see why... Allama should be a successful broker between Gandhi and

---

[42] Gandhi's words are quoted slightly differently here, than in his original letter earlier in this chapter. The press has made an error in reproducing Gandhi's words here. Regardless, the point remains the same.

[43] Also see *Dawn*, May 23, 1944.

Jinnah." He further writes that AIML "do not like the Khaksars..."
Wavell further writes, "I agree with you that as long as Gandhi and
Jinnah are in the lead there is little likelihood of a settlement or of
anything constructive being done."[44]

The Government was making every effort to keep Mashraqi out of this affair
and not allow him to broker the deal. But they knew that even if Mashraqi
arranged the meeting, nothing would come of this; they had enough power to
control the leaders and to continue to prolong the rift.

Hence, the Khaksars suggested to Mashraqi that he must meet Jinnah and
Gandhi and explain the situation face to face, so that the meeting between
Jinnah and Gandhi could materialize.

However, Mashraqi's efforts towards Muslim-Hindu unity were denounced by
the Leaguers in public and they launched a rigorous campaign to deprecate and
defame him. One such propaganda is evident from this pro-Muslim League
statement:

> "Any one who has been watching the activities of the Khaksar Leader
> very closely will come to the only conclusion that he aims at
> wrecking the solidarity of the Muslims under the cover of the Hindu-
> Muslim unity...The anti-Muslim press that hails him as a Muslim
> champion for the cause of Hindu-Muslim unity...
>
> ...To defeat him and in view, the Provincial Muslim
> Leagues should undertake vigorous propaganda work by establishing
> Provincial Propaganda Boards under the supervision of the All-India
> Muslim League Propaganda Board.
>
> Individual effort is also needed in this connection. Every
> Muslim Leaguer should expose the evil motives of the Khaksar
> Leader in the circle of his relations, friends, and acquaintances..."[45]

On June 20, 1944, *The Tribune*, Lahore reported:

> "It is learned that Allama Mashriqi, the Khaksar leader, is proceeding
> to Kashmir to meet Mr. Jinnah with a view to persuading him to meet
> Gandhi for a League-Congress rapprochement. After meeting Mr.
> Jinnah he will see Gandhiji at Poona."[46]

The Bombay Chronicle (of June 27, 1944) also reported:

> "Allama Mashriqi has sent orders for Provincial Khaksar
> Organisation asking them to keep ready for proceeding to Poona and
> to meet Gandhiji in deputation, for exerting his influence on him to
> come to terms with Muslims in order to bring about communal
> harmony.

---

[44] Mansergh 1973, P. 983.
[45] *The Deccan Times*, June 11, 1944.
[46] Also see *The Free Press Journal*, June 21, 1944. *Star of India*, June 21, 1944.

Allama will first meet Mr. Jinnah and failing to convince him the utility of his contact with Gandhiji he will proceed to Poona. The U.P. batch consisting about 15 Khaksars is waiting for a call from the Allama to proceed on his peace mission."

Dawn, Delhi (of June 26, 1944) wrote:

"The 'Orient Press' reliably understands that Allama Mashriqui will not meet Mr. Jinnah, as immediately given out in a Press report. He will decide...after consulting Mr. Ghulam Qadir [Hakimwala] and reviewing the result of his discussions with Mr. G. M. Syed."

A meeting of Ghulam Qadir (a Khaksar) with G.M. Syed indicated that Mashraqi-Jinnah meeting would bear no results. Hence, a meeting between Mashraqi and Jinnah did not take place.

On the other hand, Wavell's attitude was not encouraging a Jinnah-Gandhi meeting. The British were creating circumstances that would prevent this meeting from taking place. The British had control over the leaders as is evident from a report in the *Dawn,* Delhi of July 01, 1944:

"...Mr. Gandhi at present does not propose to write to Qaid-e-Azam, as has been suggested by Allama Mashraqi. He...first wants to know the official British reaction to his move for a settlement."

On July 02, 1944, *The Deccan Times,* Madras reported that Allama Mashraqi wrote a letter to Gandhi asking him to send a fresh invitation to Quaid-e-Azam in order to bring about Hindu-Muslim understanding. Mashraqi wrote:

"The atmosphere is tense even in League circles and Mr. Jinnah's silence is getting extraordinary if not exasperating. But being so undelightfully technical, you can still checkmate him by writing a fresh invitation and making it still more clear, if it is not already clear enough. I suggest this to you in all humility as I have come to understand that the time at our disposal is very precious."

In the meantime, on July 09, 1944, Rajagopalachariar's formula (C.R. formula) for a League-Congress settlement was made public. Rajagopalachariar had been influenced by Mashraqi's efforts for a settlement, and based on Mashraqi's influence, he had developed his C.R. formula. Rajagopalachariar had discussed his formula with Gandhi in March 1943. Rajagopalachariar had sought Gandhi's full approval.[47] The main points of the formula were:

"

1. That the Muslim League endorses the Indian demand for independence and will cooperate with the Congress in the formation of a provisional interim government for the transitional period.

---

[47] *The Tribune,* July 10, 1944.

2. After the termination of the war a commission shall be appointed for demarcating contiguous districts in the north-west and cast of India wherein Muslim population is in absolute majority. In the areas thus demarcated, a plebiscite of all the inhabitants held on the basis of adult suffrage or other praticable franchise shall ultimately decide the issue of separation from Hindustan."[48]

Anyhow, Mashraqi's pressure worked and within days of his letter to Gandhi, on July 17, 1944, Gandhi wrote to Quaid-e-Azam and expressed his desire to meet him.[49] Gandhi wrote:

> "I had invited you to meet me while I was in jail. I have not written to you since my release, but to-day my heart says that I should write to you. We will meet whenever you choose."[50]

It is important to note that Mashraqi's constant pressure on Gandhi was working, but he did not refer to Mashraqi's efforts to avoid displeasure of the British and Jinnah.

Finally, Jinnah gave way to Mashraqi's prolonged exertions. On July 24, 1944, Quaid-e-Azam replied from Srinagar and invited Gandhi for a meeting. Jinnah wrote:

> "I shall be glad to receive you at my house in Bombay on my return, which will probably be about the middle of August. By that time I hope that you will have recuperated your health fully and will be returning to Bombay…"[51]

Mashraqi's efforts and pressure were no secret, and they finally worked. It had taken a long time before the nation saw Jinnah's readiness for this meeting. The public was very hopeful and positive results were desired.

*****

On July 28, 1944, Quaid-e-Azam arrived in Lahore from Rawalpindi to attend a meeting of the Council of the All-India Muslim League. He presided over the meeting of the Working Committee at Mamdot Villa, which began its proceedings at 10 a.m. on July 29, 1944. A lengthy discussion took place on the C.R. formula. The meeting continued until the next day (July 30, 1944).[52] On July 30, Quaid-e-Azam vehemently criticized Gandhi and Rajagopalacharia's formula, which was reported in *The Tribune*, Lahore of July 31, 1944. He doubted Gandhi's intention of the proposed meeting. During

---

[48] *The Tribune*, July 10, 1944.
Additional points of the C.R. formula are listed in *The Deccan Times*, July 16, 1944.
Also see Chapter 5 for more on the C.R. formula.
[49] *Gandhi Serve Foundation web site.* (2). Also see *Dawn*, July 31, 1944.
[50] *The Tribune*, July 31, 1944.
[51] Ibid.
[52] *The Eastern Times*, July 30, 1944.

his address at the Council meeting, Jinnah said a lot of things in an attempt to prove that Gandhi's offer was nothing but a ploy to torpedo the Muslim League's demand of March 1940 for a separate homeland. In order to prove that Gandhi was a hypocrite, Jinnah said:

> "I remember when Mr. Gandhi met Lord Linlithgow in September 1939, after the outbreak of the war he broke down and tears rolled down from his eyes when he visualized the possible destruction by bombing of the Westminster Abbey and the Houses of Parliament and said 'What was the use of Indian freedom if England and France were defeated?' He in a statement declared his wholehearted and most enthusiastic support for the prosecution of the war. But hardly a week, thereafter, the Congress Working Committee decided to non-co-operate if their demand for immediate independence etc. was not met..."[53]

Criticizing the Rajagopalacharia's formula, Jinnah said:

> "formula is a parody, a negation of and intended to torpedo, the Muslim League's resolution of March [24], 1940."[54]

According to some political circles, by endorsing Rajaji's formula, Gandhi had basically accepted the partition of India. Gandhi said in an interview on July 30, 1944:

> "Rajaji's formula is intended as a help to all lovers of the country. It is the best we could conceive, but it is open to amendment, as it is open to rejection or acceptance."[55]

Gandhi's statement showed flexibility. Thus, the political circle felt that Jinnah's assumption of Gandhi's intention as well as criticism of him (within a few days of Jinnah's invitation) and the formula approved by him[56], were not the right thing to do prior to their meeting. This criticism would not be good for maintaining a congenial and favorable atmosphere for the meeting. And such an attitude on Jinnah's part would hinder a solution and would imperil the chances of settlement.

The question is why Jinnah criticized Gandhi and Rajagopalacharia? Was it to send a signal that there would be no agreement short of partition? If that is so, why was Jinnah so persistent on division? Quaid-e-Azam essentially made it clear that no negotiation except division of India would be accepted. This was validated by his statement:

[53] *The Tribune*, July 31, 1944.
[54] Ibid. Also see *Dawn*, August 01, 1944.
[55] *The Tribune*, August 01, 1944.
[56] *The Tribune*, July 10, 1944.

> "Let Mr. Gandhi join hands with the Muslim League on the basis of Pakistan in plain and unequivocal language and we shall be nearer the independence of the peoples of India…"[57]

Hence, according to political circles, it seemed that settlement was not sought by Jinnah and the only acceptable solution was partition of India. However, to the naïve commoners, Jinnah's rigidity was coming across as a fight for their rights. *The Tribune*, Lahore of July 31, 1944 wrote:

> "While the Quaid-i-Azam was busy in his 'post-mortem' of the C.R.'s formula and criticism of Mahatma Gandhi and Mr. Rajagopalachari, it seemed the logical end would be complete and outright rejection. But the shrewd League leader employed his art and without of course, using the words 'I reject' although he left little unsaid, he flung a surprise by asking his followers to 'wait and see.' This appeal of two words went home and everybody said, 'yes' perhaps in the hope that their leader would get them the promised though undefined Pakistan for he made it abundantly clear that he would not agree to anything less than the demand contained in the 1940 resolution."

Those who understood politics questioned Quaid-e-Azam's criticism. At the proceedings of a Muslim League Council meeting, a councilor, who was not happy with the answer he had received from the General Secretary, was not allowed by Quaid-e-Azam to speak and was snubbed when Jinnah said "You sit down. You have got your reply."[58] He did not agree and Jinnah again said "Well I know you have got your reply."[59]

Quaid-e-Azam was set on Pakistan and wanted no proposals and no arguments. The reason he agreed to meet Gandhi was to convince him to accept division as per the Muslim League's demand. In essence, Jinnah blocked any agreement by making such statements against the C.R. formula and Gandhi's intention.

Yet, in his letter of August 01, 1944, Mashraqi still appreciated Jinnah's agreement to meet Gandhi, thinking that a settlement might be possible. In his letter, Mashraqi could not have given better assurance than this:

> "Dear Mr. Jinnah,
>   After anxious and patient moments of the last few weeks when I finally wrote to you, I have my most sincere appreciation that you have come forward to alter the destiny of India to something better, however little, and I assure you again that I, along with every Khaksar that is in the land, will work with you in the full spirit of loyalty and friendship for the achievement of Pakistan, and consequently, the independence of India.

---

[57] *The Tribune*, July 31, 1944.
[58] Ibid.
[59] Ibid.

I deliberately ask my pardon for the harsh words spoken both in public and in my letters to you, as I feel intensely delighted over the words you uttered in Rawalpindi that you were working for the freedom, not only of 10 crores [100 million] of Muslims but of 30 crores [300 million] of non-Muslims as well. I can only say that the utterance will stand out as a pledge of your sincerity to India in the grave talks that are coming. Mr. Gandhi is to be congratulated no less for the bold and frank letter that he has written and I am sending a telegram of profound thankfulness to him today. I am also writing to him but these moves have already cleared the tense atmosphere that existed and I assure you that Hindus and Muslims are more ready for an understanding today than they were ever before.

I have purposely refrained from saying anything concerning the formula [C.R. formula] put forward by the ex-Premier of Madras, chiefly because you were silent, but also because, as I told you, I was determined to bring the matter of your meeting with Mr. Gandhi to a tangible conclusion. You are shrewd enough to see through it yourself, but as far as the Khaksars are concerned no stone will be left unturned in order to bring your conversations with Mr. Gandhi to the successful conclusion that every soul in India demands. May God help you and Mr. Gandhi as well.

On this serious occasion in the history of India I am proposing to order a batch of Khaksars to reach Bombay and shall if possible, reach Bombay myself for the purpose of begging you and Mr. Gandhi with folded hands to reach a suitable settlement satisfactory to both parties. I have no doubt that a settlement is bound to be reached with these good beginnings on both sides and that you as well as Mr. Gandhi will appreciate the reaching of this mixed batch of Hindu as well as Muslim Khaksars at the time of your conversations. I am writing to M. Gandhi also to the same effect.
Yours sincerely,
Inayatullah Khan"[60]

Hence, there was no secret of Mashraqi's good intentions. On purpose, Jinnah again remained unmoved on Mashraqi's offer. Instead he used insulting and most unbecoming language with the Khaksars who delivered Mashraqi's letter of August 01, 1944 to Jinnah; this was not suitable for the stature of Quaid-e-Azam. Mashraqi knew why Jinnah was behaving in this unbecoming manner and that he was trying to please the British. If the British were not standing by Jinnah, Quaid-e-Azam would not have behaved in this manner. The British were using Jinnah in a way that if the Khaksars posed any threat to the British, the AIML would come fully to the British side. Mashraqi's own intelligence informed him of all this. According to the Khaksar circle, Quaid-e-Azam seemed to be intoxicated with power; Jinnah admitted that people charged him with this claim.

In his letter of August 01, 1944, Mashraqi apologized to Jinnah. This should have been the other way around, as the Muslim League was causing the breach between the Khaksar Tehreek and AIML by declaring Jinnah's assailant to be

---

[60] Yousaf 2004, P. 276. *The Tribune*, August 02, 1944. *The Deccan Times*, August 03, 1944.

a Khaksar, using the incident for political reasons, banning Leaguers from joining the Khaksar Tehreek, and conducting other activities as part of an anti-Khaksar campaign.

Yet Mashraqi did not retaliate to such tactics and extended his hand of cooperation. On August 14, 1944, ignoring personal ego that would bring a political deadlock, Mashraqi sent another letter to Quaid-e-Azam and Mahatma Gandhi. The letter to Jinnah stated:

> "My Dear Quaid-i-Azam Jinnah,
>
> I send you herewith an exact copy of the letter I have written to Mahatma Gandhi to-day. The same is to you word by word with the exception of the second paragraph which relates to him and may interest you.
>
> Most unwholesome and unbecoming words were attributed to you by the distinguished messengers who undertook to take my letter of 30th July last personally to you, but I cannot believe that you uttered these words against me even in fury. My disgrace anywhere by anybody is for the good of my people and is therefore acceptable to me with good grace and without the slightest feeling of bitterness against anyone. After that letter I assure you again that not a word of bitterness has entered my heart.
>
> With these frank words I request you to come to a settlement with the Mahatama under all circumstances, and if you think that a settlement has become impossible on the conditions that you present, please have patience to inform Dr. Rafique or his assistants near Crawford Market, so that they may take steps at once to see the Mahatma and request him with folded hands to come down to an agreement. You may rest assured that the Khaksars are determined to have these conversations come to a tangible conclusion and this can only be if you do not break away abruptly and leave a loophole somewhere. I am sure that we shall prove loyal to you in your difficulties and I may at the same time warn you, if you do not already know it, that there are hundred and one difficulties in the way of actually getting Pakistan or the independence of India even after you two come to an agreement. The time is very precious indeed and the British would like it to be whiled away as long as it suits their purpose.
>
> With these brief remarks I wish you glorious success in your efforts.
> Your sincerely,
> Inayatullah Khan"[61]

Despite Quaid-e-Azam's inappropriate and wrong attitude, Mashraqi kept his cool and did not let this affect his manner. Mashraqi asked the Khaksars to create public opinion for an amicable settlement between Jinnah and Gandhi. Mashraqi's efforts were also reported in the press. His rigorous efforts and exchange of correspondence and messages finally bore fruit and the meeting between Jinnah-Gandhi was settled to take place on August 19, 1944.

---

[61] Yousaf 2004, P. 277.

*****

Now that Mashraqi's pressure had brought results and a meeting was set, Mashraqi could not let his efforts go down the drain. The public also desired a positive outcome from this meeting. There were Muslim and Hindu elements who were rejecting the C.R. formula as it conceded to the demand of Muslim League for a separate homeland. Settlement between the League and Congress parties became even more essential when according to *The Tribune*, Lahore of August 18, 1944, Wavell (Viceroy of India) in a letter to Gandhi referred to the condition for freedom that India would not be granted its freedom "until hostilities ceased."

> "The Viceroy also referred to the conditions, the fulfillment of which was necessary for the bestowal of freedom on India after the war. The object of these conditions…was to ensure the fulfillment of the duty of His Majesty's Government to safeguard the interest of the racial and religious minorities and of the depressed classes and their treaty obligations to the Indian States."[62]

Under this condition that Indians must reach a settlement, Mashraqi knew that an agreement must be reached at all costs. Other political circles shared Mashraqi's view and appreciated Khaksar efforts to bring unity and settlement. Khaksars and other political leaders were of the view that Mashraqi should attend this meeting and that there was likelihood of his coming to Bombay.

Because of the crucial nature of this meeting, Mashriqi decided to put forth every effort to see that an agreement would be reached, acceptable to both communities. Thus he ordered Khaksars to reach Bombay to form a favorable public opinion that could facilitate an agreement between Jinnah and Gandhi. Dr. Rafique Ahmed, Head of the Science Department of Aligarh Muslim University, was asked to organize Khaksar activities in Bombay that would facilitate reaching an agreement. *The Bombay Chronicle* reported that Professor Rafique had left for Bombay to talk to prominent leaders.[63]

However, the Jinnah-Gandhi meeting was postponed on August 17, 1944 because Jinnah was reported to be sick. On this date, Quaid-e-Azam sent the following telegram to Gandhi:

> "Extremely sorry. Laid up with temperature. Doctors advise it is impossible to meet you on Saturday, August 19. Will intimate the date immediately I am well enough."[64]

Gandhi canceled his scheduled trip to Bombay[65] and the meeting could not take place. Some political observers suspected that the meeting was delayed on

---

[62] *The Tribune*, August 18, 1944.
[63] *The Bombay Chronicle*, August 15, 1944.
[64] *The Tribune*, August 18, 1944.

purpose as Jinnah did not know how to justify his Pakistan scheme to Gandhi. *The Tribune*, Lahore (of September 02, 1944) wrote:

> "Mr. Jinnah suffered less from physical but more from political cold when he discovered that his Pakistan would have no legs to stand financially and in matters of defence its existence would be precarious... Mr. Jinnah wanted time to prepare his brief for Pakistan."

Meanwhile, on Mashraqi's orders, Khaksars from various areas continued to arrive in Bombay. *The Eastern Times* (of August 22, 1944) reported that a Khaksar leader [Dr. Rafique Ahmed] in Bombay sent a telegram to Allama Mashraqi stating that no more Khaksars were needed in Bombay, as the number was already more than enough for the Jinnah-Gandhi talks. The newspaper further reported that the Khaksars prayed at the mosque for Jinnah's health. Such reports illustrate how sincere Khaksars were toward Quaid-e-Azam and to a settlement. Yet, Quaid-e-Azam, never even sent a message responding to their good gesture. This could have been done via letter or through a press statement. Khaksars had come to Bombay, at their own expense, for a selfless cause — to achieve an amicable political settlement. They prayed for Quaid-e-Azam's early recovery, irrespective of the Muslim League's attitude and actions toward the Khaksars, especially since after March 19, 1940.

On August 21, 1944, Dr. Rafique Ahmed, who was in charge of the Khaksar Camp in Bombay, issued the following statement:

> "The purpose of the arrival of Khaksars in Bombay on the eve of the Gandhi-Jinnah meeting is to create by their example of brotherhood and selfless service the right atmosphere for a lasting Hindu-Muslim understanding. It is hoped that Hindus, Muslims, Parsees and other communities will extend their full co-operation in this difficult but most necessary task."[66]

On August of 22, 1944, *The Free Press Journal* reported that Allama Mashraqi was arriving in Bombay (to ensure a settlement between Jinnah and Gandhi). However, Mashraqi got the message that the meeting was postponed and that Jinnah was eager to meet Gandhi alone. Hence, Mashraqi dropped the idea and provided the opportunity to Jinnah to settle the issue with Gandhi. As in the Rajaji-Jinnah meeting,[67] Jinnah did not want to include Mashraqi in the talks, despite Mashraqi's strenuous efforts. Quaid-e-Azam's reluctance to go hand in hand with Mashraqi was viewed with suspicion in the political circle.

The Tribune, Lahore of August 25, 1944 reported that 4,000 Khaksars had arrived in Bombay; they continued to hold meetings and address gatherings to

---

[65] *The Bombay Chronicle*, August 18, 1944.
[66] *Dawn*, August 21, 1944.
[67] Read Chapter 5.

stress the urgent need for a Hindu-Muslim settlement and to ensure a successful conclusion to the Gandhi-Jinnah talks. *The Tribune*, Lahore of August 25, 1944 reporting on Khaksar activities wrote:

> "They [Khaksars] are moving in Muslim areas in batches, meeting local leaders and addressing gatherings in mosques on the urgent need of arriving at a Hindu-Muslim settlement, 'creating a favourable atmosphere for the successful conclusion of Gandhi-Jinnah talks.' They are advocating special prayers and fasts on the day Mahatma Gandhi and Mr. Jinnah meet."

A very tense atmosphere prevailed for the outcome of the talks, as the destiny of India was at stake. Mashraqi knew that if Khaksars could help reach an agreement, this would non-violently solve the biggest problem of the country. Some elements, Muslim and non-Muslim, were against an accord between Jinnah and Gandhi and tried to dislodge Khaksar efforts toward this unity. They again linked Khaksars with Nazis so that people would not listen to them. They declared Khaksars to have fascist designs, and so on. It was obviously discouraging that these anti-Khaksar elements or agents of imperialism were engaging in propaganda due to their own ulterior motives. To set things straight, on August 27, 1944, Syed Allah Bakhsh (Head of the Political Department of the Khaksar Central Organisation) issued the following statement to the press:

> "In certain quarters of the Press it is attempted to suggest that the Khaksar movement is a quasi-Nazi organisation.
>
> Let me make it clear once more that the Khaksar movement is based on the precepts of religion and is far above any racial economical or biological philosophies of life. All that the Khaksars want is the prevalence of religion, truth and justice. All that they are armed with is their selfless social service irrespective of all religions, self discipline and high individual character. The tremendous sacrifices that they had to perform in connection with the Bengal famine relief is a proof of their ideas. It is needless to say that no Fascists organisation could ever show even a fraction of this sacrifice and virtuous action.
>
> Armed with the aforesaid moral weapons they came to Bombay and are conquering it. During the week they have been in Bombay its broad-minded and sympathetic citizens have been very kind and have greeted the Khaksars with friendly smiles and sympathetic enquiries. I am glad to say that there has been no indication whatsoever that their coming was resented by anybody."[68]

No person with any sense would resent Khaksar efforts to seek unity, however agents of the colonial power had to prevent this harmony.

The Eastern Times of August 29, 1944 reported on Khaksar efforts and wrote that Khaksars met Sir Currimbhoy Ebrahim, K.M. Munshi and others to bring

---

[68] *The Free Press Journal*, August 29, 1944.

about a congenial atmosphere for the success of the talks. The Khaksars were traveling in batches to places, like mofussil areas, Ahmedabad, Ahmednagar, Khandesh, Kathiawar, Hubil and Poona, and they were meeting leaders of both parties. According to *The Eastern Times* of August 30, 1944, Khaksars said, "they are not going to disperse...until a Hindu-Muslim settlement is effected." The paper further wrote that Gandhi had accepted a salute from the Khaksars upon his arrival in Bombay. Two important things must be noted here. First, Islam does not preach hatred between Muslims and non-Muslims, thus, Khaksars, following Islam, wanted to seek unity and saluting Gandhi was a symbol of love towards all regardless of religion or color. Instead of appreciating this noble act, Muslims Leaguers condemned it. Second, Khaksars had come from every nook of India to seek this unity, despite that fact that it must have put a strain on their family budgets. How can anyone disregard this? Only people who believe in discrimination and communalism would disapprove of this.

On September 03, 1944, *The Deccan Times*, Madras wrote that out of 4,000 Khaksars, 1,000 went to various parts of the Bombay Presidency; they were meeting leaders of different parties to create a "congenial atmosphere for the impending Gandhi-Jinnah talks."[69]

When Gandhi arrived in Bombay for the meeting, over 100 Khaksars arrived in the same train in which Gandhi had traveled. The Khaksars took Gandhi to his car.[70] All of these gestures speak of their non-discriminatory and anti-communalism behavior.

On September 09, 1944, as a result of Mashraqi's hectic efforts, the Jinnah-Gandhi meeting finally took place at Bombay at Jinnah's house at 4 p.m. Mashraqi had been working to bring Hindu-Muslim unity since he was released from Vellore Jail on January 19, 1942 (for about two and half years) and his efforts finally led to this meeting. Should it have taken this long to bring two leaders living in the same country together for such crucial talks? No! This clearly indicates that certain forces were trying to prevent this meeting from happening and these leaders were succumbing to their pressure.

The momentous talks started in a cordial and friendly atmosphere and centered around Rajagopalacharia's formula.[71] Rajagopalachariar was present at Bombay and was staying at Birla House with Gandhi to assist him. Quaid-e-Azam did not invite Mashraqi to be part of the negotiations or even to seek his opinion outside the meeting, despite the fact that thousands of Khaksars had come for the success of the meeting. If he had invited Mashraqi, he would have sought British resentment that would have affected his political position. Many Muslim and Hindu leaders asked Khaksars why Mashraqi did not come to Bombay for the Jinnah-Gandhi meeting, despite the fact that he was

---

[69] *The Deccan Times*, September 03, 1944.
[70] *The Tribune*, September 10, 1944.
[71] Ibid. *Dawn*, September 11, 1944.

expected to arrive. The Khaksars replied, ask Jinnah. This raised eyebrows of the nationalists as to why Jinnah did not invite Mashraqi. On the other hand, Gandhi's attitude was somewhat different; he met Khaksar leader, Abdur Rashid Qureshi on the day of the meeting (on September 09, 1944).

> "Gandhiji thanked Mr. Qureshi and asked him to convey his best wishes to Allama Sahib and to request the Khaksar leader to pray for a settlement of the communal tangle and a solution for the political deadlock."[72]

Millions of people were closely watching the proceedings of these meetings and a situation of hope prevailed. However, the talks failed on September 27, 1944. People were shocked to hear of this, as the talks had generated hope in the hearts of well-wishers of the country who were against the dissection of British India. After strenuous efforts for a long time, the bridge that Mashraqi had successfully built to eliminate the gulf between Muslims and Hindus had broken down.

*****

Mashraqi was obviously disappointed at the failure of the meetings. It was a long effort on Mashraqi's part and thousands of Khaksars had arrived in Bombay, having spent money and leaving their families behind in the hope that talks would pave the way for freedom. But their hopes were shattered. Mashraqi directed the Khaksars to return to their respective homes.[73] The next day, on September 28, 1944, Mashraqi issued a statement regarding the failure of the Jinnah-Gandhi meeting. According to Mashraqi:

> "I do not see any failure when both leaders have been in conference for nearly three weeks and departed. The real difficulty is that neither Mahatma Gandhi nor Mr. Jinnah wishes to get out of the rut of dead theoretical politics, created round them by long years of cries for independence, on to the smooth road of living practical politics leading to immediate freedom. I must admit how ever that the Qaid-e-Azam has realised this difficulty considerably more than Mr. Gandhi and that is what makes me more hopeful of an early settlement. Our next step can only be to go on striving and I have now resolved to meet Mahatma Gandhi at the earliest opportunity available to me."[74]

Mashraqi was disappointed in both leaders' attitudes. He expected Jinnah to adopt a more cooperative approach and Gandhi to be more compromising and not allow Jinnah to leave until an agreement was achieved. But unfortunately loyal and trusted followers of the English in both Muslim and Hindu communities put forth their efforts and jeopardized this meeting.

---

[72] *The Eastern Times*, September 12, 1944.
[73] *The Eastern Times*, October 01, 1944.
[74] Ibid. News of this was also published in *The Free Press Journal*, September 30, 1944 and *The Bombay Chronicle*, September 29, 1944.

The nationalist Muslim and Hindus and other communities praised Mashraqi for his efforts for the future of India and its people. He was regarded as the most sincere and selfless person who had no personal motives behind these efforts other than to seek freedom of India as soon as possible. The historians have failed to mention this momentous effort of Mashraqi. So, you can well imagine how historians, either on purpose or out of ignorance, eliminate important events. Gandhi's overall attitude towards Mashraqi needs to be discussed separately, but since this work relates to Mashraqi and Jinnah, I have not touched upon it.

Unfortunately, Jinnah did not even thank Mashraqi for his efforts. In fact, Quaid-e-Azam did not like Mashraqi and Rajagopalachariar pushing for a settlement between Jinnah and Gandhi. According to *The Tribune*, Lahore of July 31, 1944, Quaid-e-Azam had said (without naming Mashraqi):

> "as Mr. Gandhi was no longer in prison, I requested that he should directly communicate to me..."

After this meeting Mashraqi began to work on two fronts: the Khaksar Constitution and another effort for a Jinnah-Gandhi meeting.

*****

In a press conference on October 04, 1944, Quaid-e-Azam denounced the Gandhi-C.R. formula, and according to the *Dawn*, Delhi of October 06, 1944, he described it to be an offer of "eternal burial to Pakistan." In an interview, Quaid-e-Azam said:

> "There is only one practical, realistic way of resolving Muslim-Hindu differences. This is to divide India into the two sovereign parts of Pakistan and Hindustan by the recognition of the whole of the North West Frontier Province, Baluchistan, Sind, Punjab, Bengal and Assam as sovereign Muslim territories as they now stand..."[75]

Commenting on the failure of the talks, Sheikh Abdul Majid, an ex-prominent member of the Muslim League and Member Legislative Assembly, said:

> "...the C.R. formula and the offer made by Mr. Gandhi in his talks with Mr. Jinnah constituted a fair basis for a settlement between the two communities."[76]

October 07, 1944, Latifur Rahman (Member Legislative Assembly and Member Working Committee of All India Muslim League) said:

> "While every true well-wisher of India deeply regrets the end of Jinnah-Gandhi talk... One wonders where is the hitch in his

---

[75] *Dawn*, October 08, 1944.
[76] *Dawn*, October 05, 1944.

accepting the very resolution when Mr. Gandhi asserts that his as well as C.R.'s formula are the essence and substance of Lahore Resolution..."[77]

*****

After the talks failed, it was clear that certain forces did not want the talks to accomplish any fruitful result; if the AIML and Congress could be prevented from reaching an agreement, then power would remain with the ruler. However, the world was being told that if Muslims and Hindus settled their differences, the British would transfer the power. These assertions were nothing but a stage show. If the British had sent a signal to the AIML that talks must not fail, there is no way that the AIML would have resisted this. According to political circles, it seems that there was no sincere desire to negotiate a final settlement. Who is to be blamed for the disagreement; Jinnah, Gandhi, British or all three? As matter of fact, henchmen of the British made sure that no basis of cooperation would develop between these parties and that they would all remain separately dependent upon the rulers.

Wavell commented on the failure of the Jinnah-Gandhi meeting and wrote in his journal (on September 30, 1944):

> "The two great mountains met and not even a ridiculous mouse has emerged. This surely must blast Gandhi's reputation as a leader. Jinnah had an easy task, he merely had to keep on telling Gandhi he was talking nonsense, which was true, and he did so rather rudely, without having to disclose any of the weaknesses of his own position, or define his Pakistan in any way. I suppose it may increase his prestige with his followers, but it cannot add to his reputation with reasonable men."[78]

Wavell's writing reflects a number of important points. First, the British were supporting the rift. Quaid-e-Azam's attitude was rather arrogant and he did not budge from his position of seeking division. This is exactly what the British wanted. Jinnah did not come out and discuss the Pakistan scheme in order to avoid "weaknesses of his own position." In other words, Jinnah knew from inside that his Pakistan plan was very weak and questionable and it would not be easy to convince Gandhi, thus he avoided discussing it. Quaid-e-Azam would not define his Pakistan for two reasons; first, he (and the Muslim Leaguers) was not at all clear on the idea of "Pakistan." Second, Quaid-e-Azam kept this idea vague and obscure to create a fear of the unknown in the opposite camp. This would help him in negotiations and maintain his importance. Much of the strength of his position was that he did not define "Pakistan." He never explained *how* he would secure 100 million Muslims. Another flaw in his idea was that the Muslims were already ruling in Muslim majority areas, so why would those provinces need to be separated under the

---

[77] *Dawn*, October 09, 1944.
[78] Hussain, P. 202.

pretext of Islam? Further, the Pakistan plan had increased his reputation among those who were illiterate and did not understand its ramifications. Jinnah's reputation, however, did not increase "with reasonable men." In other words people with political sense did not think that the scheme of Pakistan was a workable and good idea.

Skepticism prevailed in the political circles. W.G. Cove, Labour Member of the Parliament, remarked on the failure:

> "Cove…said he did not believe that the real cause of the breakdown of the Gandhi-Jinnah talks was religious difficulties. The difficulties lay deeper. Behind Mr. Jinnah lay the power hand of British imperialism.
> '…we shall not destroy the momentum, will and desire of India for freedom by merely stirring religious differences. It is an old old method of divide and rule.'"[79]

Gandhi said:

> "It is a matter of deep regret that we could not reach an agreement…
> My experience of the previous three weeks confirms me in the view that the presence of a third power hinders the solution. A mind enslaved cannot act as if it was free. I need not impute…motives to the rulers to prove what seems to me to be an axiomatic truth."[80]

These statements clearly implied that the cause of the breakdown were the rulers.

It was also published in the Hindu press that Sir Firoz Khan Noon, Defense Member of the Government of India, had met Jinnah at Bombay,

> "and communicated to him certain proposals from the Secretary of State for India which led to a stiffening of the Qaid-e-Azam's attitude in his talks with Mr. Gandhi."[81]

Nationalists accused Quaid-e-Azam of a pro-British attitude; he denied this and said "I cannot be accused of being pro-British."[82] Nevertheless, the Muslim League's attitude was uncompromising; it framed its demands and put them in front of other political parties, without any room for compromise or understanding. Was this rift successfully maintained to justify division? Otherwise all political matters could have been resolved through negotiations. It would not be wrong to state that the AIML right from 1940 onwards devised its propaganda in a manner to reflect that if Pakistan was not created, all the powers would fall in the hands of the Hindus, and Muslims would be in a

[79] *The Free Press Journal*, October 04, 1944.
[80] *The Eastern Times,* October 01, 1944.
[81] Ibid.
[82] *Dawn*, October 08, 1944.

miserable condition and would become slaves of Hindus. Statements and speeches of the Leaguers reflected as if they were fighting rigorously for the rights of the Muslim community. Anyone is bound to draw this impression if s/he does not know the reality behind the Muslim-Hindu conflict. But in fact, the AIML never launched any resistance or street protests. People must understand that it is typical of many politicians to mislead people. The AIML, according to many, was playing in the hands of the British and promoting their interest, in return it was reaping the benefits of working for the British. The British were smart, and to the world they were giving the impression that they were friends and well-wishers of Indians and that they sought settlement between the two major communities of India; in reality they were making the leaders of India their own puppets.

Regardless of the actual cause of the failure, the problem could have been handled if other influential leaders, particularly those who were desperately pressing for unity, were included. The question is why were Muslim and Hindu leaders not invited for the historic meeting? Why was Mashraqi not invited when he had done so much for this meeting? The answer is that anti-Khaksar pressure groups were working against this. The Khaksars as well as the public questioned why Quaid-e-Azam was reluctant to go hand in hand with Mashraqi? Was he reluctant because he did not want to send a signal to the British of a Mashraqi-Jinnah collaboration? Was he instructed by the British not to involve Mashraqi? Was he firm on partition and needed no interference from Mashraqi to bring a compromise during the meeting? All of this proves that behind this rift were imperialists who were not ready to grant freedom or at least wanted to delay freedom. This viewpoint was endorsed by Syed Ali Zaheer (President Shia Political Conference) who stated:

> "The recalcitrant attitude of its [Muslim League's] leaders has been encouraged in the hope that the League would continue to act as a stumbling block in the path of India's freedom and thus help the British Government in maintaining their domination for a little longer in this country."[83]

All along, Mashraqi kept pushing for a settlement between Muslims and Hindus and kept highlighting British intentions. Yet the non-nationalist leaders never entertained these ideas intentionally, as they knew that if they acknowledged these ideas and went against the British, their own political careers would fall; hence, they would maintain this attitude to the end.

---

[83] *The Tribune*, March 22, 1946.

Chapter 7

Mashraqi's Endeavors
After Failure of Jinnah-Gandhi Talks

Failure of the Jinnah-Gandhi talks brought disappointment to every section of the population, but Mashraqi did not lose hope. Mashraqi was likely the only leader who perfectly understood the British machinations and maneuverings, thus, he persistently asked Quaid-e-Azam and Mahatma Gandhi to settle. Mashraqi's efforts were exasperating to the British, because they never wanted any agreement between Muslims and Hindus, although they could not openly express their true intentions. Their aim was to let these leaders fight, so that they could continue ruling the poor Indians.

After the failure of the Jinnah-Gandhi talks, on October 03, 1944, Mashraqi wrote a letter to Wavell (Viceroy) to help resolve the political issues. The Viceroy replied on October 07, 1944 and wrote that India should help herself to what had already been offered in the pronouncements, that is the Indians had to come to an agreement amongst themselves before freedom could be granted. Thus, Mashraqi felt that the deadlock between Quaid-e-Azam and Mahatma Gandhi ought to end and political matters must be resolved through continuous efforts and negotiations, until both parties agreed. Mashraqi understood that personal egos had to be set aside in the interest of the nation.

Meanwhile, no progress was made by Jinnah or Gandhi to terminate the standoff. Mashraqi was compelled to renew pressure and he sent telegrams to both. Mashraqi's telegram to Gandhi was reported in the press on December 19, 1944; it stated:

> "Over seven months have passed since your release from jail and eleven weeks since you and Quaid-e-Azam parted unsuccessfully. Your attention to irrelevant matters in these precious moments is most distressing. Please take it as India speaking when I say with folded hands that you should meet Quaid-e-Azam again immediately and send a fresh invitation. India is getting unified automatically and I undertake to present you an agreed constitution soon after

settlement is reached between you both, pray give me opportunity to explain."[1]

At the same time, Mashraqi also implored to Quaid-e-Azam in his telegram, which was reported in the press on December 19, 1944; it stated:

> "With folded hands I request you to meet Mahatma Gandhi again as promised to the whole Indian public before you separated last September [27, 1944]. I have requested Mahatma Gandhi to send you fresh invitation but being as anxious for settlement it equally devolves on you to invite him. Please rest assured that the whole of India, irrespective of parties, is ready for unification for the purpose of presenting an agreed constitution before the British Government and as already most encouraging replies are being received by me. I undertake to put that constitution before you soon after you settle. Pray give me opportunity to explain further."[2]

Mashraqi's humble appeal with "folded hands" was surely a sign of his grave concern over the critical political situation in the country. His annoyance with Quaid-e-Azam and Mahatma Gandhi was not for any personal enmity or antagonism but showed his anxiety over the future of India. Allama Mashraqi's frustration was justified as these leaders were uncompromising, which was neither desired nor the need of the time. His main concern was to save India from division. He could foresee adverse consequences for the people if British India was torn apart, as was suggested by AIML. Thus Mashraqi demanded these leaders to sink their differences for the sake of the people.

Meanwhile, Allama Mashraqi had already started working towards *The Constitution of Free India, 1946 A.C.* (Khaksar Constitution) so that he could bring all communities on one platform and resolve the tangle. Committees were formed to study issues confronting the nation and then frame the constitution. They were directed to come up with a framework of the constitution that would be workable and acceptable to all. Highly qualified and competent people were made part of the committees.[3] On December 19, 1944, Mashraqi wrote to Sir Tej Bahadur Sapru, who was also working on a constitution, to "coordinate" his work with the Khaksar Constitution committee.[4]

---

[1] Yousaf 2004, P. 281. *The Sind Observer*, December 19, 1944.
[2] Yousaf 2004, Pp. 281-282. *The Sind Observer*, December 19, 1944. *The Deccan Times*, December 24, 1944.
[3] See Appendix VI for its members.
[4] See letter in Chapter 8.

While the work on the *Khaksar Constitution* was taken up, Mashraqi issued the following statement:

> "On October 3 [1944], I [Mashraqi] wrote a straightforward letter to Lord Wavell[5], telling him what I thought of Cripps' Offer and asking him to help in solving the tangle. The Viceroy gave a straightforward reply [October 07, 1944] indicating that India should help herself to what had already been offered in the pronouncements made by him and a close study of his pronouncements has revealed that an agreed constitution on the lines of what is required by the British Government is possible to attain without reference to Hindu-Muslim differences on the question of Pakistan or no Pakistan. In fact Dr. Khare, an Executive Member of the Viceroy's Council, gave a press statement to that effect a few days after my letter to the Viceroy. I am therefore confident that our efforts are not only in the right direction, but that the only way which now remains in order to make the Congress and Muslim League come to terms is to make the elements of India's national life come to an agreement. Mahatma Gandhi and Quaid-i-Azam Jinnah will only then, come to terms under duress.
>
> The Khaksar organisation has felt the existence of more or less 75 parties in the country and is already in communication with a large number of them. The replies I am receiving for the purpose of presenting a united India before the British Government are extremely encouraging. Every party seems bent on finishing the job as the end of the war is in sight and chiefly because Mahatma Gandhi and Quaid-i Azam Jinnah have come to no settlement. I am confident now in the spring of next year the Khaksar organisation should be able to present a united India before the bar of the world.
>
> I have already sent telegrams to the two leaders [Jinnah and Gandhi] imploring them with folded hands to resume their talks and relieve India from the agony of suspense. I shall continue to press these two leaders to come to settlement to the best of my power but I announce here that if in spite of the best efforts of everybody they do not come to actual settlement by the end of February 1945, I propose to release for publication the constitution [*The Constitution of Free India*] agreed to by all parties in the land as required by the British Government and shall present that constitution in negotiable form to the Government soon after that date."[6]

History reveals that the British were not serious in a settlement between the two communities. On the other hand, the leaders were also not taking practical steps to put an end to the disputes. Thus, on January 26, 1945, Allama Mashraqi sent the following letter to Gandhi from Lahore:

> "My dear Mahatma Gandhi,
>   My humble submissions and incessant wailings do not apparently make you feel ruffled…

---

[5] In a letter dated October 10, 1944, from Wavell to Amery, Wavell reported on Mashraqi's letter.
[6] Yousaf 2004, Pp. 282-283. *The Eastern Times,* December 27, 1944. *The Star of India,* December 23, 1944. *The Tribune,* December 19, 1944.

Quaid-e-Azam, in his Ahmedabad statement, has courageously come forward to say that he is ready to meet you again. It is, I humbly submit, your turn now to outdo him and come to a settlement within few hours.

...your agreement will at any rate stir India and this may prove useful. I am also daily succeeding in getting various elements of India's national life united and the British will have to think twice before they pay a deaf ear to what I am going to present them. I have already told you that I am ready to take you and Quaid-i-Azam in full confidence in case you desire.

I, therefore, request you not to lose a further moment. I told Sir Tej Bahadur [Sapru] also, when he was in Lahore lately, that I consider your evidence in his Committee inopportune at this moment and that I had already written to you to that effect. I also complained that he ought to have consulted Mr. Jinnah as he consulted you beforehand. He gave cogent reasons, but the matter of Conciliation Committee has got spoiled now.

I send a copy of this letter to Quaid-e-Azam also and send a copy of my letter to him. With best wishes, I am,
Yours sincerely,
Inayatullah Khan"[7]

On the same day, January 26, 1945, Mashraqi also wrote the following letter to Quaid-e-Azam from Lahore:

"My dear Qaid-i-Azam Jinnah,

I must congratulate you on your Ahmadabad Press statement to the effect that you are ready to meet Mahatma Gandhi again. The courage with which you initiated the move has created fresh hopes and I hope the attempt at solution this time will be from an entirely different angle and that you will mean business and business alone on this occasion.

I have to-day written a fresh strong letter to Mahatma Gandhi, of which I send you a copy. I have every reason to believe that the Mahatma will respond to my request to him to send you a fresh invitation, but as you are the initiator this time you must have sent your Press statement to him by now, if not please send it to him now.

As regards other matters I have sufficiently explained them in my letter to the Mahatma, and I hope I shall not be accused of having done anything behind the back of either of you, or hidden anything from one which I said to the other. You may rest assured that I have no sinister motives and that the only thing I wish is that you two come to a settlement.

I request that this settlement be by the end of February [1945]. I have already told you and Mahatma Gandhi that I am ready to take you in full confidence concerning the Constitution that the Khaksar Organisation is preparing if you so desire.

I am also sending you a copy of my recent statement concerning Sir Tej Bahadur Sapru.

---

[7] Yousaf 2004, P. 287.

With best wishes
Yours sincerely,
Inayatullah Khan"[8]

Yet the deadlock between Gandhi and Jinnah continued. Agents of British imperialism were at work and would not allow a settlement between these two leaders. Therefore, on February 27, 1945, Mashraqi wrote to Gandhi asking him to reach an accord with Jinnah, and that if he (Gandhi) did not agree to reach a pact with Quaid-i-Azam by March 31, then Mashraqi would command 10,000 Khaksars to proceed to Savagram and begin fasting until death. Mashraqi wrote to Gandhi:

> "Your silence my letter 26th January [1945] most distressing. If unprepared settlement Quaid-e-Azam before 31st March ordering 10,000 Khaksars fast death Sevagram."[9]

Mashraqi's correspondence with Jinnah and Gandhi clearly tells us that Mashraqi was not siding with either party. The bottom line was that he wanted to see an amicable accord between the two. Since both sides were acting stubborn, Mashraqi thought they should put aside their personal egos and think in terms of seeking freedom for the people of India. Mashraqi was taking the right course of action to keep pushing them to arrive at a truce.

*****

The problem was not just between these two leaders or the AIML and the Congress, there were other parties and groups that were frustrated on being unnoticed by the Government, AIML and the Congress. It was the responsibility of the AIML and Congress not to ignore the public behind these groups. These parties had very serious complaints and frustrations in reference to the AIML and Congress. According to them, the AIML and Congress were totalitarians, selfish and were fighting for political power. They were fighting for their seats and were ignoring everyone else. Indeed! This was among the major issues facing the country. Mashraqi was contacted by Muslims and non-Muslims regarding their grievances. Based on the aspirations of all parties, Mashraqi had taken up the task of drafting the Khaksar Constitution to redress the grievance of all groups and parties in India.

On April 05, 1945, Mashraqi sent a cable to Winston Spencer Churchill (British Premier) and the Viceroy regarding the ambition of the Indian people. This cable was referred to in the Khaksar Constitution. The constitution committee wrote:

> "Allama Mashriqi, the accredited leader of the Khaksar Organisation, having declared to the British Government in his cable to Mr. [Winston] Churchill and the Viceroy, dated the 5th April, 1945, to the

[8] Yousaf 2004, Pp. 287-288.
[9] Hussain, P. 226.

effect that declarations of interest of over 290 million people had been received by him from the various organisations in the country, and that the Government could examine his credentials in that respect, the Viceroy should have invited the Allama [Mashraqi] to represent the interest of this vast number of people in the land in the Leader's Conference, and the Second Legal Committee considers this against the spirit of the pronouncement of the Viceroy that the object of the conditions put in his pronouncement, quoted in (1) above, was to 'ensure the fulfillment of their duty to safeguard the interests of the racial minorities, the religious minorities, the depressed classes, and their Treaty obligations to the Indian States'. Political parties, or persons representing seats in the assemblies, cannot represent the interest of the voiceless communities and minorities in the true sense, and they represent only their own immediate interests. This step of the Viceroy has created intense frustration among the communities."[10]

The AIML and Congress were not the only parties in India; there were other important parties, such as the Khaksars, who had large followings and their opinion should have mattered. The British were giving the impression that they were seeking agreement between all communities in India; in reality they were willing to accept agreement between just the AIML and Congress. Mashraqi highlighted the fact that the majority of people's interests would not be represented by only the AIML and Congress.

Churchill was replaced in May 1945, so he was not in a position to do anything. The new Government followed the policy of the previous Government and continued to ignore all other parties and groups, except the AIML and the Congress.

*****

Returning to difficulties of an agreement between the AIML and Congress, when Mashraqi learned that Jinnah was not feeling well; he again took the opportunity to push Gandhi to meet Jinnah, as he had suggested to Jinnah when Gandhi was sick. Mashraqi wrote to Gandhi on April 26, 1945:

> "leave deliberating on how the next meeting with Mr. Jinnah is going to take place and meet him [Jinnah] as he is not in the best of health...simply go to him [Jinnah] for enquiring about his health... leave all ideas of personal smallness before the good of the country."[11]

This advice was necessary because leadership of the Congress and AIML possessed false egos and were seeking formal invitations, disregarding the important national issues. In his letter, Mashraqi suggested to Gandhi to leave aside formal invitation and "simply go to" Jinnah. If someone visits a sick

---

[10] *The Constitution of Free India 1946 A.C.*, Pp. 49-50.
[11] Yousaf 2004, P. 289.

person, it is bound to bring good feelings in his/her heart. Obviously, this gesture of Gandhi, if he acted upon it, would have opened the door for negotiations in a friendly and cordial manner. But Gandhi remained stubborn and did not go.

On the same day, April 26, 1945, Mashraqi also wrote to Jinnah stating:

> "I have requested him [Gandhi] to come to you to enquire about your health and this will open up the way for another meeting...leave all ideas of personal smallness before the good of the country."[12]

He wrote to Quaid-e-Azam almost in the same tone as to Gandhi so that neither felt less important. All along, Mashraqi was being impartial and was not siding with either Jinnah or Gandhi. His efforts and attitude in both directions were the same. He was only working in the interest of the people.

*****

This was the period when World War II had cost a fortune to the British and had literally broken their back. At this time, if unity was achieved, the Indians could have overthrown the rulers. But the Indians remained divided. World War II ended in May 1945. Though Churchill, Prime Minister of Britain, had brought the British to victory against Germany, he was replaced in the general elections (held on May 08, 1945). Clement Richard Attlee from the Labour Party became the new Prime Minister in a landslide victory on July 26, 1945.[13]

Right after Britain's victory, discussion on the future of India began. The British adroitly started working on a new Executive Council comprised of Indians so that, once again, it would provide them with the opportunity to continue their rule. On June 14, 1945, the Wavell Plan was announced. According to which, the Viceroy would consult Indian leaders to form a new Executive Council. According to the Wavell Plan, the Viceroy's Executive Council was to be reconstructed. The Viceroy was to select persons of his choice from the persons nominated by the political parties.

The neglected parties asked Mashraqi to take up their issue with the Viceroy. Mashraqi wrote to the Viceroy on June 21, 1945 with his suggestion regarding the distribution of seats in the Executive Council. The committee of the Khaksar Constitution endorsed Mashraqi's recommendations. Their recommendations, as they appeared in the Khaksar Constitution, were:

> "...we are of deliberate opinion that the distribution of seats in the proposed executive Council, as suggested by Allama Mashriqi in his letter No. 19216, dated the 21st June, to Lord Wavell is the most proper distribution, and we entirely endorse it. This proposal fixes two seats *each* for the Indian National Congress, the Muslim League,

---

[12] Yousaf 2004, P. 289.
[13] Ahmad 1992, P. 854.

the Hindu Mahasabha (including Arya Smaj, Brahmo Smaj, Dev Smaj, etc.,), and the Sunni Muslims; also one seat *each* for the Backward Hindu Classes, the Dravidians of South India, the Shiah Muslims, and the Momins (including Backward Muslims), thus making up the total of 12 seats for the two major communities. One each of the remaining three seats should be given to the Christians, the Sikhs and the Scheduled Castes; also out of the 12 seats allotted to the Caste Hindus and the Muslims one seat should be reserved for the soldiers."[14]

Mashraqi delivered a speech in Badshahi Mosque (Lahore) on June 22, 1945 and enlightened the people regarding the Khaksar *Constitution of Free India*. He informed them about his perspective on how India's political issues could be resolved. Mashraqi briefed the public on the salient features of his constitution, in which interest of all groups was taken care of.

The Viceroy called a meeting on June 25, 1945 to discuss his own plan with political leaders. This meeting was known as the Simla Conference and was attended by leaders of the Muslim League and Congress. The League and Congress could not agree on the question of representation in the Council. The All India Muslim League claimed that it was the only representative party of the Muslims in India. Quaid-e-Azam insisted that the League should have the *exclusive* right to nominate Muslim members for the Viceroy's Executive Council. The Congress party, on the other hand, claimed to be representative of all communities including Muslims. Wavell requested that the Muslim League and the Congress party send their nominations for the proposed Executive Council. The Congress responded swiftly and submitted a list of its nominations. It included the names of two Muslims. On the other hand, the All-India Muslim League did not send a list and insisted that Muslim members of the Council should only be nominated by and be members of the All-India Muslim League. Regardless, the matter could not be resolved.[15]

Khan Abdul Wali Khan in his book, *Facts are Sacred*, wrote:

"India's population at the time was 40 crore (400 Million), of which Muslims were only 10 crore (100 Million). Besides, of the 11 provinces in the country Muslim League did not have a ministry in a single one, whereas Congress had control over eight. Even so the Muslim-majority provinces, in Bengal the league held just 40 of 117 seats, in Punjab just one of 84 seats, and not even that in Sindh and NWFP."[16]

---

[14] *The Constitution of Free India 1946 A.C.*, P. 50.
[15] *Government of Pakistan information web site.* (2).
[16] Khan, Khan Abdul Wali. Chapter 13.

Yet according to Wavell, Jinnah's insistence with regard to the Muslim ministers in the central ministerial council was that,

> "They must all be nominated by the League and must all be Leaguers....None except himself as head of the Muslim League could nominate the Muslims on the new council... In face a communal veto."[17]

The Wavell Plan of the Executive Council was nothing but a hoax to solve the political problem of India. The Government only wanted nominations from select parties to appoint people of their choice to the Council. The Khaksar Tehreek was not invited to attend the Simla Conference. The Khaksar Tehreek had the support of Muslims and a substantial number of non-Muslims but could not speak on behalf of them. Another 75 parties in the country were communicating with Mashraqi, yet the Khaksars were not allowed to represent this large section of people at the Simla Conference. There were two reasons for not inviting the Khaksars. The British hated the Khaksars, and the AIML would also poison the British's ears to not invite them and would support the British's attitude toward the Khaksars. By not inviting the Khaksar Tehreek, the British again gave a signal to the Muslim League to stay away from the Khaksars. This suited the League very well. The AIML never raised a question of Khaksar representation in the Interim Government. In fact, they clearly stated that no other party should represent the Muslims; they did not want any Muslims, except Muslim Leaguers, to be part of the Executive Council. So how is it that the AIML was looking after the interest of *entire* Muslim community?

The Khaksar Tehreek was victimized and punished for opposing the colonial power. Wasn't the AIML working against Muslim interest and only interested in ministries for themselves? Wavell invited those leaders to Simla Conference who fit British criteria. Wasn't the Government biased? Moral principles or obligations carried little or no weight for the rulers and even for the AIML. One can only be dumbfounded at the mentality of the people at the helm of the political affairs! Anyone with little understanding of British politics can figure out the basis of their criteria. Mischief had been done to guarantee AIML prominence over Khaksars. Although the Khaksars were not to be given any representation in the Executive Council, they never cared as long as they could achieve their objective. If he was invited, Mashraqi most likely would have attended the meeting to make sure that no injustice was done to any community but would have turned down any offer to be part of the British set-up. He would not have liked to serve those who were sucking the blood of poor masses by using affluent Indians.

Anyhow, at the Simla Conference, it was a matter of seats and representation, thus, an agreement could not be reached between the AIML and Congress. The AIML and Congress were fighting for seats for their loved ones and had lost

---

[17] Khan, Khan Abdul Wali. Chapter 13.

sight of what was important. Reading through the historic papers and the newspapers of the time, it becomes very clear that the rift between Muslims and Hindus had to be maintained for British interests. The more the AIML and Congress fought, the more this legitimized the British's stay in India. This is exactly why Mashraqi kept asking the Indian leaders to settle these issues amongst themselves, outside of British influence, as he knew that the British would foster the rift to prolong their stay.

Though Mashraqi's hands were tied, he did not sit idle and kept an open eye on the manipulations in politics. Mashraqi continued his efforts for unity and to ensure that all interests were represented. He kept reminding leaders not to neglect various groups and parties within India.

On July 03, 1945, Mashraqi communicated via telegram with Jinnah, Gandhi, Maulana Abul Kalam Azad, Nehru, Pattabhi Sitaramiyya, and Patel regarding settlement between the two parties and on behalf of the aggrieved parties:

> "I pray Mahatma Gandhi and Quaid-i-Azam Jinnah both to think that their disagreement at this critical moment in the history of India will be most shameful and unbecoming. I claim unreservedly that settlement between the two parties is impossible unless both leaders think in terms of the whole of India and every element of people in the country, and not only in terms of their own parties, especially because Congress and League are invited to speak on behalf of all India. Strongest possible representations have reached me on behalf of backward and neglected classes of both Hindus and Muslims and other communities against Congress and League monopolising all seats for themselves. I have, therefore, urged the Viceroy that two seats each be reserved for Congress, League, Hindu Mahasabha (including Arya Smaj, Dev Smaj, and Brahmu Smaj), and Non-Muslim League Sunni Muslims. Also one seat each be reserved for Hindu Backward Classes, Muslim Backward Momins, Shiah Muslims, Dravidians, Christians, Sikhs, and Scheduled Classes. This will make fifteen seats in all. I strongly urge both great leaders for equitable treatment towards all parties. The claims of Congress as well as Muslim League that they represent the whole of India, or even all Hindus and all Muslims, are absolutely untenable. I shall present to Mahatama and Quaid-e-Azam both the Constitution agreed by seventy five parties representing the voice of over three hundred million people of the country as soon as Congress and League come to settlement. Pray consider the consequences of disagreement, as Khaksars will then strive to the last drop of their energies for upholding the cause of weak parties."[18]

Anyone can see, from Mashraqi's letters to the British authorities and the political leaders, that Mashraqi was not only speaking for Muslims and Hindus but also for other communities regardless of background, caste, color or creed. Mashraqi believed in fair play and his letters show how human he was. He was

---

[18] Hussain, P. 217.

speaking on behalf of all classes. Mashraqi had mentioned support of 75 parties; this cannot be overlooked, yet the British Government, AIML and the Congress ignored this. Why? This requires a thorough study.

Mashraqi was looking ahead to the future and to the consequences of this turmoil. Instead of appreciating Mashraqi's efforts for amicable settlement, the AIML constantly criticized Mashraqi for speaking for Hindu-Muslim unity. They failed to understand that if the communities were separated and two countries were born, this hatred would not be good for the region and the people would ultimately suffer. By talking against Mashraqi, they were bringing division amongst Muslims too. Obviously, not every Muslim was supporting the AIML.

*****

Returning to the Viceroy's Executive Council, Wavell decided to go ahead with the Congress to form the Interim Government. This was meant to increase the political turmoil and chaos and maintain the rift. Mashraqi immediately took up the matter and on July 10, 1945[19] sent the following telegram to Jinnah, Liaquat Ali Khan, Raja of Mahmoodabad, Viceroy, three Muslim Premiers and some members of Muslim League Working Committee:

> "To the Viceroy:- Exclusive Government by Congress alone without the participation of the Muslim League will exasperate the Musalmans, and without participation of the Hindu Mahasabha will disappoint the Hindus. If League and Mahasabha stand aloof I suggest your inviting me to propose after consultation with representative parties of Hindus and Muslims two nominees each over and above what I already suggested. The claim of the League to represent the entire Musalmans is wholly untenable, but I am urging Quaid-e-Azam Jinnah again to participate.
> To Mr. Jinnah:- I urge you to consider calmly that until Muslim League recognises liberally and wholeheartedly the claims of every section of the Musalmans for their representation, League cannot secure popularity amongst the Musalmans...I request you, therefore, to leave unreasonable claims of representation of Musalmans and not exasperate Musalmans of India by standing aloof, as Muslims would be extremely disturbed by Congress alone ruling at the Centre."[20]

Mashraqi knew that the British were stirring more trouble to maintain the rift; to understand Wavell's real intentions, he wanted to talk to Wavell directly. In his message to Wavell, Mashraqi did not disregard the AIML. He also reminded Quaid-e-Azam of his responsibility.

What came out of this telegram? Nothing! Quaid-e-Azam was unsympathetic and indifferent to everyone except the AIML. He was least concerned that the

---

[19] Date is approximated as per the source.
[20] Hussain, P. 218.

AIML was recognized by the Government out of hate for the Khaksars. If Khaksars had supported the British and compromised their principles, the AIML would have surely been pushed aside. It is important to note that until this point, the AIML had not a single ministry in any province which undermines their weak claim of representing the Muslims. The AIML forgot that the party was reaping the benefits based on someone else's sacrifice; AIML forgot the Khaksar massacre of March 19, 1940. AIML couldn't care less that Mashraqi had spent three years in detention, suffered mentally and physically and had his family suffer; AIML did not care that thousands of Khaksars had been thrown in jail and many were still rotting in jail since 1940.

Mashraqi's political activities, such as press statements and public addresses, and the Khaksars' active engagement were mobilizing the public toward independence. Indeed! It was a case of Khaksar sowing the seeds and AIML reaping the benefits. These actions could not have gone unnoticed and were obviously observed by the top British authorities; surveillance by secret services continued. Reports on Khaksar activities and other parties were not only going to Governors and the Viceroy but also to London, where they were studied and then policies were framed accordingly.

On July 14, 1945, Wavell made it public that the Simla Conference had failed.[21] On the same day, Jinnah made a statement following the failure of the Wavell Plan:

> "...we cannot consider or enter into any provisional Interim Government unless a declaration is made by the British Government guaranteeing the right of self-determination of Muslims and pledging that, after the war, or as soon as it may be possible, the British Government would establish Pakistan..."[22]

Jinnah would not agree to any proposal unless it benefited the AIML. The AIML wanted no compromise and rejected anything short of partition. Why was partition so important to them? There were many opportunities to resolve matters, but Quaid-e-Azam was not ready to take the Khaksar Tehreek into confidence. Jinnah's actions all along made nationalists suspicious of his relationship with the British.

Nationalist Muslims blamed Quaid-e-Azam for the Simla Conference's failure. Mashraqi said, "for the breakdown of the Simla Conference Mr. Jinnah alone was responsible."[23] Qazi Ehsan Ahmed Shujabadi, an Ahrar leader, also criticized the failure of the conference.[24]

*****

---

[21] *Government of Pakistan information web site.* (2).
[22] *The Tribune*, March 22, 1946.
[23] *The Tribune*, October 09, 1945.
[24] *The Tribune*, October 22, 1945.

Nationalist Muslims could not understand how the AIML could claim to be the sole representative of the Muslims. The AIML was only surviving at the hold up of the British. To legitimize AIML's representation of Muslims and to make their position solid against the Congress, elections were to be held. Otherwise, to the world, AIML appeared to be a party with no real following in the masses.

On August 21 1945, Wavell announced that elections were to be held. The British's recognition of the AIML as representative of Muslims essentially told the Muslims to vote for AIML and no other Muslim party. Hence, the Muslims had no choice but to vote for AIML and no other Muslim party. This would finally give the AIML a legal position from where they could legitimize any policy as well as their claim for representing the Muslims and would give the AIML the power to effectively oppose the Congress. The AIML's win would also allow the British to use the AIML in any direction they pleased.[25]

An article in the *Daily Herald* (London) was published a year later (on August 31, 1946). Much interest was aroused in political circles at home and in Britain in this article which was written by Michael Foot (Member of Parliament). *The Tribune* Lahore, September 01, 1946 reported the news under the title "Churchill-Jinnah 'Conspiracy.'" Referring to Foot's article, *The Tribune* wrote,

> "While the contents of the correspondence [between Churchill and Jinnah] are not revealed, there is a suggestion by Mr. Foot that they may have bearing on Mr. Jinnah's recent attitude towards the Indian Interim Government and his refusal to join it."[26]

Jinnah denied the allegation. However, nationalists would not accept Quaid-e-Azam's denial.

*****

Meanwhile, Mashraqi was not only pressing the Government and Jinnah but also Gandhi on the representation of all communities. The best solution was to take every party into confidence. On September 06, 1945, Gandhi wrote to Mashraqi from Poona:

> "... I have now read the same [your letter] and I had your telegram also about it. My personal opinion is that there should be no distribution of seats but that elections should be on a basis of adult suffrage and only one electorate. But mine is a voice in the

---

[25] To smart political analysts and observers, this appeared to be a tactic of the British and this announcement set the stage for the dissection of India. The British knew that once the AIML was elected, the Leaguers would maintain their demand for division. The British would then agree to this demand. The British's actions would be considered legitimate in world opinion, as they would be based on an elected party's demand.

[26] *The Tribune*, September 01, 1946.

wilderness. Therefore, I am afraid, it will not count among divided counsellors."[27]

Though Gandhi had a say, he conveniently slid out from making any sort of commitment by stating "mine is a voice in the wilderness."

On September 06, 1945, Gandhi wrote to Dastagir:

> "AHMED DASTAGIR SAHEB,
> As promised I am sending a letter to you for Allama Saheb. I had your letter. You can come over whenever you wish to. Today I have Allama Saheb's letter and a copy of his earlier letter...I have written to him also.
> Mohan K. Gandhi"[28]

The media wanted to know Mashraqi's views on the political issues; in an interview on September 16, 1945, on his departure from Peshawar to Lahore, he stated that he wished to see unity. He said:

> "We must work out some formula for compromise between different parties before the bitterness becomes too great for national considerations, and I have already asked my Khaksars throughout India that greater and intensive efforts should be made to smooth out these antagonisms by meeting leaders of different political parties including [Khan] Abdul Ghaffar Khan.
>
> I also wrote to Mr. Jinnah in this connection, but I have not received any reply as yet. I am even now prepared to join the Muslim League provided it definitely recognises some reasonable share for the poor masses and does not retain all the powers exclusively for certain main leaders. The first step in this direction should be to reorganise the League on more democratic lines and the League President and the Working Committee should be elected directly through a general election all over India."[29]

Jinnah avoided commenting on the letter that Mashraqi had sent earlier and Jinnah did not commit to any proposal by Mashraqi. The media was always keen to know Mashraqi's thoughts, so in talking to the press on September 25, 1945, Mashraqi mentioned what he had proposed to Jinnah:

> "Last August I proposed to Mr. Jinnah that in order to make Muslim League representative of Musalmans in any sense he should agree to my most modest proposal of giving, out of 40%, only ten percent to poor Musalmans and 5% to Shiahs, leaving 25% to Khan Bahadurs and other well-to-do individuals who overwhelm the Muslim League, otherwise, I told him, the Khaksars will help the poor Musalmans to fight for their rights, as they constituted more than 95 percent of the

---

[27] Gandhi LXXXI, P. 231.
[28] Yousaf 2004, P. 290.
[29] *Dawn*, September 20, 1945. *The Tribune*, September 19, 1945.

Muslim population. I made a similar appeal to Mr. Gandhi on behalf of the poor and depressed and suppressed Hindus.

I am not in a position to disclose yet what reply Mr. Gandhi has given, but Mr. Jinnah behaved most arrogantly with those who met him in this connection in Bombay and turned them out of his house. This event has compelled the Khaksars to come in the open field and fight for the rights of 99 percent Musalmans who do not belong to the Muslim League, and who are groaning under the tyranny of titled and rich individuals... I still adhere to the statement I made in Peshawar that I as well as all the Khaksars will join the Muslim League only if Mr. Jinnah allows us into his fold, as then he will not be able to have everything for the flatterers round him and for himself alone...

I appeal to Mahatma Gandhi publicly to think again over the reply he has given to me concerning the future fate of eighteen crores of suppressed Hindus. I am grateful to him for the reply that he has given to me in Urdu with his own hand, and this shows his conciliatory spirit, but if in Free India power is to be the monopoly of a few individuals, it is best that we remain under the British rule until parties come to know the true meaning of democracy. I feel sure I am voicing the feelings of a large majority of Hindus also in this matter."[30]

If the Muslim League was honest in its concern for the rights of the Muslims, it should have agreed to Mashraqi's proposal or at least taken steps in that direction. As a matter of fact, neither the AIML nor Congress was taking care of suppressed groups.

Mashraqi delivered a speech on October 21, 1945 in Calcutta.[31] His speech reflected that neither AIML nor Congress was sincere in solving the tangle and were actually working against the unity of people. Allama Mashraqi again addressed a public congregation on December 18, 1945 organized by the Karachi Municipal Corporation. During his speech, Mashraqi called for unity. He further stated that the Khaksars were working on a formula that would be suitable for all Indians.

To further make Gandhi realize how important it was to not ignore any class of people, the Khaksar Constitution was sent to Gandhi. Mahatma Gandhi wrote to Mashraqi on November 01, 1945:

"ALLAMA SAHEB,
I have received the printed constitution you have sent. I have gone through it. Though great pains have been taken in drafting it, I have doubts about its usefulness. I feel that if we all become one at heart, it will be easy to frame a constitution. In my view it is well-nigh impossible to achieve unity through a constitution. This is what I think.

[30] Hussain, P. 219. Also see *The Free Press Journal*, September 28, 1945.
A portion of this statement was also reported in *The Tribune*, September 26, 1945.
[31] See speech in Appendix V.

> *Yours,*
> M. K. GANDHI"[32]

No one would disagree with Gandhi that it would be difficult unless "we all become one at heart," but one has to take practical steps to move in that direction. Khaksars met Gandhi to discuss the Khaksar Constitution further. During the meeting, he conveyed to Khaksars that he would like to meet Mashraqi. In this connection, Gandhi also sent a letter to Mashraqi on November 17, 1945:

> "ALLAMA SAHEB,
> I got your letter and two Khaksar officials also came and saw me. I was very happy... On the 20th... you may come at 3 p.m. I shall wait for you then. If you want any change in the time, please send a message to me at the Birla House.
> *Yours,*
> M. K. GANDHI"[33]

Mashraqi wrote back, and Gandhi replied on November 19, 1945:

> "ALLAMA SAHEB,
>   I have your letter... The biggest problem is the condition you have laid down. I cannot speak on behalf of the Congress. I can speak for myself and I think I have already conveyed my view to you that though you have taken great pains in drafting the constitution, it is not workable and it cannot appeal to others. I still think as I have said earlier, that only if all the communities are first united at heart and wish to sit together and decide the issue will it be possible to frame a constitution. So what the Congress will do is beside the point. Personally, too, I cannot agree with you on your constitution. As I have said, though there are some good features in it and I appreciate the trouble you have taken, I am afraid we shall not be able to agree at the forthcoming meeting. I had thought and I still think, that whatever the outcome of our meeting might be, we should meet and at least try to understand each other's point of view.
>   Your letter gives me no such hope.
> *Yours,*
> M. K. GANDHI"[34]

On November 20, 1945, Gandhi wrote from Birla House to Mashraqi:

> "ALLAMA SAHEB,
> I have your letter... What I had told you was never meant for the Press and so far as I am concerned I would like to say that whatever we have been writing to each other should not be sent to the Press..."[35]

---

[32] Gandhi LXXXII, P. 5.
[33] Yousaf 2004, P. 296.
[34] Gandhi LXXXII, P. 98.
[35] Gandhi LXXXII, P. 101.

On January 01, 1946, Gandhi replied from Contai to Mashraqi's letter:

> "BHAI SAHEB,
>   I received the letter only today in Contai. I have written to you that I am not a member of the Congress. I cannot write anything on behalf of the Congress. Only Maulana Saheb can do so. I have already expressed my opinion that no one is going to accept your constitution. I personally do not accept it.
>   Write to me at the Sodepur address.
> M. K. GANDHI"[36]

Gandhi did not agree to the constitution for reasons known to him. While he appreciated some of the constitution's features, he did not agree with it. Yet he did not come up with any counter suggestion either, which indicated that he was not serious in solving the tangle. Under the circumstances, a meeting did not take place between the two leaders. Why didn't Gandhi agree? A separate study is needed on the Khaksar Constitution and Gandhi's reasons for not accepting it, despite the fact that it protected everyone's rights. If Gandhi did in fact disagree on any of the clauses, why didn't he send his disagreements or propose amendments in writing to Mashraqi? Khaksars were meeting Gandhi from time to time. Under the circumstances, the Khaskar impression, that Gandhi was not serious in resolving the issue, was legitimized.

Despite Mashraqi's attempts, the three parties — Khaksar Tehreek, AIML and Congress — could not reach a compromise.

*****

The Englishmen allowed Quaid-e-Azam and Gandhi to sit together for 18 days and let them fight between themselves. Agents of imperialism in both communities stepped in and never allowed them to settle the issue. Meanwhile the Englishmen shrugged their shoulders and maintained their position that – look gentlemen, we have put them together to settle their differences, but these Mohammadans and Hindus cannot come to any agreement, so what can we do? The world was being told that if Muslims and Hindus settled their differences, the British would transfer their power. The world was made to believe that the British's intentions were clear and they meant business. Yet this was a ploy because anytime there were hopes of Muslim-Hindu unity, circumstances were created that would aggravate the rift. The English made sure that this rift continued, so as to make it appear to the rest of the world that the Indians were fighting amongst themselves, as such power could not be transferred, and the British appeared helpless in the matter.

In fact, if the Muslim and Hindu leaders could have come together, they would have overthrown the British Government.

---

[36] Gandhi LXXXII, P. 325.

> "If they [Muslims and Hindus] joined hands the situation could become, like the one caricatured by a Hindu humourist who said that if all the Indians even pee' together these handful of British- hers would all be flooded away."[37]

Despite the fact that the AIML and Congress could not resolve their issues, the Congress went so far as to suggest to the British to transfer power to the AIML and leave.

> Gandhi, "in an article in *Harijan*, accepts the view of the Congress President and says that the Congress will have no objection to power being handed over to the Muslims League or any other party provided it was real independence."[38]

This offer was not accepted by Quaid-e-Azam. The question is why? The British would not have this and would not allow Jinnah to accept this offer. If Jinnah would have accepted it, the British would have ended Jinnah's leadership there and then. According to nationalists, he was made a leader of the Muslims so that he would keep asking for partition and maintain the rift with nationalist parties; in this way, the British could continue to exploit the quarrel. If Quaid-e-Azam had accepted the offer, then the rift would have ended, and Muslims and Hindus united would have asked the British to leave India.

There were times when agreement seemed possible as a result of Mashraqi's efforts. For instance, in November 1942, a meeting was held in Allahabad. There was a state of reconciliation and cordial relations between the two parties (AIML and Congress) and prospects of an agreement were visible between Muslims and Hindus; however, this too was soon sabotaged.

The British continued their policy of divide and rule and kept their bag of tricks handy. For instance, with regard to the Jinnah-Gandhi meeting in 1944, the British knew that the two would not come to an agreement. However, if for some reason they managed to work out their differences, then the British wanted to have another trick ready. Hence, prior to the meeting, Wavell started talking of issues of the Depressed Classes in India, Princely States and other minorities (in his letter to Gandhi written on July 30, 1944); the British did this on purpose so that in case Jinnah and Gandhi reached an agreement, then they could say that Jinnah and Gandhi alone did not represent the issues of the other minorities and that the minorities also needed to be in agreement.

Under these circumstances, rapprochement between any party was impossible. It is beyond my apprehension as to how these seasoned Indian leaders could not understand the tricks of the British, unless they too were party to them. Unfortunately, certain powerful elements in the AIML and Congress continued to play in the hands of the British.

---

[37] Khan, Khan Abdul Wali. Chapter 1.
[38] *The Hindustan Times*, August 03, 1942.

Mashraqi made his best efforts to resolve issues of all communities. His letters and statements reflect his concern about Indian political affairs and that many leaders were intoxicated with the power game and least bothered with ground reality. To many, the AIML and Congress were working for themselves and ignoring everyone else. Does this mean they were seeking freedom for a *few individuals*? At least in Pakistan, things turned out to be this way.

Mashraqi asked Jinnah and Gandhi with "folded hands" to reach an agreement; they failed. They should have realized that their struggle should have been to overthrow the rulers through a joint effort. Even if they could not have resolved their issues, they could have supported Mashraqi, and with his power, he would have brought the British rule to an end within a very short period of time. If Khaksars, Congress and Muslim League had put up a joint effort, as desired by Mashraqi, India would not have been divided and Indians would have attained freedom much earlier — probably by 1943. Mashraqi was so disgusted with their politics that on May 29, 1947, he issued a statement "asking the people to revolt against Mahatma Gandhi and Mr. M.A. Jinnah and to start a revolution against the British."[39]

If the AIML and the Congress had understood Mashraqi's wailings, mass killing at partition of India would not have occurred. If they had come to an agreement, one India could have remained intact. Even today according to Indian Muslims I have spoken to, they do not appreciate the division of India. Since Khaksar material is not easily accessible to the public in Pakistan as well as in India, this makes it absolutely evident that there are many hidden aspects of our history that have been concealed on purpose. The question is who is responsible for the division of India and the resulting massacre of innocent people; the British, AIML, Congress or all three?

Alas! The AIML and Congress did not truly understand that the British benefited from their differences and a torn apart Pakistan and India would fight forever.

History has shown that expansionists have continuously put forth efforts to weaken the Muslims. This trend has been seen throughout history with the takeover of India, crushing of the Muslims after the 1857 mutiny in India, fall of the Ottoman Empire, breakup of India and even in today's world events. Any attempts by Muslims to rise against them have been promptly crushed, and Muslims will continue to be weakened in the future. But who is to be blamed for this state of affairs? Muslims cannot continue to blame others, but instead need to look inside themselves!

---

[39] *The Tribune*, May 30, 1947.

Chapter 8

Another Attempt to Eliminate the Khaksar Tehreek - 1945-46 Elections & Khaksar Constitution

Settlement between all communities within India was a pre-condition for the bestowal of freedom on India. This was apparent from Lord Wavell's (Viceroy of India) reply to Mashraqi on October 07, 1944 (Mashraqi had written to Wavell on October 03, 1944).[1] Wavell wrote:

> "their [British Government's] offer of unqualified freedom after the cessation of hostilities was made conditional upon the framing of a Constitution agreed by main elements of India's national life, and the negotiation of Treaty arrangements with His Majesty's Government."[2]

There were also pronouncements by important men in Great Britain giving indications to help India resolve its issues. His Majesty's Government had made it clear that the constitution should be made by the representatives of the public of India.

Based on these pre-requisites and assertions of the Government regarding the future constitution, Mashraqi not only continued working for Muslim-Hindu reconciliation but also worked on *The Constitution of Free India, 1946 A.C.* (also known as Khaksar Constitution). Legal Committees (First Legal Committee and Second Legal Committee) were formed to frame the Khaksar Constitution, which would be a document of national importance. Highly qualified and eminent persons from various backgrounds were included in these committees. Behind this effort was an endeavor to nullify British schemes. The committees conducted an extensive study, including research on Indian literature, reports, conditions, religion, etc. Documents issued by other parties and constitutions of other countries were also studied. The idea was to

---

[1] Hussain, P. 202.
[2] *The Constitution of Free India 1946 A.C.*, P. 49.

frame a constitution that would satisfy and fulfill the needs of all communities. Seventy five parties as well as other organizations, groups and communities (altogether approximately 125)[3] were asked to submit their proposals to be incorporated in the proposed constitution. It was to be drafted "as far as possible, feasible and consistent with the interests of other minorities, sub-minorities, sections and sub-sections concerned."[4] This had to be done so that the British were left with no excuse but to transfer the power.

Some viewed *The Constitution of Free India* as an attempt to oust Jinnah and Gandhi from the political scene. To remove this misconception, Mashraqi stated:

> "I have not the slightest wish to outdo Gandhi and Jinnah in my attempt to bring about a settlement of the Hindu-Muslim question."[5]

Mashraqi simply wanted India to be "united on the question of freedom."[6] In fact, the Second Legal Committee of the Khaksar Constitution in its recommendation stated that seventeen parties of India, whose role was considered important in India's national life, must be represented with one person from each party. The committee recommended eminent Indians from each party that could serve as representative of that party. The following is a list of parties with recommended representatives; only one person was to represent each party:

* Hindu Mahasabha – Dr. Moonje, Veer Savarkar, Dr. S.P. Mukerjit
* Congress – Mahatma Gandhi, Jawaharlal Nehru, Sir Ardeshir Dalal
* Sanatandharmi Hindus – Swami Ganesh Dutt
* Backward Hindu Classes – Swami Sachhutanand, G.S. Pal
* Dravidians – E. V. Ramasami
* Muslim League – Quaid-e-Azam M. A. Jinnah, Nawabzada Liaquat Ali Khan
* Khaksars – Allama Mashraqi
* Sunni Muslims – Maulana Abul Kalam Azad, Maulana Zafar Ali Khan, or other Sunni Muslims
* Shia Muslims – Maharajkumar of Mahmudabad, Sir Wazir Hassan
* Backward Muslims and Momins – Mauvli Zahiruddin, or other Backward classes leaders
* Scheduled Classes – Dr. Ambedkar, R. B. Sheoraj
* Christians – Raja Sir Maharaj Singh
* Sikhs – Master Tara Singh, Sardar Ujjal Singh, Sir Jogendra Singh
* Hindu States – H.H. the Maharajah of Mysore, H.H. the Jam of Nawanagar
* Muslim States – H.E.H. the Nizam, H.H. the Nawab of Bhopal

---

[3] Hussain, P. 203.
[4] Ibid.
[5] Hussain, P. 213.
[6] Ibid.

* Soldiers – Col. Sir Sher Mohammad Khan, Jhelum; Col. Sir Hussamuddin Khan, Bhopal; Col. Nawab Mohammad Akbar Khan, Hoti, or any V.C.
* Miscellaneous (Jains, Budhists, Parsees, etc.) – Ramchandra Prasad, Rajendra Kumar Jain, Bodhanand Mahasthavir, Prof. Hiralal, Sir Cowasji Jehangir, or other representative leaders[7]

Mashraqi was not out to surpass anyone. Rather, he was seeking cooperation of everyone. Sir Tej Bahadur Sapru wrote in his letter to Sir Maharaj Singh on December 15, 1944 that he was with Mashraqi on the settlement of communal differences. Sapru had even sought Mashraqi's suggestion on the constitution he (Sapru) was developing and in the same letter he wrote: "I [Sapru] have asked him [Mashraqi] to favour me with his views or suggestions."[8]

To make a joint effort, on December 19, 1944, Mashraqi wrote to Sir Tej Bahadur Sapru:

> "Dear Sir Tej Bahadur,
> ...You will have noticed that I have appealed again to Jinnah and Gandhi to meet each other and am engaged in the meantime in getting an agreed constitution between the main elements of India's national life...considering that your work also appears identical with ours in many respects it may occur to you to coordinate your work with ours, so that we may not be running on parallel lines...I honestly think that the Hindu-Muslim problem can be solved in the way it has hitherto been attempted. At any rate my most sincere wishes are with you. With best wishes, I am,
> Yours sincerely,
> (sd/. Allama Mashriqi)"[9]

Sir Tej Bahadur Sapru interviewed Mashraqi and discussed the Khaksar *Constitution of Free India* that was in progress as well as other matters of interest to resolve issues confronting the people of British India. Allama Mashraqi told Sapru that for the sake of an undivided India, Gandhi must not ignore the AIML and must show flexibility. Otherwise, the British would continue their policy of divide and rule, and as a result, Muslims, Hindus and others would face the repercussions. Without any ambiguity, Mashraqi informed Sapru that these delays and discord between Congress and AIML leaders were politically motivated and were sponsored by the British; and that Indian leaders must not allow the British to use the Indian leadership's differences for their political ends. Thus, in the interest of the people, forming one opinion and one platform would be indispensable. Mashraqi told Sapru that if his words of warning were not heard, there would be a gross massacre of Muslims and Hindus. Communalism had taken root and was taking the country nowhere; hatred would continue and generations to come would suffer. Mashraqi knew that it was in the interest of the British that the Indians

---

[7] *The Constitution of Free India 1946 A.C.*, P. 51.
[8] Hooja, P. 424.
[9] Yousaf 2004, P. 282.

hated each other and that a rift persisted in the region. He told Sapru that these differences were taking Indians toward destruction and ultimately people would have to pay the price for the follies of their leaders. In frustration, Mashraqi asked him to convey to Hindu leaders they must seek the Muslim League's cooperation, at this critical juncture, or face consequences. Thus, Mashraqi clearly saw what lay head. His desperation was unquestionable and required utmost attention, as he thought that the AIML was playing in the hands of the British. Jinnah and Gandhi probably underestimated the havoc and tragedy that was to come, if India were to be divided. If they had understood this, they would have hopefully acted on Mashraqi's repeated suggestions and warnings. If they did not comprehend this and were playing in the hands of colonial forces, then they cannot be excused for the holocaust that took place in India.

While political events were taking a fast turn, work on the Khaksar Constitution continued. Mashraqi had received great support for his constitution from various groups and parties. Thus, on April 05, 1945, Mashraqi sent a cable to Churchill and Wavell (the Viceroy of India).[10] In his letter, Mashraqi informed both that he had received "declarations of interest of over 290 million people"[11] from various parties, groups, organizations and important people in the country. Mashraqi had based his constitution on this tremendous support. The Government was provided with the opportunity to verify this support.[12] Regardless of what the Government's attitude would be, work on the constitution continued; progress and suggestions were conveyed to Mashraqi and his advice was taken on all matters pertaining to the constitution.

On May 15, 1945, A.K. Fazl-ul-Haq wrote to Mashraqi:

> "Dear Allama Sahib,
> I have gone through the various papers I got from you last evening and have come to the conclusion that in order to expedite the work it is necessary that the report of the First Legal Committee be completed as quickly as possible on the lines indicated in the papers in order that the work of the Second Legal Committee may begin early. If there are any suggestions I wish to add to what has already been agreed, I shall send them to you from Calcutta.
> You may subscribe my name with others to the Report of the First Legal Committee, which you said would be submitted to the Second Legal Committee for further examination and for the purpose of framing the Constitution on the lines indicated in the report. I have every reason to believe that the conclusions arrived at with so much care and enormous amount of hard work and deep insight, will commend themselves to the members of the Second Legal Committee, and that the work of framing the Constitution on most sound and generally agreed lines will get much easier by this report. I

---

[10] See Chapter 7.
[11] *The Constitution of Free India 1946 A.C.*, P. 49.
[12] Ibid.

wish you success in your undertaking. I am leaving Lahore for
Calcutta to-day. With deepest regards, I am,
Yours Sincerely
A.K. Fazlul Haq"[13]

*The Khaksar Constitution was a document of utmost importance. It took into
account the interest of all parties in India ("main elements of India's national
life"[14]) and satisfied the British's condition to grant freedom.*

*****

Within almost a month of Mashraqi's letter to Churchill and Wavell (Viceroy
of India), Wavell traveled to England (in May 1945) to discuss the political
situation in India. He held discussion with the administration on the subject.
Upon return to India, Wavell announced his plan on June 14, 1945.[15]
According to which, the Viceroy would consult Indian leaders to form a new
Executive Council.[16]

"The pronouncement of Lord Wavell of 14th June 14 [1945] and the
simultaneous announcement of the Secretary of State in the House of
Commons concerning the indianization of Viceroy's Executive
Council have cleared the ambiguity that existed before, to the effect
that, for the purpose of giving unqualified freedom to India,
agreement between the two political parties, i.e. the Congress and the
Muslim League was all that was required, and this agreement
virtually meant that any constitution framed by them alone would be
taken to be the 'agreed Constitution'. The Viceroy, by proclaiming
that there would be parity between the *Caste Hindus*, and the
Muslims had affirmed that the Constitution taken to be the 'agreed
Constitution' would be that agreed by various *communities* as a
whole, and not merely by political parties claiming to represent those
communities. The interpretation put therefore, by the Khaksar
Organisation, on the words of Lord Wavell, contained in his letter to
Mahatma Gandhi of August 15, oft quoted in the letters of Allama
Mashriqi to the various parties in the country, to the effect that the
British Government at the time of Cripps' Offer made it clear that
'their offer of unqualified freedom after the cessation of hostilities
was made conditional upon the framing of a Constitution agreed by
main elements of India's national life, and the negotiation of Treaty
arrangements with His Majesty's Government,' was indeed, the
correct interpretation, and the step taken in addressing the various
organizations of the country, constituting 'elements of India's
national life' was the right step."[17]

---

[13] *The Constitution of Free India 1946 A.C.*, P. 47.
[14] *The Constitution of Free India 1946 A.C.*, P. 49.
[15] *The Constitution of Free India 1946 A.C.*, P. 48. *Government of Pakistan Information web site.*
(2).
[16] See Chapter 7.
[17] *The Constitution of Free India 1946 A.C.*, Pp. 48-49.

This excerpt indicates that despite British statements that freedom would be granted once agreement was reached by all parties in India, the British were only seeking agreement of the AIML and Congress and were basically willing to accept any constitution that they alone formed. Does this not show that the British had a special relationship with these two parties? This excerpt further shows that the Khaksar Constitution was based on the British condition and had the support of all main parties in India.

To discuss his plan, Wavell called the Simla Conference on June 25, 1945. After the failure of the Simla Conference, on August 21, 1945, Wavell announced that the Central and Provincial elections would be held in December 1945 and January 1946, respectively.[18] It was announced to have separated rather than joint electorate, meaning, Muslims voting for Muslim candidates and non-Muslims voting for non-Muslim candidates.[19] Under this method, the Muslims would have no choice but to vote for the Muslim League.

Hence, this procedure was adopted to ensure the AIML's success in the elections. The AIML had already been accepted as the only party to represent Muslims before the British, and the elections would serve to legitimize this to the world.

*****

For the AIML, this election was extremely important because earlier, in the elections in 1937, the Muslim League had miserably failed to prove that it was the sole representative of Indian Muslims.

The AIML launched its campaign, making communalism, Islam and the demand for Pakistan the prominent election issue. The main feature of this election was nothing but "communal issues" and the AIML attracted people on the "plank of Pakistan & Islam in danger and its appeal went home to the Muslim masses."[20]

Slogans were raised at public meetings to exploit religious feelings and sentiments of illiterate Muslims; these included "Pakistan ka matlab kiya, La ilaha illallah." This and other slogans implied that voting for the Muslim League and in essence voting for Pakistan, meant that Islam would be protected. The AIML even went to the extent of saying that if you do not vote for the Muslim League, you are not a Muslim. The AIML gave the election campaign a thoroughly communal color, and the Muslims' religious emotions were aroused. Under these conditions, to not vote for AIML was impossible.

---

[18] Hussain, P. 220.
[19] Khan, Khan Abdul Wali. Chapter 14.
[20] Mansergh 1976, P. 1231.

This was clearly stated in the fortnightly confidential report of February 22, 1946 sent to Viceroy Wavell by the Punjab Governor Sir Bertrand Glancy:

> "The ML [Muslim League] orators are becoming increasingly fanatical in their speeches. Maulvis and Pirs and students travel all round the Province and preach that those who fail to vote for the League candidates will cease to be Muslims; their marriages will no longer be valid and they will be entirely excommunicated... It is not easy to foresee what the results of the elections will be. But there seems little doubt the Muslim League, thanks to the ruthless methods by which they have pursued their campaign of *Islam in danger* will considerably increase the number of their seats and unionist representatives will correspondingly decline."[21]

*****

Disunity between the AIML and Congress left no choice for the Khaksar Tehreek but to participate in the elections in order to safeguard the rights of the masses and to prevent the division of India. Consequently, the Khaksar Tehreek established a Central Parliamentary Board to contest the elections. The Board comprised of:

- ❖ Barrister K.L. Gauba[22], Chairman
- ❖ Abdul Rashed Qureshi (Bengal)
- ❖ Nawab Ali Ahmad Jan (Sind)
- ❖ Dr. Ghulam Mohy-ud-Din Qadri
- ❖ Dr. Muzhar[23] Ali Abbasi (Punjab)[24]

The Khaksar Tehreek's campaign was based on unity of all communities and for a united India. The Tehreek firmly believed against using communalism in politics. The Tehreek started its election campaign on the basis of *The Constitution of Free India, 1946 A.C.* that sought a united India.[25] The Tehreek nominated candidates who agreed with the Khaksar Constitution to run under their ticket. There were supporters of the Tehreek in all parties, and thus candidates selected for its ticket included individuals from the AIML, the Unionist Party, the Ahrar Party and independents.[26] On August 31, 1945,[27] a conference was held at the Khaksar headquarters in Lahore. The conference was attended by Khaksar leaders and lasted for two days. Soon after this meeting, Mashraqi sent a delegation of Khaksars leaders to meet Quaid-e-Azam. They offered him to contest elections on the Khaksar party's ticket. Jinnah did not treat the Khaksars well and blatantly refused. He also refused to

---

[21] IOL L/P&J/5/249, P. 155.
[22] Barrister K.L. Gauba was, at one time, a member of the Punjab Legislative Assembly.
[23] This name may be misspelled as it was illegible in the source.
[24] *The Tribune*, September 21, 1945.
[25] *The Free Press Journal*, August 06, 1945.
[26] *The Civil & Military Gazette*, January 31, 1946.
[27] Akhtar, P. 565.

support the Khaksar Constitution. *The Free Press Journal* of November 16, 1945 reported:

> "Allama Mashriqui...has written a letter to Mr. M. A. Jinnah enquiring if the latter would stand for election to the Central Assembly on the Khaksar constitution ticket. Should he elect to stand on the Khaksar ticket, says Allama the Khaksar Organisation would leave no stone unturned in giving him the maximum amount of assistance."

The idea of offering a ticket to Quaid-e-Azam was to avoid division among Muslims. But Quaid-e-Azam's behavior towards the Khaksars and refusal was obviously not appreciated. According to the Khaksar circle, Quaid-e-Azam was already assured of his success by the bureaucracy, so he needed no ticket or support of any other party.

A rigorous operation was launched based on the Khaksar Constitution. Copies of the Khaksar Constitution were sent to the Viceroy, Governors, political leaders, educationists, intellectuals and the media. *The Civil & Military Gazette*, Lahore published it on September 28, 1945. (The final version of the Khaksar Constitution was published in October 1945.[28])

As mentioned, the constitution had the support of seventy five parties along with other organizations, groups and communities (altogether approximately 125).[29] It laid out a thorough plan with policies and procedures, and its features catered to every community. In general it aimed to:

❖ Create a more democratic system and ensure justice, good governance, stability and efficiency
❖ Foster cooperation and goodwill amongst different parties; end communalism and party exploitation and take the focus off of religion in order to bring the country together to work for what is best for Indians as a whole

Some of the specific elements of the constitution were as follows:

❖ India will attain complete independence and will not be divided
❖ India will not have hereditary rule and will be a democracy
❖ The country will have a fair, prompt and affordable judicial system, free press, free and secret elections, and representation for all
❖ India will ensure its security
❖ India will adopt democracy only to the extent that it is beneficial for Indians; it will not necessarily adopt Western thought and culture and will add / retract as necessary to its own way of thinking "for the purpose of developing a modern culture exclusive to her own genius"[30]

---

[28] Mashriqi [1931] 1997, P. 8.
[29] Hussain, P. 203.
[30] *The Constitution of Free India 1946 A.C.*, P. 55.

- ❖ The country will have one President (either Muslim or Hindu), with a cabinet comprised of Hindus, Muslims and other minorities
- ❖ The President will hold office for three years and will alternate from Hindu to Muslim and vice versa
- ❖ A Muslim President would be chosen by a Hindu President and vice versa
- ❖ The President would not be a party leader and must be a civil service man

- ❖ The country will have one Governor in each province (either Muslim or Hindu), with cabinets comprised of Hindus, Muslims and other minorities
- ❖ Muslim majority provinces would be under the direction of Muslim Governors and Hindu majority provinces would fall under the direction of Hindu Governors
- ❖ Governors would hold office for three years and may be re-elected
- ❖ The Governors would not be party leaders and must be civil service men

- ❖ All citizens would be equal with equal rights and duties, regardless of their caste, creed, religion, gender, wealth, rank, etc.
- ❖ Interests of all parties including minorities would be safeguarded
- ❖ The State will ensure protection of human life and fundamental rights for all individuals, including women, children and destitute persons
- ❖ The State will defend people's faith, rights and liberties
- ❖ The problem of hunger will be addressed as a top priority and no one will go hungry
- ❖ Right to free and compulsory education, liberty, property, free expression and free association will be upheld
- ❖ Compulsory labor would be ended and the interests of workers would be safeguarded
- ❖ Education would be conducted in mother tongue of region/locality
- ❖ Diseases would be exterminated[31]

The Khaksar Constitution became the focal point of the Tehreek's election campaign. Mashraqi traveled extensively and explained his constitution in huge public gatherings. Its salient features were explained in many cities such as Amritsar, Aligarh, Bombay, Calcutta, Delhi, Hyderabad, Karachi, Madras, Multan and so on. The constitution had already generated great support and this was witnessed at these public meetings. Mashraqi was congratulated for this great achievement, and the constitution earned great applause from the nationalists including Muslims and non-Muslims. Supporting slogans were a routine matter in these public meetings.

*****

Anti-Khaksar elements were quite perturbed at this support. They did not want this constitution to be implemented, as their agendas were different from the Khaksar Tehreek's. As a matter of fact, anti-Khaksar elements found their death in the Khaksar Constitution. Thus, agents of imperialism and people

---

[31] *The Constitution of Free India 1946 A.C..*

with vested interests became very active in opposition and a well-planned campaign was launched against the Khaksar Tehreek. Anti-Khaksar elements launched propaganda against Khaksars in the media. The anti-Khaksars' henchmen spread a lot of false and rotten rumors which were published in the press to mislead people. All the dirty tricks of politics were applied. False statements were even published in the name of the Khaksar Tehreek.

Witnessing the successes of the Khaksar campaign, the bureaucracy jumped in to block the success of Khaksar Movement in the elections. The deputy commissioners and police were supporting the AIML; a lot of money was also funneled in for the AIML by wealthy people. With the bureaucracy behind them, the Leaguers applied uncivilized and unethical tactics. The AIML applied all methods to convince the poor masses to not vote for the Khaksar Tehreek. The Khaksars' public meetings were disrupted by *goondas* (gangsters). These gangsters were either supporters of the AIML or were hired people. They attacked public Khaksar meetings and this became a routine matter. The AIML's harassment activities included:

- Beating the public to force them to leave Khaksar public gatherings
- Engaging in harassment to prevent masses from attending Khaksar public meetings
- Harassing Mashraqi and Khaksars to stop political activities
- Using the media for false propaganda and to throw filth on the Khaksar Tehreek
- Shouting slogans against the Khaksar Tehreek and in favor of the AIML in Khaksar meetings; these anti-Khaksar slogans were published in the newspapers condemning the Khaksar Tehreek and saying that people were not in favor of Khaksars

The purpose of these activities was:

- To create confusion and chaos
- To distract the public from understanding the constitution
- To mislead the public that Mashraqi had no support, despite the fact that many of Mashraqi's audiences were well over 100,000 in number
- To provide opportunities to the press to report that the public was supposedly disrupting these public meetings and that the Khaksars had no support
- Because the Leaguers were unable to bear any criticism of their policies

The police did nothing to stop the AIML. Meanwhile if the Khaksars had engaged in any such activity, the police would have immediately suppressed them.

The AIML was engaging in disruptive activities because they were not sure of their own success and were mainly banking on Government support. Their nervousness was reported in the press. For instance, *The Tribune*, Lahore of September 22, 1945 reported:

> "Considerable uneasiness is visible in the Muslim League circles because of the decision of Allama Mashraqi, leader of the Khaksar movement, to come to Sind in connection with the election work. The Khaksars have planned a comprehensive programme for his tour in various districts of Sind."

*****

Systematic propaganda against the Khaksar Tehreek was underway. The Leaguers were letting the British know that they were hostile toward the Khaksars, so that the AIML could continue to receive the blessings of the British.

The bureaucracy's bias was clearly visible; the public objected to this and protested against it. Partiality of the Government was noticeable from the resolution passed by the All-India Jamiat Ulema in their meetings on September 18 and 19, 1945 in Delhi:

> "This meeting of the Council of the Central Jamiat Ulema condemns the attitude of the Government of India...encouraging the Muslim League...and providing them all relative facilities, and on the other hand they are blocking the progress of freedom-loving organisations and presses by putting all sorts of obstacles in their way such as involving them in trouble and withholding permits for newspapers. Whereas on the eve of general elections in the country the Government attitude towards all parties could be desired to be similar..."[32]

The Council of the Central Jamiat Ulema also demanded release of Khaksars that were given life imprisonment because of the March 19, 1940 incident.

> "The meeting hopes that the Punjab Government will thereby be able to make good for the mistakes which the pro-Muslim League Government of the past did in that respect."[33]

A nationalist Muslim leaders' conference was also held in New Delhi on September 19 and it decided to form a Nationalist Muslims' Parliamentary Board; Maulana Hussain Ahmed Madni was elected as the Chairman.

> "The meeting passed a resolution condemning the Government of India for having yielded to the Muslim League...
> ...But, in spite of all these difficulties and handicaps...Azad Muslims should participate in all the elections...in order to...protect the Indian Mussalmans from the ruinous policy of

---

[32] *The Tribune*, September 25, 1945.
[33] Ibid.

the Muslim League, which is entirely a capitalist organisation and which has formed an alliance with the Imperialist Government to exploit the Mussalmans for their selfish ends."[34]

On September 23, 1945, Mufti Ziaul Hassan in Ludhiana, member of the Working Committee of the All-India Muslim Majlis commented on Government officials helping the AIML. He said:

"We agree that official influence in the forthcoming elections should not prevail... Sufficient proof can be given in this behalf.
Employees of the Government of India are also included in the aforesaid category..."
Hassan also talked about "rejection of the application of nationalist Muslims to start a newspaper, while the Leaguers have been given quota and permission for new papers."[35]

*****

It was an established fact that the bureaucracy was supporting the AIML. Jinnah's public meetings and addresses remained undisturbed, and he campaigned and asked people to support the AIML in the elections. On September 02, 1945, in a public address, Jinnah appealed to the public to stand behind AIML and work under its banner.

"He [Jinnah] said...the whole world was looking at the Indian Muslims...They were ready to fight for their cause.
'I do not want you to shed your blood but be prepared to fight for the Muslim League votes...We do not grudge independence for Hindus but let them be in Hindustan. Pakistan is ours. This is our own land and we should be free to rule over it.'"[36]

This statement is deplorable, as AIML attempted to gain votes on the idea of Pakistan and implied that British India did not belong to the Muslims. To Jinnah's appeal, a nationalist, Dr. Syed Abdul Latif, said in an interview:

"If the League is seriously anxious to win over those who stand aloof from it or hold a different view in any matter, the right course is not to ask them to change their view overnight as if it is just a garb which one can put on or take off at convenience...but to make an earnest attempt to understand them and to see in what honourable manner a rapproachement is possible...
Instead of wasting precious time in an arduous attempt to bring all the Indian Muslims into the League, Mr. Jinnah might do well to recognize the realities of the situation and develop the mood for a compromise."[37]

---

[34] *The Free Press Journal*, September 20, 1945.
[35] *The Tribune*, September 25, 1945.
[36] *The Free Press Journal*, September 04, 1945.
[37] Ibid.

*****

To damage the Khaksar Tehreek and to further injure the relationship between the AIML and Khaksars, anti-Khaksar elements published statements against Jinnah in the name of Mashraqi; this was not the first time this had happened, and this was not something that was particularly unusual or difficult to do.[38]

On September 24, 1945, Quaid-e-Azam issued a statement:

> "My attention has been drawn to some reports of the speeches made by Mr. Mazhar Ali Azhar and Mr. Mashriqui [Allama Mashraqi] published in some of the Hindu papers on September 17 and 18 respectively. It is not only painful and regrettable that they have stooped to such a low depth of meanness in as much as they are directed to show that I am not a Mussalman but the allegation made by them in their speeches against me and my private life are issues of falsehood.
>
> It seems that they had no other argument the creed policy and programme of the Muslim League and our stand for which we are carrying on the struggle but to resort to this mean practice in spreading this falsehood regarding me with a view to excite fanaticism and passions of some Mussalmans. I am sure that no Mussalman who has even a grain of common sense would believe in so vile speeches and false allegations against me which are sought to be broadcast in the Hindu press."[39]

Quaid-e-Azam's statement shocked people. Ever since the bogus attack on Jinnah in 1943, this campaign in the press had been part of continued efforts to oust Mashraqi from politics. It was disturbing to note that any chances of a relationship between the AIML and Khaksar Tehreek were torpedoed by the AIML; the anti-Muslim forces were bound to feel happy at this. In response to Jinnah's statement, on September 26, 1945, Mashraqi clarified his position in a statement:

> "I have seen the statement of Mr. Jinnah of September 24 [1945], issued from Quetta, today in which he virulently attacks me and another gentleman, attributing to me baseless things and using almost obscene language. My speeches everywhere are written and Mr. Jinnah will not find a word of personal attack on him. I am not responsible for what the press has written against him in my name. But if Mr. Jinnah wants to secure the sympathy of the public for himself by using such vile language, not fit for a gentleman, he may rest assured that the Mussalman public is not with him and wants to do away with all the rubbish he created around himself.
>
> I have already told Mr. Jinnah our one condition of joining the Muslim League, and we are not going to have any more humbug from him about his leadership of the Mussalmans. My speeches

---

[38] Such propaganda did not only happen during the election campaign. Concocted stories and twisting of words, to damage Khaksar reputation in the eyes of the public, was common.
[39] *The Tribune*, September 25, 1945.

strictly confine themselves to the unrepresentative character, the tyrannies and the hypocracies of the Muslim League as at present constituted, and we shall not allow that the word Muslim be exploited by the so-called Muslim Leaguers at any rate in the coming elections.

Ninety-nine per cent of the Mussalmans are groaning under the tyranny of Mr. Jinnah's self-made leadership and the way in which he justifies the Muslim League to be the sole representative of the Mussalmans is most shameful and preposterous. After we have cleared the Muslim League of these elements the Mussalmans will heave a sigh of relief and then alone the Muslim League will represent the Mussalmans. It is until now only a clique of Khan Bahadurs and Nawabs."[40]

It cannot be ruled out that the statement against Quaid-e-Azam in the name of Mashraqi was published by pro-Leaguers themselves, because false statements in the press were published to damage the Khaksar Tehreek. Such tactics, used to undermine political opponents, are nothing knew in dirty politics. Even today, with just a few thousand rupees anyone can get things published in many countries. From Jinnah's statement (of September 24, 1945), it appears that he wanted to take advantage of what was published. If he had read something in the paper against him, he could have sent a copy of the statement to Mashraqi or the Khaksar headquarters seeking clarification. He should have known that it did not take much to get such statements published. But according to the Khaksar circle, he wanted to make Mashraqi look bad in the eyes of public in order to gain political benefit.

*****

Despite all this, the Khaksar Tehreek continued its activities. On October 03, 1945, the Khaksar headquarters decided to form a Parliamentary Board in Bengal,[41] as part of their election campaign.

As explained previously in this work, Mashraqi sought unity with the AIML. Hence, Mashraqi again tried to seek Jinnah's cooperation, and on October 06, 1945, he sent Jinnah a copy of the Khaksar *Constitution of Free India* for his review.[42] This should have been taken by Quaid-e-Azam as a positive gesture. It was an opportunity for him to reciprocate, yet Quaid-e-Azam never came forward and did not even comment on the constitution. He made no attempt to support the constitution, despite the fact that it fully protected the rights of the Muslims. If Jinnah disagreed with any clause, he could have sent his suggestions to Mashraqi. However, Jinnah did not want any constitution to be discussed, as he was focused on his idea of Pakistan; this was evident from his statement of December 10, 1945:

"The British Government are putting the cart before the horse in proposing an All-India Constitution-making Body before a settlement

---

[40] *The Tribune*, September 27, 1945.

on the Pakistan issue. First we must get agreement on Pakistan. Then and only then, can we proceed to the next step."[43]

Quaid-e-Azam wanted nothing but the division of India so no efforts were put forth to seek reconciliation with the Khaksar Tehreek or any other party that sought unity of India. With this attitude, under which no united India was sought, a compromise between Jinnah and nationalists was not possible. Therefore, no study on the Khaksar Constitution was made by the AIML. The question is why could the rights of Muslims and non-Muslims not be protected through a constitution? Why did the AIML not make serious attempts to preserve India?[44]

*****

On October 07, 1945, the first meeting of the U.P. Nationalist Muslim Conference, representing the Khaksars, Muslim Majlis, Jamiat-ul-ulema Hind, Ahrars and Momin Conference, was held. According to the newspaper, about 200 delegates attended the meeting.[45] Participation in elections and other matters related to election difficulties were discussed by the delegates.

On October 07, 1945, Sheikh Hissamuddin, President of the Ahrar Party, said:

> "Pakistan was merely an election stunt of the Muslim League. Pakistan is nothing short of a fraud...which is being played upon credulous Muslims in the abnormal conditions created by the war and through direct and indirect help and encouragement by the British bureaucracy in India and the diehards in England.
> ...League wants self-determination for Muslims where they are in a majority. The question naturally arises whether this right of self-determination should be reserved only for Muslims or for the other communities too wherever they are in a minority. If so, what will happen in the Punjab? How many units will be created here? For the Muslims usually reside in a majority beyond Gujranwala district, upwards to the north and the north-west. In the Eastern Punjab the Jats are sure to claim a separate unit for themselves. Similarly the Sikhs would claim the Central Punjab. What will be left of the Punjab then? And what hope of progress will be left for Muslims? And what hope will be left for Mr. Jinnah and his Muslim Leaguers to assure the Muslims of a Pakistan, that they are promising? Why is the Muslim League silent and does not even explain its Pakistan schemes? For it knows that it cannot stand honest criticism and the post mortem that are sure to follow."[46]

---

[41] *The Tribune*, October 05, 1945.
[42] Zaman 1987, P. 186. *Al-Islah*, Edition No. 7 Vol. No. 37. June 24-July 01, 1997. P. 66.
[43] *The Tribune*, March 22, 1946.
[44] The constitution was also sent to Gandhi and Congress leaders. Another unbiased study is required as to why they did not accept the constitution.
[45] *The Free Press Journal*, October 09, 1945.
[46] Ibid.

Besides Mashraqi, others too were pointing out these factors, yet the All-India Muslim League maintained its policy of communalism and kept demanding partition. This was an extremely important statement made by Hissamuddin. Whenever a demand is put forth, it must be thoroughly investigated; however, the AIML seemed to have lacked acumen into India's problems. How could they not realize that their demand would set a precedent for various groups to claim self-determination?[47] The other important point is that, even into year 1945, people were unaware of the Pakistan scheme. Clearly the AIML kept people in the dark about the idea of Pakistan.

On October 13, 1945, Mashraqi addressed the public in New Delhi. According to the newspaper,

> "Mashriqi...described the political parties of India, including the Congress and the Muslim League, as being obstacles in the way of Indian independence. He said that Congress was a group of Caste Hindus while Muslim League represented the toadies.
>
> Referring to the coming elections, Allama Mashriqi said that they will decide the fate of the country for several centuries. If the dishonest caders of the various political parties succeeded in the elections, then Allama Mashriqi feared that they would perpetuate the worst crimes history had known. He said that while the various political parties of India had no programme of their own, Khaksars had prepared a constitution of India which is just and right."[48]

*****

The AIML turned a deaf ear to these warnings and continued with its disruptive policy and actions; this was constantly reported in the media.

On October 07, 1945, while Mashraqi was explaining the salient features of *The Constitution of Free India* to the public at Aitchison Park in Amritsar, Muslim League *goondas* attacked Khaksars and members of the public with *lathis*. They rushed to the stage and smashed a number of tables and chairs.[49] They also attempted to attack Mashraqi, however, he was protected by Khaksars. Many other Khaksars and members of the public at this meeting received serious injuries. *The Tribune* (of October 09, 1945) wrote, "Leaguers created rowdyism three or four times."

In an interview to the press on October 08, 1945, Mashraqi talked of the hostile actions of the Muslim Leaguers and stated:

> "The Muslim League seems to be employing gangs of vagabonds everywhere in order to make noise and create disturbance in our

---

[47] This is exactly what happened in the division of Punjab and Bengal.
[48] *The Free Press Journal*, October 16, 1945.
[49] *The Civil & Military Gazette*, October 10, 1945. *The Tribune*, October 09, 1945.

meetings and as they follow exactly the same technique everywhere, it is evident that the whole thing is pre-planned."[50]

On October 09, 1945, over 100,000 people gathered for Mashraqi's speech at Delhi Jamia. While he was explaining what the Khaksar Constitution was all about, gangsters arrived and created much pandemonium, commotion and uproar.[51]

Again on October 12, 1945, while Allama Mashraqi was addressing Khaksars and the public in front of Jumma Masjid in New Delhi, Muslim Leaguers indulged in disruption and tumultuous activities. They smashed bulbs and threw stones at the stage. They raised slogans against the Khaksar Tehreek and its constitution. Anti-Khaksar press took advantage of the situation and heavily wrote against the Khaksars. They made noise so that Mashraqi could not be heard.

In Lucknow on October 16, 1945, two thousand pro-League students from Aligarh University attacked Khaksars with hockey sticks, *lathis* and knives.

> The Khaksars "were making preparations for a public meeting to be addressed by Allama Mashriqui...
> Before the arrival of the Khaksar leader [Mashraqi] at the meeting place, the students smashed gas lights, tore away the tents and roughly handled the Khaksars, who received severe injuries. The Khaksars who were unarmed, remained peaceful throughout."[52]

At this event, Khaksars asked pro-Khaksar students at the Aligarh University not to retaliate. Instead of fighting back with Leaguers, Khaksars shifted the venue from Aligarh University to Jumma Masjid. Mashraqi addressed a large crowd. In this way, the Khaksars averted a potentially dangerous situation and bloodshed of Muslims. On October 18, 1945, the Vice Chancellor of Aligarh University apologized to Allama Mashraqi for the assault (on October 16, 1945) by university students that injured a number of Khaksars as they were preparing for a public address by Allama Mashraqi.[53]

The Leaguers were extremely nervous and had resorted to completely bizarre, wild and outrageous tactics. Thus attacks on the Khaksars and their public meetings continued. Nothing deterred Mashraqi and the Khaksars, however, and they continued in extensive campaigning and to building consensus amongst the public. On October 20, 1945, Mashraqi met with Khaksar leaders in Calcutta. He discussed matters pertaining to the forthcoming election. Professor Humayun Kabir and Shamsuddin Ahmad of the Krishak Proja Party

[50] *The Tribune*, October 11, 1945.
[51] Zaman 1987, Pp. 193-195.
[52] *The Tribune*, October 18, 1945.
[53] *The Tribune*, October 22, 1945. *The Free Press Journal*, October 18, 1945.
See more disruption activities in Appendix II.

also met Mashraqi to discuss the Khaksar Constitution; N.R. Sarkar (former Commerce Member, Government of India) also visited Mashraqi.[54]

On October 21, 1945, Muslim Leaguers in Calcutta again interrupted a Khaksar public meeting that was addressed by Mashraqi. On October 22, 1945, Mashraqi complained about the troublemaking crowd of Leaguers at his meeting on the previous day. Mashraqi warned Quaid-e-Azam and raised his voice that hiring gangs to shout slogans must be stopped. Before leaving for Patna, Allama Mashraqi deplored police's favoritism. He said "I feel shame in describing it."[55]

In Lucknow on October 22, 1945,

> "Muslim Leaguers, who had hitherto carried on unmolested the disgusting task of stifling the voice of Nationalist Muslims will no more enjoy their unpleasant monopoly.
> Speaking to a crowded meeting of Lucknow citizens, Mr. Abdussamad Sirujuddin Hakimullah, commander of the Bombay Presidency Khaksar Organisation, delivered a stern warning that the Leaguers would be playing with fire if they tried any further to disrupt by violence any Khaksar meeting and that 'if they do it again only one Organisation will remain on earth—either the Khaksars or the League.'
> OUTRAGES
> There was nothing, the Speaker said, the Muslim Leaguers did not do to undermine the prestige of the Khaksar Organisation in the country. Khaksar students had their legitimate scholarships terminated; they were beaten in mosques; their meetings were being raided by League members and agents who did not fight shy of stooping to naked goondaism.
> PARTY OF IDLE RICH
> Mr. Hakimullah described the Muslim League as an organisation of the idle rich, who were unprepared and unwilling to allow the poor to have their due share of the administration of the country.
> The Speaker concluded with an impassioned appeal to the Mussalmans of the country to vote only to the Nationalist Muslim candidates who, he said, on return would give battle royal to the Britishers for wresting national freedom."[56]

In Cawnpore on October 22, 1945, 10,000 people were present at a public meeting on parade grounds organized by the Khaksars. Abdul Samad Sirajhuddin Muslim of Madras Khaksar organization appealed for Muslim-Hindu unity. Leaguers arrived and attempted to stop the speech. Khaksars asked them not to disturb the meeting and requested them to leave. Their

[54] *The Tribune*, October 22, 1945.
[55] *The Free Press Journal*, October 24, 1945.
[56] Ibid.

appeals failed and a clash took place in which many people were hurt and one person died. Over 100 Khaksars were arrested on charges of rioting.[57]

On October 29, 1945, Jinnah issued a press statement asking Muslims not to attend meetings of the Khaksar Tehreek. Thus another bombshell was dropped on Muslim unity.[58] Jinnah was making every endeavor to oust Mashraqi from politics without realizing that at the end of the day Muslims would suffer. He was seeking his short term goal on the support of the British. Obviously, if the British did not want this, one warning to the AIML would have been enough to stop the disruptive activities. This strategy benefited all anti-Khaksar elements but damaged the Muslim cause. British support for the AIML is also evident from the fact that during the election period, many Khaksars were arrested, while Leaguers were not subjected to this treatment.[59]

On December 18, 1945, Muslim Leaguers again arrived at the Khaksars' public address at Rambagh and started shouting slogans in support of Muslim Leaguers. "The Allama advised the Khaksar volunteers to remain in their seats and nothing untoward occurred."[60] If Mashraqi had sent a signal to the Khaksars to react, there would have been a massacre of people.

On the same day, Allama Mashraqi addressed another public congregation organized by the Karachi Municipal Corporation. During his speech, Mashraqi called for unity between the Congress and the Muslim League.[61] The fact that Mashraqi still sought unity with these parties speaks of his character and sincerity to the cause.

In the days leading up to the elections, the Khaksars continued their campaign, while the Leaguer *goondas* and anti-Khaksar elements continued to put forth efforts to defame the Khaksars.

*****

Finally, election day arrived. When the results were announced, the AIML secured all 30 seats in the Central Legislative Assembly that were reserved for Muslims. In February 1946's provincial election, the Muslim League took 440 out of 495 seats reserved for Muslims.[62]

The AIML did not capture these seats on its own strength. The rulers converted the League's defeat in the 1937 elections into a great victory in this

---

[57] *The Free Press Journal*, October 24, 1945.

[58] Mujahid, P. 112

[59] For instance, in 1946, 300 Khaksars, who came from Punjab to Sind in connection with Sind Assembly elections, "were taken to an unknown destination in military lorries by a special police force headed by" D.V. Barty (District Magistrate). (*Dawn*, December 16, 1946. *The Tribune*, December 13, 1946. *The Star of India*, December 13, 1946.)

[60] *Dawn*, December 20, 1945.

[61] Ibid.

[62] *Government of Pakistan information web site*. (3).

election. If the rulers had pulled their crutches out from underneath the League, the AIML would have fallen on its face.

The British and the AIML breathed a sigh of relief at their win. It was necessary for the British to ensure the AIML's victory. With the AIML's win, the British were relieved, not in sympathy for the Muslims, but because they had secured Muslims in their back-pocket. To the world, the AIML was now the true representative of the Muslims.

Why did the Khaksar Tehreek not succeed in the elections? With the recognition of the AIML by the Government to represent Muslims, interference of Government officials, and encouragement to disrupt Khaksar public meetings, Muslims had no choice but to vote for the AIML. In short, the Leaguers were given all the support to win the elections and the AIML left no stone unturned to remove the Khaksar Tehreek from politics. Every conceivable method was applied to seek the Khaksar Tehreek's failure in the 1945-1946 elections; in fact all energies were exhausted to ensure that they did not even win one seat! Under the circumstances, there was no possibility of the Khaksars getting elected and opportunity to implement the Khaksar Constitution was now closed; instead, the doors to implement the British agenda were now wide open.

Allama Mashraqi and Maulana Abul Kalam Azad showed disappointment over the bureaucracy's intervention in the elections in support of the AIML. Raja Ghazanfar Ali Khan (Parliamentary Secretary to the Punjab Government in 1937-44 and, thereafter, Member of the Interim Government during 1946-47) denied this.[63] But does his denial make a difference? The Khaksar Tehreek was sabotaged and despite support from millions, there was no possibility of Khaksar candidates winning elections. It is well known in that part of the world that bureaucracy can change election results.

*****

With this win, the Leaguers' heads became swollen. Even after the elections, their hostility toward the Khaksar Tehreek continued. *Goondas* of the AIML kept up their troublemaking activities in Khaksar public meetings. They physically hurt the Khaksars and the public who came to listen to Mashraqi. Slogans against Mashraqi or the Khaksar Constitution were also raised on purpose. It was regretted that these tactics had become habitual for the AIML. This hostile and antagonistic behavior of League was considered to be hateful and childish by nationalists, Khaksars and their supporters.

On December 18, 1945, Dr. M.A. Latif Yezdani, a nationalist, said:

> "To liberate man, to elevate man, to educate man and to humanize man was the sole mission of the Muslims in the past and it is great

---

[63] *The Eastern Times*, April 11, 1946.

pity that hostile demonstrations, hooliganism, and fanaticism seem to be the share of the Indian Muslims under the leadership of Mr. M. A. Jinnah. The Muslim League is seeking honours and gifts of 'Pakistan' from those foreigners whose collar of slavery they wear on their necks...

Let it be known to such Muslims... 'Help one another in goodness and piety and do not help one another in sin and aggression' (Quran V 2). The Holy Prophet warns... 'I am not sent as a curse to mankind but as a blessing into humanity' (Muslims and non-Muslims alike). For the God in Islam is not only for Muslims, but for all mankind."[64]

In spite of the regrettable and sad behavior of the AIML, Mashraqi rose above these actions against him, and on January 13, 1946, he went to Jinnah's public meeting in Lahore to declare his solidarity with the AIML. Mashraqi took this step to go and speak publicly on unity with the Muslim League and to clarify in front of the public that the propaganda against him and the Tehreek was false and politically motivated. However, Quaid-e-Azam prevented Mashraqi from making a speech. Within minutes, Jinnah left the gathering; according to Khaksars, this was to avoid embarrassment over Mashraqi publicly seeking unity. Soon after Jinnah left, hooligans of the Muslim League attacked Mashraqi and knocked him unconscious.

On February 22, 1946, Mashraqi was addressing another gathering of 50,000 people in Bankipur (Patna)[65] and pleaded unity. Again, the Leaguers tried to disrupt this.

On March 20, 1946, *The Tribune*, Lahore reported:

"...Fazl-ul-Huq [former Premier of Bengal and Leader of the Opposition in the last Bengal Legislative Assembly] says: 'On the 16th [March 16, 1946] League hooligans fell upon peaceful Khaksars drinking tender coconuts at noon at Kadamtola, police station Backergang. Enquires now reveal that a murderous assault was made on the Khaksars, and that attack included sacrilegious handling of the holy Quran in the possession of the Khaksars...Six Khaksars, who received serious wounds, were removed to the local emergency hospital. The condition of two is precarious. Missing victims include...one Khaksar.'"

Referring to the tragic attack on Mashraqi on January 13, 1946, Mashraqi complained with dignity, without taking any revenge or filing a law suit. On March 23, 1946, he referred to

"the treatment meted out to me by thousands of hooligans after you [Jinnah] hurriedly left the meeting of January last when I arrived in

---

[64] *The Free Press Journal*, December 20, 1945.
[65] Zaman 1987, P. 305.

order to do my utmost for the purpose of creating unity among the Musalmans."[66]

Jinnah did not condemn the attack or even extend any apology to Mashraqi as a courtesy. On the other hand, Mashraqi further stated:

> "I have not the slightest ill-feeling against you or the Muslim League that you have created."[67]

Mashraqi also informed Jinnah that the Muslims suggested that all political parties in India should join hands for seeking freedom and he invited Jinnah for the same purpose. He assured Quaid-e-Azam that if he agreed to join hands, they could move mountains.

Mashraqi's gesture showed that, despite what was going on, he overlooked the AIML's behavior and still continued efforts for brotherhood and unanimity. The AIML campaign's against Khaksars was misleading and the public was not aware of everything Mashraqi was doing for an accord. Pro-Leaguer media twisted the facts and wrote that Allama Mashraqi came to the meeting of January 13, 1946 to throw Jinnah out of Lahore. This was a ridiculous and concocted story! It was also reported in the press that Unionists were using the Khaksars. But if anyone was using anyone, why didn't Quaid-e-Azam talk to Mashraqi directly to find out the reality? Quaid-e-Azam avoided every possible opportunity for unity. To place blame on others was the easiest tactic for the Muslim Leaguers to divert the attention from themselves.

*****

It is a tragedy that the *Khaksar Constitution of Free India* could not be implemented. This document may have been the closest to one that would resolve differences and look out in the interests of the majority of the people. Mashraqi's efforts were well-recognized and appreciated by the learned Khaksar Constitution committee which stated:

> "Allama Mashriqi was no doubt to be congratulated on the unique work of incomparable excellence and acumen that was being produced under his direction."[68]

A victory for the Khaksars and the Khaksar Constitution could have prevented the division of India and safeguarded the honorable position and rights of all communities.

---

[66] Hussain, P. 221. Also see Zaman 1987, P. 203.
[67] Ibid.
[68] *The Constitution of Free India 1946 A.C.*, P. 48.

See Appendix VI for "Outline of the Agreed Khaksar Constitution."

Chapter 9

Towards Freedom

The British Prime Minister Attlee announced in February 1946 that a British delegation would visit British India to discuss the future of the country. Among many leaders, this was viewed as another political game of the British, as they had been sending delegations but without any firm commitment to leave India. The Khaksar Constitution which provided a solution for British India had already been presented to the British. Yet, nothing came of this. Under these circumstances, how could any Indian think that the British were serious in leaving India?

The British had already ensured the AIML's success in the elections and now they were in a position to use the AIML in order to do as they pleased with India, while telling the world that these were the wishes of the elected party. Mashraqi and the Khaksars knew of the dirty politics that the British and the AIML were already party to. Hence, Mashraqi realized that the only option left was to make another attempt at unity and to amalgamate all Muslim parties together and form a final joint strategy. Hence, Mashraqi tried exactly this and attempted to bring all parties, including the Khaksar Tehreek, under the one flag of the All-India Azad Muslim League to overthrow the British Government. *The Deccan Times*, Madras of March 17, 1946 reported that Allama Mashraqi suggested to Muslim leaders that all Muslim parties, including the Khaksar Tehreek, be amalgamated into the All-India Azad Muslim League. He wrote to various Muslim leaders, including Quaid-e-Azam, A.K. Fazl-ul-Haq, Prof. Humayun Kabir, Malik Khizar Hayat Tiwana, Hussainbhai Lljee, Hussain Muhammad Madni, Maulana Nazar Asar, etc. On March 23, 1946, Mashraqi sent Jinnah a copy of the letter that he had written to thirteen leaders of seven Muslim organizations.[1] Mashraqi also sent an invitation to Quaid-e-Azam[2] to attend the conference of the Muslim political parties in India (to be held on April 07-08, 1946). Mashraqi also invited Gandhi to attend the conference, as he knew that Gandhi was very influential among Hindus and his support would be valuable to the overall cause. Inviting

---

[1] Hussain, P. 221.
[2] Zaman 1992, P. 70.

Gandhi was also meant to show that Muslims were not trying to join together to form a front against Hindus. According to *The Free Press Journal*, Mashraqi wrote,

> "Should you [Jinnah and Gandhi] join us we may be able to tide over the mountains of obstruction that are lying in the way of freedom."[3]

The Free Press Journal of April 03, 1946 wrote:

> "Defining the attitude of the Azad Muslim League towards Pakistan, the Allama [Mashraqi] says if we ever amalgamate ourselves into Azad Muslim League, we shall stand for Azad Pakistan." [4]

However, Liaquat Ali Khan suggested that instead of creating the All-India Azad Muslim League, Allama Mashraqi should join the Muslim League and also bring other parties under the Muslim League flag. One can well imagine why the AIML did not support the idea of the All-Azad Muslim League.

*****

On March 23, 1946, the Cabinet Mission arrived in Karachi for settlement of the Indian constitutional issue. The Cabinet Mission comprised of three cabinet ministers namely, Pethick-Lawrence (Secretary of State), Sir Stafford Cripps and A.V. Alexander. The Mission was to hold discussion with elected representatives of British India and the Indian states.

The task of the Cabinet Mission was to:

❖ Get agreement from the elected parties on a method for framing the constitution
❖ Set up a constitution body and an Executive Council

The Cabinet Mission began conducting negotiations with the AIML and Congress leaders and again excluded other parties. Obviously, it was questionable as to why they did not consider the opinion of people who supported the Khaksars and other parties in India? The British attitude was considered biased and created a feeling that justice was not being done. Why would only these two parties be invited to talks? This was a legitimate concern on the part of all others.

On March 28, 1946, a meeting was held between Wavell and the Cabinet Mission. It was discussed whether this delegation should meet "further representatives of communities."[5] They made a decision to see landholders;

---

[3] *The Free Press Journal*, April 03, 1946.
[4] It is important to note that Mashraqi's idea of Azad Pakistan was different from AIML's idea of Pakistan.
[5] Record of Meeting of Cabinet Delegation and Field Marshal Viscount Wavell on March 28, 1946 found in Mansergh 1977, Pp. 28-29.

they also decided that two Ministers would meet representatives but that these discussions would be kept "on a less formal basis" to "allay discontent."[6] They decided not to seek the opinion of the Khaksars and not to conduct meetings with other Muslim parties, out of which the most important was the Khaksar Tehreek. The parties they agreed to meet were:

❖ The Radical Democratic Party
❖ All-India Liberal Federation
❖ All-India Hindu Mahasabha
❖ All-India Muslim Majlis
❖ South India Liberation Federation (Justice Party)
❖ Communist Party
❖ Parsees[7]

The All-India Muslim Majlis party (apart from AIML) was probably invited to illustrate to the world that Muslims were being represented. However, an incredibly important party, the Khaksar Tehreek, was neglected. Was this the correct attitude of the British and shouldn't the AIML have protested to invite all Muslim groups or at least seek their opinion?

While the British were holding discussions with their recognized parties, Muslim organizations held a meeting, sponsored by Mashraqi, in Delhi from April 07-08, 1946. Delegates of various parties attended. However, those who were against Muslim unity sabotaged the meeting. The AIML did not even participate in the conference sponsored by the Khaksars to avoid British anger. Anti-Muslim forces wanted the Muslim League to stay away from the Khaksars and that is exactly what they did. It was viewed that Gandhi followed suit and avoided attending the meeting so as not to earn the bad-will of the British.

In the meantime, the Cabinet Mission continued discussion with their favorite leaders in the AIML and Congress. A series of conferences were held, however agreement between the AIML and Congress could not be reached. Disagreements are the results of stubborn attitude and when one is not willing to settle. To the world, these Indian leaders had political issues that seemed to be unsolvable. But anyone would understand that unless there were sabotaging forces at play, there was no reason an agreement could not be reached. It seemed that these Indian leaders were not serious and were victims of British intrigues to not allow any settlement.

*****

Upon failure to settle, on May 16, 1946, the Cripps Mission announced its own plan. Given these failures, anyone would know that freedom was not

---

[6] Record of Meeting of Cabinet Delegation and Field Marshal Viscount Wavell on March 28, 1946 found in Mansergh 1977, Pp. 28-29.
[7] Ibid.

forthcoming. Mashraqi asked the AIML to forget about the constitutional and pacifist fight and demand Pakistan in the battle field. Thus, on May 22, 1946,[8] Allama Mashraqi stated that the Khaksars were going to fight for Pakistan and made an unconditional offer of the Khaksars to Quaid-e-Azam in the following press statement:

> "If Mr. Jinnah is perfectly sincere about Pakistan I offer once more the services of the Khaksar organisation to him unconditionally and am ready to join hands with him in this effort. I can assure him that there is no dishonesty about my offer provided Muslim League is ready to make full sacrifices.
>
> If Mr. Jinnah agrees I shall throw the whole force into the matter unstintedly and every Khaksar will be ready to lay down his life for the cause of the country.
>
> ...To begin with, I propose to issue orders to Khaksars all over India to observe vigorously from June 9 to June 16 a mourning week in honour of Pakistan which has been buried alive by the British so ruthlessly. I shall await Mr. Jinnah's reaction and then start."[9]

It is important to note that all along Mashraqi's idea of Pakistan was different from AIML's idea of Pakistan. However, he was willing to cooperate with Jinnah as long as freedom was achieved.

This offer did not move Quaid-e-Azam at all, and he, as usual and on purpose, remained quiet. Quaid-e-Azam did not want to seek British infuriation, and he was also against fighting for Pakistan in the battle field. It is important to note, Jinnah did not issue any statement to support Khaksars, but all along he used Mashraqi's statements to impress upon the British that they could not ignore public aspiration of freedom.

On May 28, 1946, Mashraqi sent another telegram to Jinnah offering full support for attaining Pakistan. According to Mashraqi:

> "Reference my Press statement twenty second unequivocal cooperation Muslim League attainment of Pakistan also celebration ninth sixtenth June mourning week. Please wire cooperation concurrence."[10]

Yet Quaid-e-Azam remained quiet. It is important to note that all along these press statements and telegrams were in the knowledge of the British. Obviously these were not going unnoticed, and the British knew what the public was thinking. They understood that Mashraqi was a man of strong conviction and there was no way that he would allow foreign rule to continue existing in India forever; despite monitoring of his activities, Mashraqi would take the first available opportunity to end British rule. Even if the British did

---

[8] *The Star of India*, May 23, 1946.
[9] *The Free Press Journal*, May 24, 1946. Also see *The Star of India*, May 23, 1946.
[10] Yousaf 2004, P. 300.

not know what Mashraqi's mind was, his statements would have made it downright and utterly clear.

On June 06, 1946, Allama Mashraqi issued another press statement:

> "The Khaksars are prepared to sacrifice blood and undergo any amount of hardship provided Mr. Jinnah is earnest about his mission of Pakistan. But his continued silence in not acknowledging my offer proves that Mr. Jinnah is not at all sincere about Pakistan...
>
> Although I have postponed orders for a mourning week for Pakistan from June 9 to June 16 my unconditional offer to place the entire services of the Khaksar organisation for attaining Pakistan still stands."[11]

In June of 1946, Mashraqi called the Azad Hind Fauj Conference at Khaksar *Idara-i-Aliya* (the Khaksar Tehreek's headquarters) in Lahore. This was called within a few months of the mutiny at the Bombay Naval Headquarters (on February 18, 1946), about which Mashraqi was contacted from the strikers via a letter dated March 08, 1946.[12] Khaksars from all over India as well as Khaksar supporters in the defense services[13] and devotees in other organizations participated in the conference. The conference was another attempt to end foreign rule and convey to the British that the Khaksars were determined to overthrow British rule. These efforts, though they have not been highlighted by historians, never went unnoticed by the authorities right up to the Prime Minister of Great Britain. Obviously each Khaksar activity or speech by Mashraqi, that was held since he entered politics, was not only keeping the public focused on independence but sent a clear signal to the British that their rule must come to an end.

The Azad Hind Fauj Conference and Mashraqi's statement (of June 06, 1946) sent a direct word of warning and ultimatum for the British to pack up. There was no reason for Jinnah to remain quiet when Mashraqi had made open and public pronouncements through the press. Mashraqi had done just the right thing; the British had to be told what the Khaksars' *bent of mind* was. If they had not known what the Khaksars and public were thinking, they would certainly not have quit India through only drawing room politics and mere passive and peaceful protests. Is there any example in history of obtaining freedom through drawing room politics? Someone has to lay blood on the street to convey the message of seeking freedom. The Khaksars did exactly what was required and their services cannot be denied. Can anyone deny that the Khaksars' blood on the streets of Lahore on March 19, 1940 did not tell the British what the Khaksar bent of mind was? Unquestionably! It was crystal clear to British.[14]

---

[11] *The Eastern Times,* June 09, 1946.
[12] Hussain, P. 222.
[13] Thousands of Khaksars were in the army. (ORCLAD, September 23, 1942.)
[14] Mashraqi made a number of public speeches outlining the hostile actions of the British against the Muslims. For instance, on June 10, 1946, Mashraqi spoke at a public meeting at Lahore. Syed Shabbir Hussain writes in *Al-Mashriqi: The Disowned Genius* that Mashraqi "traced the genesis of

Mashraqi's *unconditional* support for attaining Pakistan[15] did not move Jinnah to form an alliance with Mashraqi. Mashraqi was openly talking of attaining Pakistan and in his press statement on June 06, 1946 said that the Khaksars were "prepared to sacrifice blood and undergo any amount of hardship,"[16] yet Muslim Leaguers kept misinforming the public that Mashraqi was anti-Pakistan; this was a tragedy and misfortune for the Muslims and they paid the price in a truncated Pakistan in the next approximately one year. Mashraqi's public pronouncements are glaring proof that he was not against Pakistan, except his concept of Pakistan was different than that of AIML.

*****

On June 06, 1946, the AIML accepted the Cabinet Mission proposal. Around the same time, the Congress also accepted it. These two parties came to an understanding on the Cabinet Mission's proposal; however, once again, the agents of imperialism came in to disrupt any settlement. Hence, after spending almost three months in India, the Mission went back on June 29, 1946 with their task unfulfilled.[17]

Another reason for disagreement was that because of the communalism and hate that had been developing between these communities for the past six years, it had become difficult to work in harmony. The conflict of these communities suited the rulers, so they perpetuated it. To a political observer, these meetings between the AIML and Congress were more for political consumption than for any real agreement.

Based on historical analyses, one can easily say that these talks were only for the world to see that the British were doing their utmost to bring settlement between these parties. This is authenticated by Wavell's words in his own book:

> "Cripps and the other ministers thought that there ought to be a meeting between Jinnah and Nehru, not with any hope of agreement, but purely for publicity value, to show that we had our best to secure agreement."[18]

Commenting on the failure of the talks, Barrister Aftab Iqbal (son of Allama Iqbal) sent the following to Jawahar Lal Nehru on July 23, 1946 from Lahore:

---

the Western trade imperialism and how with the capture of India by the British, Islamic States all over the world started crumbling. To him the emergence of Indian Muslims as a supreme factor would lead to an upsurge of Islamic renaissance everywhere." (Hussain, Pp. 222-223)

    Without any fear, Mashraqi also expressed how the imperialist power exploited all types of Indian resources, from human to economic.

[15] Mashraqi's concept of Pakistan was not the same as the AIML's Pakistan.

[16] *The Eastern Times,* June 09, 1946.

[17] *Government of Pakistan's official web site.* (2).

[18] Khan, Khan Abdul Wali. Chapter 14.

"...The failures of the Congress-League attempts to solve the political problem of India under the paternal supervision and guidance of the British Government have caused me no disappointment. The proposals of the British Cabinet Mission never contemplated the independence of India but the creation of a British India composed of the Indian States and the Muslim State under the tutelage of Great Britain. No self-respecting and patriotic Indian or Indian Muslim can ever tolerate this arrangement. I do not feel pessimistic about the future of India. I do think that freedom is coming but it will not come until after the fields of India have become crimsoned with the blood of Indian martyrs. We know how the Americans won their independence. President Kruger said that he would sacrifice every man, woman and child for the freedom of South Africa, but England never gave way until she was choked with the bloody feast which the Boers had prepared for her. To Ireland freedom never came until blood began to flow out of every single Irish artery. In the face of these great facts of history it is not possible to conceive that India can attain her freedom by mere political conferences and Acts of Parliament. It would be an ideal thing if the League and the Congress put up a united front against British Imperialism and freed India from the curse of slavery, but if this is not possible the Congress alone must be prepared to achieve the country's freedom at any cost. I believe that when the psychological moment comes for the Congress to make its next great attempt to secure the freedom of India there will be many Muslims who will wish you well and many who will be prepared to lay down their lives for the achievement of that great and noble end."[19]

This statement echoes Mashraqi's statements. For a long time, the British had been playing games with the Indians and no one knew if freedom would really be granted. People who understood politics knew that, in order to achieve independence without division, real sacrifices would have to be made, even if that meant laying down lives.[20]

*****

After the Cabinet Mission left, Wavell moved another game. He invited the Congress to form an Interim Government and on August 08, 1946 the Congress accepted this.[21] This again proves that conflict between the two rivals was desired by the British. Another reason to invite Congress was the rulers' fear of possible "mass action" against them.[22]

---

[19] *The Tribune*, July 25, 1946.
[20] Some would claim that Jinnah attained independence without fighting the British on the battlefield and without sacrificing lives. But look what the British left behind at the end of the day — a truncated Pakistan with virtually no resources and a divided Muslim population.

Any lives that were lost were lost because of communalism promoted by the AIML, not in fighting a war against the British.
[21] *Government of Pakistan information web site*. (4).
[22] *Banglapedia web site*. (1).

Obviously an Interim Government of the Congress was intolerable to the AIML. To press their terms, the AIML declared August 16, 1946 to be "Direct Action" day. As a result of this, India's bloodiest conflict, since the mutiny nearly a century earlier, broke out between the Muslims and Hindus in Calcutta. Thousands of people were killed (estimated 10,000 killed) and injured, women were raped and kidnapped, and houses and villages were burnt. Muslims and non-Muslims slit each other's throats with anger and hate for one another.

Jinnah's call for nationwide "Direct Action" did not fit with his philosophy. His fight for Pakistan had always been based on constitutional means and drawing room politics. The question is who was actually sponsoring this change in policy? What makes this even more unusual is that at least 10,000 people died, yet neither Quaid-e-Azam nor any Muslim League leader was arrested.

Now that power seemed to be falling in the hands of the Congress, the AIML all of sudden realized that Khaksar help was needed. On August 30, 1946, Jinnah reverted to the Khaksars and asked publicly for their help. He asked them to join the League in the interest of Islam and Pakistan. He made this appeal to other parties too. When Mashraqi had asked the League for an all party alliance under the All-India Azad Muslim League, the League had not even bothered to attend the conference, in order to please the British. Now when they did not get their share in the power, they began pleading with the Khaksars to join them. This is clear evidence that the Leaguers were complete opportunists.

In reply to Jinnah's fervent appeal to Khaksars to join the AIML, on September 09, 1946, Allama Mashraqi wrote a letter to Quaid-e-Azam:

> "To tell you the truth I am convinced that consciously or unconsciously you and the Mussalmans are being used by the Britishers against the independence of India. I also do not believe in the satisfaction that Mr.Gandhi or Congress feels at their entry into the Interim Government.
>
> If therefore, you can convince me by your writing to me that you mean to achieve Pakistan as a part and parcel of the independence of the whole of India and will work with Mr. Gandhi on this clear basis against British plans. I shall throw the whole force of the Khaksar organisation with you and we shall die in thousands. I also undertake that the Hindus as well as the Congress will concede Pakistan if you clearly agree to wrest India from British hands. I shall in that case work willingly with you to the last ditch.
>
> In case you do not agree to work on this clear condition, please stop 'badnaming' the Khaksars by these fa'lse appeals any more as we have resolved to work out our own destiny alone. I shall await your reply with interest."[23]

---

[23] Yousaf 2004, P. 302. *The Star of India*, September 09, 1946.

Without mincing any words, Mashraqi made it clear to Quaid-e-Azam that Quaid-e-Azam was playing in the hands of the British. Mashraqi doubted Quaid-e-Azam's intentions and felt that he wanted to use the Khaksars again for his political ambition. With the way Jinnah was behaving, it was difficult for Mashraqi to believe Quaid-e-Azam's genuineness. Mashraqi's letter was open and clear. Meanwhile, secret agencies kept a close watch on what was going on between Mashraqi and Jinnah. Once again, Jinnah remained quiet on Mashraqi's offer.

The British disregarded the AIML's "Direct Action" call and the Congress nominees were sworn in on September 02, 1946 as members of the Viceroy's Executive Council.[24] Nehru became Prime Minister of India in the Interim Government.

The AIML had lost their importance and they highly resented being left out. They knew they would be arrested by Congress Executive Council. So to avoid arrest, they resorted to just observing "Black Day." As a protest, on September 02, 1946, black flags were hoisted by pro-Leaguers. In press interviews on September 04, 1946, Quaid-e-Azam blamed the Viceroy and Gandhi for communal tension. It is important to point out that despite "Black Day," neither Jinnah nor any Leaguer was arrested. If anyone else had gone against the wishes of the British, this would not be tolerated and they would be immediately put behind bars. To Khaksars, such special treatment was reserved for Quaid-e-Azam and the top notch Leaguers. It was also interesting that Quaid-e-Azam blamed the Viceroy and Gandhi for communal tension, whereas communalism was originated by the AIML with the passing of the Pakistan Resolution.

As result of communal tension, within a few days of observance of "Black Day," riots spread to Ahmedabad and Bombay on September 05, 1946. Riots continued and India headed towards civil war. Jinnah admitted on September 10, 1946 that 400 million people were heading towards civil war.

Who was responsible for communal disunity since 1940? Yet Leaguers were sitting free and none were in jail. In the eyes of the Khaksars, why did the Viceroy make an exception for Jinnah and did not arrest him or any Muslim Leaguer, when leaders of other Muslim and Hindu parties were arrested if they went against the wishes of the British. These genuine questions are totally ignored by pro-Leaguer historians. Why? They have turned "Direct Action" and observance of "Black Day" to portray Leaguers as freedom fighters.

*****

The Leaguers could not stay without power, so they started maneuvering to find a way to enter the Interim Government. In an interview on September 11,

---

[24] Mujahid, P. 122.

1946, Jinnah said that he had not refused to enter the Interim Government. Hectic efforts started and Leaguers held meetings with the Viceroy and Nehru to enter the Interim Government. The Viceroy also, most likely, wanted AIML's participation in the Interim Government so that he could show the world that the British were not biased and were working with the Muslims and non-Muslims. Further, the Viceroy did not want all policies to be created by the Congress. In short, it suited both the British and the AIML to have the League join the Interim Government. Finally, on October 14, 1946, the AIML sent names of League nominees (Liaquat Ali Khan, I. I. Chundrigar, Sardar Abdur Rab Nishtar, Ghazanfar Ali Khan and Jogandra Nath Mandal) for inclusion in the Interim Government. A question arises that why didn't the British just include the AIML in the Interim Government from the beginning? This was all part of British maneuvering.

The Leaguers were sworn in on October 26, 1946. They managed to enter the doors of power while ignoring all other Muslim parties including the Khaksar Tehreek.

The League did include one leader from the scheduled caste from Bengal (Jogandra Nath Mandal, provincial minister). Isn't it surprising and contradictory to AIML's policy to name a non-Muslim for the ministry? But this didn't matter as long as they could get hold of power. It is likely that they took Jogandra Nath Mandal in order to use his influence in Bengal and to show to the world that they were catering to other castes as well.

It must be noticed that that there was not a single person among these nominations who belonged to the middle or lower classes. Who was the League working for? When they needed help, they would go to the public or the Khaksars, yet when the time came for power sharing, they would become strangers. What does this imply? Their entire struggle was self serving. The AIML did not care for the happiness of all Muslims; their main focus had always been to take advantage and use them for their own ends. They wanted nothing but to establish their rule on all Muslims.

*****

Though the AIML got into the doors of power, the marriage with the Congress was not going to last long. Soon the political crisis started. When the Viceroy summoned the assembly on November, 20, 1946, Jinnah declared that the AIML would not attend it. Yet again the deadlock began. The bottom line was that the agents of imperialism were intent on ensuring that harmony failed and chaos was created.

On December 02, 1946, the British asked four Indian leaders to come to London: Jinnah, Nehru, Liaquat Ali Khan and Sardar Baldev Singh. The conference lasted for four days and Lord Wavell was also in attendance.

After the talks started, it did not seem that there would be any agreement. Until leaders realize who is behind these rifts and is causing damage to their community, these rifts can never be avoided.

On December 06, 1946, the Government announced failure of the London Conference.[25]

*****

Mashraqi had been losing patience with the worthless negotiations and pacifist methods; hence, he had no choice left, but to opt for a revolt. To him these negotiations would not bring any tangible result, leave alone freedom. He was fed up by maneuverings from the side of political leaders and the Government, which had been going on forever. Thus his eyes were set on a revolt; though this was not yet publicly announced, hectic efforts to this end had been underway for quite some time. Some of the moves that were made in 1946 included:

- ❖ Communication with forces seeking freedom:
    - o Holding of Azad Hind Fauj Conference at Khaksar headquarters in Lahore
    - o Liaison with all those who supported complete independence without any further delay
- ❖ Press Statements and other communication with Quaid-e-Azam
- ❖ Other activities:
    - o Meetings and communication with Khaksars
    - o Mobilization of Khaksars in defense forces
    - o Meetings between Major General S.D. Khan of the Indian National Army, Col. Ihsan Qadir and Mashraqi[26]

Another issue that needed careful planning was the prevention of civil war and slaughter of Muslims and non-Muslims. The feeling of hate between Muslims and Hindus had been ingrained since communalism was brought into politics in India. To prevent this disastrous conflict, on December 05, 1946, Mashraqi stated:

> "London talks may fail and civil war is being openly predicted. If not restricted or averted it may prove not only the doom of India's freedom but also India's doom. I, therefore, order every Khaksar in India whether active, passive, sympathizer or reserved to stand up alert from the moment this order reaches him and gird up his loins to

---

[25] Hussain, P. 224.
[26] In the Central Legislative Assembly Debates on September 23, 1942, Dr. Sir Zia ud Din Ahmad said 3,000 Khaksars were in the Indian Army and 50 of them were Officers. Major General S.D. Khan of the Indian National Army, Col. Ihsan Qadir (Hussain, P. 226) and other officers knew Mashraqi. On July 30, 1946, Major General S.D. Khan met with Mashraqi at Ichhra and they discussed ways to overthrow the British Government. Within a few days of this meeting, Major General S.D. Khan joined the Khaksar Tehreek.

stop this slaughter even at the cost of his life. I want every man, woman and child, old or young, Hindu or Muslim or non-Muslim who has the slightest sympathy with the Khaksar Movement to come forward, and stop this wholesale slaughter by offering his life and force of his character. All Khaksars in the remotest villages as well as all Khaksars in the cities and towns must leave all personal occupations and parade the streets with or without belchas as required by the local leaders and announced to all from today that there shall be no civil war at any cost. Every Khaksar will be ready to die if Hindus and Muslims begin to fight anywhere. All newspapers will be destroyed publicly if they publish news of Hindu-Muslim riots. Children should sing poems prompting Hindu Muslim unity. Muslim and Hindu Khaksars should march side by side with their belchas and should proclaim that they have worked for sixteen years together and stand as monuments of Hindu-Muslim unity. Congress and Muslim League should be equally denounced if denounced at all. My conviction is that only Khaksars can avert such a disaster in India."[27]

Mashraqi used such powerful statements and his message was well taken. In many cities of India, Khaksars in batches started daily parades with belchas. In this way, they sent a signal to the authorities to quit India otherwise Khaksars were ready to fight. This move increased the momentum of the freedom movement. The Khaksars' activities could not go unnoticed and pressure on the Government increased.

The authorities took preventive measures immediately. As a result, Khaksars were arrested. In Hyderabad (Sind) alone, approximately 300 Khaksars were reported in the press on December 11, 1946 to have been arrested under Section 144. Their belchas were confiscated.[28]

During the same time, Mashraqi, at Khaksar headquarters in Lahore, called a meeting of Khaksars from all over India to discuss the prevailing situation and further strategy. The Khaksars had no faith in AIML's ability to fight for freedom and the AIML's negotiations so far had brought no results; at the end of the day, everything ended in fiasco or breakdown. Mashraqi's letter to Quaid-e-Azam dated September 09, 1946 and his press statements did not move the AIML.

To cut it short, Khaksars relied on their own strength and influences. Mashraqi's hectic activity had obviously enhanced pressure on the Government and it did bring results. Though historians, on both sides of the border, have ignored this.

Three days prior to British Prime Minister Lord Clement Attlee's announcement about the transfer of power, on February 17, 1947, Dr. F.K. Abra, Chief of the Khaksar Organization in Bombay, was interviewed in Poona. He was in Poona in connection with a camp of Khaksar leaders from

---

[27] Hussain, Pp. 224-225.
[28] *The Tribune*, December 13, 1946. *Dawn*, December 14, 1946.

all over Bombay Presidency. *The Free Press Journal* of February 18, 1947 reported that:

> "Dr. Abra... stated that the policy adopted at present by the Muslim League would lead the Muslim masses nowhere. In fact, he said, it was suicidal.
>
> Over 125 Khaksar leaders from the Province are attending the camp. The object of this camp, said Dr. Abra, was to train the Khaksar officers to propagate Hindu-Muslim unity and communal harmony. Also it intended to train them up as to how to act during communal strifes. Dr. Abra also revealed that at a recent meeting of Khaksar leaders from over the country convened by their leader Allama Mashriqui at Lahore the question regarding the role to be adopted during such emergencies was discussed."

Although open rebellion had not yet been declared, such statements clearly illustrate that preparation was underway. And that is why guidelines were given to avoid bloodshed of Indians.

With Mashraqi's preparations, the British finally saw their power crumbling, and they could foresee a massive revolt in India in which massacre of British people was imminent. Time had run out for the British to play any more games. The stage for the transfer of power to Indians had been set, thus, came the announcement from the Prime Minister of Britain.

Those who think that India sought its freedom on the basis of constitutional fight or non-violence are ignoring the fact that behind this was major resistance to British rule. Khaksars' and others' strong resistance and their bent of mind of personal sacrifice made the British realize that they must leave India. If these forces did not exist, India probably would have never attained its freedom. Is there any example that exists in history where freedom is obtained by begging, non-violent means or mere constitutional fights?

Indeed, sixteen years of the Khaksar struggle were finally about to bear fruit!

Chapter 10

Break-up of British India

On February 20, 1947, the British Prime Minister, Lord Clement Attlee, announced that the British Government intended to transfer power to Indians not later than June of 1948. The main points of his statement were as follows:

"

1. The British Government declared their firm resolve to take necessary steps to transfer power to responsible hands by a date not later than June 1948.
2. The British Government recognised that there was no prospect of any constitution being agreed to by all parties in India in accordance with the Cabinet Mission Plan."[1]

The British had very reluctantly conceded to quit India. However, they were to hand over the Government to leaders of their own choice, who they thought would be suitable to work in line with their policies.

With Attlee's announcement, Mashraqi could foresee that an increase in massacre, looting, plunder, abduction and all sorts of miseries would befall upon the people. In his press statement on February 22, 1947, Allama Mashraqi stated that Attlee's announcement was a

> "signal for the start of a horrifying clash between the Hindus and the Muslims. I see massacre of at least one million people."[2] (translated from Urdu)

---

[1] DFPGP, P. 34.
[2] Hussain, P. 226. Malik, P. 216. *Al-Islah*, February 28, 1947.
This was another prediction of Mashraqi's that came true.

To prevent the holocaust and to create a united front among revolutionary forces, Mashraqi wrote (on February 25, 1947) to all important people including former members of the Indian National Army (INA) of Subhas Chandra Bose. His letter to all leaders stated:

> "We are in the midst of a perplexing situation. The British have promised India freedom by June, 1948. I do not see how it can come peacefully. Most probably it will result in chaos and self-destruction.
>
> I propose that at this moment a conference be held of all elements of India which are non-communal in any sense and want a real revolution and real transfer of power.
>
> It will be indeed good for India if leaders of these elements unite for a common purpose and work for it to the successful end of it. I, therefore, invite the leaders of all such parties to join in the deliberations of the conference to be held in Delhi on 4th to 6th April [1947] in order to come to the right decision. Col. Ihsan Qadir of the INA proposes to meet some of you personally in this connection. I am also sending Major General S.D. Khan with him to convince you about my intention in this respect. I feel that unless all are united at this critical moment nothing substantial is going to come out of the separate efforts of all such parties which believe in attaining their object by revolutionary methods etc."[3]

Meanwhile, Khaksar parades continued. This was to maintain pressure on the British that they must finally leave India and to keep the Khaksars ready to fight for freedom, in case the British delayed or withdrew the transfer of power. Khaksars were directed to parade in batches, and they conducted these exercises on streets in various cities. This alarmed the authorities, and they arrested many Khaksars. For example, a batch was marching in formation in Lahore in February 1947 and was arrested under Public Safety Ordinance.[4] However, arrests had no effect on Khaksars, and parades in various cities continued.

This was the most crucial time in the history of India. Mashraqi knew he needed to take action, given the speed with which events were unfolding. As a final plunge towards freedom of India, on March 01, 1947, Mashraqi directed 300,000 Khaksars to assemble in Delhi on June 30, 1947; if they failed to assemble, he would disband the movement. His plan was that Khaksars would takeover Delhi to announce independence and prevent the disintegration of India. According to the Khaksar circle, in the case that division was unavoidable, then the Khaksars would at least ensure Pakistan's boundaries to Delhi. This assembly of 300,000 Khaksars was also meant to ensure that Atlee's announcement on transfer of power was not denied under any pretext. Hectic efforts were launched for this purpose. Khaksars enthusiastically started preparing for the day that they had been waiting for, for so long.

---

[3] Hussain, Pp. 225-226.
[4] *The Tribune*, February 28, 1947.

*****

While the Khaksars were preparing for freedom, deadly communal riots erupted in Punjab in early March. The riots took an epidemic form and spread in the entire Punjab. They brought life to misery and havoc. Stabbing, loot, plunder and burning of houses and shops were seen all over the Punjab. Women and children were kidnapped, and young women were abducted and openly raped. Many women even jumped from the upper stories of their houses or into wells to save their honor. People were subjected to torture and humiliation, and insanity prevailed in many cities. An unprecedented storm of communal hate was witnessed. It seemed that a terrible and horrific catastrophe had befallen on the innocent masses of Muslims and non-Muslims. It is hard to paint the true picture of the horror and fear that took hold.

As usual in the hour of crisis, Khaksars were put on duty to protect people and provide relief and shelter. Mashraqi visited people and they narrated their stories. Many people also came to Mashraqi's house with the stories of their sufferings, and they were given shelter. The events that took place at the time of partition were disastrous, tragic and indeed disturbing. The horror stories saddened Mashraqi and on his directive, on March 07, 1947, a Khaksar delegation met Gandhi to discuss India's political situation and to coordinate protection of the lives of Muslims and non-Muslims. Khaksars asked Gandhi to visit affected areas with them. It seemed that the situation was out of anyone's control. The riots were the result of hate between Hindus and Muslims due to religious propaganda that had infected people's minds in the previous many years.

*****

While Punjab was burning and the massacre of people was underway, Wavell left for London on March 23, 1947. Lord Louis Mountbatten replaced Wavell and came to India as the last Viceroy. Replacement of Wavell with Mountbatten, at this crucial juncture, also raises some suspicion, as to why a special personality was being sent to India at this time.

Mashraqi was observing all political developments very closely. He arrived in Peshawar on March 30, 1947 to discuss the political situation with people in NWFP.[5] Mashraqi held meetings with Khaksar leaders and others. During his stay in Peshawar, Mashraqi talked about the communal situation, as well as political developments in Britain in regards to the future of India.

During this period, some mysterious and detrimental moves were made for the division of Bengal and Punjab.[6]

---

[5] *The Tribune*, April 01, 1947.
[6] *The Tribune*, April 09, 1947.

Mashraqi was distressed with the way things were building up and he was carrying on hectic activity and using every avenue to work toward freedom. He held meetings to implement his plan for which he had called 300,000 Khaksars to Delhi. *The Eastern Times* of April 11, 1947 reported that Mashraqi was arriving in Lucknow on April 14, 1947 with Major General Dost Mohammad Khan and Colonel Khan Qadir.

Obviously, now was not the time to sit back and watch the breaking up of India. Mashraqi's hands were already tied in view of the opposition from the AIML and the British. It is sad that the AIML and Congress were not cooperating with Mashraqi. It is even more distressing to note that the AIML was issuing flowery statements, but in actuality it was sleeping while the intrigues of dividing Punjab and Bengal were at work. They were not doing anything concrete to ensure that this did not happen. The future of 100 million was at stake; mere press statements or drawing room politics would not undo British plans.

*****

Another development took place, and on April 09, 1947, Gandhi announced the first Presidentship of India to Quaid-e-Azam. Gandhi said:

> "I shall be glad if Jinnah Sahib becomes the First President of the Indian Republic. But one condition must be fulfilled before that. The best men representing all communities in this country should be found to run the administration…
> I do not even to-day know what is really meant by Pakistan."[7]

Gandhi said the same thing that Mashraqi had been saying to Gandhi and Jinnah — to give representation to all communities. Was this a serious offer to save India from division? This requires a separate discussion.

One thing that is absolutely clear is that the AIML's successes were based on the demand for Pakistan, so Quaid-e-Azam could not accept this offer as it would require him to abandon his demand for partition. People were hoping to get the promise land and paradise that the AIML had pledged. Now for Jinnah to change position was out of his control. If he did this, his political career would have ended then and there and people would have reproached Quaid-e-Azam.

The demand for partition was actually sponsored by the British. If this was not true, then Quaid-e-Azam would definitely have been jailed upon making his demand for Pakistan. The British could not have implemented their agenda without using the AIML, as no foreign power can without use of the locals

---

[7] *The Tribune*, April 11, 1947.

(people from within the community); this is why none of the Muslim League leadership was ever jailed and was kept in the forefront.

*****

When nothing came out of Gandhi's offer to Jinnah of becoming the first President of free India, the Mahasabha leader demanded the division of Bengal on April 23, 1947.[8] Frantic moves were made in the Hindu political circle to grab as much land as they could. The British wanted to damage the Muslims so they conceded to this new plan. The Khaksar circle felt that this move may have come from the British themselves.

Within days of the Mahasabha leader's demand, on April 27, 1947, Mountbatten came out with his tentative plan according to which Punjab and Bengal were to be partitioned.[9] He came up with this plan after individual and collective consultations in India as well as in Britain. The circumstances again lead one to believe that the idea of partition was British-sponsored. This encouraged the Hindus to keep pressing their demand.

On April 30, 1947, another Hindu leader, Dr. Rajendra Prasad, demanded the division of Punjab and Bengal. Prasad said:

> "Neither the Congress nor the Hindus nor Sikhs ever wanted a division of India. It is the Muslim League and Mr. Jinnah who have been insisting on it ...they [Muslim League] have demanded that 'geographically contiguous units should be demarcated into regions which should be so constituted with such territorial adjustments as may be necessary, that the area in which the Muslims are numerically in a majority as in the north-western and eastern zones of India should be grouped to constitute independent states in which the constituted units shall be autonomous and sovereign.'
>
> In terms of their own resolution, they cannot demand any areas to be included in the Muslim zone which are not contiguous and in which Muslims are not numerically in a majority. If the areas of the Punjab and Bengal, where Muslims are not in a majority, demand a fulfillment of the League's resolution how does it lie in the mouth of Mr. Jinnah to accuse them and abuse them? He cannot have it both ways. Either he wants division or he does not. If division is insisted on by him, as evidently it is, then it can only be on a basis which suits both and not him alone...
>
> The problems of minorities is not solved by the creation of Pakistan as now dreamt by Mr. Jinnah as the non-Muslim minority in the north-western zone comprising the Punjab, Sind, N.W.F.P. and Baluchistan will be 38.4 per cent and in the eastern zone comprising Bengal and Assam, it will be 48.3 per cent. If the non-Muslim majority areas are cut out and separated from the Muslim majority areas, the non-Muslim minority in the north-western and eastern

---

[8] *The Tribune*, April 24, 1947.
[9] *The Tribune*, April 28, 1947.

zones will be 24.6 per cent and 30.5 per cent respectively and the Muslim minority in the rest of India will be 13.2 per cent and the magnitude of the minority problem will be proportionately reduced."[10]

The idea was probably to put pressure on Quaid-e-Azam to come to a compromise or else Quaid-e-Azam would get a truncated Pakistan. Like nationalist Muslims, nationalist Hindu leaders too wanted to keep India intact, but in case of division, they wanted to get the maximum out of Pakistan, and they knew that the British would not help Muslims.

All along, Khaksars kept telling Leaguers what was coming, yet the Leaguers remained unmoved. However, in a statement on April 30, 1947, Quaid-e-Azam denounced the partition of Punjab and Bengal and called it "a sinister move."[11]

Now the real game had started and many leaders' (Muslims and non-Muslims) intentions were exposed. On May 03, 1947, Khaksars held a public meeting in Lahore and spoke on the critical political situation. They apprised the public that Government and political leaders of the AIML and Congress were misleading people. The Government arrested thirteen Khaksar speakers, and police applied force to disperse the crowd. Police pickets were also posted in the area.[12]

With the British and Hindus scheming against the Muslim interest, Dr. Muhammad Aslam Chisti, a Khaksar leader of Lahore, issued a statement to protect Muslim interest. He said:

> "The Khaksars who may have their differences with the Muslim League leadership as to the best method for the achievement of independence for the Muslims…pledged to oppose by every possible means the Congress-Akali move to partition the Punjab and Bengal."[13]

The AIML remained silent on this offer, despite the fact that partition of two major provinces was around the corner. It was questioned in the nationalist circle why, even at this juncture, Quaid-e-Azam remained silent on the Khaksar offer. There was a lot of suspicion that Quaid-e-Azam would finally agree to partition, because by this time Jinnah had had many meetings with the Viceroy and he knew exactly what was coming. To Khaksars, his statements were nothing but political tactics. For instance, recently at a refugee camp in Bihar (on February 23, 1947), Jinnah had said:

---

[10] *The Tribune*, May 01, 1947.
[11] *Dawn*, May 02, 1947. *The Tribune*, May 01, 1947. *The Pakistan Times*, May 02, 1947.
[12] *The Pakistan Times*, May 06, 1947.
[13] *The Pakistan Times*, May 14, 1947.

"The Muslim League will not yield an inch in their demand for
Pakistan... Nations are built through sacrifices..."[14]

Khaksars were working to ensure that British India would finally attain its
freedom and had already declared to sacrifice for independence. Even though
moves were taking place to divide Punjab and Bengal, the AIML was not
taking any action or talking of any mass movement or open revolution against
the British. Quaid-e-Azam made no moves to join Khaksars or ask Leaguers to
join 300,000 Khaksars on June 30. The Muslim Leaguers knew that the
Khaksars were working on this plan, yet they still didn't come forward to join
in; in fact the Leaguers worked against the Khaksars' plan.

*****

Meanwhile, the Khaksars were taking the necessary steps for their plan of June
30, 1947. Mashraqi kept apprising the public of dangers that lay ahead.

On May 10, 1947[15], Mashraqi issued a statement of warning in which he told
the nation what was coming. Exactly that which he warned against happened.
Mashraqi stated:

> "after the advent of Lord Mountbatten India will be a heap of
> slaughter and tyranny henceforth...the only way to get out of this
> calamity was that the Hindus and the Musalmans should unite for a
> common revolution against the dirty politics of the present day."[16]

In this statement, Mashraqi not only pointed toward a rapidly deteriorating
situation but he appealed to all nationalists to come forward and prevent the
disintegration of British India. To Mashraqi, it was "dirty politics" that was
breaking up India.

Four days later, in a public meeting in Patna, Mashraqi made an extremely
important observation in front of 50,000 people who came to listen to his
address. Mashraqi said:

> "Revolution through the united physical force of people alone can
> bring about real freedom of India. This alone will revolutionise the
> system of government hitherto in force which has so completely
> estranged the hearts of 400 million people from the British. Such a
> revolution alone will automatically change every feature of British
> Raj and will pave the way for Indian Raj of Indian make. Peaceful
> transfer of power handed over to men who have been trained in
> British way of thinking will bring nothing but worse form of British
> Raj again. This Raj will be ten times more tyrannical, more
> deformed, more ghastly, more imperialistic and non-Indian than even
> the worst form of British Raj. It will, in fact, be a travesty of all truths

---

[14] *The Free Press Journal*, February 24, 1947.
[15] The exact date was not available in the source; this is the approximate date.
[16] Hussain, P. 226.

and a parody of every good or bad thing that the British have given to India during the past 100 years. It will be, in fact, an anarchy in order, a stereo-typed tyranny, and a confusion worst confounded. It will be a perpetual reign of Atom Bomb and Rule of Terror. It will be regalised genocide and state killings. It will justify murder of children in mothers' wombs, wholesale destruction of all cultures, suppression of all true History, murder of Philosophy, total wiping out of honourable traditions, and wholesale slaughter of ideas. Handing over power to one or many political parties in India would mean a rule of worse imperialism, worse capitalism, worse halakuism than all the History has yet produced. It will, in fact, be British Raj without British traditions. It will be a reign of 'Hell on Earth'. It will decimate the beautiful culture of Asia, the beautiful code of Asiatic Moral Laws, the beautiful philosophy of Peace and Tolerance, in fact the beautiful Fundamental Truths that Asia has ever given to Mankind during the last 5000 years. I have grave doubts if 180 million of sachhut Hindus, or 95 million of poor Musalmans, or 60 million of Scheduled Castes will, under the present plan of domination ever remain virile enough to lodge even a protest against such domination. I have grave doubts if even Arabic numerals will remain, Arabic alphabet will exist, or if the scales are turned otherwise, Sanskrit language and Hindu philosophy will ever have a trace of them left. The present plan of transfer of power, to my mind, is the Diabolical Plan of the relentless rule of Birla, Brahmin and Khan Bahadur Raj where arrogance, money and tyranny will rule rather than human beings.

The last remedy under the present circumstances is that one and all rise against this conspiracy as one man. Let there be a common Hindu-Muslim Revolution in which not hundreds but millions will lose their lives by the bullets of Birla and the British. Millions will die, no doubt, in this way but hundreds of millions will be saved forever. If man has decided to kill man for sheer lust of power and with nothing to show to the world except tyranny and loot, it is time that we should sacrifice men in millions now in order to uphold Truth, Honour and Justice."[17]

In order to materialize his plan, Mashraqi traveled and worked to build support for what he had in mind. He also went to Bengal in the same connection.[18]

*****

On May 15, 1947, it was announced that Mountbatten would be leaving for London to discuss the political situation of India.[19] On the day of this

---

[17] *Al-Islah*, May 23, 1947 as quoted in Hussain, Pp. 227-228.

[18] Mashraqi also went to Bengal to oversee Khaksar relief work for refugees that was ongoing but was being hampered by the Provincial Government. He was shocked to see what the Government was doing to end the miseries of the people in Bengal. His criticism of the Government was legitimate. A lot of messages and letters were exchanged about the refugees. Some of the letters in connection with relief work can be seen in Yousaf 2004, Pp. 305-307. A detailed study is required to discuss the Bengal situation and Khaksar relief activities and humanitarian work.

[19] *Dawn*, May 17, 1947.

announcement, Jinnah had a meeting with Mountbatten at the Viceroy's House. Prior to leaving for London, Mountbatten called Jinnah and Liaquat Ali Khan for a meeting. This meeting was followed by meetings with Congress leaders, Pandit Jawaharlal Nehru and Sardar Vallabhbhai Patel. Among the main points of discussion in these meetings was the method of division of Punjab and Bengal.[20]

Jinnah, Liaquat Ali Khan and Congress leaders again met Mountbatten. In these meetings, Mountbatten was studying the reactions of these leaders about his proposal.[21] According to the Khaksar circle, prior to leaving for Britain, Mountbatten had sought the approval of his plan from Quaid-e-Azam, Gandhi and Nehru, while it was kept a secret from the rest of the world. Partition of Punjab and Bengal had to be discussed prior to Mountbatten's departure. So it is not possible that Jinnah at this stage did not know what was coming.

Before Mountbatten left for England, brisk political activity was observed. On May 17, 1947, Mountbatten and his wife left for Britain.[22] Within few hours of his arrival in Britain, Mountbatten held meetings with General Lord Ismay, Chief of Staff, and then went to 10 Downing Street and met the Premier, Clement Attlee. This visit was of utmost important as the future of India was to be finalized.

The conversations, that Jinnah, Gandhi and Nehru had with Mountbatten prior to his departure for Britain, sent a clear signal that the division of Punjab and Bengal was forthcoming. Thus, in an interview on May 21, 1947, Quaid-e-Azam, said:

> "Partition of Punjab and Bengal, if effected, will no doubt, weaken Pakistan to a certain extent. Weak Pakistan and a strong Hindustan will be a temptation for the strong Hindustan to try to dictate. I have already said that Pakistan must be sufficiently strong as a balance vis-à-vis Hindustan. I am, therefore, deadly against the partition of Bengal and the Punjab and we shall fight every inch against it."[23]

Quaid-e-Azam replied "yes" when asked during the same interview, "Will you demand a corridor through Hindustan connecting the Eastern and Western Pakistan States?"[24] Jinnah stated "we shall fight every inch against it"; he had also said so on February 23, 1947. These statements implied that the AIML would put up physical resistance and would be ready to face bullets. But no such fight came forth, so this leads one to believe that these were mere statements and nothing else. Hence, this statement was meant to prepare Muslims that partition of Punjab and Bengal was coming. Jinnah did not give a

---

[20] *Dawn*, May 18, 1947.
[21] *Dawn*, May 19, 1947.
[22] Ibid.
[23] *The Tribune*, May 22, 1947. *Dawn*, May 23, 1947.
[24] Ibid. *The Star of India*, May 23, 1947.

call for a revolt or reject the partition of British India. Instead, he basically deflected the blame for this on the British and Hindus.

On May 24, 1947, British Cabinet-Viceroy talks concluded and a blue print of Mountbatten's Plan was approved in a cabinet meeting.[25]

*****

On the same date (May 24, 1947), Khaksars met Gandhi to discuss the political situation in light of Mountbatten's visit along with other matters. Khaksars were disappointed to see that Gandhi did not say much on preventing the division of India and even on partition of Punjab and Bengal that Hindu leadership was demanding. When Khaksars asked him about the revolution by all Indians, regardless of religion, Gandhi had nothing to say.

According to some writers and political analysts, Gandhi was also responsible for division between Muslims and Hindus, and he too was playing in the hands of the British. Some of Gandhi's moves lead one to believe that he was not what he had projected himself to be. For example, he never supported Khaksars despite the fact that Mashraqi worked towards Muslim-Hindu unity. He even rejected the Khaksar *Constitution of Free India*. The Khaksars questioned why Gandhi did not come forward and work with the Khaksars in their endeavors to oust the British? Was he stopped from supporting the Khaksars or did he do this at his own? Another thing that indicates that Gandhi acceded to partition of India was when, in response to Suhrawardy's plea for undivided Bengal, he stated that the "contention of Mr. Suhrawardy could be sustained only if every single Hindu of Bengal could certify openly that he could live in any part of Bengal without fear."[26] The question is, was this a workable reply? It was impossible to get certification from every Hindu of Bengal.

Gandhi has been criticized by many writers, for example, in the book titled, *Gandhi, Behind the Mask of Divinity*. Anyhow, Gandhi is not the focus of this book, so it is inappropriate to discuss him here. But Gandhi's acceptance of partition — he used to say partition would be over his dead body — certainly disappointed and disillusioned Mashraqi and the Khaksars. They felt that at this juncture, if he was not in favor of division, Gandhi should have openly declared joining hands with the Khaksars.

*****

With these developments, on May 29, 1947, Mashraqi (who was in Patna) issued a statement asking the people to start a revolution against the British Government and revolt against Jinnah and Gandhi,[27] who he thought were

---

[25] *Dawn*, May 24, 1947. *The Star of India*, May 25, 1947. *The Tribune*, May 24, 1947.
[26] *The Tribune*, April 11, 1947.
[27] *The Tribune*, May 30, 1947.

responsible for the massacre of Muslims and Hindus and for leading the country towards destruction. He asked for a revolution against the British Government, Jinnah and Gandhi because by now he knew that all three were actually seeking their vested interests.

Both Muslim and Hindu leadership should have realized that their real enemy was the foreign rule. But unfortunately with the blessings of the rulers and lack of vision among the Muslim and Hindu leadership in the AIML and Congress, leadership on both sides chose to fight each other instead of join hands. Mashraqi was highly disappointed and disillusioned that they chose to disagree and could not see the bigger picture.

Mashraqi had devoted his life to achieving communal harmony; his embitterment should be seen in this context.

*****

While Mashraqi was working for his plan, Mountbatten returned to India after finalizing the program for the future of India. Upon his return, he called a meeting of Indian leaders (Muslims and non-Muslims) on June 02, 1947. The conference opened at 10 a.m. and Jinnah was the first to arrive. Attendees included: Quaid-e-Azam, Sardar Abdur Rab Nishtar, Liaquat Ali Khan, Sardar Baldev Singh, Jawaharlal Nehru, Sardar Patel and Acharya Kripalani. The Khaksar Tehreek was again not invited, as if India belonged only to the AIML and Congress and no one else's opinion was necessary. All these matters illustrate how the British dealt with India's division. Only those were called who Mountbatten thought would not resist his plan to be announced on June 03, 1947 and would not create embarrassment for him or His Majesty's Government.

At this conference, Mountbatten handed over the copies of the forthcoming announcement (June 03, 1946). After the meeting, Jinnah stayed back and had a discussion with Mountbatten. After this meeting, pressmen asked:

> "Mr. Jinnah, could you get what you wanted? The League President immediately made for his car and buzzed off."[28]

Then Gandhi met the Viceroy for 45 minutes. At 11 at night, Jinnah had another round of meetings with the Viceroy. The actual contents of these meetings were never disclosed to the Khaksar Tehreek or any other party. The AIML and Congress kept the proceedings of the meetings to themselves. Secrecy was maintained, although it was a moral obligation of these leaders to take all parties into confidence. The future of India was at stake, but this secrecy was maintained.

---

[28] *The Free Press Journal*, June 03, 1947.

252 | Nasim Yousaf

A press Communique was issued from the Viceroy's House on June 02, 1947:

> "His Excellency the Viceroy's meeting with the seven Indian leaders
> which was announced yesterday, took place at 10 a.m. and lasted two
> hours.
>> The Viceroy gave the meeting a full account of his
>> discussions both in India and in England which had led up to the
>> formulation of His Majesty's Government's plan, and of the
>> arguments which had resulted in its adoption.
>>> Copies of the announcement were then handed round to the
>> leaders.
>>> The Conference adjourned until 10 a.m. tomorrow, June 3,
>> to enable the respective Working Committees to consider the plan.
>>> Mr. Jinnah remained for a brief interview with His
>> Excellency after the meeting.
>>> At 12:30 p.m. His Excellency had an interview with Mr.
>> Gandhi until 1:15 p.m.
>>> At 4 p.m. tomorrow, His Excellency will meet the
>> Chancellor of the Chamber of Princes and the 14 representatives of
>> the Indian States, who formed the States Negotiation Committee.
>>> At 7 p.m. tomorrow His Excellency will broadcast,
>> immediately after which the text of His Majesty's Government's
>> announcement will be relayed over all stations of All-India Radio.
>> Thereafter Pandi Nehru, Mr. Jinnah and Sardar Baldev Singh will
>> broadcast.
>>> At 10 a.m. the following morning June 4, His Excellency
>> will hold press conference in the Council House."[29]

The Free Press Journal reported:

> "The Indian National Congress and the Muslim League High
> Command were reliably reported tonight [June 02] to have accepted
> the British Government's plan for the division of India in such a
> manner as to permit the Hindu and Sikh minority areas in Bengal and
> the Punjab provinces to be sliced off an independent Muslim state of
> Pakistan says the Associated Press of America."[30]

The Mountbatten Plan (HMG Plan) was discussed again on June 03 with all leaders and was announced on the same date. The plan was discriminatory. There was quick reaction to the Mountbatten Plan and much resentment was felt among the Muslims. The division of Punjab and Bengal sent shock waves to Muslims across India including pro-Muslim Leaguers — who were pro-partition. The fact that Quaid-e-Azam had kept this a secret and had not discussed it with other Muslim leaders including Mashraqi was a matter of great concern for all nationalist Muslims; they again felt that the British were successfully using the AIML to achieve their ends. By putting forth the June 03 plan, the British had set the stage for weakening the Muslims by dividing

---

[29] *The Free Press Journal*, June 03, 1947.
[30] Ibid.

India and the Muslims into three parts as well as giving away portions of Punjab and Bengal to the Hindus.

Mashraqi sent a telegram to Mountbatten and referred to Mountbatten's June 04, 1947 statement. Mashraqi stated:

> "foreshadowing murder and ruin of at least ten million Indians... That perhaps is being literally fulfilled and history is bound to charge the British people with responsibility for unprecedented crime in world annals. Jinnah-Gandhi personal grudges wrongfully espoused by the British Government have already worked wonders in human destruction, but repeated indication of coming war cleverly clothed in pious, or frank utterances of Mahatma Gandhi and his associates, spell complete destruction of 400 million people."[31]

On the announced plan, *The Tribune* wrote in its editorial on June 04, 1947:

> "Mr. Jinnah will have nothing but 'truncated, mutilated and moth-eaten Pakistan.' With Bengal cut up and Calcutta allotted to the non-Muslims what he will get in Eastern India will be sheer frustration. And in Western India too he will lose important and substantial chunks of earth. But he is also reported to be satisfied."

On June 04, 1947, Professor Abdul Majid Khan issued a statement:

> "After organising everything on hatred for the last seven years or so the Leaguers are now looking the gift horse of mutilated Pakistan in the mouth. They have got the husk, the shadow and the dross while the real substance and gold have been taken away by the Congress.
>
> It is high time that the Leaguers repudiated the leadership of Mr. Jinnah and expressed their willingness to accept the Cabinet Mission Plan in preference to the latest plan under which the Muslims can never rise to their fullest stature and will definitely be reduced to utter poverty. They should give up day-dreaming to put their feet on solid earth, otherwise politically they will be doomed for ever. The interests of the Muslim masses should not be sacrificed at the altar of Mr. Jinnah's vanity."[32]

The Professor said exactly what Mashraqi had been telling the Muslims — to stop day-dreaming or they will never rise. The Professor also echoed Mashraqi's repeated warnings regarding partition.

Maulana Zafar Mehdi (a Shia leader) also denounced the plan and said:

> "The H.M.G.'s plan for the partition of Punjab and Bengal is injurious to the hundred million Mussalmans of India...Muslim areas in Hindu majority provinces such as U.P., Bihar, Madras, etc., are not

[31] Hussain, P. 235.
[32] *The Tribune*, June 05, 1947.

partitioned from the Hindu majority areas on the principle of non-coercion which is accepted by the Congress."[33]

The Eastern Times of June 07, 1947 criticized partition and provided an analysis:

> "The Pakistan areas, particularly in the Punjab and Bengal, have been reduced and crippled economically and their resources have been weakened in more than one way. There was no justification whatsoever for the grouping together of Amritsar, Jullunder and Ferozepur districts as part of a non-Muslim province, especially as the Muslim population in each of these districts exceeded the combined population of caste Hindus and Sikhs...
>
> The Pakistan State, as envisaged in H.M.G.'s plan, will have a far smaller population than what Muslims are entitled to even on their population basis in British India."

These voices should have been heard and the Muslim Leaguers should have realized what the British were up to. They should have understood that Muslims were losing their land and their population too. Another trick was played that the transfer of power would take place in 1947 instead of 1948. This was again not without a reason. Speed was of the essence to divide India without giving much time for retaliation.

*****

The AIML had not yet approved the plan, but Jinnah had already accepted it. According to political circles, he had accepted it in the meeting he had with Mountbatten on June 02, 1947; news of this was published in the *Dawn*, Delhi of June 04, 1947:

> "The Muslim League President, M.A. Jinnah called on the Viceroy at 11 p.m. tonight [June 02, 1947]. It is understood that the League President assured the Viceroy of his acceptance of the plan and that he would throw his weight in favour of getting the Muslim League Council to accept it."[34]

In fact, Jinnah's acceptance of Punjab was reported in *The Eastern Times* (of April 19, 1947) as well. The paper wrote:

> "The Congress demand for partition of the Punjab has, it is understood, been accepted in principle by Mr. Jinnah.
>
> There is reason to believe that the Muslim League leader has informed the Viceroy that he is willing to detach the Ambala Division from the Punjab.

---

[33] *The Eastern Times*, June 07, 1947.
[34] Also see *The Free Press Journal*, June 03, 1947.

According to a reliable source Mr. Jinnah may even go further and accept the principle of predominantly Muslim and non-Muslim areas..."

According to *News Week*:

"Mr. Jinnah had already half resigned himself to a truncated Pakistan without parts of Bengal and the Punjab, on the basis that half a loaf would be better than none...and he had already been thinking of Dominion Status[35] as the best way of strengthening numerically inferior Pakistan against independent Hindustan — this analysis of the rationale of Mr. Jinnah's acceptance of Lord Mountbatten's scheme is not very flattering to the Leaguers political intelligence."[36]

*****

According to the press, Jinnah had already accepted the plan in a meeting with the Viceroy, but he still had to maintain an appearance that the plan was up for discussion within the League. Hence, Jinnah invited a meeting of the Leaguers on June 09, 1947. The All-India Muslim League Council held meetings at the Imperial Hotel in New Delhi. Quaid-e-Azam arrived

"and was mobbed by a hysterical crowd. He lost his temper and threw away a garland pushed on to his neck by an enthusiastic Muslim lad.
When he was ascending the staircase some Muslim League National Guards volunteers shouted 'Shahenshah (Emperor) Pakistan Zindabad.'"[37]

Despite the fact that many Leaguers were praising Quaid-e-Azam's achievement, he lost his temper. He was nervous and upset that there was quite a large opposition to the HMG plan. He was also expecting resentment from the delegates at this session.

The morning session started at 10 a.m.[38], under a very tense atmosphere; the session was to discuss the Mountbatten Plan. More than 400 Leaguers[39] from different provinces attended the session that would open another chapter in the history of India, as it would discuss the fate of 100 million Muslims. There were 20 special invitees but the League did not invite anyone from the Khaksar Tehreek to this session. Quaid-e-Azam made a brief speech on HMG's Plan. When Jinnah was asked to comment on safeguarding the rights of minorities,

[35] One of the self-governing nations within the British Commonwealth.
[36] *The Tribune*, June 14, 1947.
[37] *The Free Press Journal*, June 10, 1947.
[38] *The Tribune*, June 10, 1947.
[39] *Dawn*, June 10, 1947.

"Jinnah reiterated…in Pakistan…their [minorities'] rights would be protected in every possible manner. He expected the same would be the case in regard to minorities in the Indian Union too, but pointed out that it was obviously a question for the minorities in the Indian Union to take up in their Constituent Assembly."[40]

In other words, Muslims, including other minorities in India, would be at the mercy of Hindus.

There were many Leaguers who opposed the plan. It was reported in the newspaper:

"…during the morning session opinion was divided regarding the British plan. Prof. Abdur Rahim (Bengal) and Mr. Z.H. Lari, Deputy Leader of the United Provinces Muslim League, are stated to have strongly opposed to the acceptance of the plan. While Prof. Rahim did not think that the plan was economically self-sufficient to support the proposed Pakistan, Mr. Lari criticised the plan because it afforded no protection to the Muslim minorities in Hindustan."[41]

Bengal Muslims, who had specially come from Calcutta, raised slogans outside the Imperial Hotel; they shouted "Down with the Division of Bengal!"[42]

Khaksars and their supporters held a protest at the Imperial Hotel to urge the Muslim League not to accept a *truncated* Pakistan, which was not even in line with the Lahore Resolution (Pakistan Resolution). Khaksars demanded a complete Pakistan. They raised slogans such as "Azad Pakistan Zindabad" and "Truncated Pakistan Murdabad."[43] The Khaksars proclaimed that they were with the League, provided that the unjust plan was rejected and they urged them to demand at least fair treatment from the British Government. The Khaksars wanted to meet the Leaguers to present their concerns, but they were denied entry into the hotel. The Muslim League National Guards, instead of appreciating their concern, refused to even listen to them. On top of this, the Leaguers called out the armed police guards that had already been posted around the hotel for their safety prior to the start of the session. Khaksars were *lathi* charged by police, fiercely beaten by police and Muslim League National Guard and arrested upon the green signal from the Leaguers. It seemed that the Government was on the side of the AIML and there was no denying this fact.

The morning session ended at 1:45 p.m.[44] To discuss the matter further, another session of AIML was held in the evening.

---

[40] *The Star of India*, June 11, 1947.
[41] *The Free Press Journal*, June 10, 1947.
[42] Ibid.
[43] Ibid.
[44] *Dawn*, June 10, 1947.

The evening session started around 8 pm on the same date. Khaksars continued with their protests at the Imperial Hotel. Khaksars wanted to meet Quaid-e-Azam and the League delegates to present their concerns before them and offer their support if the League was prepared to reject the plan. The Khaksars also wanted to discuss the assembly of Khaksars on June 30th.

Yet again, the Khaksars were denied entry into the hotel for no legitimate reason. The Muslim League National Guard again refused to even listen to them. The Guard resorted to violence and pushed the Khaksars back with *lathis* to remove them from the hotel premises. This created an ugly scene for no reason, and many Khaksars were seriously injured. The Leaguers also called armed police. The police authorities stood with the Muslim League and wanted no protests. Those who managed to enter the hotel were chased by the police and the League Guards and were brutally beaten. On that evening, police fired shots, used tear gas bombs and arrested many Khaksars. Many Khaksars were injured and those arrested were thrown in police trucks and whisked away. Can anyone believe the treatment that Muslims gave to their brother Muslims? No Muslim can ever appreciate the way Khaksars, who had risked their lives for freedom, were treated by the AIML.

It is important to note that these Khaksar protests have been grossly distorted in many history books; this has been done on purpose to suggest that the Khaksars were against the creation of Pakistan and that they tried to attack Quaid-e-Azam at this meeting. However, the reality is that the Khaksars were only opposing the *truncated* Pakistan. How can anyone say that this protest was not justified? The Khaksars' only crime was that they protested against the unjust Mountbatten Plan. It is the basic right of the citizens of a nation to be able to protest against any injustice or leaders who are making wrong decisions. To turn the story around and accuse the Khaksars of being against Pakistan is highly unethical.

*****

While injured Khaksars were suffering in pain, the Leaguers continued with their meeting. Finally, by an overwhelming majority, the Council of the All-India Muslim League accepted the HMG's Plan for the transfer of power and passed a resolution.[45] The following resolution was passed on June 09, 1947 and forwarded to the Viceroy:

> "The Council of the All-India Muslim League after full deliberation and consideration of the Statement of His Majesty's Government dated the 3rd of June, 1947, laying down the Plan of transfer of power to the peoples of India, notes with satisfaction that the Cabinet Mission's Plan of May 16th, 1946 will not be proceeded with and has been abandoned. The only course open is the partition of India as now proposed in H.M.G.'s Statement.

---

[45] *Dawn*, June 11, 1947. Also see *The Free Press Journal*, June 10, 1947.

The Council of the All-India Muslim League is of the opinion that the only solution of India's problem is to divide India into two — Pakistan and Hindustan. On that basis, the Council has given its most earnest attention and consideration to H.M.G.'s Statement. The Council is of the opinion that although it cannot agree to the partition of Bengal and the Punjab, or give its consent to such partition, it has to consider H.M.G.'s plan for the transfer of power as a whole.

The Council, therefore, hereby resolves to give full authority to the President of the All-India Muslim League, Qaid-e-Azam M.A. Jinnah, to accept the fundamental principles of the Plan as a compromise and to leave it to him, with full authority, to work out all the details of the Plan in an equitable and just manner with regard to carrying out the complete division of India on the basis and fundamental principles embodied in H.M.G.'s plan including defence, finance, communications, etc.

The Council further empowers the President, Qaid-e-Azam M.A. Jinnah, to take all steps and decisions which may be necessary in connection with and relating to the Plan."[46]

This AIML meeting was nothing but a mere formality. Not much opposition or speeches were allowed; the Mountbatten Plan was accepted in a *hush hush* manner without resistance and without protest by the high command. Jinnah did not give a chance to anyone to put up resistance to the plan.

The Free Press Journal of June 11, 1947 wrote under "Sample of Pakistan Democracy - Jinnah's Rough Riding Disgusts Leaguers:"

"The manner in which Mr. Jinnah put down the opposition during the session of the All-India Muslim League Council has left most of the delegates disgusted and disappointed.

When the Free Press of India correspondent met some of the progressive Leaguers who were refused permission to address the meeting, they all agreed that their work for the last ten years has only ruined the Muslim community.

...Maulana Hasrat Mohani the veteran Khilafatist...was many times interrupted by Mr. Jinnah, when he vehemently attacked the League's ten years campaign of hatred and the achievement of a Pakistan dominion in a truncated form. The revered Maulana was finally removed bodily from the dais by the Muslim National Guards.

The delegates from the Muslim minority provinces were the most vehement in denouncing the plan for power transfer. Mr. Jinnah, while complimenting them for building up the League could not guarantee them any safeguards.

The Baluch delegates too were dissatisfied...

Mr. Abdul Hashim [another Leaguer] asked about the possible attitude of the Muslims in Hindustan told the Free Press of India that the Muslim League here should be wound up and the Muslims should not look to Pakistan for any protection. They should,

---

[46] *The Star of India*, June 12, 1947.

he said, try to live in amity with their Hindu brethren and support the Leftist movements."

It is extremely unfortunate that Muslims in India (where Muslims were now hated) were asked to live at the mercy of Hindus. The Muslims obviously felt completely betrayed and depressed.[47]

*****

Quaid-e-Azam had enjoyed a dictatorial position, particularly since after 1940, when he was elevated by the British to be the leader. He was essentially made the speaker of the Muslim community by the rulers. The League councilors feared Jinnah, who was the only strong leader in the AIML and few had the guts to raise a voice against him. It is a fact that if anyone had fiercely objected to Jinnah, then new opportunities in Pakistan would have been closed for that person. Some even feared undergoing political victimization[48] and having their political careers come to an end in Pakistan, if they opposed the Mountbatten Plan. This was one of the reasons why many Leaguers kept quiet and accepted the plan.

The high command of the AIML, including Quaid-e-Azam, also feared arrest for launching an aggressive movement or for rejecting or resisting the Mountbatten Plan. Although, no person with even little political wisdom would ever accept splitting up of Punjab and Bengal, such pressures kept the Leaguers from speaking against the plan. Hence, they basically pleased the Government by accepting it with little verbal protests. It would not be wrong to say that the AIML never fought against the British, it fought against the nationalist parties such as Khaksar Tehreek.

According to the Khaksar circle, the AIML was completely exposed when it accepted the partition of Punjab and Bengal. The Leaguers were incapable of resisting authorities and they basically surrendered. All their statements, claiming that the AIML would fight for every inch, turned out to be fake. Khaksars believed that all the Leaguers' speeches and proclamations that were made against the British in the previous years were exposed; they were nothing real and were only meant for public consumption. In fact, Linlithgow's comments to Amery show that Jinnah was not a threat to the Government and endorses the Khaksars' view that his statements were for public consumption. Linlithgow had written to Amery on June 10, 1943:

> "Your comments on Jinnah's attitude....I think he probably looks a little more alarming from London than he does here. I don't however, think he wants a row with the government, though on the other hand (like unfortunately all these leaders) he exists on being as rude to

---

[47] After partition, Muslims in India became even more depressed as they were leaderless and had become second class citizens in their own country.
[48] This is exactly what was done to Mashraqi after the creation of Pakistan. His life was made miserable through arrests and maltreatment. His family and Khaksars were also victims.

government (and to his political opponents) as he thinks he dares. I doubt if anyone takes it very seriously, and his threats do not cause me any sleepless nights. As I have consistently felt and said both to Zetland and you, Jinnah would be quite as bad a master as Gandhi. But Jinnah is not in as strong a position as Gandhi's and Congress' and he is never likely to be in the near future, since he represents a minority that can effectively hold its own with our assistance. Nor of course is his organisation as deep rooted as is that of the Congress. I would expect him to be likely to continue to be not merely non-constructive but positively destructive, and to endeavour to play his hand so as to get the maximum in the way of commitments favourable to his community and the maximum in the way of hurdles to be taken by the Hindus, but without facing a showdown with the Government."[49]

Amery seemed to be concerned and worried at Jinnah's anti-British statements, but Linlithgow had written to Amery and comforted him on October 04, 1943:

"But I believe as I have often said to you in these matters that the Muslims (i.e., Mr. Jinnah) though they are bound to abuse us in the interest of keeping their place in the public eye and so safeguarding their reputation as good nationalists, have nothing to gain from the disappearance of the British connection or from a further weakening of that connection, and do not want any such weakening."[50]

These letters were written in 1943 and completely expose the AIML. The high command of the AIML was, as a matter of fact, pampered by the rulers. What the AIML leadership discussed with the British was different than what was said publicly. It is no big secret to anyone who understands a bit of politics that what goes on behind closed doors between leaders is different than what is said in the public. Leaders who did not follow the policy of the British were generally harassed and arrested. Main Leaguers were never arrested and never faced any brutality, despite anti-British statements; isn't this enough to show that there was a clear understanding between them and the British?

*****

Mashraqi, who was in Delhi at the time, was very upset at the acceptance of a truncated Pakistan. He was also annoyed with Congress leadership and issued the following statement on June 09, 1947. According to the newspaper:

"He [Mashraqi] said original Pakistan had made 60,000,000 Muslims safe at the sacrifice of 40,000,000 in non-Pakistan areas. He declared Khaksars had always stood for united Hindu-Muslim India but now stood for full Pakistan territorial independence because 'British themselves have decided the fate of Musalmans through Mr. Jinnah

---

[49] Khan, Khan Abdul Wali. Chapter 8.
[50] Ibid.

and because Congress has also forsaken its life-long ideal of Hindu-Muslim unity for good by accepting the divided India.'"[51]

Apparently, Mashraqi's complete statement was not published in *Dawn*. The British Government was nervous owing to the Khaksar protests at the Imperial Hotel, thus on June 11, 1947, Allama Mashraqi was arrested. They soon realized that Mashraqi's arrest might invite Khaksar reaction and deteriorate the situation, and thus released him.

The Jamiat ul Ulema also condemned the Mountbatten Plan at a meeting on June 24, 1947:

> "Maulana Kakhri [Fakhri] reprimanding these persons said that in discussing and deciding the fate of ten crores of Muslims, the Muslim Leaguers could not claim sole monopoly. 'We have had enough of rowdyism our patience has been strained to the last limits...'"[52]

Jamiat ul Ulema passed a resolution demanding rejection of the Mountbatten Plan,

> "...since it sought to destroy the political unity of the Muslims and divided them into three areas. This was highly injurious to the interests of Muslims in both the Pakistan and Hindustan zones...
> ...It has by creating a sense of hatred and mutual abhorrence among Indians facilitated the intervention of Britain or any other foreign power at any stage of the history of India."[53]

Tribal leaders (Maliks, Afridis and Mahmands) were not happy with Quaid-e-Azam; they protested against his visit to their territories in connection with the referendum there and issued a statement:

> "It has come to our knowledge that Mr. Jinnah is coming to the Frontier Province [NWFP]. It is no concern of ours as to whatever is done in British territory. But we must warn him that it will be a most unwise step for him to come to our territory because we consider Shias as the enemies of Islam. We also hereby warn the Government of India that they will be responsible for any consequences in this connection."[54]

*****

Meanwhile, the Bengal Legislative Assembly approved the division on June 20, 1947.[55] On June 23, the Punjab Legislative Assembly also approved partition.

---

[51] *Dawn*, June 11, 1947.
[52] *The Free Press Journal*, June 26, 1947.
[53] Ibid.
[54] *The Tribune*, June 18, 1947.
[55] *The Tribune*, June 21, 1947.

No Muslim could be happy at this discrimination against Muslims. In the state of tension that persisted in the country, on June 22, 1947, Shahalmi Gate and Paper Mandi in Lahore were "razed to the ground."[56] Property worth crores of rupees was damaged. This was a result of hate, retaliation and anger towards partition. Human destruction continued and countless cases of stabbings and burning were reported. The situation was very serious in the heart city (Lahore) of Punjab. The Governor of Punjab visited the affected areas in Lahore (but his visit had no positive effect).[57] Riots continued in different parts of the province and leaders appealed to the public to remain calm.[58] But nothing seemed to work, and stabbing, firing and bomb explosions were reported.

The tragedy did not end with human and property destruction. With the division of Punjab and Bengal, the richer parts (East Punjab and West Bengal) of these provinces went to India. Efforts were made to not include NWFP in Pakistan, and the Congress in NWFP demanded to make the province independent (Pathanistan). On June 28, 1947, Jinnah condemned this and declared it in violation of the Congress's acceptance of HMG's Plan of June 03, 1947.[59] On the same day, Khan Abdul Ghaffar Khan, a leader in NWFP, in his public address said:

> "We have decided to establish Pathanistan, which will be an independent State of all Pathans."[60]

When criticism was made that Pakistan would be deficient on resources and "would not be a practical proposition from the economic point of view"[61], the Muslim League Planning Committee Secretary issued a statement to prove that Pakistan will be a sound economy.[62]

*****

Mashraqi was against breaking India into pieces. After the acceptance of the Mountbatten Plan, Mashraqi continued working to implement his plan of having the Khaksars take over Delhi in order to stop disintegration of India and its people. In the case that division was unavoidable, then through this action, the Khaksars would at least extend Pakistan's boundaries to Delhi. Mashraqi was mobilizing the Khaksars and other forces[63] that supported him in this effort. He wanted to *undo* the injustice to the country and its people. Mashraqi had not forgotten that there was a time when the Muslim Ottoman Empire had a strong hold across continents from Africa, to Europe to the

---

[56] *The Tribune*, June 23, 1947.
[57] Ibid.
[58] *The Pakistan Times*, June 25, 1947.
[59] *The Pakistan Times*, July 01, 1947.
[60] Ibid.
[61] *The Star of India*, June 14, 1947.
[62] Ibid.
[63] See Chapter 9.

Middle East. The British plan was to ensure that Muslims never rose as a power again. This was Mashraqi's last attempt to stop the British from dividing India and to foil their plan.

This was the time when AIML support was badly needed, yet they did not come forward. The Leaguers knew that Mashraqi had issued a call for 300,000 Khaksars to assemble in Delhi on June 30th and they could have used this golden opportunity to fight the unjust partition plan. But they did no such thing, as they did not want to seek British resentment and were not ready to be jailed.

Further, the most upsetting part is that anti-Khaksar elements and agents of the British relayed information on the Khaksar plan to authorities. Accordingly, *severe* preventive measures were taken by authorities, and many Khaksars were beaten, loaded in trucks and taken to jail.

Despite the Government's preventive measures, on June 27, 1947, a Khaksar meeting was held at Idara-i-Aliya (Lahore) to discuss the Khaksar Camp in New Delhi to be held on June 30, 1947. Khaksar activities were closely monitored and the Government did its best not to allow entry of the Khaksars into Delhi. Section 144 had already been imposed in Delhi. Under this section, no more than five people could gather at one place. Despite all these restrictions, a very large number of Khaksars had gathered in and around Delhi. According to the press, 70,000 to 80,000 Khaksars had assembled in Delhi.[64] However, as per the Khaksar circle, the figure of Khaksars was much greater and many had reached the outskirts of Delhi but were facing difficulty in entering the city owing to rigorous Government restrictions in Delhi. The influx of Khaksars from across the country continued as did the massive arrests and Government checks, which hindered them from reaching their destination.

None of the Leaguers or Congress members protested against Section 144 to help the Khaksars; they did nothing to facilitate the gathering of this assembly. While Khaksars were assembling, Muslim Leaguers were working for the division of India and Quaid-e-Azam was hoping to become the first Governor General of Pakistan; on July 02, 1947, Jinnah finally conveyed his intentions to Mountbatten. The Viceroy was taken aback and it made the Viceroy's blood boil, because the Viceroy could not even imagine that Jinnah would make such a demand.

*****

---

[64] *The Tribune*, July 02, 1947.

Due to the restrictive Government measures and intrigues against this assembly, 300,000 Khaksars could not come together, and under the circumstances, Mashraqi's plan could not materialize. *Dawn*, Delhi reported:

> "Khaksars were not allowed to hold their rally which was scheduled to take place today [June 30, 1947] in Delhi."[65]

On purpose, very little coverage was provided by Muslim (pro-League papers) and Hindu press to such a large gathering. Even the *Dawn*, a pro-Muslim League paper, remained virtually silent on what was going on with Khaksars. The paper made no effort to bring people on the street to support Khaksars. It did not even condemn the Government for Khaksar arrests.

Mashraqi had made it clear in his call on March 01, 1947, that if the 300,000 Khaksars, for any reason, failed to reach Delhi, he would not implement his plan and disband the Khaksar Tehreek. Mashraqi was disheartened by the fact that Khaksars could not assemble, despite their attempts. On July 04, 1947, with a heavy heart, Allama Mashraqi disbanded the Khaksar Movement.[66] His message to disband the Khaksar Movement was announced in Delhi in front of hundreds of thousands of masses. Upon hearing this, the public cried hysterically, as people were completely shocked and saddened. They chanted slogans such as, "Delhi is Ours," "Lal Fort is Ours," "Allama Mashriqi Zindabad," "Khaksar-e-Azam Zindabad" and "Khaksar Tehreek Zindabad." Khaksars and the public pleaded to Mashraqi to reconsider his decision. But it was too late.

The Tribune, Lahore (of July 05, 1947) reported that Mashraqi stated:

> "About three and a half months ago I announced that if three lakhs of Khaksars would not have rallied in Delhi there would be no revolutionary power left in the movement and, therefore, it would be necessary to disband it. Now with the establishment of Pakistan, which has been bestowed upon the Muslims by the British, the last hope that ten crores [100 million] of Muslims who have been divided into various parts would continue their struggle for freedom has been lost. I, therefore, disband the movement."

On July 04, 1947, *Al-Islah* published Mashraqi's statement regarding the disbandment of the Khaksar Movement. Mashraqi said:

> "Ah! After 17 years of intense and honest struggle to which I gave the best part of my life and resources, the nation has not been able to develop qualities which could enable it to re-establish its authority in India"[67]

---

[65] *Dawn*, July 02, 1947.
[66] Zaman 1987, P. 325.
[67] Hussain, P. 234.

The disbandment of the Khaksar Tehreek was a not an easy decision for Mashraqi, and he was highly saddened and disheartened when he made the decision to dissolve it. Mashraqi had spent the best part of his life working toward his goal and had faced a lot of personal sufferings. However, he came to the understanding that the Muslims were not yet ready to change their future and lacked the spirit that was needed to revolutionize their lives. If this plan had materialized, either India would have remained intact or the map of Pakistan would have been different.

None of the Leaguers showed any regret on the disbandment; instead they were happy that Mashraqi had removed himself from the political stage. They immediately asked the Khaksars to join the AIML.[68]

*****

Even after disbandment of the movement, Khaksar men and women continued to stay in Delhi. People sent thousands of messages requesting Mashraqi to reconsider his decision, but Mashraqi did not withdraw his verdict. The Khaksars continued to march and hold demonstrations against the Government. At times, police used tear gas to disburse them and many were injured and arrested. For instance, on July 09, 1947, police used tear gas to disperse the Khaksars and arrested many for violating Section 144. Despite police action, Khaksars continued to stay in Delhi in the hopes that Mashraqi would withdraw his decision. On July 11, 1947, Khaksars marched in formation in Delhi. In order to disperse them, armed police beat them with *lathis* and many Khaksars were injured. They were tear-gassed and arrested. Cases were registered against Khaksars. In the mean time, on July 18, 1947, the Indian Independence Bill was passed, barely in 15 minutes, by the British House of Lords. Khaksars protested against the bill. On July 24, 1947, police opened fired on the Khaksars in Delhi. Many Khaksars were wounded and arrested. Police entered the mosques wearing shoes to chase the Khaksars and arrest them; police officials denied this.

Khaksars could not reconcile losing India and there were still thousands of them in Delhi; police were combing the area. Among Muslims, those who supported AIML did not hesitate to go after Khaksars without realizing that it was hard for anyone to see their own people and country disintegrating into pieces.

"The Chief Commissioner of Delhi, Sahibzada Khurshid Ahmed Khan, personally supervised the raids."[69]

---

[68] *Dawn*, July 08, 1947.
[69] *The Pakistan Times*, July 26, 1947.

There were clashes between Khaksars and the police. Khaksars were

> "...opposed to the present partition and were engaged in a
> propaganda campaign for the inclusion of Delhi and other adjoining
> districts in Pakistan... Khaksars had made known their intention to
> prevent the authorities from hoisting the tri-colour flag on the Red
> Fort on August 15 [1947]. Local Muslim League leaders refused to
> evince any sympathy with the activities of these Khaksars...
>   Apprehending trouble, the Provincial authorities began to
> disperse the Khaksars late last night and the recalcitrant ones were
> taken into custody."[70]

During these days, many Khaksars were arrested, brutally beaten or killed in
prison. The firing, in jail, took place many times.[71] Those injured were not
properly treated. In jail, Khaksars continued to be mishandled and tortured.
Mashraqi's son, Inayatullah Khan Asghar, was also imprisoned.[72] As a young
boy, he was kept in solitary confinement in jail in Delhi and was mishandled
(he was released but was banned from going to India for ten years).

On July 30, 1947, Khaksars wrote to Mountbatten criticizing his partition
formula stating it was the

> "most unfortunate and one-sided division of India... It is most
> amazing...a people who ruled India for centuries and up to whose
> standard of rule even the British could not reach should be so
> ignominiously treated and thrown to the dogs."[73]

*****

None of the Leaguers were concerned with the Khaksars. None of them issued
any statement, even to sympathize with them.

However, *after the creation of Pakistan*, Dr. Zakir Husain (who later became
the President of India) at least brought the subject up with Nehru, and Nehru
showed his concern.

The treatment meted out to the Khaksars is self explanatory from Jawaharlal
Nehru's letter to Vallabhbhai Patel dated October 09, 1947:

> "My dear Vallabhbhai,
>   Dr. Zakir Husain mentioned to me that he had received
> information about the ill-treatment of Muslim prisoners in the jail
> here. According to report they are being manhandled, are beaten
> severely and are kept in solitary confinement...

---

[70] *The Pakistan Times*, July 26, 1947.
[71] Hussain, P. 235.
[72] Ibid.
[73] Hussain, P. 234.

>Many of these prisoners are the old Khaksars... I am told
>that among the Khaksar prisoners there is Allama Mashriqui's son
>Asghar Inayatullah [Inayatullah Khan Asghar], aged eleven years. If
>this fact is correct, the boy need hardly be kept in prison. His sister is
>in the Jamia.
>Yours sincerely,
>Jawaharlal Nehru"[74]

Mashraqi was upset at how the Khaksar prisoners were being treated. On October 10, 1947, he sent a telegram to Mountbatten regarding the treatment meted out to the Khaksar prisoners. He wrote that Khaksar detainees were

>"being terribly tortured...firing occurred on four occasions killing 21
>and wounding over 150...I disbanded Khaksar Movement for my
>own reasons but hope that Indian Government will not take
>advantage and release all including my son immediately."[75]

*****

Returning to the period *before Pakistan's creation* and the brutal situation that the Khaksars were undergoing, as stated the Leaguers were least concerned of this. Quaid-e-Azam too was not bothered with what the Khaksars, including Mashraqi's child, were going through. Quaid-e-Azam addressed Muslim members of the Indian Constituent Assembly and never raised any concern about the Khaksars. Further, Muslims who were left behind in India felt abandoned by the AIML. On Quaid-e-Azam's address, *The Eastern Times* on August 02, 1947 wrote:

>"Mr. Jinnah addressed a private meeting of the Muslim members of
>the Indian Constituent Assembly and exhorted them to co-operate in
>its work and be loyal and law-abiding citizens of Hindustan.
>   ...It is said that a large number of Muslim members asked a
>series of questions as to their position in India. They should not
>expect any help from the Pakistan State, he said and must rely on
>themselves and fit in the new conditions.
>   Replying to one question, he said, it is reported, that they
>should learn Hindi if it became the 'lingua franca', just as they learn
>English, which was also a foreign language."

According to *The Eastern Times* of October 14, 1947, Jinnah said:

>"My advice to Muslim brethren in India is to give unflinching loyalty
>to the State in which they happen to be."[76]

The Muslims in India felt orphaned. Did it ever bother the AIML high command that these poor Muslims were now left at the mercy of the non-

---

[74] JNMF, Pp. 134-135.
[75] Hussain, P. 235.
[76] Also see *The Pakistan Times*, October 12, 1947.

Muslims, who were now hostile? Among these Muslims were those who had supported the League in hopes of a better future and those who were anti-partition. Regardless of their political preference, they were left to fend for themselves and became second class citizens in their own country. After the establishment of Pakistan, these same leaders who had benefited from Muslim support, all of a sudden abandoned the Muslims and asked them to be loyal to India.

On August 07, 1947, Mountbatten gave his plane to Jinnah to travel to Karachi. On the same day, dressed in a silk Shirwani, Quaid-e-Azam landed in Karachi, where he was given a rousing welcome. Jinnah drove a 15 mile distance (from the airport to the Government House) with hundreds of cars in a three miles procession. Upon arrival at the Government House, Quaid-e-Azam was accorded the Guard of Honor.[77]

On August 13, 1947, a State dinner was given by Jinnah in honor of Viceroy and Lady Mountbatten. At this event,

> "...Declaring that such voluntary and absolute transfer of power of this kind was unknown in the whole history of the world, Mr. Jinnah remarked today it falls to the lot of King George VI the good fortune of fulfilling the promise and the noble mission with which his great-grandmother assumed the reigns of this sub-continent nearly a century ago. The reign of King George will go down in history by the performance of this act voluntarily of transferring power and handing over the Government of India which was rightly characterized as the brightest jewel in the British Empire and by establishing two sovereign Dominions of Pakistan and Hindustan...
>
> Mr. Jinnah played a glowing tribute to the Viceroy and said: 'Your Excellency Lord Mountbatten, how much we appreciate your having carried out whole-heartedly the policy and the principle that was laid down by the Plan of June 3...passed by the British Parliament and received the assent of His Majesty the King on the 10th of July with grace, dignity and great ability. You are the last Viceroy of India but Pakistan and Hindustan will always remember you and your name will remain cherished not only in the history of these two Dominions but will find a place in the history of the world as one who performed his task and duties magnificently.'"[78]

This was not a voluntary transfer of power. In fact, behind this was a massive struggle for which many innocent Khaksars laid their lives.

According to Khaksar circle, indeed, it was a transfer of power to the AIML with no sacrifice on the AIML's part. The Khaksars who died had no place in the speech, whereas Quaid-e-Azam went on to appreciate others in the said speech.

---

[77] *The Pakistan Times*, August 08, 1947.
[78] *The Free Press Journal*, August 14, 1947.

*****

Pakistan declared its independence on August 14, 1947 and India on August 15, 1947. Though Mashraqi had disbanded the Khaksar Movement when he thought that India could not be kept undivided (in light of AIML and Congress accepting division), his efforts of almost two decades had brought fruit and British rule in India had finally ended. Mashraqi would have been the happiest man if he had managed to foil the schemes of the British which sought to weaken the Muslims. With the emergence of India, the golden period of Hindus and their political domination in the region began.

To cut the story short, British India obtained independence and two countries emerged on the world map with harrowing tales of murder and loot. Minorities were left to the mercy of *goondas*. Many were displaced having to leave behind their friends, property and values. Abandoned properties of evacuees were taken over by plunderers. Trains and means of transportation continued to be stopped by stabbers and looters. A general atmosphere of panic and horror prevailed. It seemed that there was no law and order and no steps were taken to protect the lives and properties of the people. People's stories and general incidents presented a heart rendering spectacle.

Nationalist political circles continued to denounce the truncated Pakistan. This plan had not only divided the country into three parts, but it had divided the Muslims too. With the emergence of two new countries, India's history, economy, strategy and policy were changed. In the nationalist circle, it was wondered why Quaid-e-Azam and Gandhi could not settle in their meeting in 1944. Why were the people forced to accept division of their beloved country? And could so much loss of blood due to the riots between Muslims and Hindus have been prevented?

Nationalists were of the view that Jinnah was backed by the British. He was their friend and in return the British had treated him well. In the end, however, the British literally betrayed Quaid-e-Azam's trust by dividing Punjab and Bengal. According to nationalists, the only reason that Jinnah accepted a mutilated and disfigured Pakistan was because he wanted to emerge as the Champion of the Muslim cause. This was his last chance to do so, and his only option was to accept a truncated Pakistan or let the idea of Pakistan go. The only way that Jinnah could have gotten a better Pakistan would have been by putting forth fierce resistance, which of course the Khaksars were ready to support him in. In the process, however, he most likely would have ended up in jail. If Quaid-e-Azam had shown courage and sought Mashraqi's help, the shape of Pakistan would have definitely been different. Unfortunately, Quaid-e-Azam was not willing to end up in prison and did not pay any attention to Mashraqi's offers. In a nutshell, if the British wanted to keep India intact, no one in the AIML had the courage to even present the Pakistan Resolution.

Owing to the non-existence of the nationalist point of view, Pakistan's history is grossly distorted, and the unfortunate part is that the Khaksar struggle toward independence has been treacherously eliminated from the history of Pakistan and India. Absence of Khaksar material in the libraries is glaring proof that history has been distorted. In Pakistan, the AIML and, in India, the Congress took full credit for independence. No credit has been given in either country to the Khaksar Tehreek's long struggle for the freedom of British India. As a matter of fact, all parties, regardless of religion, that took part in the freedom movement should have been given credit in both countries. The Pakistani and Indian authorities are to be blamed equally for gross misrepresentation.

After Pakistan's creation, the Muslim League ensured that only its role was projected in the history books, thereby wiping out almost two decades of long and unparalleled services of the Khaksars Tehreek to the freedom movement.

Hence, those who truly suffered for freedom were eliminated from history, while AIML leaders who arrived in Pakistan in planes became the sole founders of the nation.

Chapter 11

Consequences of Partition

Partition divided both the Muslims and the country of India into three parts. Though there were jubilations in Pakistan, no Muslim could be happy on the division of their loved ones and the land they had once ruled.

Slightly prior to independence, two Boundary Commissions were appointed under the Indian Independence Act 1947 for the demarcation of boundaries between India and Pakistan. One Commission was to manage the partition of Bengal and the other was to deal with the partition of the Punjab. Both Commissions were to have a Chairman and four members. Lord Cyril Radcliffe was to head both Commissions.[1]

Radcliffe prepared his report, known as the Radcliffe Award, which announced the final boundaries between Pakistan and India on August 18, 1947. Punjab and Bengal were divided.

> "Although numerical majority and contiguity were to be a fundamental basis for the allocation of border areas to Pakistan and India, large areas of the Punjab and Bengal containing Muslim majorities, and contiguous to other Muslim majority areas, were given to India. Even this award, although it was condemned by the people of Pakistan as manifestly unjust, was accepted by the Muslim League."[2]

According to this award, Muslim majority areas, including Ferozepur, Jullundhar and Zira, were treacherously handed over to India.[3] In district Gurdaspur, two Muslim tehsils (Gurdaspur and Batala, a rich Muslim Industrial town) with a clear Muslim majority were awarded to India. On the Eastern wing, again highly objectionable demarcation was done.

---

[1] *Government of Pakistan's official web site.* (3).
[2] DFPGP, P. 35.
[3] *Government of Pakistan information web site.* (5).

The Commissions turned out to be a one man show. They were supposed to be impartial yet they crossed all limits of justice. Boundaries of villages, tehsils and districts were demarcated as if a child was given the map of British India to draw the lines to suit his/her desire. It is mind boggling to understand the principle or logic under which the Boundary Commissions allotted Muslim majority areas to India. Yet no one could challenge the Radcliffe Award, as per the "word of honour"[4] given by the leaders.

It was the unkindest demarcation anyone could think of. Sardar Abdur Rab Nishtar (a Muslim Leaguer), admitted:

> "We believe it is a parting kick of the British."[5]

Begum Shah Nawaz, a member of the Muslim League Working Committee, said:

> "The award is most unfair and unjust. Predominantly Muslim majority areas have been handed over to the other parties. This shows that the British have gone back on their words. The award given is based on no principle at all."[6]

It seemed that the intentions of the British were finally revealed; they took revenge on the Muslims and did the maximum damage they could. It also seemed that the award was meant to sow seeds for a war between Muslims and Hindus. This would open up a large market for sale of arms and ammunition and keep both countries dependent on the West. Thus, lasting peace in the region was destroyed on purpose. The division of India clearly embodied the interests of the Western powers. The award was nothing but a *fierce blow* to the All India Muslim League.

*****

With division, Muslim heritage was lost and their chances of ruling India again were eliminated. Not only were their priceless jewels taken by the British, but their monuments such as mosques, mausoleums, tombs, forts and other historical places were lost to India. Massive numbers of families and members were displaced, separated, killed and injured. People lost their properties, valuables and other belongings; they lost their homes where they were born or bred. A scene of horror prevailed in many parts of the country. Dislodged, people were starving due to no money or lack of food, and riots and violence continued. The division of India not only resulted in mass migration across the new borders of Punjab and Bengal but an estimated one million deaths throughout India. Tens of thousands of girls and women were raped and/or abducted. The primary reason for these massive atrocities was the

---

[4] *The Free Press Journal*, August 19, 1947.
[5] *The Pakistan Times*, August 19, 1947.
[6] Ibid.

hatred that had been built over the previous seven years (from 1940 to 1947) between Muslims and non-Muslims. Partition had finally set the stage for never-ending hate, long-term conflict and other problems in the region.

Partition was without a doubt one of the bloodiest massacres in human history. Though Mashraqi and Khaksars' efforts were successful in preventing an India-wide civil war, communal violence and riots in parts of the country could not be prevented.

In Quaid-e-Azam's words:

> "...Unfortunately, the birth of Pakistan was attended by a holocaust unprecedented in history.
> Hundreds of thousands of defenceless people have been mercilessly butchered and millions have been displaced from their hearths and homes. People, who till yesterday, were leading a decent and prosperous life, are today paupers with no means of livelihood..."[7]

Nationalists felt that despite such massive atrocities, the Pakistanis were made to feel proud to have achieved a truncated Pakistan.

*****

Despite partition, more than one half of the Muslims did not move to Pakistan. A vast majority of nationalist Muslims did not want to abandon their homeland. For others, it was probably not feasible to leave.

The loyalty of more than one of half of the Muslims who stayed in India was confronted with an extremely complex situation. They now had to prove their loyalty to India, where they were looked upon with utmost suspicion, regardless of how loyal they were. The outcome of this suspicion was nothing but violent retaliation, harassment, persecution, oppression and discrimination. Muslims were in a pitiable situation. India was no longer their homeland, and their actual home country, by virtue of the Two-Nation Theory, was now Pakistan. Precisely, they became second class citizens in a country to which they and their forefathers belonged.

Quaid-e-Azam himself admitted:

> "When I turn my eyes to the sister Dominion of India, I find that the Muslim minority there has suffered grievous wrongs. Not content with having uprooted Muslims from East Punjab, certain sections in India seem to be determined to drive Muslims from the entire Dominion by making life impossible for them. These helpless victims of organised forces feel that they have been let down by us. It is a thousand pities that things have come to such a pass. The division of

---

[7] *The Eastern Times*, October 14, 1947. *The Pakistan Times*, October 12, 1947.

India was agreed upon with a solemn and sacred undertaking that minorities would be protected by the two Dominion Governments and that the minorities had nothing to fear, so long as they remained loyal to the State. If that is still the policy of the Government of India and I am sure it is, they should put a stop to this process of victimization of Muslims, which, if persisted in, would mean ruin for both States.

...I further hope that the Government of India would see that their fair name is not sullied by ill-advised action on the part of those who are bent upon eviction, or extermination, of the Muslims of India by brutal and inhuman methods. If the ultimate solution of the minority problem is to be mass exchange of population, let it be taken up at Governmental plane and should not be left to be sorted out by blood thirsty elements.

The establishment of Pakistan, for which we had been striving for the last ten years, is, by the grace of God, an established fact today, but the creation of a State of our own was a means to an end and not an end in itself. The idea was that we should have a State in which we could live and breathe as free men and which we could develop according to our own rights and culture and where the principles of Islamic social justice could find free play..."[8]

Jinnah had finally come to this realization, but it was too late. Hatred that was being built since 1940 was not going to end now. These statements did not matter to the people who continued to suffer. What bothers one's mind is why didn't the Leaguers realize that this would happen, when Mashraqi had warned and requested them to not dupe people and refrain from dividing their country?

It is hard to understand how Quaid-e-Azam could not know the ramifications of partition. He was constantly being reminded of them by Mashraqi and other Muslims. In an interview on February 29, 1944 to *News Chronicle* (London), Quaid-e-Azam had said:

"If the British Government is sincere in its desire for peace in India it should now frame a new constitution dividing India into two sovereign nations — Pakistan for Muslims, representing one quarter of the Country, and Hindustan for Hindus, who would have three-quarters of All-India."[9]

When the interviewer had asked if the Congress and Hindus will not accept partition and if there will be violence or possibly a civil war in India, Jinnah replied:

"...nothing like that would happen. If the British Government announced its intention of setting up Pakistan and Hindustan, Congress and Hindus would accept it within three months."[10]

---

[8] *The Eastern Times*, October 14, 1947.
[9] *The Bombay Chronicle*, March 02, 1944.
[10] Ibid.

The interviewer had again asked: "But surely there would be a civil war."[11] Jinnah had replied "I DON'T AGREE."[12] It is beyond comprehension as to how Quaid-e-Azam could say such a thing in his interview.

*****

According to a rough estimate, at least one million people died as result of the mass killings. The British rulers watched indifferently as India was engulfed in horrible devastation of mankind. Think of those women who jumped from the upper stories to save their honor! Think of those whose throats were slit. When I read those stories in the newspapers of the time, it brought tears to my eyes.

No Muslim could ignore the anguish, deprivation and wretchedness that had fallen on the people of India. The miseries on Muslims were visible outside the country and aroused resentment in the Iranian Parliament. The sufferings of the Muslims of India were debated in the Parliament on November 11, 1947. Amir Teimur, member of the parliament requested the "Government to do whatever lay in their power to reduce the miseries of the Muslims of Pakistan."[13] Another prominent member, Faramarzi, requested the Iranian Government to do something "against the barbarities committed by Sikhs and Hindus."[14]

Mashraqi too was disgusted with the mass killing of innocent people and the ruining and disintegration of his country. This could have been easily avoided if Mashraqi's wailings for unity had been mulled over. Who was responsible for such misery and flames across India? The Indian Muslims did not know who to look up to — Pakistan, India or some foreign country — for the protection of their rights? What was there for these people to celebrate?

The Muslim League was indifferent to the disintegration of their Muslim brethren in India. Jinnah told them to be loyal to India. And the Muslims' position in Hindu India was bound to become worse.

An author in *Dawn* of April 24, 2005 wrote:

> "Are we obliged to believe that our leaders were so shortsighted that they could not apprehend the dreadful consequences of partitioning a country? Did they ever think what would happen to the Muslims who would be left behind in India after the partition of the subcontinent in the name of religion? None of our leaders was prepared to accept the responsibility for the holocaust of unparallel magnitude people had to face after the creation of Pakistan. For our leaders what happened to the humanity was a part of the game. They created Pakistan, arrived in chartered planes, and became its rulers. With them arrived the ICS,

---

[11] *The Bombay Chronicle*, March 02, 1944.
[12] Ibid.
[13] *Dawn*, December 31, 1947.
[14] Ibid.

fortune hunters, and the men in khaki who were the backbone of the British during their two hundred year rule over India. They amassed fabulous evacuees' property, acquired vast agricultural and urban land, and secured lofty jobs for their kith and kin. Then came the uprooted, devastated and the wounded in teeming millions on foot, on bullock carts, buses, trucks, and the trains. Upon witnessing their misery did our well-entrenched leaders in cosy comforts feel embarrassed? It is anybody's guess."[15]

Regarding sacrifices for the creation of Pakistan, if we are talking of the people who died, were injured or otherwise suffered due to communal disturbances or at the time of partition, indeed, we have tremendous amount of sympathies and respect for them. In actuality, were they not victims of the power struggle?

The nationalists question, but what about the main leadership of the Muslim League? What was the sacrifice on their part? In their history of existence, did any of them put up any resistance? Were they ever arrested? Did any elite member of the League suffer in a dingy and dirty prison cell in British India for the cause of freedom? So the question is, what price did they pay for seeking freedom? When such questions are raised, there is no redeeming answer.

In the nationalist view, the Muslim League leadership was neither prepared nor capable of putting forth any resistance against the British. They were recipients of titles and other benefits from the British, so for them to resist against their masters was neither conceivable nor workable. As a matter of fact, throughout the freedom struggle, Muslim Leaguers elevated themselves. They not only gained prominence but the creation of Pakistan brought a lot of benefits to the members of the elite class of the AIML. So again the grilling question is, was Pakistan created by the rich for the rich?

*****

On the other hand, Mashraqi had given everything he had to the fight for freedom. He gave up his life of luxury, wealth, property and future capital gains. Mashraqi rejected all honors that were offered to him by the British, and he worked for the downtrodden to reform the nation and build its character to finally achieve his goal of the revival of the Muslim glory. On the Muslim side, it was without a doubt Mashraqi and the Khaksars who paid a very heavy price for obtaining freedom. Mashraqi and the Khaksars put up the longest fight to undo the designs of the rulers. Anyone who denies this is manipulating the facts of history for vested reasons.

After the creation of Pakistan, Mashraqi said on May 28, 1950 at Iqbal Park, Lahore (translated from Urdu):

[15] Jaleel, April 24, 2005.

"...Twenty years ago I called upon the Muslims to adopt soldierly way of life so that they could frustrate the enemy designs to destroy us. For 20 years the Muslims did not listen to me with the result that the Hindu, by owing this call, won the battle. For the first time during the 1300 years of their existence, the Muslims fled before the most coward nation and vacated the entire East Punjab. After this defeat of ours, the Hindus have become far bolder, and the happenings in Kashmir, Hyderabad and Junagarh have demonstrated not only the cowardice of the people of Pakistan but have also exposed the weakness of the Government...

During the last one hundred years, the Hindu through intensive struggle in every field of learning and emulating good qualities of the British, attained such superiority in intellect and knowledge, amassed such wealth and created such an indomitable organisation as enabled him to turn out the British through a constitutional and a non-cooperation movement. This is a unique event in the history of mankind and undoubtedly the world is perplexed over it. Not only that, the Hindus also succeeding in pushing to the extreme corners of 'Maleecha Pakistan' the Muslims who had held sway over India for 1145 years, who had left throughout the length and breadth of India the marks of their culture, civilisation and the hoofs of their steeds on which they rode into this vast country. Now, after all this, the Hindu is oppressing the five crore Indian Muslims and then sweeping them off to either wing of Pakistan so that at some later date it destroys both the Wings and completely annihilates the Muslims from the subcontinent. The Hindu believes that Bharat should be free from the 'Maleechas'; Bharat is no Bharat if it is inhabited by a single 'Maleecha'.

Listen and ponder that the Hindu used the same methods to free Bharat from the Jains and the Budhists. The resurgence of Hinduism after Asoka is replete with similar happenings as are taking place today in India in respect of the Muslims. When the Hindus decided to banish Budhism, hundreds of thousands of Brahmans became Sadhus and Yogies and spread throughout India like the present day Hindu Mahasabha and Rashtrya Sevak Sangh..."[16]

*****

There is no denying the reality that a large number of Muslims and non-Muslims opposed division. Even in Pakistan many people mourned and cried when their country was torn apart. The fact that the majority of Indian Muslims stayed back is in itself evidence that they did not approve of division. Those who remember losing East Pakistan can relate to the feelings of the nationalists at the time of the division of India.

People, who died at the time of partition, did not die because they were fighting against the British to seek independence; they died because they were civilians caught up in the politics of the time. Nationalists question, was this a

---

[16] Hussain, Pp. 279, 280, 284.

278 | Nasim Yousaf

sacrifice for Pakistan on the part of those who suffered or were they victims of their leaders' political adventures and quest for power?

By dividing the country, the Muslim League sowed the seeds of hatred between Muslims and Hindus and even among Muslims. How could they not anticipate that a huge number of lives would be lost and millions would lose their brothers and sisters? Anyone who studies historical documents and the newspapers of the time with an open mind would fail to understand AIML's vision.

The British damaged Muslim interests brutally. They could not have done this if the AIML had joined hands with the Khaksars, who were a threat to the British. Further, it must not be forgotten, that in light of World War II, the British were terribly weakened and to continue their hold in India was impossible. Decolonization after World War II had to take place. A world revolution was progressing and nations were no longer willing to accept imperialism. To hold on to India for a long period was no longer possible. Hence, if the AIML had joined the Khaksar Tehreek, at least a more complete Punjab, Bengal and Kashmir would have been part of Pakistan, if not the entire India.

Yet instead of supporting Mashraqi, who had the ability to end British rule, the AIML opted to fight the Khaksars. Mashraqi had made up his mind and made it clear that he would not sit until the British had left India. The British knew that their suppressing attempts against the Khaksars had already failed. However, the Khaksar Tehreek's hands were tied in the face of opposition from the British, AIML and Congress, and it was not possible and pragmatic for them to fight three forces simultaneously and to keep India intact. The tragedy is that the AIML had divided the Muslims. If the Muslim League had supported Khaksars, things would have been different. But the Muslim Leaguers were so worried of Mashraqi's abilities that Mashraqi's offers were disregarded on purpose, without realizing the repercussions and what could have been achieved if unity was demonstrated. As a result, Muslims suffered heavily and lost many areas that could have been part of Pakistan. According to the Khaksar circle, by accepting the truncated Pakistan, the rulers' agenda was finally met through the courtesy of the AIML. The AIML intrigues against Khaksars are deplorable and provide a lesson to learn from.

From the nationalist perspective, by accepting the Mountbatten Plan (HMG's Plan), the AIML had proven that it had no resisting power. The Muslim Leaguers were power hungry and division was a short cut to power and material benefits, so the plan was quickly accepted.

The British deprived the Muslims of the region that they had ruled for almost 1,000 years. Division literally broke the Muslims' spine, and the Muslim block from India to Turkey had ended. The world knows that, throughout history, Muslims of India had shed their blood and sacrificed. Yet the majority of India had been handed over to Hindus through the courtesy of the AIML. The fact is that the policy of the British Government was anti-Muslim all along. This was not only in India but in other parts of the Muslim world too. For example, they aided the Dutch in their invasion of Indonesia. When Indonesia wanted their case to be heard in the Security Council of the United Nations, the British opposed this.[17] There are many other instances that can be quoted from history to support this assertion.

*****

The height of injustice was that Muslim majority provinces of Bengal and Punjab were partitioned. On the other hand, the Hindu majority provinces were kept intact. The injustice did not end there; in Muslim majority provinces even districts were divided and made part of India.[18] Twenty one Muslim states were made part of India besides Jummu and Kashmir.[19]

Muslims ended up where Muslims were already in majority. So the questions are:

❖ Why was division sought when the AIML version of Pakistan would only provide protection to Muslims in areas where they were already in the majority? How could the AIML believe that it would be practical for Muslims from all over India to migrate to Pakistan?

❖ What was the League's plan to accommodate the entire Muslim community? If they had no plan, then on whose instructions were they sacrificing more than half of the Muslim population? What was the sense in partitioning India if all Muslims could not be secured?

Does any of this sound credible or persuasive to anyone who thinks logically? It would not be wrong to state that the Two-Nation Theory was not even applicable in Muslim majority areas. If there was an issue of Muslim rights, it was in the provinces where Muslims were in minority. All those areas went to India.

With this division, Hindus were consolidated, where as Muslims were torn apart.

According to nationalists, the reality is that the British used the AIML for their own ends; once their objective was achieved, the British discarded the Muslim League, partitioned Punjab and Bengal and left Kashmir a disputed territory.

*****

---

[17] *The Eastern Times*, August 20, 1947.
[18] Hussain, P. 238.
[19] Ibid.

The AIML even failed to put up any proper resistance or pressure to obtain Kashmir. On October 26, 1947, Maharaja of Kashmir sent a letter to Mountbatten (who had become the first Governor General of India on the day of partition) via V.P. Menon declaring accession to the Indian Union. He also requested to send forces to help him. Mountbatten wrote back on October 27, 1947 accepting Kashmir's accession to India. On the same day, Mountbatten sent his forces to Kashmir. Mountbatten also accepted the suggestion of Maharaja to invite Sheikh Abdullah to form an Interim Government.[20] According to *The Eastern Times* (of November 11, 1947), from October 24-26, 1947, Mountbatten had consulted with the chiefs of three defense services and worked out a complete plan of occupying Kashmir. Despite declaring impartiality, Mountbatten personally supervised the operation. If he had become the Governor General of Pakistan, all these injustices that were done to Pakistan could have been avoided. *The Eastern Times* of November 11, 1947 reported that Mountbatten was

> "...no longer the constitutional and impartial head of the Indian Government. He, as India's Supreme Commander, is also planning the operations, maturing military schemes and supervising their tactical execution. The British people have played many a black role in history before, but this will go down as the blackest on record."

According to the Khaksar circle, if he had been the first Governor General of Pakistan, Mountbatten would have been morally obligated not to do injustice to Pakistan. He took revenge on Pakistan because it was his desire to be the first Governor General of both countries. Obviously, Radcliffe must also have been influenced by him. The question is was Quaid-e-Azam's demand of becoming the first Governor General right?

Anyhow Indian forces had already landed in Kashmir. Mashraqi alarmed the Government and pointed out the conspiracy between Gandhi and Mountbatten in a statement on December 03, 1947 he said:

> "We have seen the dire consequences of the partition of Punjab and Bengal...This idea [partition of Kashmir] is now being vigorously pursued in high Congress circles and Mr. Gandhi and Lord Mountbatten are the co-conspirators of this deadly game."[21]

Mashraqi again warned the Government that it must not take half-hearted actions or Pakistan would lose Kashmir forever. He suggested obtaining Kashmir forcibly for which he offered Khaksar services for military operation. He had already established links in Kashmir with many freedom seeking forces. Khaksar camps were also established in Sialkot,[22] but despite requests from Mashraqi for support, the Government again created problems for him and did not come forward to support Khaksars. To Mashraqi, it was time for

---

[20] *The Eastern Times*, October 29, 1947.
[21] Hussain, Pp. 235-36.
[22] Hussain, P. 237.

immediate action and any delays would have had serious consequences, but the Pakistani Government prevented Mashraqi from moving any further.

Mashraqi made another effort to mobilize world opinion and undo the injustice in Kashmir; in this connection, he wanted to travel abroad but was denied by the Government of Pakistan. On December 30, 1950 at Iqbal Park Lahore, Mashraqi stated:

> "Our rulers [Pakistani Government] were coward, ease-loving and fearful of the Hindus, and therefore failed to take proper action in time."[23]

Mashraqi's assessment turned out to be true and Pakistan has not yet been able to liberate Kashmir.

---

[23] Hussain, P. 240.

Chapter 12

Conclusion: All India Muslim League's Thirst for Power

To nationalists, the AIML sought partition to seize power! Most of us believe that the AIML put up a great fight to seek a homeland for Muslims. Is that true? To ascertain the correct answer one must not ignore the point of view of Muslim and non-Muslim nationalist leaders, who were against the division of India. Their point of view has been concealed on purpose. In this work, I am making an endeavor to bring forth their perspective, which changes the entire complexion of Pakistan's history and allows one to see the AIML in a different light. This perspective enables one to reach the conclusion that the AIML struggle was for power and they misled the illiterate masses.

During my research, I read the correspondence and statements of important people, including Indian leaders and the British high ups, as well as intelligence reports, fortnightly reports of Governors, articles, books, various old newspapers (primarily from late 1930's to 1963) and so on. My findings are further substantiated when one studies and contemplates world politics, particularly the West's overall relationship with the Muslim world.

I had been debating over the idea of enlightening people about the AIML's real motive behind seeking partition of India. I have substantiated my examination of this area with evidence. The idea is not to disparage anyone, rather it is to reveal the nationalist point of view, so that readers may learn from the past and make more informed decisions.

I would certainly seek pardon from those who might be hurt; my intent is not to injure anyone's feelings as this would bring nothing to me but their resentment.

*****

Let's briefly take into account the AIML's background. Since its establishment in 1906, the AIML could not succeed in organizing the Muslims. The party comprised of elite Muslims, primarily beneficiaries of the British. It would not be wrong to state that the AIML had the least interest in the masses. If one studies the history, there is nothing that supports that AIML had done anything concrete to lift the masses. It was more of a club of the elite than a political party. They were mainly focused on looking after their own interest. In few words, this club lacked direction, unity, sincerity, organization and most importantly roots in the masses. Thus, they lost miserably in the 1937 elections.

There is no denying the fact that in the late 1930's, the Khaksar Tehreek had emerged as the most powerful Muslim organization in the entire British India. After the League lost elections in 1937 and the Congress party emerged victorious, the Muslim Leaguers felt that they were nowhere in comparison to Khaksar Tehreek and Congress party. The Leaguers were nervous and highly perturbed at this state of affairs. With Khaksars having roots in the masses and Congress winning the 1937 elections, the AIML was fearful of their popularity. A Jinnah-Sikander pact, signed on October 15, 1937, was a result of this nervousness. The Jinnah-Sikander pact suited both and was formed to contain the Khaksar Tehreek in the Punjab, one of the most important provinces where the Khaksar Tehreek had its headquarters and was extremely popular. The All India Muslim League National Guard and the demand for a separate homeland for Muslims were also results of this thought process. Both of these came after the League badly lost the 1937 elections.

The Muslim League's high command was extremely jubilant when the Congress withdrew its support of Khan Bahadur Allah Bux Ministry in Sind province in 1938, because they saw a hope of creating their own *first* League Ministry ever.[1] However, negotiations in this regard broke down between Jinnah and Khan Bahadur Allah Bux, Premier of Sind. Khan Bahadur Allah Bux refused "to form a purely Muslim League Ministry."[2] The newspaper further reported: "Mr. Jinnah persuaded a majority of the members to sign the League pledges. This was objected to by the Khan Bahadur who left the meeting along with his followers in protest."[3] *The Tribune*, Lahore of October 13, 1938 also reported "Later, Sir Abdulla Haroon and other prominent Muslim leaders dashed to the residence of" Allah Bux and persuaded him.[4] Another meeting was held the next day and Allah Bux informed Jinnah that the "Ministry shall not be called a League Ministry."[5] This was not acceptable to the League. Thus, the talks broke down.[6] These talks were not successful primarily because the AIML wanted to be dominant in the Sind Ministry.

---

[1] *The Tribune*, September 12, 1938.
[2] *The Tribune*, October 13, 1938.
[3] Ibid.
[4] Ibid.
[5] Ibid.
[6] Ibid.

In 1939, the AIML tried to win over the Khaksar Tehreek by making offers to settle their dispute with the U.P. Government over the Shia-Sunni riots. In 1939, when Congress Ministries throughout India resigned, the AIML celebrated in the hope of forming its own Government. The AIML all along was making desperate attempts to gain ground and establish Ministries wherever they could.

Meanwhile, the Tehreek had already emerged as an extremely powerful force in India. To contain the movement, Sir Sikandar Hayat Khan (member of the Working Committee of the AIML) imposed a ban on the Khaksars and Mashraqi was arrested.

*****

The AIML was generally criticized for its poor policies and lack of political vision. Based on the heavy disapproval, the League realized that in order to gain power, it had to develop a program which would bind and give direction to the Muslim community. The League decided to use Islam and communalism as tools to achieve their ambition; thus the Two-Nation Theory (dividing India into two nations for Hindus and Muslims) was devised and thought to be the best and easiest solution to meet their aims. This theory was an expression of political aspirations of the AIML; it was never a demand of the majority of the Muslims and non-Muslims. In other words, religion and communalism were brought into politics to seek control over Muslim masses by arousing Muslim communal sentiments. The Two-Nation Theory was meant to use religious sentiments for political motives. This was regarded as a mischievous concept by many nationalist politicians with long term vision.

The British supported this theory for their own vested reasons as it would promote their divide and rule policy. This was evident from the fact that on March 24, 1940, only a few hours before passing of the Pakistan Resolution (which called for the establishment of Pakistan under the Two-Nation Theory), the Punjab Governor attended a party thrown by Premier of Punjab, Sir Sikandar Hayat Khan, in honor of Jinnah. If this theory was not under British tutelage, do you think Sikandar would have thrown a party for Jinnah and that the Governor would have attended it? This showed that the British gave the official signal in favor of the Pakistan Resolution.

Thus, the Pakistan Resolution, based on the Two-Nation Theory, would not have gone through if it did not have the blessings of the British. Jinnah had discussed it in his meetings with the Viceroy.[7] The British knew this demand was forthcoming. The Viceroy wrote to the Secretary of State on March 12, 1940, "document has been prepared for adoption by the Muslim League with a view to be given the fullest publicity."[8]

---

[7] See note of interview between Jinnah and Linlithgow on September 04, 1939 and Viceroy to the Secretary of State on March 16, 1940 in Singh, Pp. 56-57.
[8] Khan, Khan Abdul Wali. Chapter 5.

After the Lahore session on March 22-24, 1940, which resulted in the passing of the Pakistan Resolution (Lahore Resolution), the stage was set for Quaid-e-Azam to emerge as the leader of the Muslims. The AIML was recognized by the British as the party to represent the Muslims.[9] After the resolution, the AIML was treated at par with the Congress.

The Pakistan Resolution was a bargaining card for the AIML to negotiate for power with the Congress. The Pakistan Resolution enhanced the rift between the AIML and the Congress and created a rift between the AIML and nationalist Muslims. The AIML happily accepted the role to confront the Congress and the Khaksars (who were nationalists) to gain prominence and seek power. The Pakistan Resolution was to benefit the League whether Pakistan was to be created or not. The British did not elevate the AIML to help Muslims, but for their vested reasons. In short, the Two-Nation Theory suited the British and the AIML very well.

Professor U.N. Ball wrote under the title, "Mr. Jinnah's Fallacies":

> "The communal spirit has been fanned by those who do not want to part with power."[10]

Quaid-e-Azam himself admitted that his position was elevated in his statement during the historic AIML session (March 22-24) in 1940. *The Hindustan Times*, on March 23, 1940, reported Jinnah's words:

> "But after the war was declared, the Viceroy naturally wanted help from the League. Suddenly, there came a change in the attitude of the Viceroy towards me. I was treated on the same basis as Mahatma Gandhi... I was wonder-struck why all of a sudden I was promoted and given a place side by side with Mahatma Gandhi."

In essence, Jinnah was elevated to be the sole representative of Muslims and to fight the Khaksar Tehreek and undermine Mashraqi's position in politics. Quaid-e-Azam achieved this position soon after Mashraqi was arrested and a ban was imposed on the Khaksar Tehreek in March 1940. Quaid-e-Azam never admitted this fact.

On March 24, 1940, the AIML took a position, from which the League never again budged, without considering the overall ramifications for the entire Muslim community or the role of Pakistan and India in the world as two separate countries. The AIML maintained the rift with non-Muslim and Muslim parties all in order to please the British. If all parties had joined hands against the rulers, British rule would have ended there and then.

---

[9] In the Viceroy's speech of October 17, 1939, within weeks of start of World War II, the Viceroy recognized the AIML as the representative of the Muslims. This was just a few months before the passing of the Pakistan Resolution.
[10] *The Tribune*, December 01, 1945.

*****

The British had their own interest in the Two-Nation Theory, thus, they did not object to it. It would enhance the rift between the Muslims and Hindus and also among Muslims, thereby allowing the British to prolong their stay in India. Meanwhile, to the outside world, the British were implying that they were sympathetic to the needs of the Muslims. Thus, the British did not put any resistance to Lahore Resolution (Pakistan Resolution).

Without a doubt, the British wanted to implement their own agenda; hence they recognized the AIML, who they knew sought wealth, fancy titles and power, as the representatives of Muslims. History is witness to the fact that powerful nations have been appointing people in developing countries who will implement their agenda. India was no exception to the rule. The Viceroy had picked the AIML and made Quaid-e-Azam powerful so that no one could challenge his authority. The Viceroy had written (on May 14, 1940) to Zetland, "Indeed I am sure that Jinnah remains the man to deal with on Muslim side."[11] It is important to note that the Viceroy's letter was written soon after the ban on the Khaksars was imposed. The British chose to deal only with the AIML, regardless of how powerful and popular the Khaksar Tehreek was at the time. This is because they knew that the AIML's nature was to seek power and political gains and that they (the British) could use this to achieve their own ends. The British used the AIML to confront the Khaksar Tehreek and the Congress in order to prolong their stay in India. The British fed the AIML from behind the scenes, implying their demand to be the public stand. From public pronouncements and speeches by the AIML leaders, it seemed that the AIML was putting up a rigorous fight to protect Muslims rights.

*****

The question is why did many Muslims[12] support AIML's Two-Nation Theory? Muslims supported this idea because they were led to believe that they could no longer live with Hindus, that Islam was in danger and that Pakistan would solve their problems. These factors obviously made sense to people who were primarily uneducated. To the illiterate masses, the creation of Pakistan would equal protection of their interests and a brighter future.

History is witness to the fact that people can be riled up on the basis of religion and hopes of a better future, however false the proclamations might be. Even today, many politicians apply this technique and do not hesitate to provoke communalism or sectarianism in their greed for power. People can be driven with slogans and this is what was done, through slogans such as "Islam in

---

[11] Khan, Khan Abdul Wali. Chapter 5.
[12] In the history books, it is implied as if all Muslims supported the AIML and its theory. This of course is incorrect.

danger." The AIML propagated communalism and misled the Muslim public to believe in the Two-Nation Theory; by inciting emotions, the AIML hypnotized the public.

*****

Nationalist Muslims knew that the general Muslim population was being misled and that the Two-Nation Theory was impractical. From its passing in 1940 until partition in 1947, the Pakistan Resolution was highly criticized by Muslims and non-Muslims. If the Two-Nation Theory had been the only solution to the political problems of India, there would not have been so much resistance from nationalists. Nationalist Muslims and non-Muslims regarded the AIML to be pawns in the hands of British as it would bring them fame, power, wealth and other benefits. The AIML disregarded all opposition to its partition plan.

Mashraqi did not support this scheme as he knew that it would bring hatred and suffering of the people, and he believed that communal bias and abhorrence were indeed un-Islamic. The Khaksar Tehreek was meant to serve the entire human race, which is the *essence* of Islamic teaching, and end all evil forces that created disunity, hatred and sectarianism. The Two-Nation Theory, on the contrary, promoted division in all sister communities. This is one of the reasons why the Khaksar Tehreek and Muslim League could not reconcile.

Maulana Moulvi Mohammad Syed (General Secretary of the Jammu and Kashmir National Conference) referred to the Muslim League's scheme of partition.

> "Maulana Mohammad Syed…said…the Partition scheme put forward by Mr. Jinnah amounts to waging a war against Islam."[13]

Other leaders also condemned the theory. Khan Bahadur Shaikh Mohammad Jan (MLC) issued a press statement which appeared in *The Hindustan Times* (April 03, 1940) under the title:

> "Jinnah's 'Impracticable and Absurd' Scheme."

Dr. Saifuddin Kitchlew criticized the Pakistan Resolution, as reported in *The Hindustan Times* dated March 28, 1940:

> Dr. Kitchlew said: "The separatist resolution passed at the Lahore session of the Muslim League is a wild-goose chase. Mr Jinnah and his satellites are obviously playing into the hands of the British imperialists and making it easier for them to continue their rule by dividing India into the so-called religious zones. The scheme…most

---

[13] *The Tribune*, May 01, 1940.

impracticable, and I am sure no sane Muslim will be taken in by such a scheme."

According to the newspaper, "he [Dr. Kitchlew] opined that ...the League disregarded the fact that religion had been relegated to its proper place and the sense of religiosity is being entirely discouraged. It is the purely economic and political forces that are guiding the destinies of nations today...

...He wanted the leaders of the Muslim League, majority of whom obviously represented British Imperialist interests — or their personal interests — if they had the least sense of patriotism in them, to carefully study the trend of public opinion and the conditions prevailing in the country...He was sure...many of the responsible Muslim leaders were themselves not satisfied with all that was said in the Muslim League session... resolution ... was... mischievous... derogatory to the self-respect of the Muslims."

Mohammad Rashid Ali Baig (member of the Muslim League and President of Indian Progressive Group) resigned from the Muslim League. According to the newspaper,

"Baig says that now that the partition of India has been accepted as its official creed by the Moslem League he has no alternative but to resign as he believes that partition will make communal unity impossible of achievement, and will leave the minority problem unsolved."[14]

Another leader, K.B. Allah Bux (Baksh), former Premier of Sind, addressing 25,000 people, talked on the Muslim League scheme of partition for a long time. He said:

"The Pakistan scheme is about the most indiscreet approach to a serious problem." According to the newspaper, "Bux sets it [partition scheme] down as grotesque and mischievous."[15]

A big conference was held in Delhi. Muslim speakers opposed the Muslim League's Lahore Resolution.[16] Arbab Abdul Rahman, Member Legislative Assembly (NWFP) said:

"Pakistan scheme was an absurdity... He condemned the false cry of 'Islam in danger' raised by the Muslim League...Muslim Leaguers had raised the bogey of Islam in danger in order to secure ministerships."[17]

At the Delhi conference, a resolution on the Pakistan scheme was passed unanimously characterizing it

[14] *The Statesman*, March 26, 1940.
[15] *The Hindustan Times*, April 28, 1940.
[16] *The Hindustan Times*, April 29, 1940.
[17] The *Hindustan Times*, April 30, 1940.

"as impracticable and harmful to the country's interest generally and those of Muslims in particular."[18]

Abdul Qaiyum Ansari, President Bihar Provincial Jamiat-ul-Momineen made a statement. According to the newspaper,

> "...Ansari said that the League's Pakistan scheme would not only divide India into Hindu and Muslim Indias, but would also divide Muslims into several factions and sections...Mr. Jinnah's reactionary and power-hunting leadership would bring nothing but shame and disaster to Muslims...
>
> ...a body like the Muslim League which consisted of rich and upper class people and which was brought into being at the instance and for the purpose of the Imperial masters... League which was...unpatriotic body and which consisted of those whose sole object was to dance attendance on their foreign rulers and keep India as bondage.
>
> *Speaking on the Pakistan scheme, he severely condemned it and said that such a mischievous proposal could only emanate from a fevered brain.*"[19]

The Muslim Majlis manifesto added:

> "The attempt to create a geographical barrier has been a gigantic political blunder on the part of the propounders of Pakistan. While the whole world is improving upon the most advanced ideas of political solidarity, enslaved India is being compelled to make suicide in the name of Pakistan.
>
> ...The Muslim leaders have always thought more of themselves and the common Muslims have all along been exploited. The self-styled leaders made them constantly feel that they had been deprived of their legitimate rights and privileges by the Hindus. But they were never induced to aspire for the freedom of their country.
>
> Mr. Jinnah's leadership of the Muslim League is one of the numerous links of the reactionary chain of the selfish and self-styled leaders. He is indeed one of those leaders who have blocked the way to the goal of freedom and national unity. As long as such leaders are allowed to reign supreme there is no chance of any compromise among the two great communities in India... This reactionary leadership is powerful weapon in the hands of the British Government to resist the aspiration of 400 million people in their struggle for freedom. We must make an end of reactionary leadership to save our community from its baneful effects. Mr. Jinnah is now and then haughtily insisting that all his demands must be accepted verbatim by the Hindus, but does not explain and clarify the issue underlying this absurd and ridiculous demand."[20]

---

[18] The *Hindustan Times*, April 30, 1940.
[19] *The Hindustan Times*, June 22, 1940.
[20] *The Bombay Chronicle*, August 02, 1943.

At a meeting on December 06, 1943 in Lahore, Syed Attaullah Shah Bukhari, leader of the Ahrars party, questioned Jinnah and said:

> "What is there of Islam in you? Do you have faith in the holy Quran? Are you prepared to live the life ordained by the holy Quran?"
>
> According to the newspaper, "Syed Attaullah Shah and Maulana Mazhar Ali Azhar, M.L.A. [Member Legislative Assembly], who spoke on the occasion, characterized the cry of Pakistan as a big hoax and vote-catching device."[21]

A resolution by Nationalist Muslim Parliamentary Board was passed that stated:

> "...Muslim League which is entirely a capitalist organisation and which has formed an alliance with the Imperialist Government to exploit the Mussalmans for their own selfish ends..."[22]

H.N. Brailsford in his book titled, *Subject India*, referring to the Two-Nation Theory wrote:

> "Mr. Jinnah denies the existence of an Indian Nation and maintains that two distinct nations inhabit this peninsula...If so, it is strange that this able man should have discovered this basic fact of Indian life only in the last phase of a long public career."[23]

Nationalists believed that the Muslim League misled the people in the name of Islam; this is evident from the open letter of Barrister Aftab Iqbal (son of Allama Iqbal) sent to Jawahar Lal Nehru on July 23, 1946 from Lahore:

> "...during the last election they were duped by the League propagandists in the name of God and the Holy Prophet and that Islam, after all, is not so much in danger of being wiped out as they were persuaded to believe...with well organised Congress propaganda it will not be difficult for the Congress to enlist the sympathy and support of the Muslim masses who were grossly misled by the provincial henchmen of the League aristocracy. If the League High Command, which is composed primarily of Nawabs, landlords and Muslim capitalists prefers to remain a mere tool in the hands of British Imperialism the Congress must go ahead and win the freedom of India...Unfortunately the men who form the League Working Committee and the League provincial bodies lack intellectual culture, patriotism, political farsightedness catholicity of outlook and sympathetic understanding of the problems, hopes and fears of millions of starving Muslims with whom they seldom come in personal contact. Their one principal aim is to capture power with the assistance of the ignorant Muslim peasant with whom they have nothing in common and whose economic welfare is, to them, a matter

---

[21] *The Hindustan Times*, December 09, 1943.
[22] *The Tribune*, September 20, 1945.
[23] *The Tribune*, March 22, 1946.

of indifference. My observation and experience have convinced me that now is the time for the Muslim masses to capture the League and then to co-operate with the national forces in freeing India from the yoke of foreign rule. If this is not done now there will be nothing in store for them later but kicks and insults from their feudal lords and aristocratic masters.

When in the year 1936 Mr. Jinnah came to the Punjab and sought the assistance of my late father in consolidating the League in this province the latter made it perfectly clear to him that he was only interested in a people's Muslim League wherein the voice of the masses would predominate and believing that Mr. Jinnah was also working to the same end offered him all his support. He then threw himself heart and soul into the League movement and overhauled the entire body of the Punjab Provincial Muslim League purging it of all its undesirable elements. Had he then the slightest suspicion that soon after his death a few half educated, selfish and ambitious Nawabs and Muslim capitalists from Muslim minority provinces under the leadership of Mr. Jinnah would capture the League by exploiting the ignorance and poverty of the Muslim masses he would have taken strong precautionary measures to prevent the League Organization from falling into such hands. Had he lived the Muslim League would have been quite different from what it is to-day for he would never have tolerated the callous indifference with which public spirited Mussalmans of liberal and progressive views and with profound sympathy with the hopes and aspirations of the Muslim masses are being treated by the League High Command and their provincial subordinates who have no will of their own..."[24]

Edward Thomson wrote in his book, titled, *Enlist India*, about his interview with Jinnah on the League's theory:

"Two nations. Mr. Jinnah! Confronting each other in every province? every town? every village?... That is a very terrible solution, Mr. Jinnah!"[25]

On December 12, 1946, Sheikh Abdul Majid spoke at the Inter-Cultural Association. According to the newspaper,

"Majid said...The division of India meant division of Islam. The Muslims now claimed to be 10 crores, but, if India was divided, Muslims of one part of India would be divided from the other part of India."[26]

*****

It is interesting to note that the Muslim League leadership was secular and hardly inclined towards Islam, yet they were seeking division on the basis of

---

[24] *The Tribune*, July 25, 1946.
[25] *The Tribune*, November 09, 1945.
[26] *The Tribune*, December 13, 1946.

religion. According to political circles, Quaid-e-Azam wanted to emerge as champion of Muslims and acquire national stature. The Two-Nation Theory was used to meet this aspiration. Otherwise, he was a secular person and his appreciation of Ataturk (who separated state from religion) also supports his belief in secularism. His belief in secularism was further proven by his speech in the Constituent Assembly on August 11, 1947. Jinnah said:

> "You may belong to any religion or caste or creed – that has nothing to do with the business of the State...Now, I think we should keep that in front of us as our ideal and you will find that in course of time Hindus would cease to be Hindus and Muslims would cease to be Muslims, not in the religious sense, because that is the personal faith of each individual, but in the political sense as citizens of the State."[27]

Quaid-e-Azam's speech was an utter surprise to the nationalist. He finally declared to the world that he was a secular minded person. It seems that, in the heart of his heart, he knew that his scheme of the Two-Nation Theory was not workable. His speech deviated from the basic principle and stance of the Muslim League on which division was demanded. This causes controversy and confusion and raises many questions. There are various justifications that are given to support Jinnah's statement of August 11, however, these do not satisfy one's mind. Those who justify it are providing unnecessary protection to the theory. Even if it is agreed that the theory was the only alternative solution to the problems of the people, then the question is did the Two-Nation Theory bring desired results?

It is also important and strange to note that the parameters of the demand for Pakistan were never properly explained to the people. The Muslim League never explained their theory and kept the nation in the dark. The definition of Pakistan remained a mystery to many. *The Tribune*, Lahore of September 13, 1943 called the demand of Pakistan a "stunt." It further wrote:

> "Mr. Jinnah has cleverly evaded the issue so far. He has consistently refused to define either the geographical limits of his Pakistan or the political, military and economic implications of his pet scheme. He knows well enough that as soon as he is compelled to define what his Pakistan means in effect and what its final implications amount to, his idol will be found to have feet of clay."

Even in 1947, this was the case. Sir Evan Jenkins, the Punjab Governor, met Khawaja Nazimuddin on February 18, 1947 and later wrote in his fortnightly report to the Viceroy:

> "In our first meeting Khawaja Nazim-ud-Din admitted candidly that he did not know what Pakistan means, and that nobody in the ML knew..."[28]

---

[27] Government of Pakistan 1989.
[28] March 1947, IOL L/P&J/5/250, P. 379.

*****

The Two-Nation Theory was flawed from the beginning. It embodied the idea that the Hindus were dominating Muslims and Islam was in jeopardy, hence a separate homeland was needed for the Muslims. This was untrue and did not make sense given the circumstances.

For ages, Muslims have lived with people of different religions, cultures and languages in different countries. Similarly, Muslims and Hindus had been living alongside in India for a long period; how is it possible that all of a sudden in 1940, they could not co-exist? This is not by any imagination a convincing reason for the creation of a separate country.

The preaching of Islam was not prohibited in India, so Islam was not in any danger. Islam can be spread more so by Muslims living with other communities, rather than by segregation or isolation. Further, how could Hindus be dominating in Muslim majority areas? If they were, then there must have been something wrong with the Muslim leadership. We cannot blame Hindus or non-Muslims for everything. To put blame on others is the easiest thing to do in order to provide an excuse or justify an act. Hence, the logic behind the Pakistan Resolution that Islam was in danger or that the Hindus were dominating Muslims does not make sense.

The Two-Nation Theory did nothing but propagate communalism, which is completely un-Islamic. Remember! It is the responsibility of the leader to teach the nation what is best for its interest. However, the AIML misled the public without realizing the overall repercussions.

This theory, as it appeared to the public, was that it would unite and provide security to Muslims. In reality, there was no way that this plan could secure 100 million Muslims.

With the creation of Pakistan, the theory did not secure Muslims and instead divided them into three parts. If the Muslims had known that this plan would divide them and more than half would have to live in India under Hindu domination, they would not have supported it. In the end, more than half of the Muslims could not migrate to Pakistan for different reasons.

If the intent of the theory really was to secure the entire Muslim community in India then why were Indian Muslims denied entry into Pakistan soon after creation? *The Pakistan Times* reported:

"Pakistan opposed to mass migration of Indian Muslims."[29]

---

[29] *The Pakistan Times*, October 16, 1947.

Nawabzada Liaquat Ali Khan, Prime Minister of Pakistan, said:

> "If such conditions are created as to lead to a mass exodus from any part of India other than the East Punjab, the Pakistan Government will have to review the whole situation and adopt such measures as may be necessary to resist any such design, for they are firmly of the opinion that it will be disastrous to the interest of both Dominions.
>
> The programme of mass evacuation of Muslims is strictly limited and applies only to the East Punjab for reasons mentioned above..."[30]

A final ban was imposed on immigration of Indian Muslims in the early fifties. Why was this done? Wasn't Pakistan created for every Muslim living in British India?

Further, Quaid-e-Azam stated on October 11, 1947:

> "My advice to Muslim brethren in India is to give unflinching loyalty to the State in which they happen to be."[31]

Those who support the Two-Nation Theory say that division was indispensable and power was not the motive, however they cannot explain how partition secured the entire Muslim community.

The Two-Nation Theory stood the test of time and failed! This plan led to disaster and hatred – the displacement of Muslims, divisions within Muslims and between Muslims and non-Muslims, loss of loved ones and property for the Muslims, and more. Further, partition secured the Hindus and unsecured the Muslims. Indirectly, the communalism policy resulted in a gift for Hindus, and Pakistan became a less important country in world politics, as compared to India. The Muslim League received a truncated and weak Pakistan. The Two-Nation Theory further died after the creation of Bangladesh, as the religion, Islam, could not keep the two wings of the country together.

*****

Upon reflection, it is true that much hatred had been bred between the Hindus and Muslims in the years prior to 1947, however this was instigated by forces, who had their own reasons to perpetuate conflict. This conflict was not real reason to divide the country and could have been resolved, given the fact that the Muslims and Hindus had ties that significantly outlasted the conflict itself.

In the years prior to partition, WWII was crippling the British and demand for freedom in India was gaining strength. Nationalists, like the Khaksars, would no longer allow the British to continue their rule. The Two-Nation Theory legitimized division of India, thus leaving behind an even weaker Muslim

---

[30] *The Pakistan Times*, October 16, 1947.
[31] *The Pakistan Times*, October 12, 1947. *The Eastern Times*, October 14, 1947.

population. The British did not want to leave behind a strong Muslim population which could potentially rise to become a Muslim Empire, hence division of India was key to their interests. A weaker and smaller Pakistan was acceptable to the British. Thus, the British did not put any resistance to Lahore Resolution (Pakistan Resolution).

Further, the British ensured the AIML's win in the 1946 elections; in this way, the AIML appeared to be the legitimate representative of the Muslim community. Hence, the AIML's politics, including the Two-Nation Theory, automatically gained legitimacy.

It is important to note that the British did not actively support the Two-Nation Theory, rather they did it from behind the scenes. The British completely understood that this theory was impractical.

In the end, the British did what they had to do. They divided India to maintain the balance of power in the region; further a rift in the region was essential to enable the British to sell warfare equipment, arms and ammunition, technology and so on.[32]

---

[32] The main objective of dividing India was to keep any regional power from rising against the West. The intricacies of this are described as follows.

First, the aim was to weaken the Muslims so that they would not rise again. Muslims were spread in many countries across the world, from East Asia to Africa. A Hindu state was created to prevent the formation of a Muslim block.

On the other hand, Pakistan was also created as a buffer state to prevent the rise of Hindus. If the Hindus decided to rise, then the West could use the Muslims sitting on either side of India as a force to suppress Hindus. Through East and West wings of Pakistan, the world powers could pull India's strings as and when desired.

India was also divided to thwart the spread of communism. It was felt that India might go far left, and communism might spread into India, which would pose a significant threat to the West. Communist influence on the Muslim oil states would also pose a danger to the West. Hence, the West wanted to prevent the influence of communism from spreading into the region. Under the circumstances, an Islamic state was indispensable to prevent the spread of communism. Pakistan would serve as a barrier against Soviet advancement into India.

The Tribune of June 04, 1947 in its editorial wrote: "...the unity of India has been planned to be broken...

The position is this British Imperialists chanakyas gain and we fools lose all along the line. They are in mortal dread of the deepening and expanding influence of the Soviet Union and Communism. They wanted to create a buffer State between them and the progressive forces in India and link up their reactionary Muslim allies in Egypt, Turkey, Arab countries, Persia and Afghanistan with those in this country. Pakistan would serve this particular purpose of theirs admirably. That is why the British plan is designed not only to bring into existence, but also to strengthen it by compelling the Pushto-speaking area to join it."

Hence, the West did not want any power rising against them, whether Muslim, Hindu or communist. Breaking up the region would create buffer states, avert alliances and keep the region's power in check. This has played out since the independence of the region. For instance, in the 1950s, USA created Badaber base facility near Peshawar in NWFP, in exchange for assistance to Pakistan. This was done to contain Russian advances; hence, Pakistan was needed to contain Russia. In 1971, India wanted to weaken Pakistan but was stopped from attacking West Pakistan; here, Pakistan's presence was important to contain India. On the other hand, today, India is being used to contain Pakistan and China. A US think tank, Stratfor, recently confirmed:

In Pakistan's history books, we do not find an analytical view of the Two-Nation Theory. Views of nationalist Muslims on Two-Nation Theory have been eliminated on purpose and criticism is not tolerated. People even fear arrest, if they criticize Quaid-e-Azam or the Two-Nation Theory. This is a gross violation of the right of speech. It is not advisable to ignore opinions; other perspectives are important to further our country's learning.

*****

According to nationalists, the Leaguers wanted power, and in 1947 right before partition, Jinnah voiced his demand to be the first Governor General of Pakistan. Mountbatten was furious when he heard of Quaid-e-Azam's desire to be the first Governor General; he conveyed to Jinnah to not think along those lines as it would cause problems for Pakistan. In other words, he made it clear to Jinnah that Mountbatten himself wanted to go down in history as the common Governor General for the two countries.

Mountbatten attempted to explain to Quaid-e-Azam that this might cause problems for Pakistan and

> "Jinnah solemnly assured me [Viceroy] that he realised all the disadvantages of giving up the common governor general... but he was unable to accept any position other than the Governor-General of Pakistan on 15th August..."[33]

The Viceroy made a final attempt to be the first Governor General of Pakistan as reported in a book by Khan Abdul Wali Khan titled, *Facts are Sacred*:

> "I [Viceroy] asked him [Jinnah], 'Do you realise what this will cost? He sadly said, 'It may cost me several crores (Several Million) of rupees in assets, to which I replied some what acidly, 'It may well cost you the whole of your assets and the future of Pakistan'."[34]

Mountbatten basically conveyed that if Jinnah did not accept Mountbatten as the common Governor General, then Jinnah should be prepared for the consequences. Yet, Jinnah ignored this warning. Jinnah's desire was conveyed to Attlee. Speaking at the reading of the Indian Independence Bill in the Commons, Attlee said:

> "It had been intimated to us that it would be most convenient to all concerned to have one Governor General at least in the initial stages, and for some time we proceeded on this assumption. It recently

---

"The United States is grooming India into a junior partner to balance China's influence in the Indian Ocean region and to keep a check on a 'recalcitrant' Pakistan, says a US think-tank." ("US grooming India...", June 11, 2006.)

[33] Khan, Khan Abdul Wali. Chapter 21.

[34] Ibid.

became clear, however, that the Muslim League was in favour of a separate Governor General to be appointed for Pakistan."[35]

With all of the factors mentioned earlier, no one can say that the AIML did not seek division of India in order to gain power.

*****

After its creation, the challenge was upon the High Command of the Muslim League to prove that Pakistan was indeed created for the uplift of the Muslims. It seems that soon after the creation of Pakistan, the leadership completely forgot what Pakistan was created for. The leaders completely disregarded their priorities and had no idea where they wanted Pakistan in the next 10, 20, 30 or 50 years. They became bigger *sahibs* than the previous masters.

From the very beginning, the leaders of Pakistan overlooked the fact that they needed to strengthen civil liberties. Nothing was done on any of the core issues. Instead, the high command of the AIML ran after power. The people in power chose extremely high profile lifestyles. An atmosphere of greed for power and wealth, loot and plunder, and selfish attitudes was witnessed. The nationalistic approach was set aside and snatching a piece of the pie prevailed. Properties were taken over; in many cases, fraudulent claims of properties were lodged. As children follow examples set by their parents, the nation follows examples set by its leaders. Hence, all of these factors, including the leaders' extravagant lifestyles, became the icon for the average Pakistani. Over time, this led to a "get rich soon" mentality and acquiring wealth through unfair means became the norm. Even today, the Pakistani system is extremely corrupt.

From the beginning, even principles of Shariat were not implemented. *The Eastern Times* (of July 22, 1947) reported on the "statement of the Qaid-e-Azam that the Pakistan State would be governed by the principles of Shariat." The Muslims in India expected that the Islamic system would be implemented in Pakistan. It was supposed to be a country where equality and justice would exist. Pakistan was promised to be a model Islamic state for the rest of the world to cherish. However, this did not happen.

If Pakistan was created for what the AIML had promised, then from day one, the Leaguers should have first adopted simplicity and a modest way of life and then asked others to follow suit, because the country could not afford luxury.

Right after the creation of Pakistan, the high command of the AIML should have taken *immediate* steps including the following:

❖ Abolished the feudal system and introduced land reforms
❖ Established a compulsory education program for all

---

[35] *The Free Press Journal*, July 11, 1947.

- ❖ Formed a separate, independent and powerful judiciary
- ❖ Separated the judiciary, legislative and executive branches of Government
- ❖ Abolished the British system of bureaucracy and red tape
- ❖ Made public servants accountable and instituted strict punishments for corrupt or unfair use of authority
- ❖ Formed a new constitution, without which a country cannot function
- ❖ Formed an election commission for holding the first general elections

It was definitely possible to *at least* begin to move in these directions, in order to put the country on the right track. Quaid-e-Azam did have the power and the popularity to easily take at least the first four steps, and no Muslim Leaguer had the courage to challenge Jinnah. The nationalists question why Quaid-e-Azam and his successors did not take such crucial and practical steps.

Instead, right from the beginning, the country saw nothing but their leaders engaging in a power struggle. The AIML was exposed and soon lost its popularity, as its original strength was derived from British support. The AIML had no serious agenda and no direction for the nation and a series of problems were observed. In short, the new state shattered the expectations of the people. Elections were held in March 1954 and in East Pakistan (now Bangladesh), the Muslim League could only win eight seats.[36] The AIML crumbled fast and Pakistan deteriorated. It could not put Pakistan on the right track, and today Pakistan, according to many, is almost a failed state.

Taking a brief look across the border, the Indian leaders adopted a nationalistic approach and took the following steps:

- ❖ Maintained simplicity within their leadership
- ❖ Demolished the feudal system
- ❖ Strengthened the education and justice systems
- ❖ Strengthened the political system and democracy

India and Pakistan started their journeys with similar circumstances, but varied widely in their approaches beyond partition. The results of this are evident today.

*****

After fifty nine years of independence, religion has not bonded the people into one nation of Pakistan. Pakistanis have always been representing themselves as Pathans, Punjabis, Baluchis, Sindhis and so on. Now people are talking of a five nation theory in Pakistan; Pathans, Punjabis, Baluchis, Sindhis and Mohajirs. So does this mean that Pakistan should be divided into five countries? Religion is no reason to bond people into one nation. Otherwise from Morocco to Indonesia, there will be one nation. As a matter of fact, religious beliefs do not constitute the basis of nationhood. There are many

---

[36] *Banglapedia web site.* (2).

countries around the world where people from different faiths and beliefs live together. In North America and Europe for example, people from all over the world come and live together. People living in USA are Americans and people living in Britain are Britons, regardless of their faith or country of origin. Hence, one does not have to be a rocket scientist to understand that division on the basis of Islam was not practical and was politically motivated; to understand this, all one has to do is to study historical maps of that time illustrating areas where Muslims and non-Muslims resided. One would see that the Muslims were spread out and not located in one area or region and it was not possible that Pakistan could be carved out to protect all. The country could not be sliced based on where Muslims and non-Muslims could live separately. The wholesale exchange of population was impractical. There is no denying the fact that Two-Nation Theory failed when East Pakistan, in 1971, opted for independence.[37]

Many in Pakistan are homeless and hungry, and a lot of people live below the poverty line. Pakistanis continue to be ruled by political parties who claim to change the fate of Pakistanis. Yet, Pakistanis have heard nothing beyond slogans. We need to step back and ponder what is wrong, and where and why?

What does one gather from this state of affairs? The events in Pakistan since its creation are highly disturbing and depressing for any patriot. Now after fifty nine years of its creation, the question is did the majority of people get what they were promised or hoped to get in Pakistan? No! Only a very small percentage of the population benefited, and for the rest, life remained the same or deteriorated. So the questions are:

❖ Were people misled?
❖ Was Pakistan acquired by the privileged for the privileged?
❖ Did the majority in Pakistan gain what they were promised?

In closing, I would like to reiterate that the purpose of this book is not to demean Jinnah or ignore his role in the creation of Pakistan. Whatever Quaid-e-Azam's true intentions were, no one can say for certain. I would be the last person to condemn the father of our nation, or anyone else for that matter.

My intention with this book is to convey the nationalist point of view, which has been ignored. This will hopefully prompt a truly honest national debate on our history. Many scholars agree that Muslims have been looking up to the West for gaining or retaining power in their respective countries for more than 200 years; however, people overlook this point when it comes to the partition of India.

My point is that we must not *dwell* on the past, but rather learn from it for the future. I believe that in doing so, we can resolve our internal and external issues and formulate policies that support unity and growth for the future.

---

[37] See reference note on Mashraqi's predictions in Chapter 5.

Internally, leaders must adopt a humanistic approach and end corruption and the like to work in the interest of their people. External differences must also be resolved. Since the independence of the sub-continent, significant funds have been spent in defense rather than development, and the Kashmir issue has not ceased to be a problem. For the sake of their people, India and Pakistan must remember their heritage and unite — whether as good neighbors or eventually as one country again. If the Berlin Wall can come down, then why can Pakistan and India — which share a rich history, culture and language — not join hands? Working together rather than against one another will bring peace and prosperity to the region. Today, there have been efforts toward reconciliation, which means that there is some realization that hatred between the two countries has been destructive for the people; hence, these efforts must be intensified.

These learnings are the essence of Mashraqi's vision; if applied according to his direction, they can put an end to animosities and the region can discover prosperity.

Epilogue

Allama Mashraqi and the Khaksar Tehreek suffered heavily — physically, emotionally and financially — for the sake of bringing freedom. Mashraqi and the Khaksars worked day and night to mobilize the nation towards this cause. Unfortunately, as has been shown in this book, the historiography of Pakistan and India has, on purpose, eliminated Allama Mashraqi and the Khaksar Tehreek's role.

While I have attempted to expose many of the hidden truths in Pakistan's history in this book, a number of questions still require further research. For instance:

- Was it really necessary to divide India?
- Why would Muslim majority provinces need to be separated to secure Muslims, when the Muslims were already in the majority in these provinces?
- Was Islam and policy of communalism a political gimmick to seek power?
- Most importantly, was partition done on the behest of the colonial power? Was Pakistan created by the privileged for the privileged?

It is hence the need of the hour that Pakistani and Indian historians, who have thus far hesitated to elaborate on the Khaksar Tehreek's role, come forward and unlock the role of Mashraqi and the Khaksars towards the independence of British India. The present and future generations deserve to have knowledge on the Khaksar Tehreek's untiring efforts.

Extensive material that belongs to Mashraqi, the Khaksar Tehreek and the Islam League (the party that Mashraqi founded after the creation of Pakistan) has been missing. What is extremely disturbing is that no one in Pakistan seems to know the whereabouts of this material dating from 1930 to 1963. This material is of extremely high value and was confiscated during raids in the pre- and post- partition era. I was told that leftover material was taken over by the Government of Pakistan. Where is this material? This needs to be investigated.

In the absence of Khaksar materials, Indo-Pakistan history will remain distorted and incomplete. Allama Mashraqi's sons and daughters have, from time to time, reminded the highest authorities of this negligence, yet nothing concrete has been done. Only lip service has been given in my family's personal meetings with the Heads of the State and Federal Ministers. My mother and I met Prime Minister Zulifiqar Ali Bhutto (when he was in power and was a great fan of Mashraqi), Federal Secretary Qudrat Ullah Shahab and other dignitaries in the same connection; I personally met Maulana Kauser Niazi (when he was Information Minister). In recent years, I have written letters to the President, Prime Ministers, Federal Ministers, Chairman of Senate and Speaker National Assembly reminding them of their duty.[1] Yet there is little action. The results of our efforts are yet to be seen. Hopefully the Government authorities will recognize that the position they enjoy today is because someone else sacrificed for it.

It is true that if Mashraqi's works are published and if Khaksar material is revealed, this will create considerable controversy and open debate surrounding the partition of British India. Some hard truths that are hidden under the dust shall be revealed. Yet it is in the interest of the nation to know the truth, and then learn from history.

---

[1] See letter in Yousaf 2004.

Photographs

Photographs

Allama Mashraqi — a great visionary and freedom fighter.

Mashraqi's son, Ehsanullah Khan Aslam, died of injury due to the tear gas grenade that hit him during the police raid at the Khaksar headquarters on March 19, 1940.

Jinnah visits Mashraqi. From left to right: Liaquat Ali Khan, Allama Mashraqi, Quaid-e-Azam, Barrister Mian Ahmed Shah, Dr. Sir Zia ud Din.

Sir Sikandar Hayat Khan (in the background, wearing a sherwani and shalwar [long Indian style coat and pants]) at a Khaksar camp.

Pir Elahi Buksh (Chief Minister of Sindh Province) greeting Mashraqi.

Sir Abdul Qayyum (Premier of NWFP) witnessing the activities at a
Khaksar camp in Peshawar.

Mashraqi expected no disparity among Khaksars.
Nawab Bahadur Yar Jung (Salar of Hyderabad, sitting
second from left in the first row) with the Khaksars.

Ch. Mohammad Ali (Prime Minister of Pakistan) hosted a dinner
for political leaders who attended the All-Parties Kashmir
Conference in November of 1957. In this photo,
Ch. Mohammad Ali is seen standing with Mashraqi at the dinner.

Hussain Shaheed Suhrawardy (Prime Minister of Pakistan) invites
Mashraqi for a dinner. In this photo, Mashraqi is talking to his host.

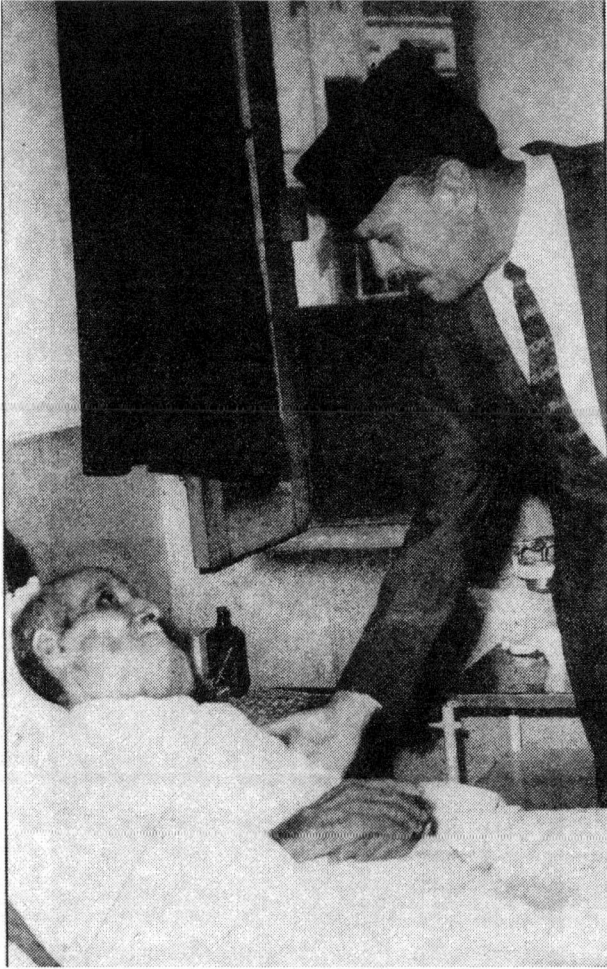

President Ayub visits Mashraqi in the hospital.

Standing: Allama Mashraqi with Khaksars and Raja Muhammad Afsar Khan (extreme left). Sitting: grandsons of Mashraqi (center: Nasim Yousaf, author).

From left to right: Syed Younus Ali Shah (Mashraqi's son-in-law), Raja Mohammad Afsar Khan, Inamullah Khan Akram (Mashraqi's son), Raja Mohammad Akbar Khan (Mashraqi's granddaughter's husband), Mohammad Yousaf Khan (Mashraqi's son-in-law), Zawar Haider.

First batch of Khaksars near Lahore. Mashraqi is in front row on the right. Mashraqi, a world-renowned scholar from Cambridge University picked up the spade, a tool of the poor man, to revolutionize the lives of the masses.

Mashraqi delivering speech at Badshahi Mosque, Lahore (1936).

Crowds gathered to hear Mashraqi speak.

Mashraqi (first row, second from left) leads and directs the nation to
rise for freedom. Mashraqi believed in equality. Here, he parades
with fellow Khaksars.

Mashraqi does not require expensive setup to address his people. Here he stands on an ordinary table and talks to Khaksars.

Allama Mashraqi with Khaksars at a Quetta Khaksar Camp.

Mashraqi goes to Khaksars and delivers his message. He does not require a fancy stage to address his people.

Left to right: Dr. Muhammad Ali, Raja Sher Zaman, Allama Mashraqi, Dr. Nazar Muhammad and other Khaksars at the Rawalpindi (Punjab) Khaksar Camp in 1936.

Mashraqi witnesses Khaksar activity at a Khasar camp. He is standing on the right with his children.

Khaksars parade at a Khaksar Camp in Peshawar.

A scene of a mock war.

Khaksars were always engaged and were ready to perform any duty may it be for the cause of community service or the message to rise for freedom, unity, or brotherhood.

A smart turnout of Khaksars, standing in formation at a Khaksar Camp. Public witnesses Khaksar activities. Such camps were held in different parts of India at various times. These camps were not only a source of training but also a great source of motivation for the public to rise for freedom.

Smartly dressed Khaksars standing outside their camp.

A group photo of the robust Khaksars.

A robust Khaksar.

Khaksar salars at a Khaksar camp.

Khaksar leaders at a training camp.

Khaksars determined to bring freedom to their country.

Khaksar parades generate great enthusiasm amongst the public.
(Photo courtesy of Khaksar Sher Zaman.)

Khaksars mobilize the public for freedom.

Khaksars stand proudly in formation.

Khaksars parade in protest through the streets of Lahore on March 19, 1940.
Many of these Khaksars became victims of the brutal
Khaksar Massacre on that day.

Khaksars listen to a lecture.

Khaksar followers in London (United Kingdom).

Khaksars perform community services on a daily basis. They engaged in services of all kinds and toward others, regardless of religion, color, caste or creed. This was a source of building the nation and bringing love and unity among the people.

Barrister Mian Ahmed Shah (a Khaksar leader).

Injured Khaksars are treated at a Khaksar Camp. No injury could stop the Khaksars from striving toward their cause.

LATE MORNING
EDITON

SUBSCRIPTION RATES

The Tribune

VOL. LX. NO. 77 — LAHORE, WEDNESDAY, MARCH 20, 1940 — PRICE:—ONE ANNA

SERIOUS CLASH BETWEEN KHAKSARS AND POLICE

HERR HITLER'S PEACE PROPOSALS

ELEVEN POINTS

TERMS HANDED OVER TO POPE

New York, March 19.

SEVERAL OFFICERS WOUNDED

FIRE OPENED

26 KILLED : 70 INJURED

CURFEW ORDER PROMULGATED AT LAHORE

BAN PLACED ON KHAKSARS

Lahore, March 19.

CURFEW ORDER PROMULGATED

CARRYING OF ARMS PROHIBITED

ALLAMA MASHRAQI TO BE ARRESTED?

WARRANTS ISSUED

Lahore, March 19.

INDIAN NATIONAL CONGRESS MEETS

Open Session

RAIN UPSETS ALL ARRANGEMENTS

THOUSANDS OF PEOPLE WAIT IN KNEE-DEEP WATER

Ramgarh, March 19.

Session Opens

Rain Breaks Out

NO PRESIDENTIAL PROCESSION

BUT LEAGUE SESSION WILL BE HELD.

The Tribune (Lahore), March 20, 1940

Author's comments:

The above news of March 19, 1940 about the Khaksar Massacre (only three days prior to passing the Pakistan Resolution) sent shockwaves to Muslims of the entire India and united them to rise for freedom. Great enthusiasm at the Muslim League Session from March 22-24, 1940 was a result of this massacre. Behind any freedom, there are always many martyrs. Thus, the Pakistani nation must not forget its Khaksar freedom fighters who laid their lives and suffered otherwise for the sacred cause of freedom.

LATE MORNING EDITION

The Tribune

REGISTERED No. L 4.

EDITOR'S OFFICE
Telephone No. 3676.

MANAGER'S OFFICE
Telephone No. 3663

SUBSCRIPTION RATES

VOL. LX. NO. 78   LAHORE, THURSDAY, MARCH 21, 1940   PRICE:—ONE ANNA

ALLAMA MASHRAQI ARRESTED

ENGAGEMENTS ON WESTERN FRONT

SHARP FIGHTING

GERMANS SUFFER HEAVY LOSSES

Paris, March 20.

Patrol engagements have been the only noteworthy incidents on the Western Front during the past 24 hours.

NOT A SUPPORTER OF PEACE AT ALL COSTS

DUCE'S POSITION

London, March 20.

MR. SUMNER WELLES LEAVING FOR AMERICA

Paris, March 20.

FRENCH CABINET

Paris, March 20.

MR. JINNAH LEAVES NEW DELHI FOR LAHORE

New Delhi, March 20.

He Will Be Kept Under Detention

Raids In Different Places

KHAKSARS TAKEN INTO CUSTODY IN LARGE NUMBERS

LAHORE CITY QUIET : SITUATION UNDER CONTROL

New Delhi, March 20.

NO BAN ON MUSLIM LEAGUE

RESTRICTIONS ON KIRPANS REMOVED

Lahore, March 20.

"Al Islah"

LAHORE CITY QUIET

No Further Demonstrations

Lahore, March 20.

MR. JINNAH'S APPEAL TO KHAKSARS

"KEEP PEACE"

LEAGUE LEADER DEPLORES LOSS OF LIFE

New Delhi, March 20.

Mr. M. A. Jinnah, President of the All-India Muslim League in a statement to the Associated Press says—

AIR RAIDS ON SYLT ISLAND

British Bombers In Action

WHOLE OF WEST COAST OF GERMANY ATTACKED

HINDENBURG DAM HIT

London, March 20.

Second Raid

FIRST SCIENTIFIC ELECTRIC LAUNDRY
ON A LARGE SCALE IN LAHORE.

EQUIPPED WITH MOST MODERN MACHINERY
UNDER DIRECT SUPERVISION OF A FOREIGN QUALIFIED EXPERT

SHORTLY STARTING WORK

THE PUNJAB ELECTRIC LAUNDRIES LIMITED,
65, THE MALL, LAHORE.

The Tribune (Lahore), March 21, 1940
Author's comments:
Allama Mashraqi's detention for a significant period
of time directed the Muslims that no solution other than
freedom would be acceptable. Mashraqi was the only prominent
leader at the time who suffered the most at the hands of the
rulers of India. The sufferings of Mashraqi did not go
to waste and resulted in independence.

Police continues its actions against the Khaksar Movement, while the Muslim
League Session is in progress. The photo on the left depicts the use of tear gas
by the police to arrests Khaksars. The photo on the right
shows the Muslim League Session.

forces before they surrendered. The arrows show the main objectives of the Ger

Khaksars Parade. In
Military Formation

They Refuse To Surrender "Belchas"

POLICE PARTY SURROUNDED BY MOB

ALLEGED FIRING OF SHOTS BY S. I. IN SELF-DEFENCE

1 PERSON KILLED: 2 INJURED

(From Our Own Correspondent.)

Lahore, May 29.

A Sub-Inspector of Police is alleged to have fired a number of shots in self-defence this afternoon in Dabbi Bazar when he was surrounded by a large number of Khaksars eleven of whom were seen parading in military formation against the orders of the Punjab Government.

These shots it is alleged resulted in the death of one person and injuries to two others. The deceased Abdul Rehman, a youth of 22, was a passer-by, while of the two others admitted to the Mayo Hospital, one was the son of a watch merchant of Dabbi Bazar and the other a Khaksar. A number of policemen who were alleged to have been attacked by the Khaksars before the firing by the police also received injuries.

The Tribune (Lahore), May 30, 1940.

Allama Mashraqi addressing a public meeting in Bombay in November 1945.

Officers of the Indian National Army with Allama Mashraqi.

Major General S.D. Khan (left) with Allama Mashraqi.

The Star of India (Calcutta), May 23, 1946.
Author's comments: Mashraqi's offer to Quaid-e-Azam to fight
for Pakistan is also reported in the media.

FOUNDED BY QUAID-I-AZAM
MOHAMMAD ALI JINNAH

KARACHI

Sunday, May 11, 1958
21 Shawwal, 1377

Editor: ALTAF HUSAIN

DAWN

MASHRIQI, HIS SON & 4 KHAKSARS HELD

Identified by assassin

MORE ARRESTS EXPECTED

From KHURSHIDUL HASAN
Dawn Lahore Correspondent

LAHORE, May 10: The 70-year-old Khaksar leader, Allama Mashriqi, his younger son, Inamullah Khan, and four of his followers were arrested in the early hours of the morning today and sent for interrogation to Lahore Fort, where Dr Khan Sahib's alleged murderer, Ata Mohammad, is also being detained.

Since British days Lahore Fort has continued in the public mind as a place for police interrogations in

Allama Mashriqi

Mirza lays wreaths at Mazar

Jail filling continues in Kashmir

NEW DELHI, May 10: About 40 persons have been arrested during the last few days in Bhadarwah as a sequel to the demonstrations and protests that followed the re-arrest of Sheikh Mohammad Abdullah, according to a report reaching here.

Those arrested include Maulana Syed Ahaullah Subrawardy, President, Jammu Provincial Plebiscite Front, and Niaz Pardil, a poet and Plebiscite front worker of Bhadarwah.—APP.

Lakhanpal's house searched by police

NEW DELHI, May 10: Police today conducted a search of the residence of the Chairman of the 2nd Kashmir Dispute Committee, Mr Lakhanpal. They were looking for copies of a book "Captive Kashmir".

No copy or objectionable material was found at the residence of Mr Lakhanpal. Police also raided a number of other places for

Qayyum slates Mardan ban under Sec. 144

From Dawn Peshawar Correspondent

PESHAWAR, May 10: The President of the Pakistan Muslim League, Khan Abdul Qayyum Khan, has said in a Press statement that he was setting out for Jahangira boat bridge on river Kabul, where the Mardan Muslim League workers had arranged a public reception for him, when he was informed that Section 144 had been promulgated throughout Mardan district. The reason given for this measure, he said, was that there was tension there.

The League President said: "These receptions and meeting had been fixed long ago, and a local workers of the Muslim League had made arrangements for roadside meetings in villages, a workers' meeting at Adina, a procession followed by a public meeting at Swabi and a huge procession and public meeting at Mardan.

"I had to comeback and set out for Shaidu village where I met Sardar Bahadur Khan and quite a number of other League workers including Mukarram Khan, Mohammad Ashraf Khan, MPA, besides, Muslim League workers of Mardan district continued to pour in.

BORDER MEETING
"I was told that a large number of workers were waiting on Peshawar-Mardan district border as we set out for meeting

Dawn, Karachi of May 11, 1958 reports Mashraqi and his son's arrest.
They are arrested on fabricated charges in Dr. Khan Sahib's
(Chief Minister of West Pakistan) murder case.

Mashraqi is adorned with flowers from his followers.
In this photo, his face can hardly be seen.

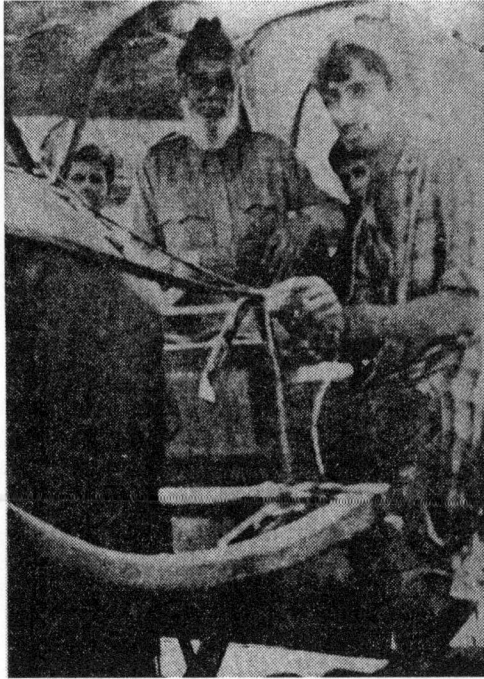

Mashraqi, a Cambridge University (U.K.) scholar, unlike his peers, does not
feel belittled traveling on the transport of the common masses (*tonga*).

Jang, Karachi of August 29, 1963 reports Allama Mashraqi's death.

DAWN

Mashriqi dies of cancer in Lahore hospital

BURIAL TO TAKE PLACE TOMORROW

Khaksars gathering for last rites

LAHORE, Aug 27: Allama Inayatullah Mashriqi, 75-year-old leader of the Khaksar movement, died here today at 9-05 p.m. in the Mayo Hospital, after a prolonged illness due to the cancer of rectum.

The dead body of the aged Khaksar leader will be laid to rest in the Idara-i-Aliya-Hindia, the headquarters of the Khaksar movement, at Ichhra, on Thursday morning. Nimaz-i-Janaza will be offered at the Badshahi mosque on Thursday at 10 a.m. ......

Allama Mashriqi's body has been placed in the morgue of the Mayo Hospital, where it will be kept in cold storage till the burial.

VIGIL BY KHAKSARS

Workers of the Khaksar movement will stand guard over the body of their leader in the morgue till it is taken on its final journey for burial.

An armed military policeman Faculty of Law, Saigon Univer city-wide roundup aimed at

INDIAN LAWS DON'T AFFECT PAKISTAN

Move to block air

Dawn (Karachi), August 28, 1963.

Imroze (Lahore), August 30, 1963.

JUTE
INDUSTRIES
A vital national
industry where B.O.C.
oils play a vital part.

The Eastern Examiner

ESTD. 1952

Chittagong's Pioneer English Daily

Acting Editor : ZAFAR AHMAD KHAN JAWEED.

REG. NO. D.A. 227. VOL.XI NO. 249 : CHITTAGONG WEDNESDAY, AUG. 28, MUFASSIL AUG. 29, 1963 RABIUS SANI 8, 13!

ALLAMA MASHRAQI
PASSES AWAY

Eventful Career Comes To An End

Lahore, Aug. 27 (APP): The founder of the Khaksar Movement Allama Enayet-Ullah Khan Mashraqi expired in the Albert Victor Hospital at 21.08 tonight.

Allama Mashraqi, who was followers, relatives, friends

On behalf of the American National Institute of Health, Mr. John F. Mc Jennett acting chief of mission of the American Consolate General on Monday presented a cheque of Rs. 1,81,360 to Dr. M.O. Ghani, Vice-Chancellor, Dacca University, who turned it over to Dr. Kamaluddin Ahmed, Head of the Bio-chemistry Department for a bio-chemical study of nutritional problems in East Pakistan specially related to effects of ind-genous oils and fats. Mr. Mc Jennett is wishing success to Dr. Kamaluddin's project as the Vice Chancellor looks on.

GOVER

POL

Gov
In

E.PAK CEN

Murree. high-le under Pres the govern opposition ble line-up some of the

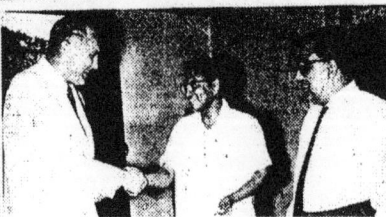

The Eastern Examiner (Chittagong), August 28, 1963.

'Mashriqi was eminent scholar'

MORE CONDOLENCE MESSAGES

LAHORE, Aug 28: People from various walks of life in the country have expressed their deep sense of sorrow over the death of the founder of the Khaksar Movement, Allama Inayatullah Khan Mashriqi.

In their messages of condolence, they have paid glowing tributes to Allama Mashriqi and described him as a "stalwart political leader and an eminent scholar."

The Khaksar leaders have also appealed to the management of the business concerns in Lahore to close their business on Thursday to enable their employers to participate in the funeral prayers of Allama Mashriqi.

Mr Mohammad Anwar, Speaker of West Pakistan Assembly, said he was shocked to hear the sad news. "The late Allama Sahib was a distinguished scholar and got world fame due to his extra-ordinary academic qualities."

Sardar Mohammad Alam, President of the Lahore Circle of All-Jammu and Kashmir Muslim Conference, and Mr Manzar Masud, Secretary-General in a joint statement, paid rich tributes to the late Khaksar leader. The services rendered by Allama Sahib for the liberation of occupied Kashmir would be written in

Muslim League, Organising Committee: Mr Sadruddin Ansari, Joint Secretary of the Conventionist Muslim League; Nawab Yamin Khan, Joint Secretary of the Sind Muslim League Organising Committee; Mian Mohammad Shaukat, Amir of Jamaat-i-Islami, Hyderabad also expressed grief over the sad demise of Allama Mashriqi.

Mr Faiz Mohammad Sandal, Chairman Sind Conventionist Muslim League Organising Committee, said that the country had been deprived of a great scholar.

Agha Ijaz Hussain, Salar-e-Ala of the Pakistan Muslim League, said the Allama Saheb was a man of letters and a great organiser.

In Peshawar elder Khaksars, Mian Sahibnishan and Hakim Sahib, though full of grief, told Pressmen that God-willing the movement will get a suitable successor because its principles were true.

Ghaibana Namaz-i-Janaza was

Dawn (Karachi), August 29, 1963.

VALIANT FIGHTER FOR FREEDOM

MASHRIQI'S DEATH CONDOLED

Political leaders and educationists have expressed their deep sense of sorrow over the death of Allama Mashriqi.

Ch Mohammad Hussain, MNA, said that the Allama was a great organiser and valiant freedom-fighter. After the establishment of Pakistan he concentrated his efforts on the liberation of Kashmir from the Indian yoke.

He expressed his sympathies with the bereaved family.

The Principal of the local Islamia College, Civil Lines, Prof. Hamid Ahmad Khan, said that he was shocked to hear the news of Allama Sahib's death.

PPA adds: The Speaker of the Provincial Assembly Mr Mohammed Anwar, when con-

capital.

The Rawalpindi Bar Association at an emergency meeting condoled the death of Khaksar leader, Allama Mashriqi.

In a resolution the Association termed his death a great national loss.

Ch Ghulam Abbas, a veteran Kashmir leader, expressed a deep sense of grief on the death of a "great revolutionary" and a scholar.

HYDERABAD

Begum Tahira Agha, Chairman of the Sind Provincial Muslim League (Councillors), said in Hyderabad that Allama Mashriqi was a great soldier.

Muslim resurgence in the Sub-Continent.

Paying glowing tributes to the late Allama Ch Khaliquzzaman said that it was a sad loss for "the work of great men has to be judged not only by its success but even by failures in a laudable cause."

Mr Manazar-e-Alam, General Secretary of All-Pakistan Muslim League (Conventionists) said that he was deeply grieved to hear of the sad demise of an "old political worker". He sympathised with the bereaved family.

Mr Z. H. Lari, president of the Karachi Muslim League (Councillors) in a message of condolence said that in the death of Allama Mashriqi, the country had lost a distinguished and self-sacrificing leader. Allama Mashriqi, he said, was endowed with a great intellect. The Khaksar Party, which the late Allama founded in pre-partition days, Mr Lari said, was organised in a "marvellous way" which created in its followers a spirit of sacrifice which was unrivalled. He hoped that the spirit of the Allama

The Civil & Military Gazette (Lahore), August 29, 1963.

A man with courage of convictions

President condoles Mashriqi's death

Continued from page 1.

said, "With his demise a chapter of the history of Indo-Pakistan Muslims has closed."

Maulana Maududi said at a time Allama Mashriqi's movement had brought into its fold the whole Muslim nation and had greatly aroused the Muslims to fight for their freedom. That he said, was the outcome of his ability as a great organiser.

He prayed for the enternal peace of his soul and offered sympathy with the bereaved family.

Political leaders and educationists expressed deep sense of sorrow over the death of Allama Mashriqi.

Ch. Mohammad Hussain, MNA, said that Allama was a great organiser and a valiant freedom fighter. After the establishment of Pakistan, he concentrated his efforts for the liberation of Kashmir from the Indian yoke, he added. He expressed his sympathies with the bereaved family.

The Principal of the local Islamia College, Civil Lines, Professor Hamid Ahmad Khan, said i-Ahrar, Pakistan, Sheikh Hissamuddin, said Allama Mashriqi through his Khaksar Movement, considerably influenced the course of the Indian history. He had tremendous organising capacity which he fully utilised in influencing the Muslim youth, he added.

The Ahrar chief said Allama Mashriqi might not have been completely successful in his mission to organise Muslims to bring near the ideal of Islamic domination, but he did make mighty efforts to take Muslims of the Indian sub-continent towards that goal.

'PINDI BAR'S RESOLUTION

APP continues from Rawalpindi:

The Rawalpindi Bar Association at an emergency meeting held today condoled the death of Allama Mashriqi.

In a resolution, the Association termed his death a great national loss.

A message from Hyderabad says:

Begum Tahira Agha, Chairman of the Sind Provincial Muslim League (Councillors), said in her condolence message on

President Ayub mourns Mashraqi's death.

Giant Among Men

Lahore, Aug. 27 (APP): Allama Inayetullah Khan Mashriqi, rose to fame in the thirties as the leader of the Khaksar Movement — a social service organisation.

The parades and camps of Khaksars aroused the suspicion of the British Government and soon after the beginning of the World War II action was taken to suppress the movement.

Allama Inayetullah Mashriqi, was born at Ghulamabad near Amritsar on August 25, 1888. He passed his M. A. in Mathematics in first class from the Punjab University at the age of ninteen.

Later Allama Mashriqi proceeded to United Kingdom During his stay abroad, he also took keen interest in journalism and wrote in the "Empire Views', "West-Minister Reviews "and London Times" mainly about the Indian political scene. It was perhaps there that seeds were sown, which took him into active politics despite his study of a disinterested and terse subject like mathematics. The A'lma was endowed with an amazing memory.

On return to India Allama Mashriqi joined the Indian Educational Service and was appointed Vice-Principal of Islamia College, Peshawar. He acted as Principal for sometime.

In 1917 Allama was appoin-

The Eastern Examiner (Chittagong), August 28, 1963.

Mashriqi's Death Shocks Leaders

(From APP/PPA) Karachi received the news of Allama Mashriqi's death with a sense of shock and grief.
MAULANA ABDUL HAMID

Special Broadcast

Radio Pakistan, Karachi, will broadcast the following special programme today:
7.30 a.m. In our programme Quran-e-Hakeem Aur Hamari Zindigi: In the series Tableeghi-Deen Ke Usool, talk by Maulana Qazi Abdul Rehman.
8.45 p.m. Kaisay Kaisay Log: In this series of documentary programmes based on the interviews with typical characters "Hath Dekhne Wala".
8.45 p.m.: Admi Nama: Weekly serial programme.
8.15 p.m.: A talk by Mr. Ovals Ahmed Adeeb, on Two new loans of the Central Government.
Broadcasts to Schools: In the programme Broadcasts to Schools, Radio Pakistan, Karachi will broadcast a feature in English entitled 'Direct and Indirect Speech' in the series 'Grammar and Composition', for Matric students today at 11.35 a.m. and again at 4.35 p.m. It will be followed by a recorded talk on

KHAN BHASHANI on Tuesday night sent a condolence telegram to Mr. Akhter Hamid Khan, son-in-law of the departed Khaksar leader. He said that in Allama's death the country had been deprived of a 'mojahid'. He had rendered great services for the cause of the country. "I pray to the Almighty to grant peace to the soul of Allama Mashriqi", he added.

MR. Z.H. LARI President of the Karachi Muslim League (Councillors) in a message of condolence said that in the country had lost a distinguished and self-sacrificing leader. He was endowed with a great intellect. The Khaksar Party, which the late Allama founded in pre-partition days, was organised in a 'marvellous way'. It created in its followers a spirit of sacrifice which was unrivalled. He hoped that the spirit of the late Allama would serve as a source of inspiration for his followers.

CHAUDHRI KHALIQUZZA-MAN, Chief Organiser of the Pakistan Muslim League (Conventionist) said that Allama Mashriqi's death will be mourn-

Retracing the history of the Khaksar movement Chaudhri Saheb said that the movement was crushed by the British for fear of Muslim resurgence in the sub-continent. His death was a sad loss for "the work of great men has to be judged not only, by its success but even by

Trade Team Leader Flies To Delhi For Consultation

Morning News REPORT

Leaders of the trade delegations of Pakistan and India left yesterday for their respective capitals for consultation with their Governments.
Negotiations for a fresh agreement between the two countries were started on Thursday last. Mr. S. Vohra, the leader of the Indian team and Mr. Ejaz Ahmed Naik, leader of the Pakistan delegation are expected to return to Karachi in the afternoon today.
The trade talks are expected

failures in a laudable cause".
MR. MAHMOODUL HAQ USMANI, A National Democratic Front leader, said that in the death of Allama Mashriqi the nation had lost "a great patriot".

MR. ZAIN NOORANI, General Secretary of the Karachi Provincial Muslim League (Councillors) Organising Committee, expressed his sense of shock at the death of Allama Mashriqi who was one of the first few who realised the importance of making the Muslims of India conscious that they were a separate nation".

MR. MANZAR-E-ALAM, General Secretary of the Conventionist Muslim League, said he was deeply grieved to hear of the sad demise of an "old political worker".

Firing Warning

The Pakistan Navy will carry out AA firing on Thursday from 1.30 p.m. to 3.15 p.m. in the Golf Area with the safety range and the height 11,000 yards and 18,000 ft. respectively. Live ammunition will be used. All concerned are advised

Morning News (Karachi), August 29, 1963.

Leaders pay rich tributes to Mashriqi

Khwaja Nazimuddin, President of the Pakistan Muslim League, said in Dacca that Allama Mashriqi's death has ended the career of "a very interesting figure who took prominent part in the politics of the Indo-Pakistan Sub-Continent."

He said: "I pray to Allah that his soul may rest in peace and grant patience and courage to his children to bear the loss."

Maulana Abul Ala Maudoodi, Amir, Jamaat-i-Islami, condoling the death of Allama Mashriqi in Lahore said: "With the death of Allama Mashriqi a chapter in the history of the Muslims of the Indo-Pakistan Sub-Continent has closed today".

Maulana Maudoodi said that Allama Mashriqi possessed extraordinary organisational capabilities and inspired the Muslims of the Sub-Continent before partition.

Maulana Abdul Hamid Khan Bhashani, leader of the defunct National Awami Party, sent a condolence telegram to Mr Akhtar Hamid Khan, son-in-law of the deceased. He said that in the Allama's death the country had been deprived of a "Mojahid".

Maulana Bhashani said in Karachi that Allama Mashriqi had rendered great services for the cause of the country.

"I pray to the Almighty to grant peace to the soul of Allama Mashriqi," he added.

Mr Nurul Amin, a former Chief Minister of East Pakistan, said in Dacca that he was much grieved to learn the sad news of the passing away of Allama Inayetullah Khan Mashriqi.

He said: "I pray to Allah for his "Maghferat".

Chaudhri Ghulam Abbas, a veteran Kashmir leader, in Rawalpindi expressed a deep sense of grief on the death of a "great revolutionary" and a scholar.

Mr Akhtaruddin Ahmad, MNA, said in Dacca, Pakistan had lost a great patriot and it was a "great loss" for the nation.

Allama Mashriqi, he said, was a devoted, selfless and sacrificing personality. Mr Akhtaruddin wished the nation had more people like him.

Shah Azizur Rahman, an NDF leader, said he was an intellectual leader with a thinking of his own and consistent in the pursuit of his ideals.

Large number of Chinese still detained in India

PEKING REJECTS DELHI ASSERTION

PEKING, Aug 27: China today rejected a reported Indian assertion that there were no longer any Chinese in India who wanted to return to China, according to the New China news agency.

In a Note delivered to the Indian Embassy here the Chinese Foreign Ministry recalled a Note handed over in New Delhi on July 31 saying China would send a ship for a fourth batch of repatriates.

The agency said India had replied that no Chinese in India wished to return, but today's Note described this as "an utterly baseless assertion".

The Note said India still held large numbers of Chinese in concentration camps and prisons and added that the Embassy in New Delhi had been instructed to discuss arrangements for shipping them to China.—Reuter.

Mobin's concern over move for Press curbs

LAHORE, Aug 27: Mr Mobinul Haq Siddiqui, ex-Speaker of the West Pakistan Assembly, today expressed great concern over the reported move to impose curbs on the freedom of the Press.

He said in a statement that freedom is the very essence of democracy. The Press has to play an important role in the national life of a country and therefore it should be allowed to function in a free manner.

"The freedom of expression and freedom of thought will be meaningless without a free Press. Ac-

Dawn (Karachi), August 28, 1963.

Mashraqi's funeral.

Streets are filled with mourners.

MILE-LONG FUNERAL PROCESSION

Continued from page 1

career of a person who fought valiantly throughout his life against the British and the Hindus by organising the Khaksar Movement some 23 years ago.

According to a conservative estimate, 50,000 people attended the funeral prayers for Allama Mashriqi at the Badshahi Mosque. The courtyard of the Mosque was almost packed. The prayers were led by Maulana Abdus Sattar Khan Niazi at 10-23 a.m. Maulana Abul Ala Maududi

killed in the ruthless firing on that occasion.

The procession reached Badshahi Mosque at 9-50 a.m. It took 33 minutes to begin the funeral prayers in order to allow the rear of the procession stretching right up to Shahi Mohalla, to enter the Mosque.

After the prayers, the procession started its six-mile march to Ichhra. It grew thicker and thicker as it passed through Tehsil Bazar, Bazar Hakiman,

Mashraqi is showered with flowers from the people.
The Civil & Military Gazette (Lahore), August 30, 1963.

Mashriqi's Death Casts Pall Of Gloom Over Country

From APP & PPA

The death of Allama En-yatullah Khan Mashriqi, leader of the Khaksar movement in Lahore last night cast a pall of gloom over whole of Pakistan.

The mortal remains of the 75-year-old leader will be laid to rest on Thursday in Idara-A'ala-Hindia, Ichhra, Lahore, near his residence. The Namaz-i-Janaza will be held at 10 a.m. The Badshahi Mosque at 10 a.m. The body of Allama Mashriqi, whose parades of spade-carrying followers were a feature of pre-partition days will be kept in the cold storage of the Mayo Hospital, Lahore till Thursday morning.

A brilliant mathematician, eduationist and author a graduate of Christ College, Cambridge Allama Mashriqi made transition to politics in 1931 when he founded the Khaksar Movement which grew to the strength of several hundred thousand before the British Government.

Acting Chief Of Khaksars Named

LAHORE, Aug. 28 (APP)—Mr. Bashir Ahmad Siddiqi, a lieutenant of Allama Mashriqi, was chosen as Acting Chief of the defunct Khaksar Movement by the Khaksar leaders here last evening, it was announced late last night.

Mr. Siddiqi had led the Movement during Allama Mashriqi's detention in Vellour Jail in 1940.

The Khaksar leaders will meet after the burial of their leader on Thursday at Ichhra, the headquarters of the Movement, to decide about the future programme of the organisation.

The Acting Chief has announced that a camp has been established outside the Mochi Gate to lodge the late Allama Sahib's followers who will come to Lahore to attend funeral of their leaders.

Nazim Mourns

DACCA, Aug. 28 (APP)—Khwaja Nazimuddin, President of the All-Pakistan Councillors Muslim League, last night said that Allama Mashriqi's death has ended career of 'a very interesting figure who took prominent part in the politics of the Indo-Pakistan sub-continent'.

He said: 'I pray to Allah that his soul may rest in peace and grant patience

imprisoned him during the Word War II.

He was also imprisoned after the Partition during the Prime Ministership of the late Quaid-i-Millat Liaqun Ali Khan for opposition to his Government's foreign policy and later in 1957 on charge of abetting in the murder of former Chief Minister of West Pakistan, Dr Khan Sahib, but was acquitted.

In 1957 he organised a 'Lashkar of former Khaksars near the Wagha border to fight for the liberation of Kashmir. One hundred and one tents were pitched near Wagha but the idea of crossing the border was dropped on the presuasion of the authorities.

Leaders of various shades of opinion on learning the news of his death described him as 'an interesting figure who played prominent part in the freedom movement of the Indo-Pakistan sub-continent'.

The following are the condolence messages received from all over Pakistan mourning the death of Allama Mashriqi:

Hyderabad

BEGUM TAHIRA AGHA, Chairman of the Sind Provincial Muslim League (Councillors), said that he was a great soldier and persued on his mission with the courage of a lion, He faced countless difficulties in the way of the Khaksar Movement but he met with them courageously and boldly, she added.

NAWAB MUZAFFAR ALI KHAN, Chairman of the Sind Provincial Muslim League (Councillors) Organising Committee; MR. SADRUDDIN ANSARI, Joint Secretary of the Conventionists Muslim League; NAWAB YAMIN KHAN, Joint Secreary of the Sind Councillors Muslim League Organising Committee; MIAN MOHAMMAD SHAUKAT, Convener Nizame Islam Party; also expressed grief over the sad demise of Allama Mashriqi.

MR. FAIZ MOHAMMAD SANDAL, Chairman of the Sind Muslim League (Conventionist) Organising Commitee, said that the death of Allama Mashriqi had deprived the country of a great scholar.

AGHA IJAZ HUSSAIN, Salaar-i-A'a of the Pakistan Muslim League said that the Allama Sahib was a well-known personality in the Muslim world and was a man of letters and great organiser.

Lahore

CHAUDHRI MOHAMMAD HUSSAIN, MNA said the Allama was a great organiser and a valiant freedom fighter. After the establishment of Pakistan he concentrated his efforts for liberation of Kashmir from the Indian yoke, he added. He expressed his sympathies with

KHAN Principal of the Lahore Islamia College, Civil Lines, said he was shocked to hear the news of Allama Sahib's death. He said the Allama, a great organiser, took leading part for the glory of Islam before the Independence.

MAULANA FAZAL HUSSAIN DILAWAR, a prominent social worker and Basic Democrat, said that the Allama, besides being a top educationist, was a great statesman of the sub-continent. Before Independence he fought for the freedom of Muslims against alien rulers and the Hindu capitalists. After creation of Pakistan, he added, the Allama disbanded his Movement and worked mainly for the freedom of Kashmiri Muslims and security of country's borders.

SARDAR MOHAMMAD SADIQ, the Organising Secretary of the West Pakistan Muslim League (Conventionist) said the sad demise of Allama Mashriqi was an irreparable loss to the nation. He was a great freedom organiser, He prayed for the peace of his soul.

MIAN MEHRAJDIN, the Provincial Parliamentary Secretary for Basic Democracies, said Allama Mashriqi's death had deprived the people of a true statesman and a true Muslim.

MR. ABUL HASSAN ABU ALI, a member of the Council Muslim League, Lahore City, said that the Allama Sahib had struggled hard for the freedom of the Indian Muslims and recapitulating the glory of Islam.

MAULANA ABUL ALA MAUDUDI, Amir of the Jama'at-i-Islami, in his condolence message said: 'With his demise a chapter of the history of Indo-Pakistan Muslims has closed.' Maulana Maududi said at the time Allama Mashriqi's movement had brought into its fold the whole Muslim nation and had greatly aroused the Muslims to fight for their freedom. This he added, was the outcome of his ability as a great organiser. He prayed for the eternal peace of his soul and offered sympathy with the bereaved family.

MR. MOHAMMED ANWAR, Speaker of the Provincial Assembly of West Pakistan, said he was shocked to hear the sad news of the death of Allama Mashriqi.

SARDAR MOHAMMAD ALAM, President of the Lahore Circle of All-Jammu and Kashmir Muslim Conference; and MR. MANZAR MASUD, General Secretary; in a joint statement also paid rich tribute to the late Khaksar leader. They said the services rendered by Allama Sahib for the liberation of Occupied Kashmir would be written in golden words in the history of struggle for freedom in Kashmir.

Allama Inayatullah riqi rose to fame in as the leader of th movement—a social nisation.

The parades and Khaksars aroused th of the British Gove soon after the beginn War II action was t press the movement.

Allama Inayatullah was born at Ghulam Amritsar on August passed his MA in Ma First Class from the versity at the age of

Later Allama Ma ceeded to the Unite for higher studies o Tripos Honours' fro College, Cambridge period he was a Foundation and Bacl ships by the Univers

In 1912, Allama M ed his B.Sc. (Hons taining the highest Mechanical Engine (Hons) from the sam

During his stay al took keen interest i and wrote in the 'E 'London Times' mak Indian political scen hape there that seed which took him into ties despite his stud terested and terse Mathematics. The endowed with an

On his return to Mashriqi joined the eational Service and ed Vice-Principal of lege, Peshawar. He cipal for some tim

In 1917 Allama Under-Secretary, G India, Education De later on was poste NWFP. Before he the I.E.S. in 1931 as Headmaster, Gov School, Peshawar.

In 1920 he began International Cong talists, Leyden.

Allama Mashriqi Ichhra at Lahore after he founded Movement with a lims to unite for

The movement spr out India and clai lakh members by World War II durin ment aroused the s Government of Ind was arrested. Allama Mashriqi sent to jail in 1940.

During his impri lama wrote four 'Harem-i-Ghaib', 'I disul Quran' and Hakeem'.

After independer disbanded the Kha ment and started l ment under the na lam League' which named as 'Muslim

In 1957 Allama 'Lashkar' of form near the Wagha bo for the liberation Tents were pitched der was dropped o sion of the authorit

Allama Mashriqi mained convinced moment that only v rate Kashmir from dian. hold.

Allama Mashriqi prison for anothe

۱۹۔ میری تثلیث

تثلیث کا قائل تو نہ پہلے تھا نہ اب ہوں
لیکن مجھے اک آن نہ بھولے گی یہ تثلیث

اسلم تو ہوا اندرِ ستم ہائے فرنگی
میں قید تھا، اور یاد یہ لگتی تھی بڑی مِس
بیٹا تھا وہ اک فردِ زماں، ماتے پہ جس کے
اک لاٹ عیاں علم کی جوں ہالہ بر جبیں، دا)
ہر روک اُٹھتی تھی اِن ظلم پہ گوہر جاں ہے مری سخت
دعوے ہے کر لےگا کوئی کیا اس میں مری رِیس
پُر خیر، وہ قصہ تو فرنگی کا ہوا پاک
سات ایک برس میں ہی کہ سن اسکا تھا پانسیس (۲)

Mashraqi mourns his sons' (Ehsanullah Khan Aslam and
Majeed ud Din Amjad) deaths, who died while Mashraqi was
still in jail. Mashraqi was not allowed to attend their funerals.
He expressed his feelings of sorrow in two poems.

٩۷ ۔ ترانۂ پاکستان

مسلماں کی تمناؤں کی دنیا، ارضِ پاکستاں
مسلمانوں کی دنیا کی تمنا، ارضِ پاکستاں
صلہ ملنا تو تھا مسلم کو خونِ بے گناہاں کا
یم خونِ ناب کا لولوئے لالا، ارضِ پاکستاں
اٹھو اے مردِ جواں! تلوار سے رتبے کو سلامی دے
رضائے حق کا انعام مویّدا، ارضِ پاکستاں!
چل اے بطلِ وطن! مردوں کی پہلی صفی میں تو آجا
کہ تونے بی بنانی ہے توانا، ارضِ پاکستاں!
ادھر مکیاں نہیں سب! اہلِ اسلام کی ہاں پر حکومت ہے
ہر اک انساں کی ہے کیکیاں شناسا ارضِ پاکستاں!
تو پھر اے مسلمِ خستہ! مسلماں بن کے دکھلا دے
کہ مسلم کے لئے ہے اک تقاضا! ارضِ پاکستاں!

An excerpt from a poem by Mashraqi
(see *Armughan-i-Hakeem* for full text of poem).

Imroze, Lahore of August 29, 1963 reports on Mashraqi's burial.

Allama Mashraqi waiting to address a public meeting in Lahore. Sikh and Hindu Khaksars also present. Mir Ali Ahmed Talpur (without cap/headress in the center with his face towards the right).

A Sikh Khaksar.
The Khaksar Tehreek did not discriminate against anyone based on religion,
caste, color, or creed and many non-Muslims were part of the movement.

Khaksars conduct training exercises.

Khaksars parading on the streets and spectators watching the parade.

Allama Mashraqi addresses Khaksars at a Khaksar Camp. Onlookers are
listening to Mashraqi.

Khaksars undergoing military training at a Khaksar Camp.

Khaksars marching in front of Lahore Assembly Chambers.

Ikramullah Khan Anwar (Mashraqi's son) in Khaksar uniform.

The Khaksars came out on the streets to wake the nation from a deep slumber.

A smartly dressed Khaksar batch.

A Khaksar holds the Movement's flag with pride and leads the contingent.

Appendices

Appendices

Appendix I

Bogus Attack on Quaid-e-Azam by a Muslim Leaguer

On July 26, 1943, Rafiq Sabir Mazangavi, who according to Jinnah's nephew's book, *Jinnah Faces an Assassin*,[1] was the Propaganda Secretary of the All India Muslim League (Mozang Branch, Lahore) in 1939,[2] attacked Quaid-e-Azam at his residence in Bombay at 1:30 p.m. This was a *phony* and *bogus* attack. But this attack was crucial to the Muslim League interest.

*****

By the early 1940s, the power of the Khaksar Tehreek had been revealed, and anti-Khaksar forces in the Muslim League, British and non-Muslim organizations had become panicky at the Khaksars' strength. The Muslim League originally desired to bring the Tehreek under its flag, or else it would not tolerate the movement's existence (except for purely social service). The British did not want any collaboration between the Khaksars and the Muslim League, and they could not tolerate the Khaksars' militant character or any role on the political stage. They made it clear that the Khaksars were to perform purely social service, otherwise the movement would face repercussions. But the Khaksars continued their activities and efforts of anti-Khaksar elements failed to eliminate it. Anti-Khaksar forces became extremely eager to finish Mashraqi politically; therefore a conspiracy was hatched to achieve this aim — this attack was indispensable to crushing the Khaksar Tehreek.

In light of this plot, an attack on Jinnah by Rafiq Sabir Mazangavi took place on July 26, 1943. Rafiq Sabir Mazangavi used a *small* knife, not a dagger, pistol or gun, to inflict a very minor injury ("a cut on the bend of his palm and

---

[1] The book titled, *Jinnah Faces An Assassin*, was written by Barrister Akbar A. Peerbhoy, nephew of Quaid-e-Azam. Peerbhoy was a son of Jinnah's sister, Mariambai. (Peerbhoy, P. 1 Introduction)
[2] Peerbhoy, P. 70.

some scraps on the left jaw"[3]) on Quaid-e-Azam, in his home in broad day light and in the presence of his staff members. Right after the attack, Rafiq Sabir Mazangavi was alleged to be a Khaksar, without any investigation. The main witnesses in the court included Quaid-e-Azam and his staff.

Upon hearing of the attack in the news, only after an hour of the incident [4], Khaksars visited Quaid-e-Azam at his bungalow in Bombay and sympathized with him and sternly condemned the attack. It is surprising that Jinnah "never suspected them."[5] How could Quaid-e-Azam have met with Khaksars, when the attacker was alleged to be one of their movement? Mashraqi and the Khaksars were shocked to learn that Rafiq was accused of being a Khaksar, and they viewed the allegation as a deep conspiracy against the Khaksar Tehreek. Dr. Mohammad Sadiq (a Khaksar leader) stated:

> "We went to Mr. Jinnah's bungalow as soon as we learnt that a cowardly attack was made on his person by a Muslim who said that he was a Khaksar. We congratulate the Qaid-e-Azam on his escape, and strongly condemn that man who has done such a mean action which is absolutely against the Khaksar principles. We cannot believe that such a person could be a Khaksar."[6]

After the Khaksars visited Quaid-e-Azam, they were convinced that the attack was pre-planned and everything seemed fictitious. Quaid-e-Azam was the only person who could have set the record straight and stated that the attacker was not a Khaksar, or at least his affiliation was unknown. However, he did no such thing.

Instead, Muslim Leaguers issued press statements and great publicity was launched, which was enough for anyone to understand that political advantage was meant out of this incident. In the Khaksar circle, this was seen as a high level conspiracy against the Khaksar Tehreek. It was arranged by anti-Khaksar elements to defame the Khaksar Tehreek and to finish them politically. According to the Khaksar circle, these anti-Khaksar elements included the Muslim Leaguers as well as intelligence/secret services.

On the day of the attack (July 26, 1943), Quaid-e-Azam's Secretary issued a statement to the media. *The Star of India*, Calcutta of July 27, 1943 wrote:

> "Mahmood Rasikh [Rafiq Sabir Mazangavi], stated to be a Khaksar, came to Mr. Jinnah's residence at about 1-30 p.m. today. The Pathan watchman asked the visitor whom he was and what he wanted. On being informed that he wanted to see Mr. Jinnah, the watchman brought him to my room. I asked him why he wanted to see Mr. Jinnah and he said that he had come from Lahore to discuss with Mr. Jinnah about the League and other matters. I told him that Mr. Jinnah

---

[3] *The Star of India*, November 03, 1943.
[4] Hussain, P. 193.
[5] Ibid.
[6] *The Bombay Chronicle*, July 27, 1943.

was busy and that he should fix an appointment to meet him. The visitor took a paper and wrote on it in Urdu that he wanted to see Mr. Jinnah to discuss some important matters and that he would be grateful if he met him.

While we were discussing the possibility of getting Mr. Jinnah to agree to see him immediately, Mr. Jinnah chanced to come into the room to take a file. Mr. Jinnah asked me who the visitor was and what he wanted. I told Mr. Jinnah the purpose for which the visitor had come. Mr. Jinnah then told the visitor that he was busy and that he should arrange an appointment. The visitor was not, presumably, willing to do this and he picked up a quarrel with Mr. Jinnah, in the course of which he drew out a knife and attempted to stab him in the neck. Mr. Jinnah caught his hand and thus prevented the knife striking him in the neck. The assailant, however, succeeded in inflicting minor injuries on Mr. Jinnah's chin and left hands. The Pathan watchman and myself overpowered the assailant and with great difficulty we snatched away the knife from his hands. The Police were immediately summoned and the assailant was handed over to them.

Mr. Jinnah was bleeding in the face and his left hand. The wounds are slight and Mr. Jinnah is now resting."

As soon as Mashraqi heard (on July 26, 1943) of this incident, he vigorously condemned the attack on Jinnah. *The Star of India*, Calcutta of July 27, 1943 reported Mashraqi's statement:

"Quaid-e-Azam Jinnah is the most revered leader of the Mussalmans at this moment and all hopes are centered in him. I may differ from him in his methods of getting something for the Mussalmans but I have always considered him as a most essential person at this moment. I cannot believe the allegation that the assailant is a Khaksar from Lahore as no Khaksar of the name Mohamed Rafiq exists in Lahore excepting Mohammad Rafiq Ghauri, who is [at] present in Lahore, nor a Khaksar would ever think of such a thing. But the crime whosoever has done it is most dastardly and mean. I would simply say that, my personal sympathy apart, the young devil who has tried issues with an old man of the personality of Mr. Jinnah has done the greatest disservice to the immediate task before the Khaksar Organisation concerning which I was about to say something very substantial. The culprit must be brought to book but I would appeal to Qaid-e-Azam as well as everyone in India not to give this incident the slightest political tinge for the sake of the most important things that are happening and the most immense results involved. I would have taken it as a mere accident if the thing had happened with me and perhaps would not have cared to give it to the press or even get the culprit arrested, on account of the vital issues before the country."

Mashraqi was sorrowful of this attack, but he did not blame anyone for the conspiracy. Instead he requested Quaid-e-Azam to concentrate on the major issue of freedom.

*****

According to the Khaksar circle, the British never wanted the AIML and the Tehreek to collaborate; this attack would widen the gap between the two and also help eliminate Mashraqi from the political scene.

In the weeks prior to the attack, Linlithgow (Viceroy of India) had written to Amery (Secretary of State for India) on July 05/06, 1943:

> "I am not by any means happy about the Khaksar position…we shall have to deal with these people… It would not, in my opinion, be prudent to disregard the possibility that the Muslim League may one day adopt a more bellicose policy towards Government. If, when that time comes, the League finds a powerful instrument, such as the Khaksars, may well become, ready to its hand, we might well be faced with a most dangerous position. I am quite sure that this is a real danger which should be most closely watched."[7]

Linlithgow's words reflect that they saw the Khaksar Tehreek's power as a danger to them. This clearly illustrates that the British had an interest that Mashraqi and Jinnah should not join hands under any circumstances. It also shows that the AIML did not have a "bellicose policy" against the British.

One day after the attack, on July 27, 1943, Linlithgow wrote another letter that shows his interest in this Mashraqi-Jinnah relationship. Linlithgow sent a private and secret letter to Amery and wrote that Jinnah was "slightly injured" and that he had "at once" sent him a "telegram of sympathy." He added that he was "much relieved" as Jinnah was not seriously injured, and that Jinnah had issued a press statement which was very "sensible" and "short." He stated "But the business will not improve relations between" the Khaksar Tehreek and AIML.[8]

It is interesting that the Viceroy was so concerned with Jinnah's condition. Why would this make a difference to the Viceroy unless the British had some special relationship with him, which was causing this concern? Many Indians were of the view that Quaid-e-Azam worked at the behest of the British and that is why Linlithgow was compassionate and concerned. Further, the Viceroy was relieved that no patch-up between the parties was possible.

*****

On July 27, 1943, Rafiq Sabir Mazangavi (Jinnah's assailant) was produced before the Chief Presidency Magistrate in Bombay, who remanded him to police custody.

---

[7] IOL L/P&J/8/680.
[8] Mansergh 1973, P. 127. IOL MSS EUR F125/12.

The fact that the injury was not life threatening, yet so much publicity and hype was stirred around it, creates more suspicion of a high level conspiracy. Jinnah's secretary stated on July 28, 1943, "There is no need for any anxiety as he [Jinnah] is progressing very favourably."[9] Yet large scale publicity was launched and meetings were convened by Muslim Leaguers to condemn the attack.

Within days of the attack, a court case was filed.[10] A case for such a minor injury established that political motives were to be derived and thus a well planned conspiracy was confirmed. If political elimination of Mashraqi and division of Muslims was not meant out of this attack, then this case would not have been filed. It was established that AIML wanted to take political advantage of the situation.

Oscar Brown, the Chief Presidency Magistrate, recorded Quaid-e-Azam and his secretary's (Syed Ahmed Syed Yaqub) statements. The following was Jinnah's statement in the court as it appeared in *The Bombay Chronicle* of September 08, 1943:

> "I live at Mount Pleasant Road in a bungalow with no name. Mr. Syed is my Secretary. His office is on the ground floor of my house. I work on the ground floor. I have a Pathan watch-man at the gate. Anybody who wanted to see me was allowed to come in if I was free. I willingly saw people. Recently I was getting threatening letters apart from the Khaksars. I was, therefore, obliged to be a little more careful. I told my Secretary and watchman that anybody who called without appointment should be taken first to the Secretary before I saw him.
>
> I got a copy of the instructions and orders issued by Allama Mushriqi, leader of the Khaksar organisation in the first or second week of June. Thereafter, I received telegrams, postcards and letters daily, both in Bombay and in Sind and Baluchistan during my tour in June and July and on my return till the incident on July 26. All of these letters ordered me to see Mr. Gandhi at once and contained an insinuation that I was in the way of the freedom of India and a tool in the hands of British Imperialism.
>
> On July 26, I was working in my study on the ground floor. I was engaged on something very important. At 1-30 p.m. I got up and went to my Secretary's room for a particular file. I saw the accused there. He was sitting and writing at my Secretary's table. On seeing the accused, I asked who he was. The Secretary said that he was a visitor who wished to see me. The accused said it was urgent

[9] *The Hindustan Times*, July 29, 1943.
[10] According to the book titled, *Jinnah Faces An Assassin*, the particulars of the case are as follows:
In The High Court of Judicature at Bombay.
Crown Side
Case No: 35
Fourth Session, 1943
Emperor v/s Rafiq Sabir Mazangavi alias Mohammad Sadiq

business and he must see me at once. This was in spite of the fact that my Secretary had already told him that I was engaged on an important matter at the time. I was standing by the edge of the table. The accused stood up. He had a paper on which he had written something. I told him that I was very sorry that I could not see him at once. I told him to write out whatever he had to say. I assured him that I would look into the matter and would be glad to see him the following day or the day after to fix up some time. My mind was on the matter I was attending to. I moved to leave the room. Suddenly, in the twinkling of an eye, the accused sprang at me and gave me a blow with his clenched fist on the left side of my jaw. I reeled back a little. Simultaneously, the accused whipped out a knife and held it in his clenched hand."

When the Magistrate questioned whether it was an open knife, Jinnah responded:

"Yes, it was an open knife. The accused wanted to strike at my throat. The accused took it out from his vest. The knife was open already. My instinct of self-defence made me parry the blow with the knife which the accused aimed at my neck. Fortunately, I seized the accused's wrist and broke the momentum of the blow. The knife only reached my chin and made a small cut. I forced back the accused's hand holding the knife and seized his other hand. A scuffle ensued. It was all a matter of a few seconds. My Secretary rushed up and my watchman came up and seized the accused. I received an injury on my left hand. In the struggle my coat also received a cut on the left shoulder.

The Secretary and the watchman pulled the accused away from me. I let go the accused's hand. My Chauffeur also came on the scene and disarmed the accused by taking away the knife. I was bleeding from my cuts. I went up to my room and sent for Dr. Masina. He dressed my injuries. The police were informed and they arrived. They took charge of my coat, waistcoat, trouser, shirt, and collar. The police also took charge of the knife. My statement was recorded. I did not know the accused before.

Between the time of the attack on me and the arrival of the police, the accused said it was a misfortune that he had failed in his mission. He said he had done this because I had refused to carry out the orders of Allama Mashriqui to meet Mr. Gandhi. He said that I was in the way of the freedom of the country and that I was a tool of British Imperialism. The accused was holding forth this way because it had been suggested to him by someone that he was a hired assassin."

Quaid-e-Azam clearly implicated the Khaksars when he stated, "I was getting threatening letters apart from the Khaksars." Jinnah's statement in the Court was highly deplored in the Khaksar circle, because his statements implicitly put the blame on Mashraqi and the Khaksars without any solid proof. Mashraqi's request to not turn this into a political scandal was ignored. This was again a reason for this incident to be viewed as a conspiracy to destroy Mashraqi and the Khaksars politically.

On September 08, 1943, the trial of Quaid-e-Azam's assailant was resumed in Bombay. Dr. Dinsnaw Masina (who had seen Jinnah after the attack) and other people recorded their statements. *The Bombay Chronicle* of September 09, 1943 reported that:

> "A large crowd thronged the Court...among the crowd were some European ladies also. An unusual feature was that by the side of the Magistrate to his left sat a European Honorary Magistrate on the Bench watching the proceedings with keen interest."

What were these European people doing in the court? Were they there to influence the court or were they spying on the court proceedings? It was very unusual to see Europeans in India, particularly at that time, watching the proceedings of an Indian person's trial. This obviously raised eye-brows. The case was postponed until September 14, 1943.

*****

It was already known that the attacker was an ex-Muslim Leaguer. On September 13, 1943, a meeting was held in Jamia Masjid in Delhi. Liaquat Ali Khan presided over the meeting. Professor Inayatullah Lahori, the editor of *Pakistan* newspaper (a Muslim League paper published in Delhi), addressed the session and admitted that Rafiq Sabir Mazangavi was not a Khaksar, but was a Muslim Leaguer. Lahori said:

> "I state with regret that Mr. Jinnah's attacker was from amongst us and has been working for the Muslim League for a long time. It's even more regrettable that Mazangavi belongs to the same area where I come from. When I see that this is the same Rafiq Sabir Mazangavi whom we used to consider one of our valuable companions, I bow my head in shame."[11]

On November 01, 1943, the trial of Jinnah's assailant, Rafiq Sabir Mazangavi, continued before Justice Blagden and a common Jury at the Criminal Sessions of the Bombay High Court. The court recorded evidence from Jinnah, his secretary (Syed Ahmed Syed Yaqub), the Pathan watchman, and the doctor (Dr. Dinsnaw Masina). On November 02, 1943, Rafiq Sabir Mazangavi's trial again resumed in the court of Justice Blagden. Rafiq Sabir Mazangavi cross-examined Jinnah. *The Bombay Chronicle* (of November 03, 1943) reported:

> "...letters received by Mr. Jinnah after 5th June [1943] threatening him if he should refuse to see Mr. Gandhi were put in as exhibits by Mr. Jinnah and read out in court by his counsel.
> The accused having dispensed with the services of his counsel proceeded in person to cross-examine Mr. Jinnah. On being asked whether these threatening letters could have been written by persons other than Khaksars, Mr. Jinnah replied that that was a matter

---

[11] *Al-Islah*, 1997. P. 26. Translation from Urdu.

of opinion. In reply to further questions from the accused Mr. Jinnah stated that he did not remember the accused having handed him a letter at Lahore in 1935 when he went there in connection with some dispute relating to a mosque and stated that there was no personal enmity between him and the accused."

On November 03, 1943, the trial of Jinnah's assailant, Rafiq Sabir Mazangavi, almost came to an end and the court was crowded with people. Jinnah was present and was cross-examined by Rafiq. However Justice Blagden did not allow Rafiq to raise certain questions to the witness (Jinnah). The accused stated that he was a member of the Muslim League (Propaganda Secretary of the Muslim League) and therefore he was entitled to ask the questions to the President (Jinnah) of the Muslim League. However, Jinnah stated that he did not know if the accused was ever Propaganda Secretary of the Lahore District Muslim League. Rafiq further stated in court,

> "There is no dispute between me and Mr. Jinnah over any property or a woman. I looked upon Mr. Jinnah as a leader and I went to his bungalow on July 26, 1943 thinking he was a leader."[12]

This was a high profile case and drew great attention in the public. It needed careful decision and Justice Blagden reviewed the case proceedings. Blagden and the Jury found nothing in the evidence submitted by Jinnah to prove that the assailant was a Khaksar. Obviously, Justice Blagden and the Jury had to thoroughly examine the case, and besides that, they had no sympathy with Mashraqi. If they had any sympathy, it may have been toward Jinnah as he was not in the bad books of the British; in fact the British liked him. Regardless of all this, Justice Blagden and the Jury did not accept the assertion that the assailant was a Khaksar.

On November 04, 1943, in front of a packed courtroom, Justice Blagden announced his verdict.[13] Addressing the Jury he said:

> "Well, Gentlemen of the Jury... I have to tell what the law is...If you should convict the man, the responsibility for passing sentence on him — which is going to be a very difficult problem in this case...
> ...I have no doubt that this case, which has a certain political background, has excited a good deal of comment and description in the newspapers...Gentleman, anything you have seen in the newspapers, anything you may have heard about this case from the source outside the four walls of this room, you must please put completely out of your minds. You are to give a true verdict 'according to the evidence' which is what you have heard from the witnesses here and what you observe from the exhibits that have been proved [produced]. Evidence, Gentleman, is not what is written in newspapers, it does not consist of gossip, it does not even include the statements made to you by learned Counsel at the Bar.

---

[12] *The Bombay Chronicle*, November 04, 1943.
[13] *The Leader*, November 06, 1943. *The Bombay Chronicle*, November 05, 1943.

You will remember that in opening his case Mr. Somejee for the prosecution told you that he intended to prove that the accused was not only a member of a body called the Khaksar movement but held a certain position in it called 'Jan Baz', which I gather to mean a person prepared to sacrifice his life in that cause. People who go in for movements involving the wearing of shirts of a particular colour and other such demonstrations of solidarity seem to like adopting rather sensational titles like the expression 'Storm Trooper' which I believe is in use in Germany. But as the evidence has come out learned Counsel's anticipations have not been fulfilled, a thing which quite often happens. Actually, you have no evidence at all that this man is a member of that movement, though you may well think that he is acquainted with its ideas, sympathetic towards them, and possibly ready to go a great deal further than, apparently, the leader of that movement has ever asked his followers to go. However that may be you have no evidence that he is a member of the movement, still less that he holds any particular position in it...

Let us take the story, if we may, in the order in which the events are supposed to have occurred, which is a little different from the order in which the witnesses were called, I am not going to take you through the past history which the accused has sought to introduce into this case, and I may say, it matters extremely little whether the accused had taken part in politics at a very young age, or whether at the age of seventeen he had the impertinence to address a letter to Mr. Jinnah to alter his opinions. Let us go to a little bit of more recent history. Apparently on or about the 22nd June last somebody purporting to be the leader of the Khaksar movement issued a circular, which is Ex. C, — I am not going to bother you by reading the whole of it, — in which in rather verbose terms he exhorted his followers to pester Mr. Jinnah with letters urging him to go and see Mr. Gandhi. Whatever the policy of the author of that circular was right or wrong, or whether Mr. Jinnah's view as to the proper procedure in the circumstances were correct or not, matters no more to this case than to the man in the moon. What is noticeable is that the circular was a perfectly legitimate document, as far as I can see, because it did not ask anybody to do anything which they were not legitimately entitled to do...

The chauffeur says that he gave the knife on the stairs. What does it matter? It again shows that these people have not put their heads together and concocted a story. He says further:

'I am definite the knife was handed to me within a minute, but precisely where I am not sure'

He says the injury was caused to him by the knife and by nothing else.

He was quite sure that he did not bump his head against the accused, and he cannot say, as no honest witness could say, whether he was stabbed from the front or the side; he cannot say the precise angle of his jaw in the knife's path. He says the accused pulled the knife from his left hand side with his right hand, as one draws a sword from its sheath, and he is positive that the knife was open when pulled out. It was suggested that he may have coached the witnesses, and he said, 'I never spoke to a single servant of mine as to his evidence.' Finally he said that the injury to his face was not a scratch but a cut, and finally (to me) he emphatically denied that he first saw the knife when the chauffeur brought it to him, and said that the chauffeur did not suggest that they should foist the story of the knife on the accused. He said that he was not excited when he saw the accused, and that he did not lay hands on him and try to chuck him out. On the contrary, he said that after the accused was overpowered and he was separated from him he gave strict instructions that the accused was not to be hurt in any way, but merely detained.

If you have one witness whom you can believe it does not matter how many other witness there are. If you believe that one you have got the truth, and truth does not become more true if 20, 40 or 100 people tell it. In this case the principle witness is Mr. Jinnah. You and you alone are judges to decide whether it is right and safe to believe his story."[14]

In his verdict, the Judge sentenced Jinnah's assailant, Rafiq Sabir Mazangavi, to five years of rigorous imprisonment. However, Justice Blagden refused to accept that the assailant was a Khaksar.[15] Anti-Khaksar elements were highly disappointed. The verdict proves how weak their case must have been. All that was presented in the court was no more than a *cock and bull* story. Quaid-e-Azam, a seasoned attorney from Lincoln's Inn, could not prove that Rafiq was a Khaksar. This proves how flimsy and baseless the case must have been.

*****

On November 05, 1943, Mashraqi issued the following statement:[16]

"...the 26th [July 26, 1943]. On that day some rascal from the blue attempted to spoil the game, drive his zeal for Pakistan against the brusqueness which is Quaid-e-Azam's habit with almost everybody, fought the issue of achieving separate kingdom for the Musalmans amidst pushes, kicks, insults and angry words, and finally, when outnumbered, over powered and at bay made the most shameless attempt to get at the throat of that veteran leader whose yes or no spoken in a bolder mood can yet change the destinies of India. The Quaid-e-Azam, immediately after the event and as if in a fit of revenge against me, announced it as a 'serious and well-planned attack', had it announced that the assaulter was a Khaksar from Lahore, had been sent there, had been loitering round his house, had been following him in the railway train and so forth... I possess patience enough not to have commented upon these allegations as I never met or even knew about the assailant and it is well-known now that he never set his foot in Lahore during the last two years, that he

---

[14] Peerbhoy, Pp. 90-107.
[15] On November 07, 1943, *Zamindar* newspaper, Lahore stated in an article that Rafiq Sabir Mazangavi was not a Khaksar. (*Al-Islah* 1997, Pp. 7, 31).

Al-Islah reported that Justice Blagden stated in his verdict that Jinnah, his attorney and witnesses had all failed to prove that Rafiq Sabir Mazangavi was a Khaksar. (*Al-Islah* 1997, P. 59).
[16] See Appendix IV for more of this statement.

is more a Muslim League office-bearer than a Khaksar, that after arrest he gave an undertaking not to be a Khaksar again. But the most unanswerable suggestion given to me by a person in close touch is that the Quaid-e-Azam could not have possibly meant the words 'well-planned attack' as referring to the Khaksar organisation as only an hour after the event he met a deputation of Bombay Khaksars who had come to express their sympathies and he never suspected them. I have my own reasons to say that having occurred on the 19th [March 1940] and the 26th July [1943] both were 'well-planned attacks' on the Khaksar organisation, the one from the side of the Government and the other from the side of Mr. Jinnah.

As regards the assailant being a Khaksar, it is unthinkable that Khaksars who spared Sir Sikandar Hayat Khan for three years after his massacre of them and were the only organisation who attended his funeral after his death, could conspire to attack Quaid-e-Azam for whom they have the greatest reverence and respect.

Hostility between the Khaksars and the Muslim League is indeed impossible under any circumstances, as Khaksars have not been organized to oppose any political or non-political party in the land. They are, in fact, to serve all and serve for the good of the country. I also declare here that I am no rival to Quaid e-Azam and will not think of taking his place, but I have the right to ask him to hurry up. I am fully aware of the discontent against him in the inner circles and the grave differences that are slowly appearing but the Muslim League cannot have a better leader at this moment.

As a next step towards the achievement of Pakistan, I respectfully suggest to Quaid-e-Azam that even in case the British Government is formally disinclined to let him meet Mahatma Gandhi, the question of Hindu-Muslim settlement cannot be much postponed owing to the fact that the British victory in war is now measurably within sight. I request him that as he has roused extraordinary enthusiasm in Musalmans of India on account of his slogan of Pakistan he should write formally to the Viceroy to allow him to see Mahatma Gandhi for the purpose of settlement and in case the Viceroy refuses, ask in the next letter the name or names of those Congress or Hindu gentlemen in India, who in the eyes of the British Government are best fitted to make that Hindu-Muslim settlement which the British government thinks as essential to the grant of complete independence to India immediately after the war. I, with the due respects, suggest to him that this is the most essential next step and that Pakistan can only come if he is up and doing..."[17]

*****

Reverting to the case, obviously, each and every step was methodically and meticulously prepared by Jinnah and his aids to prove that Rafiq Sabir Mazangavi was a Khaksar. Yet still the Judge did not accept this.

The Judge stated, "I have no doubt that this case, which has a certain political background." What does this statement reflect? The Judge understood that

[17] Hussain, Pp. 192-194.

case was politically motivated. The verdict of the Judge and the Jury is in itself glaring proof that this attack was pre-planned.

The attack seemed planned for a number of reasons:

❖ The assailant was declared to be a Khaksar right after the attack without any proof
❖ Desperate and systematic efforts were made in the court to prove him to be a Khaksar
❖ The assailant turned out to be a Propaganda Secretary of the Muslim League as well as editor of the League's official newspaper, *Pakistan*
❖ The attack was majorly publicized. If political motives were not at play, why was the attack publicized so much that it would cause division amongst Muslims?
❖ Soon after the attack, the Bombay Provincial Muslim League passed a resolution "to enjoin upon all members of the Muslim League Organisation to disassociate themselves from the Khaksar Movement forthwith and not to support it any more"[18]
❖ Another resolution in November 1943 banned Leaguers from joining the Khaksar Tehreek; this resolution was passed after the verdict

The Khaksar circle also questioned why Quaid-e-Azam came to the secretary's room, where the assailant was sitting? If a file was needed or Jinnah had any question, the secretary would generally have been asked to come to his room. High profiled personalities, particularly in the sub-continent in those days, never came to their secretary's room; it was always the other way around. Hence, why did Jinnah bother to come to the Secretary's room? This is a legitimate question that raises eye-brows.

If political motives were not to be derived from this sensitive case, Jinnah could have spoken to Mashraqi right after the attack and sought clarification or requested an inquiry. Instead, Quaid-e-Azam ignored Mashraqi's statement and request, "not to give this incident the slightest political tinge." Jinnah did not even suggest to those Khaksars, who were with him soon after the attack, to have an inquiry conducted by the Khaksar Tehreek. Most importantly, if political benefits were not meant to be drawn out of this attack, Quaid-e-Azam should have respected the court's decision and Mashraqi's plea. Jinnah should have issued a public proclamation in the press stating that the assailant was not a Khaksar, but he never issued any such statement.

The Khaksar Tehreek, obviously, would not have attacked Jinnah, as this would have damaged their party politically; and there was no history of them ever doing anything of this sort with anyone. They did not attempt to even harm Sir Sikandar Hayat Khan (Punjab Premier), who had proven to be their deadly enemy. Sikandar's brutalities on the Khaksars were unforgettable, yet Mashraqi issued a statement on his death praising him. Khaksars even attended

---

[18] Hussain, P. 194.

his funeral. The Khaksar Tehreek was an organization that sought unity even with non-Muslims and purification of the spiritual side of one's personality. Mashraqi taught his followers that one's salvation was through good deeds and service to humanity. Hence, an organization of this type could never perform such a heinous crime.[19]

*****

Quaid-e-Azam made a big mistake by rigorously making an effort to prove that the assailant was a Khaksar. This incident was one of the biggest blows to Muslim unity. He did not write to Mashraqi apologizing for whatever damage had been caused to the Khaksar reputation. Soon after Blagden's decision, the AIML passed a resolution barring its members from joining the Khaksar Tehreek. If anyone maintained any type of connection with the Khaksars, that person was highly resented and considered a traitor. It is so unfortunate, that for political ends and vested interests, overall Muslim unity and interest were compromised. Throughout history, such decisions have weakened the Muslims and have given strength to opponents.

Although with this bogus attack on Jinnah, Mashraqi was stabbed in the back, he was brave and least concerned with what the anti-Khaksar forces were doing against him. Regardless of this phony attack, the Khaksar Tehreek retained its importance, influence and glamour. It remained a source of fear for the British; this of course was important to end foreign rule. Despite the AIML's violent and vicious politics, the Khaksar Tehreek did not retaliate and did not impose any restrictions on its members from joining the Muslim League. They were open to join both parties at the same time. In fact, the Khaksar Tehreek encouraged this in order to bring unity among the Muslims. There were many Khaksars who were also members of the Muslim League.

On the other hand, the AIML's consistent behavior was straining its relations with the Khaksar Tehreek. There is nothing concrete that suggests that Quaid-e-Azam was a well-wisher of the Khaksars. For instance, when the Khaksars met Quaid-e-Azam in Quetta, during the course of discussion, they asked him why the League was causing a breach between the two parties. Jinnah told

---

[19] Shan Muhammad wrote in his book titled *Khaksar Movement in India*:
"Greater enemy of the Khaksar than Jinnah was Sir Sikandar Hayat Khan, the Premier of the Punjab, who mobilized his forces against them causing the death of many Khaksars. But Khaksars did not take any action against him" and actually attended his funeral. "How could then they go against the Qaid-i-Azam?...to say that the assailant was selected for a murderous attack by the organisation does not appear to be true...

Mashraqi and Jinnah differed only on the question of communal settlement...it was Mashraqi's earnest desire to bring about a settlement between Gandhi and Jinnah, and for that he asked the Khaksars to send letters, telegrams and messages to Jinnah latest by July 26, 1943. Mashraqi regarded it a great sin that Indian independence should be delayed on account of the obstacle of Pakistan and more than two lakh [200,000] letters, telegrams and resolutions were sent to Jinnah and Viceroy. Had he thought otherwise, he would not have waited for such a long time. But Mashraqi loved conciliation and throughout the whole course of the movement he stuck to it even at the time of much critical moments in the history of the movement." (Muhammad, P. 155.)

Khaksars that Mashraqi should have contacted him or met him to resolve the issues. This message was conveyed to Mashraqi.

Quaid-e-Azam arrived in Lahore on March 18, 1944; the next day was the Khaksar massacre's anniversary, yet Jinnah did not utter a word about the Khaksar massacre. He did not even say anything about those Khaksars that were still rotting in jail since 1940.

As Jinnah had suggested to Khaksars in Quetta, Mashraqi wrote to Jinnah upon Jinnah's arrival in Lahore on March 18, 1944[20]:

> "Dear Mr. Jinnah,
> I have learnt just this minute that you are in Lahore and attending some occasion. Events of the past some months have made you cause a breach between the Khaksars and the Muslim League and I have yet to know if I am to blame for that. My conviction is that Mussalmans and Hindus must come to an understanding at this critical moment, in order to gain Pakistan as well as independence for India; but you in your fury are losing these precious moments amidst despair and inaction.
> I am open to conviction if you can convince me otherwise. You told Khaksars in Quetta that I should have written to you or met you if I thought you were mistaken. I have persistently written and do write again. I shall be pleased to meet you if you come to Ichhra, but if my humble invitation does not suit you I do not feel at all small if I come over to you.
> Please let me know per bearer as I think we must come to an agreement. I hope you are well.
> I am & c.
> Inayatullah Khan"[21]

Despite Jinnah's own suggestion, he did not come over to meet Mashraqi nor did he call to discuss any matter. So Quaid-e-Azam's suggestion to the Khaksars in Quetta was nothing but a statement to avoid embarrassment. As a matter of fact, Quaid-e-Azam wanted no alliance with Mashraqi and he took no serious steps in this direction. All statements and letters were merely for public consumption and for taking political advantage.

On March 19, 1944, Quaid-e-Azam sent the following reply to Mashraqi's letter, which generated further resentment and friction:

> "Dear Mr. Inayatullah Khan,
> I am in receipt of your letter of the 18th of March, late last night, and I regret very much indeed to note that you have thought fit to accuse me for having caused the breach between the Khaksars and the Muslim League and further you convey and insinuate that I am, to use your own expression, 'in my fury' opposed to Hindu-Muslim

---

[20] *The Tribune*, March 19, 1944.
[21] Yousaf 2004, Pp. 271-272. *Dawn*, March 20, 1944. *The Star of India*, March 20, 1944.

understanding under any circumstances. There is no truth whatsoever in these allegations that you make against me, and you should know that there is no justification for it. I have repeatedly made my position clear by my statements and speeches that have been broadcast in the press.

However, as you say you are open to conviction, may I draw your attention to the fact that now, the All-India Muslim League has appointed a Committee of Action, in whom are vested all the powers of organising the Muslim League, and request you to get in touch with the chairman, Nawab Mohamed Ismail Khan, whose address is Mustafa Castle, Meerut, U.P. or the convener Nawabzaba Liaquat Ali Khan whose address is, 8B, Hardinge Avenue, New Delhi as they are free from accusations and reflections that you have cast on me both in this letter under reply and by your previous writings and statements that you have issued to the press heretofore; and I hope that in that atmosphere they may be able to convince you that the policy and the principles and the programme of the League are in the best interest of Muslim India. I am informed that the full Committee of Action is going to meet at Delhi on the 25th instant. I am releasing this letter to the press as I notice that you have already published yours without waiting for my reply.
Yours sincerely,
M.A. Jinnah"[22]

In his letter, Jinnah also denied that he was "opposed to Hindu-Muslim understanding." He wanted understanding of partition and nothing else.

A breach between the Khaksars and the Muslim League was in fact the result of the continuous actions of the Muslim League for years, yet Quaid-e-Azam denied this. Further, Quaid-e-Azam caused a breach by showing arrogance to Mashraqi by asking him to contact Nawab Ismail Khan, instead of appreciating Mashraqi's gesture of contacting him. Anyone, particularly a person of Mashraqi's stature, would have been offended by his words (directing Mashraqi to talk to someone other than himself). In this letter, Quaid-e-Azam tried to show his importance; it was common for the Leaguers to show their importance and this attitude was more visible in personalities close to the British.

Yet Mashraqi, humble as he was, did not make this a matter of prestige; he wrote back to Jinnah the same day (March 19, 1944) and suggested that he reconsider his decision:

"Your reply to my letter of last night, received after much persuasion after sixteen hours, settles that I am not to blame for not meeting you for an understanding between the Mussalmans and the Hindus, or even between the Mussalmans themselves. My assertion, therefore, that you made an attempt to cause the breach between the Khaksars and the Muslim League stands true. Please reconsider the position in which you have involved yourself by this refusal. I can assure you that the Khaksar is not against the Muslim League in spite of everything that has happened.

Your reference to the 'Committee of Action' as having been given powers to organise the Muslim League is most amusing as this means that you consider the Muslim League to be a disorganised body so far. I assure you that the disorganisation is solely due to your inaction and despair, also, if I may add, to the expectant sentiments you arouse at the shows you make in public and the high words you give to them. I can respectfully assure that the Mussalman public is tired of all this.

I have asked you to reconsider your decision not to meet me, but I confess here that I shall be one of your lieutenants if you show real action. As regards your 'Committee of Action' I shall certainly give my best attention to it if it shows any action.

As a last word I can only say that if you, as the Quaid-i-Azam of the Mussalmans of India do not show any real action in the matter of Hindu-Muslim understanding or in getting Pakistan for the Mussalmans, I shall be compelled to the conclusion that the Mussalmans of India must leave you alone and try their luck elsewhere.

With best expectations that I shall get a more prompt reply."[23]

Mashraqi was bound to be embittered and disgusted by what Quaid-e-Azam had stated in his letter; yet Mashraqi had a generous heart and didn't let personal ego get in the way when critical national issues were more important. Despite Quaid-e-Azam's behavior, Mashriqi wrote "I shall be one of your lieutenants." If Jinnah had any grudges, he should have put them aside and taken Mashraqi's offer of being his lieutenant in the overall interest of the community. Yet Quaid-e-Azam avoided meeting Mashraqi for political reasons. So who is responsible for the breach?

The breach between the Khaksars and the Leaguers was created on purpose through this conspired attack. Despite this, Mashraqi put forth efforts for unity, but Quaid-e-Azam made no attempt to join hands with Mashraqi.

*****

It is important to note that those writers who continue to mention Rafiq Sabir Mazangavi as a Khaksar are responsible for distorting history. This is a clear misrepresentation and a distortion of the facts; it is a continuation of a well thought-out, organized assassination of Mashraqi and the Tehreek's character, political role and reputation.

Mashraqi's family has refrained from suing the authorities or the ones who are behind Mashraqi's character assassination, for this would spill a lot of mud on

---

[23] Yousaf 2004, P. 273. *The Tribune*, March 20, 1944.

the father of the nation (Quaid-e-Azam). I urge all persons and the authorities to straighten the record and not distort history.

Appendix II

Muslim League
as Seen in Late Thirties & Forties

It is unfortunate to note that, in Pakistan, only the Muslim League's version of history is publicized. It is difficult to access any materials that contradict the League's version of events, and even in history books, criticism of the League is avoided. This has led to a distortion of the nation's history. To find the real truth, one must also understand the anti-Leaguer and nationalist perspectives. Only then can one form a truly educated opinion. Therefore, I have included below a few comments that show the other side of the story. Note: These comments are included for educational purposes only and are not intended to demean anyone.

On May 15, 1937 Mohi-ud Din Maraikayar, Member Legislative Assembly, issues a statement regarding the strength and popularity of the Muslim League: "Can Mr. Jinnah prove that today there are not more Muslims in the Congress than in the Muslim League. Is there any organization under the League's auspices even in his Bombay Presidency and what efforts, if any, he makes for bringing the Muslim masses into closer contact with the League and what are his performances in this connection...How is it that more people are drifting from the League than joining it? Does it not show that the general feeling that the League can serve no useful purpose, least of all in politics..."[1]

The Tribune, Lahore of April 23, 1937 publishes Prof. Abdul Majid Khan's statement. "...in four provinces the Muslims are in a majority, while in the remaining seven they are in a minority. And Mr. Jinnah is too apt to ignore this aspect of the question. In the N.W.F. Province the Muslims are in an over-whelming majority; while in C.P. they are just a small minority. Therefore, it behoves the Muslims in the N.W.F. Province, the Punjab, Sind and Bengal to be over careful about the rights and interests of the non-Muslim minorities in these provinces...

---

[1] *The Tribune*, May 16, 1937.

The only difficulty with Mr. Jinnah is that the question of personal equation is simply insoluble for him. Extraordinary and exaggerated notion of self importance and the incurable itch of posing as the sole saviour and spokesman of the Muslims..."

Mir Abdul Qayyum, Chairman of the Reception Committee of the Provincial Ahrar Conference, at a meeting held on May 21, 1937. *The Tribune*, Lahore of May 22, 1937 reported that he stated:

"[Muslim] League from its very inception had been a coterie of few knights, Khan Bahadurs and Nawabs. 'It never was nor is an organisation of the masses,' added Mir Abdul Qayyum. During the last thirty-one years of its existence it had not led a single popular movement among the Muslims nor had it educated the Muslim masses in any political or social matter. With the advent of the new Act, political power along with political importance had passed from the hands of these self-imposed leaders, who were egged on and supported by the Government to those of the leaders chosen by the people... Muslim League, with its present restricted membership and undemocratic constitution could not be expected to attract the attention of the masses."

Qayyum pretty much explained what the Muslim League's position was. Muslim League leadership was also considered job hunters and away from masses. This impression prevailed among those who understood the Muslim Leaguers. Jinnah tried to wash that impression by speaking in Bhendy Bazar in Bombay in Hindustani and refuted that the Muslim Leaguers were "job hunters."[2] The impression of "job hunters" prevailed because they never worked for the masses and had no support from them, which was reflected in the 1937 election. The League's poor position in the Muslim majority provinces triggered their demand for partition.

In a press statement, Prof. Abdul Majid Khan describes the Muslim League's position after the 1937 election: "1/3 (one-third) India is being represented by the non-Congress Muslims. Out of these five provinces, in four, namely Sind, N.W.F.P., the Punjab and Bengal, Muslims form the bulk of population. Consequently, it is but significant to inquire as to how many Muslim League M.L.A.'s [Member Legislative Assembly] there are in all the four provinces together. In the N.W.F.P., there is not a single Muslim M.L.A. who was elected on the Muslim League ticket. The same is true in the case of Sind. In the Punjab the story is slightly different. One Muslim Leaguer was elected exclusively on the Muslim League ticket but immediately after his election he either with the knowledge or the connivance of Mr. Jinnah joined the Unionists. The second Muslim who was elected to the Punjab Legislative Assembly had a sort of joint ticket of Ittihad-i-Millat plus the Muslim League, a peculiar combination of hot potatoes and ice cream. In Bengal, of course, there were 40 M.L.A.'s elected on the Muslim League ticket but they have now merged themselves in the Proja Party of Mr. Fazl-ul-Haq [A.K.Fazl-ul-Haq]."

---

[2] *The Tribune*, May 23, 1937.

Prof. Abdul Majid Khan further states: "...the four Muslim Premiers, of Sind, the N.W.F.P., the Punjab and Bengal respectively who command clear majorities in their respective Legislative Assemblies not only owe no allegiance to the Muslim League but on the contrary are in a definite manner opposed to it...

At present his [Jinnah's] claim to speak on behalf of the Muslims is nothing short of 'sounding brass and tinkling cymbal'...Muslim Leaguers not only disowned Mr. Jinnah and started a separate League but actually participated in the deliberations of the so-called All-Parties Muslim Conference which met at Delhi on 1st January, 1929...Mr. Jinnah who represents but a microscopic minority of the upper middle classes among the Muslims and who generally speaks on behalf of a handful of the communal leaders who play the role of Dr. Jekyll today and of Mr. Hyde tomorrow. So Mr. Jinnah can do anything but deliver the goods on behalf of the Muslim masses. His oft-trumpeted solicitude about 'the fate and future of eighty millions of Muslims' leaves a bad taste in the mouth. To quote his very words 'service, suffering and sacrifice are absolutely essential conditions before we can achieve anything.' The tragedy of it all is that most of the Muslim Leaguers are stuffing themselves while the Muslim masses are starving. 'Service' and 'sacrifice' are words which are non-existent in the dictionary of arm-chair leaders and academic scholars of politics. Nay Muslim masses have been deliberately betrayed by the political lotus-eaters known as the Muslim Leaguers who have all along been drugging the gullible and credulous Muslims with the opiate of myopic communalism."[3]

The Tribune, Lahore October 20, 1937 reports the speech of Maulana Habibur Rehman, President of the Majlis-i-Ahrar-Hind. The speech was delivered on October 17, 1937. The newspaper reported, "Maulana Habibur Rehman strongly criticised the Muslim League and said the presidential speech of Mr. Jinnah...contained no practical programme for the amelioration of the condition of the millions of Muslims of India. He observed that the leaders of the Muslim League owing to their aristocratic mentality and narrow outlook were utterly incapable to lead the Muslim masses."

On June 16, 1938, Dr. Abdul Aziz Khan, General Secretary, Anjuman Nasir-ul- Musalmin issued a statement in Lahore: "Some self-styled Muslim leaders are shouting at the top of their voice that 'Islam is in danger.' But they should know that Islam can never be in danger because Allah has himself assured all protection to Islam. On the other hand the leadership of these so-called protectors of Islam is in danger. They do not know what Islam is. They are quite ignorant of Islamic principles, yet they raise the cry in the name of Islam. They boast to be the leaders of 9-crores of Muslims of India, but they must know that the Muslims are aware of the fact that these communalists care more for their own interest and leadership than for the safety of Islam or for the matter of that anything else. They are responsible for retarding the progress of the country...

---

[3] *The Tribune*, July 31, 1937.

The leaders of the Muslim League, whose business it is to pass paper resolutions, are nowhere to be found when the time comes for solid work. They try to follow a hole and corner policy and put forward unreasonable demands."[4]

Muslim Leaguers had a bad reputation because of their past. People were saying that it was difficult to expect knights and Nawabs to fight the battle for freedom, as they had never known struggle. According to *The Tribune, Lahore* of June 24, 1938, Professor Abdul Majeed "characterized the Muslim League as a body of imbeciles."

The newspaper further reported: "'The League' he [Professor Abdul Majeed] said, 'is an un-quranie body because it is most undemocratic, while democracy is the basic principle of Islam'...it was an insult to the Musalmans themselves to say that in spite of their being...crores, their religion, their language and their culture were in danger. All this was the excuse of wearied men who were unwilling to suffer but anxious to retain power in their hands. 'Mr. Jinnah and his Muslim League,' said Prof. Majeed, 'are out to protect what nobody in India has threatened'...the opposition of the League to the Congress was the opposition of self-seekers some of whom wanted dominate without paying any price for their domination. Mr. Jinnah wanted to be a Caesar or nothing; he appeared to believe that it was better to be the cockhead than to be a lion's tail...

The Gandhi-Jinnah and Jinnah-Jawaharlal correspondence had shown clearly, and beyond any doubt that Mr. Jinnah was not really so much anxious to protect the rights of the Muslims as to protect his own self and keep intact his leadership of innocent Musalmans. The brave fighters of freedom never stopped to ask for shares and privileges."[5]

The Tribune, Lahore June 15, 1938 reports on a debate that was held in Lahore on June 13, 1938. The newspaper states, "The Punjab University students at a largely attended meeting...under the auspices of the University Union, unanimously voted against the policy and politics of Mr. M.A. Jinnah...

The resolution 'that this House strongly disapproves of Mr. M.A. Jinnah's policy and politics'...

Mr. Mazhar Ali made it perfectly clear that they were concerned with Mr. Jinnah's politics and not his person because his politics were responsible for retarding the anti-imperialist forces in the country. All the supporters of the resolution characterised Mr. Jinnah as an arm-chair politician, a bulwark of Imperialism in India.

'This self-styled leader [Quaid-e-Azam] of the Muslims of India cares more for the crease of his trousers than anything else,' said Nawabzada Mahmud Ali. Mr. Abdulla Butt's reply to Maulana Chisti was both convincing and crushing. Mr. Butt's speech was punctuated with wild applause.

He said 'I challenge the so-called protector of Islam to recite the holy *Kalema* correctly.' Mr. Butt quoting from the Holy Quran called it a sin to say

---

[4] *The Tribune*, June 17, 1938.
[5] *The Tribune*, June 24, 1938.

that Islam was in danger because Allah had himself assured all protection to Islam...

Mr. Mahmud said that it was an irony of fate that knights and Nawabs claimed to speak in the name of masses whom they exploited...Can these Nawabs and Khan Bahadurs represent the people whose blood they have been sucking."

Syed Attaullah Shah Bukhari, Bar at Law, spoke at a largely attended conference on June 25, 1938. *The Tribune, Lahore* of June 28, 1938 reported that he stated that "the Muslim League was dominated by Mr. Jinnah and a group of autocrats of his school of thought. He said that the Muslim League was a mere sham in the present political atmosphere of the country..."

It is interesting to note that the Muslims Leaguers were never ready to give up their privileges may it be for freedom or any other issue. A press statement was issued by Maulana Mohammand Miyan Farooqi, Sayed Muzaffar Hussain, Maulana Shahid Fakhri, Dr. K.M. Ashraf and Syed Sajjad Zahir on behalf of the organizers of the Allahabad Palestine Conference:

"On the eve of the meeting of the Council of the All India Muslim League we, in a press statement, briefly reviewed the history of the Palestine movement in India and expressed a hope that on this issue a most wide-based programme would be adopted to make possible and effective cooperation from every section of Mussalmans and anti-imperialists. We also mentioned the triple boycott and offered a most practical and effective programme for a united front on the Palestine issue.

It is unfortunate that the Council of the All-India Muslim League did not see its way to adopt the resolution moved at its Delhi meeting for the boycott of British goods and the surrender of titles and contended itself with fixing August 26 as the Palestine Day."[6]

Nawabzada Mahmud Ali condemned Sikandar and the Muslim League forcefully at a public meeting in Campbellpur on September 25, 1938. He stated: "He [Sir Sikandar Hayat Khan] is not the champion of the poor, which he poses to be..." According to *The Tribune, Lahore* of September 27, 1938, "Continuing further the Nawabzada vehemently criticized the action of the Muslim League, and the activities of its leaders who were determined to perpetuate the bondage on the country. They had got no programme except to mislead the poor people and to further the ends of the British Imperialism. They were exploiting the illiterate masses in the name of religion and diverting them from the true path..."

In 1937, the Muslim League was an absolutely disorganized party with no agenda. It needed to be organized. Jinnah admitted in his interview to the Associated Press on October 19, 1937 that "The task before us now is to organise Mussalmans all over India...I expect every member of the League

[6] *The Tribune*, August 14, 1938.

and Mussalmans generally all over India to strengthen the All-India Muslim League."[7]

The reason the League could not organize itself for the past many years and frame a solid agenda was because of lack of direct contact with the masses as well as lack of sacrifices for and sincerity to the cause. These were the chief reasons behind the League's failure in the elections. To succeed, a party has to have a concrete agenda, like the Khaksar Tehreek had, as well as high ideals behind every movement so as to bind people together. The League had no concrete social, economic or even political program to uplift the masses; this was also stated by Asaf Ali, Secretary, Congress Party in the Central Legislative Assembly in his press statement.[8]

Jinnah's interview, in which he stated that the Working Committee of All-India Muslim League would be chosen,[9] reflects there was no participation from the masses in the political process. If a party seeks public participation, it has to invite members to contest elections within the party, not choose them itself.

Dr. Syed Mahmud, in his press statement on October 25, 1937, stated: "Will Muslim League succeed in organising the Muslims? It will not succeed because it has placed no programme before the community. It has no band of selfless workers who will go the masses and live and work with them. It has preached hymns of hate and it has threatened the Hindus and done nothing else. With such poor equipment no community can be organized. Have they really a spirit of service? Do they really want to serve the cause of Islam? Do they want to save Islam from ruin and destruction?...

History also tells us that by sufferings and sacrifices for an ideal a nation or a community can only hope to organize itself. There is no royal road to organize a community. Will it be too much to expect from Mr. Jinnah or Mr. Fazlul Haq to lead us...

Alas! It is a vain hope. The Muslim League meeting was not held at Lucknow to save Islam or even to help the Muslim masses from utter helplessness and misery in which they find themselves today. It was nothing but a gathering of reactionaries. They always unite when they find that their power or prestige is threatened. It is the case with the Hindu reactionaries and so it is with Muslims."[10]

Prof. Abdul Majid Khan issued a statement on October 26, 1937: "We know what the Nawabs, the Knights and the Khan Bahadurs have accomplished in the past. Is it not a fact that both in the N.W.F.P. as well as in the United Provinces most of them have been removed from the political arena?

...Mr. Jinnah by delivering an incoherent and poisonous address and

---

[7] *The Tribune,* October 20, 1937.
[8] Ibid.
[9] Ibid.
[10] *The Tribune,* October 27, 1937.

the League by purging itself of the 'undesirables' have themselves precipitated the crisis."[11]

At the Ranchi Momin Conference held on October 6 and 7, 1938, Abdul Qaiyum Ansari, President Bihar Provincial Jamiat-ul-Momineen, criticized the Muslim League and talked about its behavior. According to *The Tribune, Lahore* of October 14, 1938, he "referred to the death of Abdulah Ansari who was mortally wounded at Cawnpore at the hands of several Muslim Leaguers. Mr. Ansari asked his community not to be led away by the cries of 'Islam in danger' raised at the moment by the Muslim League."[12]

Khan Abdul Qayyum Khan (Member Legislative Assembly, Central) said at a large public meeting in Peshawar: "The Muslim League movement is led and manned by the members of the gilded gentry and of vested interests. The only aim of their lives is to stand in the way of Hindu—Muslim unity. They are out to strengthen British Imperialism and tighten the bonds of slavery for their own countrymen. They are now yearning after Ministerial chairs."[13]

Maulana Habibur Rehman Ludhianvi, ex-President, Majlis-i-Ahrar Hind in a statement said "…it is quite in the tradition of the Muslim League to welcome the Viceroy's declaration…

The Muslim League has been recognized by the British Tory class to be the sole representative of Mussalamans… It is a matter of pride for us that we do not derive our representative character from British Imperialism.

It will not be forgotten that some time ago the Muslim League declared that it stood for full independence. However, the course which the Muslim Leaguers have now adopted will henceforth be, as it has always been to impugn those who struggle for the independence of the country. It is for the first time in the history of the Muslim League that it has after due consideration and complete unanimity given the pledge of loyalty to the British Government."[14]

Abdur Rehman Siddiqi, Member Legislative Assembly and member of the Working Committee of the All-India Muslim League, criticized Jinnah's appeal for the observance of a "Day of Deliverance"[15] and said: "He cannot be allowed to play havoc with the fundamental principles of the Muslim League or run riot with the cherished ambitions and ideals of the progressive section among his co-religionists. He has to realize that the attitude of respectful silence and anticipation adopted by a vast majority of Muslims in India despite their resentment against the dangerous and demoralizing channel in to which

[11] *The Tribune*, October 31, 1937.
[12] *The Tribune*, October 14, 1938.
[13] *The Tribune*, August 03, 1939.
[14] *The Tribune*, October 25, 1939.
[15] On the resignation of the Congress ministries in British India, the All India Muslim League appealed to the Muslims and other minorities to observe December 22, 1939 as the "Day of Deliverance."

the League is drifting...A leader must, undoubtedly, give the lead to his people, but he must also voice their true feelings."[16]

Shaikh Mohammad Jan (M.L.C.) criticized Jinnah's appeal for the observance of a "Day of Deliverance" and said: "I am glad to note that Mr. Abdur Rehman Siddiqi [Member Legislative Assembly], a prominent member of the Working Committee of the All-India Muslim League, has in his statement voiced the feelings of younger and progressive sections of the League against the humiliating and un-Islamic statement of Mr. Jinnah, and I appeal to...progressive elements in the League to give a true lead to the Mussalmans of India...and not be led away by those, however influential they might be, who cannot conceive of anything but destructive methods and are pursuing the policy of self-aggrandisement at the sacrifice of the best interest of the country as well as their community."[17]

The Tribune, Lahore of December 11, 1939 reports that Mr. Mauhammad Bhoy (I. M. Rowjee, J.P., ex-Sheriff of Bombay and President of H.H. the Agha Khan's Supreme Council of Bombay Presidency) criticized Jinnah's appeal for the observance of a "Day of Deliverance." Mr. Bhoy stated:
"Mr. Jinnah must realize this is not the time for political propaganda but for courageous *action*; and all his oratory and rhetoric will fail to convince the Muslims of his political wisdom, if he is merely satisfied with abusing all and sundry without practical and concrete proposals..."
The newspaper further reports: "Concluding, the ex-Sheriff earnestly appeals to the accredited leaders of the Muslims in India to come out from their silence and give correct lead to their community...'in case Mr. Jinnah continues his obstructive attitude and suicidal policy.'"[18]

Maulana Habibur Rehman (President, Majlis-i-Ahrar-i-Hind) addressed a public meeting in Jullundur on December 8, 1939. According to *The Tribune, Lahore* of December 11, 1939, Maulana Habib-ul Rehman said that the "Muslim masses of this country are being misled in the name of religion by the Muslim Leaguers..."

On December 12, 1939, Dr. M.S. Ansari (Vice President, All-India Momin Conference) issued a statement saying: "Mr Jinnah's appeal for the observance of a 'day of deliverance' is most unjust and unfair and is very much being resented by poorer classes of Muslims. Educational and economic problems of the poorer Muslims had never been the concern of Mr. Jinnah and his friends...we consider that Mr. Jinnah's appeal is inspired by the desire to perpetuate the dominance of the upper class Muslims over the vast working and poorer classes, who are about eighty millions in number...who are so far,

---

[16] *The Tribune*, December 08, 1939.
[17] *The Tribune*, December 09, 1939.
[18] *The Tribune*, December 11, 1939.

being exploited politically and being starved for the benefit of a favoured few the so called shareefs – upper class Muslims."[19]

Dr. Syed Mahmud (Ex Minister of Education, Bihar) criticized Jinnah's appeal for the observance of a 'Day of Deliverance.' According to *The Tribune, Lahore* of December 14, 1939, Dr. Syed Mahmud said that Jinnah's "statement was in sharp contrast to the sermon of goodwill and tolerance preached by him on the occasion of the last Id day…this demonstration was bound to widen the gulf between the two major communities and aggravate the unfortunate communal disharmony."

On April 09, 1941, Muhammad Suleman Cassum Mitha in his press statement said: "…For the last few years, I have heard of the Muslim League shouting of Congress 'zulum' in the Congress governed provinces but for the last one year and more, Congress Ministers have left office and the respective provinces are run by the Governors with the help of advisors.

What has the Muslim League done to redress the grievances of the Muslims, except pass pious resolutions in public meetings and indulge in big speeches and big talk by the so called leaders. Where is the evidence of any sacrifice? It is all talk and no result. Have they represented their grievances to the proper authorities? If not, why not? And if the authorities refused to redress the grievances, what steps have they taken or contemplated to get the grievances redressed? Can it be done only by big talk to ignorant masses?

Has the Muslim League no programme except Pakistan, which is impracticable and is neither in the interest of Muslims nor of the Hindus nor India in general?

What about economic condition of the Muslim masses; education, services, industry, business, unnecessary expenses of the community and the adoption of a simpler life? What have they done for all this?

I will leave it to the Muslim masses to give the answer for themselves."[20]

Maulana Obaidullah Sindhi also opposed the division of India.

Sahibzada Faizul Hassan (a prominent Ahrar leader) stated at an Ahrar Conference held on August 31 and September 01, 1941: "Neither Islam nor Hindustan is in danger. As religion is truth, it can never be in danger. The real danger is to the leadership of certain people, and for this reason they want to exploit the religious sentiments of the people. Capitalists make the poorer people fight in order to permit the leadership of such selfish people being maintained in tact."[21]

On February 26, 1942, Khan Bahadur Allah Buksh (Premier of Sind) said: "Mr. Jinnah knows that he reflects the opinion of only a section of the Indian

---

[19] *The Tribune*, December 14, 1939.
[20] *The Tribune*, April 10, 1941.
[21] *The Tribune*, September 03, 1941.

Muslim community. There is unquestionably a larger section of the Mussalman community who do not see eye to eye with Mr. Jinnah and his political organisation..."[22]

On May 02, 1942, Maulana Abul Kalam Azad stated at the All-India Congress Committee Session: "Pakistan is against the spirit of Islam" He further said, "The details of Pakistan have not been clarified. If Sir Sikander Hyat Khan is asked, he says one thing. Mr. Jinnah says something else, and the resolution itself means something else. The whole thing has been kept vague."[23]

On May 02, 1942, Maulana Nur-uddin Behari spoke at the All-India Congress Committee Session. *The Tribune*, Lahore of May 03, 1942 reported that he said that "Pakistan would harm the interests of not only the Hindus and the Muslim League but Pakistan would harm the interest of not only the Hindus but Muslims also in general."

On May 02, 1942, Yusuf, Meherally stated at the All-India Congress Committee, "The slogan is disastrous. The whole thing is politically retrograde, economically unsound and culturally ridiculous.[24]

The Tribune of June 21, 1942 reported that A.K.Fazl-ul-Haq (popularly known as Sher-i-Bengal) stated, "The policy pursued by the present Muslim League is neither Islamic nor patriotic. It serves neither the Muslims nor anybody else. It pretends to be exclusively Muslim, but is really leading even the Muslims to political ruin and disaster."

Maulana Mazhar Ali Azhar (Member Legislative Assembly) "accused Mr. Jinnah and his League of not fulfilling their assurances and promises made during the last elections. He then criticised vigorously the claim of Mr. Jinnah to be the accredited leader of the Muslims...

...He declared that the slogan Pakistan on which election was to be fought was a farce and simply invented to deceive the Muslims. Muslims could not accept Mr. Jinnah as the Quad-e-Azam of India or the League as their sole representative body, as Mr. Jinnah's life was totally un-Islamic."[25]

Mashraqi addressed a public meeting in Golbagh at Amritsar, on October 07, 1945. *The Tribune*, Lahore of October 09, 1945 reported that Mashraqi said: "He [Jinnah] was playing in the hands of the British Government...Continuing the Allama said that the Muslim League was composed of Nawabs, Khan Bahadurs, etc...They had their own personal interests to achieve and do nothing for the poor Muslims...

The only qualification Mr. Jinnah has is that he is an obstacle in the way of freedom of the country and is playing in the hands of the bureaucracy."

---

[22] *The Tribune*, February 27, 1942.
[23] *The Tribune*, May 03, 1942.
[24] Ibid.
[25] *The Tribune*, September 20, 1945.

According to the newspaper, the CID was present and took notes of Mashraqi's speech.

The Tribune, Lahore of October 18, 1945 reported that Chaudhri Nurul Hassan Sandilivi (Editor of *Paigham*) said: "I have been a silent Muslim Leaguer for a decade, but recent events have forced me to the conviction that the League at least in the U.P., with its leadership of Rajas, Nawabs and Knights is incapable of doing any good to the Muslim masses. In this province where they form only 15 per cent of the total population, the cry of Pakistan is unreal. The real question for Muslims here, however, should be what steps Government are taking for the amelioration of Muslim peasants, shopkeepers and workers."

On October 20, 1945, Qazi Ehsan Ahmed Shujabadi (an Ahrar leader) spoke at the Amritsar District Ahrar Conference. *The Tribune*, Lahore of October 22, 1945 reported that Shujabadi said: "The Muslim League had no programme in the past, none now, nor will it have any programme in the future. It is an organisation of Nawabs and knights, who are anxious to seize power without making any sacrifices...He [Shujabadi] referred to the cheap leadership thrust on Mr. Jinnah, who did not even observe the tenets of their faith...It was strange that Mr. Jinnah who himself defied the tenets of their faith and thereby disobeyed the holy Prophet was a leader. He said that Mr. Jinnah who himself was misled, was now misleading the Muslims...He asked Mr. Jinnah to come out in the open and make sacrifices if he wanted Pakistan. They would only be destroyed by their own misdeeds...He [Shujabadi] described how the Simla Conference failed, because Mr. Amery wanted that Mr. Jinnah should not be displeased."

On October 20, 1945, Maulana Abdus Salam Hamdani spoke at the Amritsar District Ahrar Conference and criticized the Muslim Ministry for the heavy death toll resulting from the Bengal famine. *The Tribune*, Lahore of October 22, 1945 further reported: "He [Hamdani] said that in view of the past misdeeds of such gangs, there was no guarantee that they would work for any improvement in the lot of the poor Muslims. He regretted that at the time Muslims were dying, the capitalist leaders were making money in the black-market. He asked as to where Mr. Jinnah was at that time...He advised the Muslims to learn to distinguish between right and wrong."

Maulana Mazhar Ali Azhar of the Ahrars made a statement: "All his life Mr. Jinnah has opposed the programme of courting imprisonment... But I ask Mr. Jinnah to enlighten me as to how he would reconcile his programme of courting bullets when according to the creed of the Muslim League he is bound to use constitutional means[26]...

But he has not made it clear when that time would come. During 70 years of his life the time has never come for Mr. Jinnah to go to jail... People like myself are eagerly awaiting the moment when the time would come for

---

[26] Jinnah is quoted under news titled, "Muslim League will not follow unconstitutional methods" (*The Tribune*, October 21, 1938.)

Mr. Jinnah to court a bullet... I remind the people... 'Judges and other Government Officers attended the meeting in large numbers.' If Mr. Jinnah relies on these Judges and these Government Officers then he must know that these are the people who showered bullets on the Muslims during even Islamic movements and ordered Muslims to be hanged by the neck until they were dead...

If you [Jinnah] do not like to go to jail I do not wish to draw you there... You are ready Mr. Jinnah to court bullets...

I fear, however, that your declaration to court bullets would prove similar to the one made by the late Sir Sikandar Hayat [Punjab Premier].[27]

Syed Ali Zaheer (Bar at Law) wrote: "Some statements have recently appeared in the press on the question of Pakistan by the President [Quaid-e-Azam] and the Secretary [Liaquat Ali Khan] of the All-India Muslim League. One wonders how long will the Mussalmans take to realise the futility of the propaganda of hatred and animosity against the Congress and the Hindus... How easily both these gentlemen assume things which have no existence in fact... Every nationalist Mussalman and practically every Congressman is agreed that Muslim religion, culture, rites and their autonomy in majority provinces must be guaranteed and is ready to negotiate on these terms. Why then confuse the issue...? Such statements of Mr. Jinnah only succeed because the average Indian is incapable of drawing a true picture of a free India... In a Federated State of India, it will be impossible for the Centre to interfere with the internal and economic problems of various units... After all the Muslims and Hindus have to live as neighbours... Is it wise to continue to harp on this song of animosity and bitterness..."

Referring to the idea of Pakistan, he said: "The entire conception is not only absurd but merely an attempt to deceive the common Mussalman, who is not fully aware of its implications." He stated if a genuine desire for settlement with Congress exists it could be achieved. "The coming generations will look upon them as tools in the hands of the British bureaucracy, and either consciously or unconsciously playing their game, and thwarting the aspirations of the Indian people... What will be their gain if Pakistan is achieved is difficult to say and none of the League leaders care to explain to the Mussalmans. If Pakistan is followed by the acceptance of the two-nation theory, then the Mussalmans in Hindu majority provinces will be in a far worse position than they are today. But the questions like this are conveniently ignored by the Nawabzada and all League leaders. The Mussalman is asked to vote blindly for the League, whatever may be the consequence for him in the minority provinces. Is this politics or sheer fraud? ...the poor Mussalmans are being exploited in the name of religion by a few well-placed and well-to-do leaders who desire to gain their object without any sacrifice or honest service for the community... A man can deceive some people for all time and all people for some time but not all the people for all the time... so long as this intransigent attitude is maintained by the League High Command, it will lead the country nowhere. It is only when an equitable just and fair attitude is

---

[27] *The Tribune*, October 31, 1945.

adopted towards other communities and political parties that the League can achieve something for the Mussalmans, as well as for the country as a whole."[28]

Dr. Khan Sahib [who after the creation of Pakistan became Chief Minister in Pakistan] said "I think it is an insult for an Indian to call Mr. Jinnah 'Qaid-e-Azam'"[29]

On January 27, 1946, the title "Promoters of Pakistan are Playboys of British Imperialism" appeared in the *The Free Press Journal* with Khan Abdul Ghaffar Khan's address. He said: "I warn those agents of the British Government who do not allow us to concentrate our attention on our only objective, freedom, but divert it towards Pakistan and other things...We want Hindustan, while the others try for Pakistan..."[30]

Under the title, "Shias Opposed to Pakistan," Syed Ali Zaheer (President Shia Political Conference) wrote: "Among other sections of Mussalamans, the Shias have been and are even now opposed to the Pakistan demand."[31]

On December 12, 1946, Sheikh Abdul Majid in his speech at the Inter-Cultural Association said: "The division of India meant division of Islam. The Muslims now claimed to be 10 crores, but if India was divided, Muslims of one part of India would be divided from the other part of India.

Mr. Majid added that leadership being in the hands of certain persons who pose to be great leaders, anything could happen..."[32]

On April 18, 1947, Dr. Syed Hussain, Chairman of the National Committee for India's Freedom, Washington "stated that 'India is an organic whole and a living body and it cannot be dissected in the insane manner which some hysterical propagandists are asking for.'

He added: 'The time has come for all sober elements of Indian population to assert themselves against the frenzy Fanatics and the machinations of selfish for short-sighted politicians.'

The foundations of Hindu-Muslim unity, said Dr. Syed Hussain, lay deep in time, history and culture. The present sectarian differences and dissensions, however acute, had nevertheless, been artificially generated...

---

[28] *The Tribune*, December 01, 1945.
[29] *The Tribune*, December 04, 1945.
[30] *The Free Press Journal*, January 28, 1946.
[31] *The Tribune*, March 22, 1946.
[32] *The Tribune*, December 13, 1946.

The very fact that Hindus and Muslims have lived together as friends and neighbours for the better part of a thousand years and have built up common traditions and an essentially common culture is a positive guarantee that under happier conditions of freedom and progress their association will not only endure but become closer and more fruitful."[33]

---

[33] *The Tribune,* April 19, 1947.

Appendix III

The following was written on December 20, 1942 and was published in *The Radiance* (Aligarh) on February 06, 1943:[1]

"With this tragic close of the drama of the Satanic hatred created by the leaders of the political parties in India between the Mussulmans and the Hindus in order to attain their purely selfish gains, the first chapter of the history of slavery of one-fifth of human race closes so miserably at such an opportune moment. We are too near the focus of events yet to judge the harm done, but the future historian will not characterise the happenings in India this year as anything but the doings of those who had lost all sanity and sense of proportion in their pigmy greatnesses, petty prides and puny prejudices. The above correspondence clearly shows, between the lines, the violence, the haughtiness, the spite and the lordly indifference to stern and real facts, of those whom God, the Good Lord, has not entrusted the physical power even of the captain of an army. Even Hitler would not have shown this bluff and bluster if he had come to know that there was an advantage for his National Socialist Germany in coming to terms with the Jews. Even Churchill, the arch-enemy of communist Russia, has climbed down to meet Stalin in his own capital, by the pressure of events, but these so calmly 'armyless generals' of India have only, like Nero, fiddled away their opportunity in a most heartless fashion, while Allama Mashriqi, the Khaksar leader, has been asking them, on bent knees and with folded hands, to unite for the sake of India. The only conclusion one can draw is that Dame Destiny has yet ruled that India shall be slave for ever!

The reactions in Government circles of Allama Mashriqi's efforts for Hindu-Muslim unity have been very marked and revengeful. The Khaksar Chief's telegram to Sir Stafford Cripps on the 23rd March was most bitterly commented on by the Government of India again and again, as an obstruction to war effort and there was a clear indication in the manner in which the Government of India explained as to why the ban on the Khaksar Organisation was not to be lifted within the promised time that the Allama's telegram had made a profound impression everywhere and was indeed a cause for the failure of the Cripps mission. The Allama was indicted in clear terms by Government for making negotiations with the Congress, which obstructed war effort, for

---

[1] "[?]" denotes an illegible word in the source.

publishing his telegrams inculcating political leaders to unite, for allowing political pamphlets on Hindu Muslim unity to be published by Khaksars all over India, *and last of all but not the least* the Government of India severely complained that in his telegram of July 21 to Mr. Gandhi, Allama Mashriqi did not advise him not to launch his mass civil disobedience movement, *but only urged that it should be postponed.*

...This sympathy with the ideal of the complete independence of India through Hindu-Muslim unity finally led the Government of India in a later communication to say that 'they have information to the effect that the Allama has been with the Congress.' At any rate these stricture character of the Allama Sahib clearly show that [the role] which the Khaksar Organisation played in the [purpose] of Hindu-Muslim unity during the year was [?] extremely dreaded by the Government, but that [?] certificate to the effect that Allama Mashriqi's [?] voice might effect such a unity. It is the great [tragedy] that even under such circumstances that voice [was not] heeded by the political leaders in the blind fury [of] selfish interests.

Finally, before the curtain is lifted for another [?] and the Indian political leaders make other [Historical] blunders in order to seal the destiny of India to [?] damnation and slavery, also before the general [?] Public come to realise after the turmoil of war [?] and Imperialism in its worst form again reigns [supreme in] the country, the point to note in the above [panoramic] events of this year is that the only way in which [India is to] gain its freedom at this critical juncture is that which [?] Mashriqi has suggested...and [the] only refuge at this moment for every Hindu, M[uslim], Sikh, Parsee and others is that they leave every [political] party of the Country for the moment and attend [to the] immediate need of the country of saving the civil [?]tion from destruction by joining the KHAKSAR MOVEMENT in MILLIONS.

As a last word to remember, there was [some]thing dreadfully and prophetically true in the [warning] of Allama Mashriqi last August that the mass [civil] disobedience movement of the Congress was the [?] ill-considered and suicidal movement..."

Dated Aligarh,
the 20th December, 1942

Syed Allah Bukhsh, M.A. Aligarh
Ahmed Dastagir, Journalist[2]

---

[2] *The Radiance*, February 06, 1943. Pp. 21-22.

Appendix IV

On November 05, 1943, Mashraqi issued the following statement:

"Two lakh fifteen thousand telegrams, letters, resolutions, petitions, memorials, etc., involving amiable contact of Khaksars with at least 70 lakh intelligent people, have been sent to Quaid-e-Azam Jinnah and His Excellency the Viceroy urging settlement with Mahatma Gandhi on the Pakistan question. I am satisfied with the enormous work done by the Khaksars during these six weeks, although at the very heavy cost levied from us by Government as well as Quaid-e-Azam that all know, and I can say with confidence that real amity between Hindus and Muslims has now begun to be established because of the realisation that the matter of Pakistan is as essentially fundamental as that of the freedom of India, that is not possible to attain one without the other and that, as in Egypt, the British Government will never fulfil the promise or grant even a shadow of independence unless Hindus and Muslims came to a joint agreement. In fact, our stand for the Mahatma at the time of his worst troubles after his regrettable efforts to crush Khaksars in 1940 and thereafter, has convinced the Indian public that ours is the most sincere and selfless mission for peace between the two communities and that the Khaksars have no personal grudges. The Khaksar now stands for Pakistan more zealously than Quaid-e-Azam or Muslim League because it is most criminal to let the great British promise of complete independence immediately after the war fritter away on account of this obstruction.

Twenty fifth July was the last day of sending messages and I was expected to take the next step on the 26th [July 26, 1943]. On that day some rascal from the blue attempted to spoil the game, drive his zeal for Pakistan against the brusqueness which is Quaid-e-Azam's habit with almost everybody, fought the issue of achieving separate kingdom for the Musalmans amidst pushes, kicks, insults and angry words, and finally, when outnumbered, over powered and at bay made the most shameless attempt to get at the throat of that veteran leader whose yes or no spoken in a bolder mood can yet change the destinies of India. The Quaid-e-Azam, immediately after the event and as if in a fit of revenge against me, announced it as a 'serious and well-planned attack', had it announced that the assaulter was a Khaksar from Lahore, had been sent there, had been loitering round his house, had been following him in the railway train and so forth... I possess patience enough not to have commented upon these allegations as I never met or even knew about the assailant and it is well-known now that he never set his foot in Lahore during the last two years, that he is more a Muslim League office-bearer than a Khaksar, that after arrest he gave an undertaking not to be a Khaksar again. But the most unanswerable suggestion given to me by a person in close touch is that the Quaid-e-Azam could not have possibly meant the words 'well-planned attack' as referring to the Khaksar organisation as only an hour after the event he met a deputation of Bombay Khaksars who had come to express their sympathies and he never suspected them. I have my own reasons to say that having occurred on the 19th [March 1940] and the 26th July [1943] both were 'well-planned attacks' on the Khaksar organisation, the one from the side of the Government and the other from the side of Mr. Jinnah.

As regards the assailant being a Khaksar, it is unthinkable that Khaksars who spared Sir Sikandar Hayat Khan for three years after his massacre of them and were the only organisation who attended his funeral after his death, could conspire to attack Quaid-e-Azam for whom they have the greatest reverence and respect.

Hostility between the Khaksars and the Muslim League is indeed impossible under any circumstances, as Khaksars have not been organized to oppose any political or non-political party in the land. They are, in fact, to serve all and serve for the good of the country. I also declare here that I am no rival to Quaid e-Azam and will not think of taking his place, but I have the right to ask him to hurry up. I am fully aware of the discontent against him in the inner circles and the grave differences that are slowly appearing but the Muslim League cannot have a better leader at this moment.

As a next step towards the achievement of Pakistan, I respectfully suggest to Quaid-e-Azam that even in case the British Government is formally disinclined to let him meet Mahatma Gandhi, the question of Hindu-Muslim settlement cannot be much postponed owing to the fact that the British victory in war is now measurably within sight. I request him that as he has roused extraordinary enthusiasm in Musalmans of India on account of his slogan of Pakistan he should write formally to the Viceroy to allow him to see Mahatma Gandhi for the purpose of settlement and in case the Viceroy refuses, ask in the next letter the name or names of those Congress or Hindu gentlemen in India, who in the eyes of the British Government are best fitted to make that Hindu-Muslim settlement which the British government thinks as essential to the grant of complete independence to India immediately after the war. I, with the due respects, suggest to him that this is the most essential next step and that Pakistan can only come if he is up and doing. Quaid-e-Azam must be aware that nearly two crores of Musalmans also Hindus here and abroad are now helping in this war in some capacity or other and their joint effort alone has turned the tables in Europe and brought British victory near at hand."[1]

[1] Hussain, Pp. 192-194.

Appendix V

Mashraqi's Address:

Where Leaders Fail
A Dispassionate Dissection of Indian
Politics from a Non-Party Point of View

Delivered at the University Institute Hall, Calcutta on 21st October, 1945, with a discussion on the AGREED CONSTITUTION OF FREE INDIA prepared under the auspices of the Khaksar Organisation with the agreement of over three hundred million people of India.

Published under the authority of Idara-i-Aliyyah
by N.M. Anwell
66, Coolootola Street, Calcutta

Printed at the Calcutta Phototype Company
6, Chowringhee Road, Cal.

"Hindus, Muslims and other Brethren of Calcutta and Bengal! At this moment the failure of Leaders' Conference at Simla, after the unsuccessful talks of the two political leaders Messrs. Jinnah and Gandhi in the September of last year, has cast a fresh gloom and created a spirit of deep frustration and bitterness from one corner of India to the other, and everyday the political Hindu is angry with the political Mussulman and the political Mussulman angry with the political Hindu that the question of freedom of India is being spoiled by the opposing party. The British Government had put down the one and solitary condition of freedom of India to the effect that Indians should 'frame a Constitution agreed by the main elements of India's national life' and had explained that 'the object of putting forward this condition was to ensure the fulfillment of the duty of the British Government to safeguard the interest of the racial minorities, i.e., (the Anglo-Indians, Europeans, etc.), the religious minorities (i.e., the Mussulmans, the Christians, the Sikhs, the Parsees, the Jains, the Budhs, etc., etc.) the Depressed classes minorities, and lastly the Treaty obligation of the Indian States.' Under this circumstances the first and foremost duty of the leaders of the two great communities was to fulfil this condition, but the politics of this unfortunate country in the eyes of political parties in the country is that the personal prejudices and pet politics of the political parties are a thousand times more important than the question of Freedom of India. Now let me know, Gentlemen, is it possible for a country to touch even the fringe of freedom whose supposed political leaders prefer going on fighting in slavery with one another to attaining freedom by coming to terms? Is it possible that a country should attain freedom when the leaders are overwhelmed with fear to the effect that before attaining freedom it is more essential to get our share distributed in the presence of those who are going to give us the gift of Freedom? Is it possible that a country should attain freedom under leaders who think that in case the shares are not distributed now and here, they did not know what would happen after the Britishers had departed? Is it possible to attain freedom under the leadership of men of such low ideas and childish character who after having shown complete distrust of each other in the presence of freedom-Givers, actually prove to the world that in order to keep peace among these people the presence of the Britisher is absolutely necessary, nay actually prove that these two people would remain at drawn daggers with each other in case the British departed? Does not, after this childish move, the first question arise that in case your first fear is that the other brother may not give you your share afterwards where is the guarantee that the divided share may not be snatched by the aggressive brothers? Does not this ridiculous and childish move of your political leaders produce the natural impression on the mind of the world that you would be ready to re-invite the British people from London in case the aggressive brother snatched away your share afterwards and you will say to the Britisher; 'please Father! Do not go away from here, because every time you go away the stronger brother mischievously takes away my share and I am left with nothing except your good will and sympathy; so the best thing for you, please, is to stay on here forever!'

Friends! Think what a shameful picture of your dirty politics you are presenting to the world at large. After an incessant and indefatigable effort of two and a half years, the Khaksars were able to compel Messrs. Gandhi and Jinnah to meet each other and come to terms. After a ridiculous talk lasting for twenty five days these two 'bankrupts of wisdom', in their words, did not come to any terms whatever, and the impression they created on the rest of the world was that not only these two men but the two great nations of India, i.e., the Hindus and the Mussulmans were so low and mean that they fought with each other, that their differences were so deep-seated and fundamental that they could not be rooted out even after a talk lasting for 25 days together, that hundreds of kinds of differences must have existed in these 25 days, that as agreement on not even a single point had been announced the differences must have been something impossible of solution, and that as no result was arrived at the problems must have been something impossible to death with. The impression has been that the Britishers who have held India for the last one century and a half were very much right in saying that the two peoples of India, viz., the Hindus and the Muslims were permanently antagonistic to each other, that they were perfectly right in claiming that in case they left, India would become a slaughter-house, perfectly right in telling us that India was yet unfit for freedom, perfectly right in claiming that they were very generous and so on. Friends! Think what golden opinions the British people won from the world during this worthless talk lasting for twenty-five days, what good the British people achieved and what tremendous loss of prestige was the lot of India. The Britisher no doubt held India on the point of sword, but think that even the most tyrannical and aggressive Government in the world could not hold power for a long time without the good opinion of the world at this moment. Think what satisfaction the British people would have felt after these Bombay conversations and they would have become indeed gratified to know that the world acknowledged them to be just, good and generous rulers and that their hold over India was indeed fully justified.

Gentlemen! After the Bombay talks of September of last year the British people made another very deep move in calling the Simla Conference. Lord Wavell's trip to London in the mist of the war had drawn the plebiscite of the world to the impression that the Britishers meant to give freedom to India even before the War terminated. A Conference was called immediately after his return and there was no indication whatever that the Britisher did not mean to give freedom to India. In fact the declaration of giving parity to the Caste Hindus and the Muslim gave the direct indication to all that whether the Hindus and the Muslims were pleased over it or not at any rate the British people had a heartfelt desire to get over the Hindu-Muslim tangle, and that they sincerely wanted to get away from here. It is possible that the Hindus may not have been fully satisfied at this parity, but there was clearly no general dissatisfaction among them, also the Muslims were distinctly pleased that the demand concerning which they had been waiting so long had at last been accepted. Not only this, but the Leaguers with great pomp and show, considering this parity to be the latest and the most exclusive achievement of their Qaid-i-Azam, cried hoarse with joy at the announcement. At last this Simla Conference also finished after a few days' show, and the world outside got convinced once more than there was no possibility of peace between the unfortunate Hindu and the Muslim. The world was convinced once more without a shadow of doubt that the Britisher not only intended to give freedom to India but had actually been anxious about it.

Gentlemen! You naturally ask: Where did the trouble lie after this grant of parity to Hindus and Muslims as equal brothers in the distribution of shares? In fact, you say, the Mussulmans should have gone farther and said that this equal distribution among brothers was right even from the point of Islamic religious law. Yes! It may have been right from your domestic or religious point of view, but I tell you that in the dirty mud slinging that is going on in

India during the last quarter of a century it is *not* right, in fact, it is criminal that these two political parties out of which one is claiming that it is the 'sole representative' of 400 million people and the other that it is the 'sole representative' of 100 million people, yes, it is *not* right that they should ever come to terms at any cost. I affirm that for these two parties to bring India to the threshold of Freedom is to make them sign their own death-warrant. Friends! Do you remember how it was that these two parties came to be called, rather self-styled, as the 'sole representatives' of us four hundred million Indians. They styled themselves as our political representatives, because they claimed that they had come forward in the field in order to secure Freedom for us. They cried from the house-tops that they had no other purpose in view in order to exist. Could you ever imagine that these few hundreds or few thousands who now actually constitute the Muslim League or the Congress, could possibly have been accepted as the representatives of 400 or 100 millions of people of India if they had not made this very tall claim? Could they ever have secured our sympathies without this boast? No Hindu in India would ever have paid a little of attention to Congress if Congress had not claimed that. None would have known the name of Congress if it had not cried hoarse that the only reason of its existence was the Freedom of India. The Congress remained in the corner of utter oblivion for full forty five years and no Indian ever knew about its existence until it put forward that its sole aim was the Free India from the clutches of the British people. The Muslim League was unknown altogether until it came out with its slogan of Pakistan. It was till then a clique of unknown individuals hunting for individual favours from their masters. It holds no considerable power among the Mussulmans even now with this empty slogan but tell me that if the Muslim League had not put forward Freedom as the reason of its existence could it possibly have secured any recognition among the Mussulmans? Could Congress have obtained any recognition among the Hindus if it had remained a mere debating society? Now if these parties with these credentials of their existence as the sole representatives of 400 dumb and voiceless millions, secure freedom for India after coming to terms with each other, are they not signing their own death-warrants? Will not India, after securing freedom, put the first question to them- 'Well, Gentlemen of the Congress and Noblemen of the League, we agree that Freedom has been secured after all and we are probably thankful to you for this trouble. But as you told us that you existed as our sole representatives because you claimed to secure Freedom for us, and freedom has come, we people of India would like you to disperse and cease to exist. The necessity of you existence is over and the people of India shall themselves take up the trouble of ruling India now.' Gentlemen and Ladies, that is the reason why the existence of these political parties in the country is a veritable obstacle in the path of Freedom. As long as these parties do not make peace with each other they will remain but the moment they come to terms they commit suicide or rather hari-kari for themselves. That is exactly the reason why even after the parity between the Caste Hindu and the Muslim the Muslim League has set up a new quarrel altogether that the Mussulman will still remain unsafe because there is the possibility of all the remaining elements joining against him, thus wiping out his existence from the face of India. So this well-wisher Qaid-i-Azam of the Muslims is trying his level best to save his people further. On the other hand, in spite of the fact that there are no more Muslims in the Congress that can be counted on fingers, the Congress has set up a new quarrel in order to prolong its existence to the effect that the Congress must have its due share of the Muslims from among the share of the Muslim League. In other words these two organisations with shameless audacity are claiming a share strictly for themselves alone deceiving the people of India to the belief that the Britishers have not given parity to the Caste Hindus and Muslims in the capacity of their being two great communities of India, but that the parity has as a matter of fact been given to these two political parties alone, and that their representatives alone would count. Could you, gentlemen, ever think of a more audacious falsehood or greater deceit to the people of India? Could possibly any one think how vilely these two parties, who do not actually represent even a thousandth or a hundred thousandth part of the population of India, are silently claiming that only the Congressite or the Leaguer is the true representative of the Caste Hindu or the Muslim, silently managing that these two parties alone shall exist even after the attainment of freedom and that the whole population of four hundred millions for which freedom has really been obtained must go to the dogs! Are not these two organisations by setting up these new quarrels silently managing among themselves, like two dacoits that, in the first place, we shall see that no freedom ever comes, and even if it ever comes we alone shall be the equal partners in the loot. Is not there a clear conspiracy of the most vile and vicious kind between these two arch-conspirators of the destiny of India?

Brothers! In the March of 1942 after Japan had reached almost the borders of India and Singapur had fallen, the British people sent one of their ministers, Sir Stafford Cripps, with the stipulation that if we Indians helped the British in the War the British would give India full freedom provided the Indians among themselves 'framed a Constitution agreed by the main elements of India's national life.' It was never said in this promise, nor, in fact, in any previous or subsequent utterances of the British Government that the agreement was to be between the Congress and the League, or between Messrs. Gandhi and Jinnah, or between any political parties. As a matter of fact the agreement of the various elements of the national life of India was repeatedly emphasised. In the above announcement the *object* of this condition was mentioned to be 'to ensure the fulfillment of the duty of the British Government to safeguard the interests of the four groups of Communities comprising the national life of India,' and not any groups of political parties, and these four groups were (1) the racial minorities of India, (2) the religious minorities of India, (3) the Depressed Classes, (4) the treaty obligations of the British Government to the Indian States. The announcements, as a matter of fact, most clearly stated that the British people wanted the safeguarding of interests of all these communities before they departed from India, and wanted to ensure than no community, major or minor, was molested. The Britishers refused to recognize in these announcements the existence of any political parties which they knew had sprung up of themselves and without any popular sanction except in the sense that they managed to send, by hook or by crook, their representatives in the assemblies to a certain extent. It is most extraordinary that these organisations now claim the representation of total populations of the country with an audaciousness unsurpassed anywhere, and instead of securing the freedom of India for which they originally stood, they seem to obstruct its way by screaming at every possible prospect of agreement that in case such and such a demand were not accepted by the opposing party the Mussulmans will get destroyed, the Hindus will get crushed, the whole of India will get atombombed and so forth. Nay, the matter has gone so much forward and selfishness of parties has advanced so mischievously that the Muslim League now claims that that very person represents the Muslim Community who is a member of Muslim League, rather a member of Muslim League holding the pleasure of Mr. Jinnah. Any person who does not belong to the Muslim League or belongs to another Muslim political or other party cannot claim to represent in any sense the Muslims. On the other hand although Mussulmans in the Congress can be counted almost on fingers, and whatever number there is in the Congress, it is either paid or is there for its individual benefit, the Congress is putting forward the most brazen-faced claim that the person appointed by the Congress is the only person that can claim the representation of the Mussulmans. This I submit is a chicanery of the first magnitude and to disacknowledge that for all time is the first duty of the people of India. The manifest object underlying this fraud is to train the people of India most cleverly to the belief that the political parties alone represented the *communities* and that it is essential for the representation of communities that political parties should remain even after freedom is achieved. The net result of this amazing move will necessarily be that India will always remain a theatre of incessant warfare and endless dissensions throughout ages, the parties will rule and represent India and each party will try to crush other party and the unfortunate people of India will be fooled by these parties without a moment's respite into throwing down ministries overnight and these devilish ministers will earn their illegal wealth, commit rapes on their own communities, and create a tyranny in India unparalleled in the whole history of the world. In the course of our framing the future Constitution I discovered the most remarkable fact that 180 millions of Backward Class Hindus were groaning under the tyranny of the Congress, groaning that the Congress was at best a *Brahmin Raj* and that this terrible Raj had almost crushed ever portion of their community, that the Raj had not safeguarded even remotely the interest of any community of Hindus it posed to represent. This very Congress out of sheer fraud and faithlessness to their own kith and kin now claims that only that person who is a member of the Congress or rather that person who is in the *good books of Mahatma Gandhi* or the Brahmin Clique it represents, can represent the 200 millions of Hindus in British India. No other person can claim this representation in accordance with the announcements of the British Governments. In short the whole population of 400 millions of unfortunate India is groaning under the unparalleled tyranny of these political parties of the country and every sensible person is amazed at the fraud that is being openly perpetrated in broad daylight everywhere.

Brethren! For the last twentyfive years these political monsters in the country have been rending India to pieces in every possible manner putting one small section against the other, till we Khaksars after getting convinced that any approachment between them was not only not possible but that it was not possible to make Messrs. Jinnah and Gandhi come to terms for another twentyfive years, began to draft a Constitution exactly in accordance with the requirements of the British Government. We addressed almost every important element of India's national life requesting it to send its declaration of interests so that in case the interests did not clash with those of other parties in the country they might be incorporated in the body of the Constitution 'as far as possible, feasible and consistent with the interests of other parties.' We addressed more or less 75 parties and over three hundred million people in the country accepted our invitation through their accredited leaders. During the course of these communications we came to the startling fact that the claim of the political parties to represent these voiceless millions was a grand humbug. We found it repeated times without number that the Muslim League was a body composed of Khan Bahadurs, titled individuals, posthunters, pensioned Government servants, irreligious and even immoral persons who had formed themselves into a clique with the object of representing Mussulmans of India, in spite of fact, that these worthless individuals had not the slightest affinity with Islam or with any section of Mussulmans constituting the Muslim Community of India. We found that 99 millions out of 100 millions of Mussulmans did not show any connection with Muslim League in any sense, nor was the Muslim League connected with them by fraternal connection, postal communication or otherwise. The Parties openly asserted that they had not received the slightest benefit from the League in any direction ever since its inception, that the office-holders of the League had not been elected by them on any occasion, and that they had been crushed under the tyranny of those who snatched their votes from them under force by telling them beautiful tales of what they would do in case their member got elected. The Congress about which it is notorious that it poses as the most democratic, most constitutional and most systematic organisation in the country, and which most frequently claims at least on paper that such and such a thing could not be altered, amended or abrogated without the regular and official consent of such and such committee, it was disclosed in heartrending voice by Hindu associations in the country that the Congress representation of Hindus was a mere fraud, that the Congress was a terrible slaughter-house of Hindus belonging to castes lower than the Brahmins or high caste Khattris and that Hindus belonging to the working classes were very badly treated by it. These people told us in so many clear words that 'under the garb of the most fraudulent spider's web termed 'democracy' and 'Government by people of the Congress' this most prominent organisation of the country was perpetrating such unparalleled fraud on the destinies of the backward classes of the Touchable Hindus of India coming under the classification of High

Caste Hindus, that in case measures were not taken to stop this tyranny the Touchable poor Hindus even would be compelled to separate themselves from the Upper Class Hindus, just as the Untouchable Scheduled Castes had already separated themselves from them', and in case powers is entrusted to these tyrants in future 'all people in India with the exception of Brahmins will live the life of Gonda and Bhils of Central India within the space of a few decades.' In short, ever since the British people have striven their utmost to efface from the memory of the people of India the beauties of the *Ram Raj*, the *Dharam Raj* and the *Parja Raj* of the olden times and have tired to substitute instead the beauties of 'democracy' and 'Constitutional Government' in their minds, these clever political parties in the country have become cliques, of deceit, fraud, hypocrisy and tyranny under the garb of democracy and constitutional progress, and have devised hundred and one tricks in order to play the part of Ali Baba and Forty Thieves in ever phase of political life of India to the extent that if power is handed now to these parties the population of 400 million people in the country will not have been left with an ounce of flesh on their bones, a shred of cloth on their bodies or a drop of blood in their veins. Friends! This is an aspect of the present situation which one shudders to see and I can assure you that there is not the slightest exaggeration in the picture that I have presented to you.

Brethren! It is with this end in view that we have come in the open field in order to stand for the rights of the poor, the oppressed and the suppressed people of India and send only those people to the Assemblies who most nearly represent the common people and the poor people. We frankly want to do away with the *Brahmin Raj* and the *Khan Bahadur Raj*, and we want to substitute instead the real *Parja Raj* of olden times in which everybody lived in peace and plenty and when India was a land of Milk and Honey. Democracy in our estimation is decidedly not the rule of certain selected individuals belonging to certain mysterious circles of the Communities, rather, it is the equally distributed rule of every section of every community and every people. We have come to the most emphatic believe that no political party in the country can represent in any manner all sections of a community and that the very existence of political parties after the attainment of freedom is a standing menace to India that these political parties will wage endless warfare in the country and will be the cause of endless bloodshed for all time. There shall be no peace at any time if this is allowed to happen and the chief engagement of these parties will be to overthrow ministries of the opposing denominations by rousing the prejudices of one community against the other and make this India and this motherland of ours a most veritable Hell on Earth. We want most particularly to stand in the way of these unrepresentative bodies in these coming elections as the future Constitution of Free India is going to be framed by the next assemblies and in case this Constitution is framed by these undemocratic and unconstitutional bodies, and in case that Constitution is not the voice of the people of India, it is going to prove a veritable Hell for all time to come. We have come to the definite conclusion that the ideology of every political party in the country is most strictly communal and although every party puts forward beautiful political ideals before the country the real interest of every political party is to crush not only the opposing political *party* but the opposing *community* to which that political party belongs. On this basis we believe it almost criminal to hand over the reins of Government to any single political party for any time.

Brothers! It was with this view that we prepared an agreed Constitution which is now in your hands. Our programme as to get this Constitution agreed by as many members of Assemblies as possible irrespective of caste or creed or any political organisation. Let all leaders and organisations fight amongst each other as much as they please but let us present a united front before the British Government as far as this agreed Constitution is concerned. Let everybody belonging to any political party owe allegiance to his party throughout the life of the future Assemblies in matters concerning their particular matters and aims but in the matters of presenting this Constitution before the British Government let all people in Assemblies speak with one voice or at any rate with a predominant voice, so that the British people who jeeringly said to us that for India to present an agreed Constitution to the British Government, not only extraordinary brains are required but that it was an altogether 'impossible feat'. That 'impossible feat' I am glad to tell you is an accomplished fact now and I am going to give you its details as far as possible in the short space of time at my disposal."[1]

---

[1] Mashriqi 1945. Pp. 1-13.

Appendix VI

Outline of the Agreed Khaksar Constitution

"The foundations of the Constitution were laid on the following utterance of Lord Wavell in his letter to Mahatma Gandhi of August 15, 1944, which contained for the first time in the history of British utterances the words '*unqualified freedom* after the cessation of hostilities' and other unequivocal conditions regarding the attainment of freedom, and attention to which was drawn by Lord Wavell in his letter to Allama Mashriqi:—

'His Majesty's Government at that time (meaning Cripps' Offer), made it clear (a) that their offer of *unqualified freedom* after the cessation of hostilities was made conditional upon the framing of a Constitution *agreed by the main elements of India's national life*, and the negotiation of necessary Treaty arrangements with His Majesty's Government, (b) (This relates to no change during the war and therefore does not concern us now.)

'The *object* of these conditions was to *ensure* the *fulfilment* of their *duty* to *safeguard* the *interests* of the *racial* and *religious* minorities and of the *Depressed classes* and their *treaty obligations* to the Indian States.'

In this utterance in which italics are ours: —

(a) there is no question of the Constitution being agreed by any political party or political leaders but by the main *elements* of the national life of India, i.e., by all the principal communities, sections, subsections, constituting the population of 400 millions.

(b) if Constitution becomes agreed and a Treaty is negotiated, unqualified freedom will follow. These are the two conditions of freedom.

(c) Constitution can only become *agreed* if all *elements* agree to it, therefore Lord Wavell says that the *object of these conditions* is to *ensure* that the *interests* of four groups of communities viz., (1) racial minorities, i.e., Anglo-

Indians, Europeans, etc., (2) religious minorities, i.e., Muslims, Indian Christians, Sikhs, Jains, Parsees, Budhs, Jews, etc., (3) Depressed classes, and (4) Indian States, with which the British Government is treaty-bound, are safeguarded in the Constitution. *The British call this their duty which they have to fulfil before they leave India.*

(d) if interests of these four groups are safeguarded, the only *remaining elements* are the various sections of the *Hindu community*, who have got to agree to these interests and *at the same time safeguard their own interests*, and then the Constitution because 'agreed' in the above sense.

(e) the word '*interests*' is put, *not* the words 'claims' or 'rights' or 'shares' or any other thing; the word is most cautiously put in order to minimise extravagant claims of parties and to secure that *minimum* for every party in the land which renders it safe from the aggression of other parties.

Exactly in accordance with the above scheme suggested by Lord Wavell, also by all previous British utterances on the freedom of India, all the four above groups constituting, over 75 parties, various sections of the Hindu community, and many other considerable or voiceless or important organisations in the country, in all about 125 in number, were addressed by Allama Mashriqi, and he told them that they were to send their 'declarations of interests' on the condition that their interests would be incorporated in the body of the Constitution 'as far as possible, feasible and consistent with the interests of other minorities, sub-minorities, sections and subsections concerned.'

Over and above this, vast amount of literature issued by the various political parties, voluminous reports of Khaksars all over India concerning grievances of poor, afflicted, suppressed and depressed sections of the people of India, large number of books by European and other authors on India, books on the Constitutions of almost every notable country in the world,—comprising about 50,000 pages of reading matter,—were utilized in preparing this Constitution and almost every demand or claim of the Indian National Congress, the All-India Muslim League, the Hindu Mahasabha, and other well-known political organisations of all the communities was accommodated in the Constitution to the satisfaction of all parties concerned. Over sixty well-known men of unassailable reputation, political leaders, professors of universities, high court judges, barristers, advocates, journalists, Europeans, Muslims, Hindus, Christians, in fact, most outstanding non-party men available in the country have contributed to make this Constitution the most unique ever devised by any human agency. The most prominent features of the Constitution are very briefly as follows: —

1. The keynote of the Constitution is simplicity of administration, its *efficiency and complete absence of Hindu Muslim tension* in any quarter. For this purpose *one* President at the Centre, whether Muslim or Hindu, and *one* Governor in the provinces, whether Hindu or Muslim, for three years, with *no*

Prime Ministers, vice-premiers, vice-presidents, etc., of opposite denominations to make government a tug-of-war between political parties, has been made the rule. The President of India and the Governors shall be men above all parties and shall be chosen from the Indian Civil Service (as the Governors are chosen now by the British) after a thorough experience of the whole machinery of Government extending over 25 to 35 years. For three years the Hindu President shall rule India, to be followed by the Muslim President for three years. The out-going Hindu President shall choose a panel of five Muslim names from among Provincial Governors or Ex-Governors fit in his estimation for the post of President, and shall put this panel before a grand assemblage of the Central and all Provincial Assemblies and the Muslim who secures the highest number of votes in this grand assemblage shall be the next President for three years, and *vice versa*. For the Hindu Provinces of Bombay, Madras, U.P., Bihar, C.P., and Orissa there shall always be Hindu Governors and for the remaining five provinces always Muslim Governors, thus giving full 'Pakistan'. As the choice of Muslim President rests of the Hindu President and *vice versa* from among the provincial Governors, no Hindu or Muslim Governor shall ever deal with Muslim or Hindu minorities unjustly.

The President as well as the Governors shall choose their cabinets of 15 minister from among the parties in the assemblies in fixed proportions of the communities, and being the *elected* non-party heads of vast experience who have served India throughout their lives, shall possess wide veto-powers over their cabinets and assemblies, in order to see that no party crushes the other party or community. Thus they will possess kingly qualities along with their being fully elected rulers. In the Centre Hindus and Muslims shall get 40 per cent seats each Scheduled Castes 10 per cent, Christians 3 per cent, Sikhs 4 per cent, Jains 1 per cent, Parsees 1 per cent, Buddhists 1 per cent, in the Provinces the *same* percentages of seats as now given in the Government of India Act with the *non-communal* seats *equally* divided among the Hindus and the Muslims. Thus the condition of Hindu and Muslim minorities in the Provinces will greatly improve by this device.

There is virtually *joint electorate* at the top of the Administration as the Hindu President is chosen by the Muslim President and *vice versa*. In the Assemblies there shall be separate electorates as before, because very few parties in the country agree to joint electorates. In order to remove the oppression of the rich over the poor there shall be three classes of constituencies, class I for the very poor class of a community, class II for the middle class and class III for the very rich class, and no voter from any class shall be elected by the vote of the inferior class. Franchise shall be on the basis of qualified adult suffrage. Village Panchayet System shall be introduced everywhere. Distinction between martial and non-martial races will be abolished. Compulsory military training for three years for all and compulsory military service in the time of dire necessity for all. Every Province in India shall have the right to secede from the Central Government and form a *totally independent unit*, thus providing *full* '*Pakistan*' for all time. Treaties with States shall be transferred intact to the Central Government, but they will be annulled as soon as a State becomes as fully democratic as a Province, and then new treaties will become bi-lateral. The merger scheme shall *not* be enforced, but small States can join the Province adjacent to them as 'districts' of that Province permanently ruled by the hereditary rulers. The administration of all States shall be through a Council of Princes of 15 members almost exactly on the line of the Council of Ministers of the President of India.

Currency shall be measured by the WHEAT standard, a Rupee being *always* that coin which buys *at least* sixteen seers of wheat everywhere in India for all time and all economies of the State shall be adjusted so as to solve the problem of HUNGER in India. Within 15 years from the attainment of freedom, a rupee shall buy thirtytwo seers of wheat everywhere. The external value of the rupee shall be three times this value in case of manufactured export and four times this value in case of raw exports, so that no foreign country may exploit the labour and raw materials of the country unduly.

Besides all the usual Fundamental Rights we have in this Constitution: every destitute mother to get Rs. 2 per month for her infant for 2 years, every destitute family of dead breadwinner to get Rs. 2 per month per person, every destitute above seventy to get pension up to Rs. 5 per month, every unprotected child to be maintained by State by grant up to Rs. 10 per month; adequate measures for the protection of cows, improvement of general health by the establishment of Unani and Vedic systems, measures for extermination of tuberculosis, malaria, leprosy; no person to be detained without trial, none to be kept under police vigilance without his knowledge, imprisonment of under-trial person to be counted in his punishment, prohibition of corporal punishment, abolition of capital punishment, freedom for use of *jhatka* for Sikhs, Muslim's right to call *Azan* everywhere, and for cow-slaughter in private places, the prohibition of *Bande Matram* song in mixed public gatherings, option for a boy to attend adverse religious instruction lectures in denominational schools and hospitals; abolition of all forced labour and *begar*, for a labourer decent living wage, healthy conditions of work, limited hours of labour, sickness and casual leave, indemnities for diseases incident to professions, sanitary quarters and facilities for education of children, also suitable machinery for settlement of disputes with employees; adequate measures for protection of women-workers; prohibition of child-labour; for the small peasant no land-revenue establishment of equality between the urban and the rural tax-payer, abolition of incapacities to buy land, effective revival of small industries in villages, special pensions for children of soldiers who have fought in the recent world wars and measures to help their re-settlement; special measures to make justice prompt, cheap and *in situ*, curtailment of litigation among peasants, and general separation of the judiciary from the executive; full freedom of the Press; full recognition of Religious Heads of communities; adequate measures for the protection of Services; adequate measures for reduction of agricultural indebtedness; among the Caste Hindus the High Caste Hindus to get 25 per cent share, backward Hindus to get 10 per cent share, and Dravidians to get 5 per cent share out of the 40 per cent fixed for them; among the Muslims the well-to-do Sunnis to get 25 per cent the well-to-do Shiahs 5 per cent, and the Backward Muslims (including Momins) to get 10 per cent out of their 40 per cent share; the protection of personal law of the Hindus; the protection of personal law of the Muslims, the institution of *Shariat* courts, the management of *waqfs*, the passing of *Zakat* Acts everywhere and the proper management of incomes from *waqf* properties and *zakat*; for Backward classes of all communities adequate shares in State services, free education to their children up to 12 years, protection of handloom industry, free use of vacant land in village *abadis* and of *shamilat-i-deh* and *patti* lands for their cattle; for Scheduled Castes over and above all these rights protection from disgrace due to exhibition of untouchability, provision of drinking water well in every village, free education to children up to 12 years; for Indian Christians and Anglo-Indians all privileges given to others in the same position, protection of English language, family law and personal status, protection of appointments in public services and of educational and other grants, due facilities for acquisition of land; for the Sikhs the protection of Punjabi language in Gurmukhi script, adequate facilities and concessions for grants-in-aid, education and franchise, protection of Sikh officials from humiliation by superior officers, special provisions for *Mazhabi*, *Ramdasia* and *Ramgarhia* Sikhs, etc., etc.; adequate provision for Jains, Parsees, Buddhists, Jews and Tribes.

If it is possible to condense a Constitution covering 150 pages of close print in this short space then it is done here. It is now the business of every well-wisher of India to stand for such a Constitution in which the interests of every conceivable community of India are preserved."[1]

---

[1] Mashriqi 1945. Pp. 14-20.

Other Features of the Constitution

Some facts about *The Constitution of Free India:* [2]

Report of the First Legal Committee, As Amended and Endorsed By The Second Legal Committee, With Part II and a Portion of Part III of *The Constitution of Free India 1946 A.C.*

As agreed by Main Elements of India's National Life and Framed Under the Authority of the Idara- I-Aliyyah, Ichhra, Lahore.

- ❖ First English Edition: Printed October, 1945
- ❖ First Hindustani Original Edition: Printed November,1945
- ❖ Reprints English Edition: November, December 1945 & January, 1946
- ❖ Reprints Hindustani Original Edition: December, 1945
- ❖ Total number of copies: 50,000
- ❖ Number of pages: 140

*****

This constitution protected the rights of everyone such as Muslims, Hindus, Scheduled Castes, Sikhs, Jains, Parsees, Budhists, Jews and Christians (including Europeans and Anglo-Indians). The quality of the constitution can be observed from the Khaksar Constitution committee's comments:

"The care with which adjustments, adaptions and elaborations were made in the body of the Constitution was commendable, and this reflected to a great extent the ability of those who were engaged in drafting the work."[3]

Note: After partition, the Khaksar Constitution, with some modification, was implemented by Nehru in India.[4]

---

[2] *The Constitution of Free India 1946 A.C.*
[3] *The Constitution of Free India 1946 A.C.*, P. 48.
[4] Mashriqi, Allama. [1931] 1997. Pp. 23-24.

Members

Members of First Legal Committee[5]

Dr. George A. Arundale
President, First Legal Committee
(M.A. LL.B., D. Litt., F.R. Hist. S., President Theosophical Society, International Headquarters, Madras)

Members:

Barrister K.L. Gauba (M.L.A. (Member Legislative Assembly), Bar-at-Law, Author of *Uncle Sham* etc., Lahore) *Vice President*

A.K. Fazl-ul-Haq (M.A., B.L., ex-Chief Minister, Bengal)

Professor Humayun Kabir (M.A., Professor, Calcutta University, General Secretary, Krishak Proja Party, Bengal)

Bulusu Sambamurty (B.A., LL.B., Speaker, Madras Legislative Assembly)

Rafiq Ahmed Khan (M.A., Ph.D., D. SC., Head of the Department of Biology, Muslim University, Aligarh)

Lt.-Col. Dr. Sir Zia ud Din Ahmed (Kt, C.I.E.., M.A., D.SC., Ph.D., Vice Chancellor, Muslim University, Aligarh)

A.H. Siddiqui (M.A., Ph.D., Principal, Sind Madrissah, Karachi)

Obaidullah Durrani (M.A., D.SC., Ph.D., M.I.E.E., Principal, Engineering College, Muslim University, Aligarh)

Lady Members:

Syeda Sardar Akhtar (President, All India Women's Muslim League, Member Defence Council, U.P., Author and Poetess)

Fatima Begum (Munshi Fazil, Principal, Jinnah College for Women, Lahore)

Ex-Offico Members:

Justice Sir Jailal (late Judge, High Court of Judicature, Lahore, Chief Justice, Kapurthala State)

---

[5] *The Constitution of Free India 1946 A.C.*

Associated Members:

Nawah Sardar Dr. Nawazish Ali Khan (B.A., Ph.D., Taluqdar, Oudh, Nawabganj, Aliabad, Bahraich)

Barrister Wahidud Din Hyder (B.A, LL.B., Bar-at-Law, Taluqdar, Oudh, Lucknow)

Ibrahim Ali Khan (Nawab of Kunjpura)

Pir Bukhsh Khan (M.A., LL.B., M.L.A., Peshawar)

Raja Sarfraz Khan (M.L.A., Chakwal)

Rai Faiz Muhammad Khan (M.L.A., Hoshiarpur)

Amar Nath Chopra (B.A., LL.B., ex-President, Bar Association, Lahore)

Barrister Brij Lal (B.A., LL.B., Advocate, Bar-at-Law, Lahore)

B.L. Rallia Ram (B.SC., B.T., General Secretary, All India Conference of Indian Christians, Lahore)

Dr. Muhammad Sadick (L.R.O. & V., German Clinic, Specialist, Mahim, Bombay)

Reader Members:

Professor Sultan Bukhsh (M.A., Government College, Hoshiarpur) *Secretary*

Muhammad Ibrahim Sharar (B.A., LL.B., Ellichpur, Berar) *Secretary*

Ahmed Dastagir (Journalist, Hyderabad, Deccan) *Secretary*

Professor Abdul Aziz (M.A., Professor, Jinnah College for Women, Lahore) *Secretary*

Syed Allah Bukhsh (M.A.)

Barrister Mian Ahmed Shah (B.A., LL.B., Peshawar, Founder, Red Shirt Movement)

Habib ullah Khan (B.A., LL.B., Advocate, ex-Deputy Speaker, Frontier Legislative Assembly, Bannu)

Professor B.D. Verma (M.A, M.F., A.F., Professor Fergusson College, Poona)

Mir Hazrat Shah (B.A., LL.B., Campbellpur)
Khawaja Muhammad Afzal (B.A., LL.B., Lyallpur)

Qazi [Kazi] Abdul Baqi (M.A. LL.B., Lucknow)

Akhtar Hameed Khan (M.A., I.C.S., Retired, late Asst. Collector Netrokona, Bengal, Aligarh)

S. Shamim Ahmed (M.SC., Lecturer, Muslim University, Aligarh)

Professor Karrar Husain (M.A., Professor Meerut College)

S. Qamarud Din (B.A., LL.B., Advocate, Lahore)

Agha Ghazanfar Ali Shah (M.A., LL.B., Advocate, Delhi)

Mazahar Husanain (B.A., LL.B., Advocate, Ambala)

Faiz Muhammad Khan (B.A., LL.B., Pleader, Halani Nawabshah Sind)

Khawaja Ghulam Sadiq (B.A., LL.B., Pleader Ludhiana)

Mehr Muhammed Sadiq (B.A., LL.B., Advocate, Lyallpur)

Allah Dad Shujra (B.A., LL.B., Pleader Shikarpur, Sind)

Ikramullah Khan Anwar (B.A., Lahore)

Members of Second Legal Committee[6]

Sir Currimbhoy Ebrahim
President, Second Legal Committee
(3rd Baronet, J.P., M.L.C. President, Reception Committee, All-India Muslim League, Bombay)

Members:

Justice, Sir Dalip Singh (Kt, B.A., (Cantab), Bar-at-Law, Judge High Court of Judicature, Lahore, 1925-42)

Sir Frederick E. James (Kt., M.A., O.B.E., M.L.A., Whip of European Group, Founder of Indian Institute of International Affairs, New Delhi)

Mr. Nalini Ranjan Sarker (Ex-Member, Governor General's Executive Council, Ex-Finance Minister, Government of Bengal, President, Federation of Indian Chambers of Commerce and Industry, 1935)

---

[6] *The Constitution of Free India 1946 A.C.*

Malik Khuda Bukhsh Khan (B.A., LL.B., Ex-Speaker Frontier Legislative Assembly, Advocate-General and Secretary to Government, Legislative Department, Frontier Province)

Peer Ilahi Bukhsh (M.A., LL.B., Education Minister, Sindh)

Nawab Makhdum, Sir Murid Hussain Quraishi (Kt., M.L.A., (Central) Sajjada Nashin, Multan)

Sir Syed Wasif Ali Meerza (Khan Bahadur, K.C.S.I., K.C.V.O., Nawab Bahadur of Murshidabad, Member, Bengal Legislative Council)

Khan Bahadur Saadullah Khan (Honorary Secretary, Islamia College, Peshawar, Ex-Minister and Deputy Commissioner, Peshawar)

Dr. Syed Zafarul Hassan (M.A., Ph.D., Head of the Department of Philosophy, Muslim University, Aligarh.)

Nawab Bahadur, Sir Habibullah of Dacca (K.C.I.E., Ex-Minister, Bengal Government)

Lt.-Col., Sir Muhammad Nawaz Khan (Kt. M.L.A., Khan of Kot Fateh Khan, Representative in the Central Legislative Assembly of Punjab Landholders)

Barrister Nawabzada Allah Nawaz Khan (Bar-at-Law, M.L.A., (Central) Dera Ismail Khan)

Associated Members:

F.W. Bustin (Journalist, Editor, *Civil and Military Gazette*, Lahore)

Saint Nihal Singh (Journalist and Author, Dehra Dun)

Sardar Labh Singh (M.A., LL.B., Advocate, Gujranwala)

H.R. Batheja (M.A., I.E.S., Principal Patna College, Bankipur)

Joachim Alva (Journalist, Editor, *Forum* Weekly, Bombay)

Hafiz Aslam Jairajpuri (Author and Historian, Professor, Jamia Milliyyah, Delhi)

Reader Members:

Malih Ahmed Siddiqi (M.A., LL.B., Advocate, Gorakpur)

Barrister K. A. Hamid (Bar-at-Law, Advocate, Author and Historian, Lahore)

Appendix VII

1937 Elections

Table of the 1937 elections to the provincial assemblies[1]

Province	Total Seats	Congress Seats	Muslim Seats	Muslim League Seats	Muslim Seats besides Muslim League
Bengal	250	54	117	40	77
Assam	108	33	34	9	25
Punjab	175	18	84	1	83
Sindh	60	7	36	0	36
NWFP	50	19	36	0	36
Bihar	152	98	39	0	39
C.P.	112	70	14	0	14
Orissa	60	36	4	0	4
Madras	215	159	28	11	17
Bombay	175	86	29	20	9
U.P.	228	134	64	27	37

[1] Khan, Khan Abdul Wali. Chapter 3.

Bibliography, Glossary
& Index

Works Cited & Bibliography

Ahmad, Waheed, Editor. 1992. *Quaid-i-Azam Mohammad Ali Jinnah The Nation's Voice Towards Consolidation*. Karachi, Pakistan: Quaid-i-Azam Academy.

Ahmad, Waheed, Editor. 1996. *Quaid-i-Azam Mohammad Ali Jinnah The Nation's Voice, Vol. II: United We Win*. Karachi, Pakistan: Quaid-i-Azam Academy.

Ahmad, Waheed, Editor. *Jinnah-Linlithgow Correspondence (1939-1943)*. Lahore, Pakistan: Research Society of Pakistan, University of Punjab.

Akhtar, Sana ullah. 2003. *Khaksar Tehreek Ki Inqalabi Jiddo-Juhad: 25th August 1931 to 4th July 1947*. Rawalpindi, Pakistan: Sana ullah Akhtar.

Baljon, J.M.S. 1961. *Modern Muslim Koran Interpretation*, 1880-1960. Leiden: E.J. Brill.

Banglapedia web site.
(1) http://banglapedia.search.com.bd/HT/C_0004.htm
(2) http://banglapedia.search.com.bd/HT/M_0423.htm
(Last accessed in March 2006)

Barrister Mian Ahmed Shah's letter to the Chief Secretary to the Government of United Provinces (U.P), Sir Francis Mudie, October 17, 1940. File Number: IOL L/P&J/8/680.

Copland, Ian. "'Communalism' in Princely India: The Case of Hyderabad, 1930-1940." *Modern Asian Studies*, Vol. 22 No. 4 (1988). UK: Cambridge University Press.

DFPGP (The Director of Foreign Publicity, Government of Pakistan). 1949. *Pakistan: The Struggle of a Nation*. Washington, D.C., USA: DFPGP.

Encyclopedia Britannica Online. "Chakravarti Rajagopalachari." http://cache.britannica.com/eb/article-9062513 (Last accessed in March 2006)

Gandhi, Mahatma. 1980. *The Collected Works of Mahatma Gandhi* (LXXXI, Jul. 17, 1945-Oct. 31, 1945). New Delhi, India: The Director, The Publications Division, Ministry of Information and Broadcasting Government of India.

Gandhi, Mahatma. 1980. *The Collected Works of Mahatma Gandhi* (LXXXII, Nov. 1, 1945-Jan. 19, 1946). New Delhi, India: The Director, The

416 | Nasim Yousaf

Publications Division, Ministry of Information and Broadcasting Government of India.

Gandhi-Manibhavan.org. "1942- 'Quit India Movement.'" http://www.gandhi-manibhavan.org/activities/quit_india.htm (Last accessed in April 2006)

Gandhi Serve Foundation web site.
(1) http://www.gandhiserve.org/cwmg/VOL083.PDF
(2) "Chronology 1944" http://www.gandhiserve.org/information/chronology_1944/chronology_1944.html (Last accessed in May 2006)

Gauba, K.L. 1974. *Friends and Foes.* New Delhi, India: Indian Book Company.

Government of Pakistan. 1989. *Quaid-I-Azam Mohammad Ali Jinnah, Speeches and Statements as Governor General of Pakistan 1947 - 48.* Islamabad, Pakistan: Government of Pakistan, Ministry of Information & Broadcasting, Directorate of Films & Publications.

Government of Pakistan information web site.
(1) http://www.infopak.gov.pk/14august/chronology.htm#6
(2) http://www.infopak.gov.pk/14august/chronology.htm#4
(3) http://www.infopak.gov.pk/14august/chronology.htm#17
(4) http://www.infopak.gov.pk/14august/chronology.htm#23
(5) http://www.infopak.gov.pk/14august/chronology.htm#43
(Last accessed in April 2006)

Government of Pakistan's official web site.
(1) "Cripps Mission 1942" http://www.pakistan.gov.pk/Quaid/leader7.htm
(2) http://www.pakistan.gov.pk/Quaid/leader12.htm
(3) http://www.pakistan.gov.pk/Quaid/leader18.htm
(Last accessed in March 2006)

Governor of U.P.'s letter, November 08, 1939. IOL MSS EUR F125/102 (Microfilm Number: IOR NEG 1289). Pp. 380 - 385.

Hooja, Rima. *Crusader For Self-Rule: Tej Bahadur Sapru & The Indian National Movement - Life and Selected Letters.* Jaipur, India: Rawat Publications.

Hussain, Syed Shabbir. 1991. *Al-Mashriqi: The Disowned Genius.* Lahore, Pakistan: Jang Publishers.

Jaleel, Amar. "Academic overview of partition." *Dawn Internet Edition.* April 24, 2005.

http://www.dawn.com/weekly/dmag/dmag13.htm;
http://www.dawn.com/weekly/dmag/archive/050424/dmag3.htm
(Last accessed in April 2005)

JNMF (Jawaharlal Nehru Memorial Fund). 1986. *Selected Works of Jawaharlal Nehru* (Second Series, Volume 4). New Delhi, India: JNMF.

Kane, Albert E. "The Development of Indian Politics." *Political Science Quarterly*, Vol. 59 No. 1 (March 1944). P. 68.

Kazi Abdul Baqi's letter to Jinnah. *Note on the Khaksar Movement,* February 27, 1941 (prepared by British authorities). File Number: IOL L/P&J/8/680.

Khan Bahadur Shaikh Fazl-i-Haq Piracha's speech in the Central Legislative Assembly, September 23, 1942. *Official Report of the Central Legislative Assembly Debates.* File Number: IOL L/P&J/8/680. Pp. 460-486.

Khan, Khan Abdul Wali. *Facts are Sacred.*
http://www.anp.org.pk/factsAreSacred.htm
Chapter 1: http://www.anp.org.pk/factsAreSacredchapter1.htm
Chapter 3: http://www.anp.org.pk/factsAreSacredchapter3.htm
Chapter 5: http://www.anp.org.pk/factsAreSacredchapter5.htm
Chapter 6: http://www.anp.org.pk/factsAreSacredchapter6.htm
Chapter 8: http://www.anp.org.pk/factsAreSacredchapter8.htm
Chapter 13: http://www.anp.org.pk/factsAreSacredchapter13.htm
Chapter 14: http://www.anp.org.pk/factsAreSacredchapter14.htm
Chapter 21: http://www.anp.org.pk/factsAreSacredchapter21.htm
(Last accessed in April-May 2006)

Malik, Rasheed. 1993. *Allama Mashraqi aur Musser.* Gujrat: Idara-e-Maurif Afkar Al-Mashraqi.

Mansergh, Nicholas, Editor. 1973. *Constitutional Relations Between Britain and India - The Transfer of Power: 1942-7* (Volume IV The Bengal Famine and the New Viceroyalty 15 June 1943-31 August 1944). London, England: Her Majesty's Stationery Office; Oxford University Press.

Mansergh, Nicholas, Editor. 1976. *Constitutional Relations Between Britain and India - The Transfer of Power 1942-7* (Volume VI The Post-War Phase: New Moves by the Labour Government 1 August 1945-22 March 1946). London, England: Her Majesty's Stationery Office.

Mansergh, Nicholas, Editor. 1977. *Constitutional Relations Between Britain and India - The Transfer of Power: 1942-7* (Volume VII The Cabinet Mission 23 March-29 June 1946). London, England: Her Majesty's Stationery Office; Oxford University Press.

Mashriqi, Allama (Khan, Inayat Ullah). [1931] 1997. *Isha'arat*. Lahore, Pakistan: Khaksar Hameed ud Din Ahmed (son of Allama Mashriqi) c/o Al-Tazkirah Publications.

Mashriqi, Allama (Khan, Inayat Ullah). 1945. *"Where Leaders Fail - A Dispassionate Dissection of Indian Politics from a Non-party point of view."* (Speech delivered at the University Institute Hall, Calcutta, India on October 21, 1945). Published: 66, Colootola Street, Calcutta: under the authority of Idara-i-Aliyyah by N.M. Anwell. Printed: 6, Chowringhee Road, Calcutta: Calcutta Phototype Company.

Merriam, Allen Hayes. 1980. *Gandhi vs. Jinnah: The Debate Over the Partition of India*. Calcutta, India: Minerva Associates (Publications) Pvt. Ltd.

Muhammad, Shan. 1973. *Khaksar Movement in India*. Delhi, India: Meenakshi Prakashan.

Mujahid, Sharif Al and Yousuf Saeed, Editors. 1981. *Quaid-i-Azam Jinnah: A Chronology*. Prepared by Riaz Ahmad. Karachi, Pakistan: Quaid-i-Azam Academy.

ORCLAD (*Official Report of the Central Legislative Assembly Debates*). File Number: IOL L/P&J/8/680.

Peerbhoy, Akbar A. 1986. *Jinnah Faces an Assassin*. Karachi, Pakistan: East and West Publishing Company.

Pirzada, Syed Sharifuddin, Editor. 1977. *Quaid-e-Azam Jinnah's Correspondence*. 3d ed. (Revised and Enlarged). Karachi, Pakistan: East and West Publishing Company.

Punjab Criminal Investigation Department (C.I.D.). *Addendum to the Note on the Khaksar Movement*, March 31, 1943. File Number: IOL L/P&J/8/680.

Quit India Movement web site. http://quit-india-movement.biography.ms (Last accessed in May 2006)

Report on Public Instructions of NWFP Quinquennium 1917-22. P. 16.

Saeed, Muhammad. 1989. *Lahore - A Memoir*. Lahore, Pakistan: Vanguard Books Pvt. Ltd.

Singh, Anita Inder. 1987. *The Origins of the Partition of India 1936-1947*. Delhi, India: Oxford University Press.

Sir Richard Tottenham's, Additional Secretary to the Government of India, letter, May 08, 1943. File Number: IOL L/P&J/8/680.

Sir Richard Tottenham's, Additional Secretary to the Government of India, letter to Allama Mashraqi and all Provincial Governments, July 19, 1943. File Number: IOL L/P&J/8/680.

SQS (*Secret Quarterly Survey of the Political and Constitutional Position in British India No. 12 for the period May 01-July 31, 1940*). Pp. 10, 11, 20. IOL MSS EUR F125/143 (Microfilm Number: IOR NEG 1330).

The Constitution of Free India 1946 A.C. (full title: *Report of the First Legal Committee, as Amended and Endorsed by the Second Legal Committee, With Part II and Portion of Part III of The Constitution of Free India 1946 A.C.*). Ichhra, Lahore: Authority of the Idara-i-Aliyyah. (also known as Khaksar Constitution).

The Ottomans.org. http://www.theottomans.org (Last accessed in March 2006)

"US grooming India as a junior partner: think-tank." *Dawn Internet Edition.* June 11, 2006. http://dawn.com/2006/06/11/int1.htm (Last accessed in June 2006)

Wolpert, Stanley. 2002. *Gandhi's Passion: The Life and Legacy of Mahatma Gandhi.* USA: Oxford University Press.

Yousaf, Nasim. 2003. *Allama Mashriqi & Dr. Akhtar Hameed Khan: Two Legends of Pakistan.* New York, USA: Nasim Yousaf.

Yousaf, Nasim. 2004. *Pakistan's Freedom & Allama Mashriqi: Statements, Letters, Chronology of Khaksar Tehrik (Movement), Period: Mashriqi's Birth to 1947.* New York, USA: AMZ Publications.

Zaidi, Z.H. *M.A. Jinnah: Ispahani Correspondence 1936-1948.* Karachi, Pakistan: Forward Publications Trust.

Zaman, Sher. 1987. *Khaksar Tehrik Ki Jiddo Juhad Volume 2.* Rawalpindi, Pakistan: Khaksar Sher Zaman c/o Al-Tazkirah Publications; Sher Zaman Khaksar, Madni Clinic, Chah Sultan.

Zaman, Sher. 1988. *Khaksar Tehrik Ki Jiddo Juhad Volume 3.* Rawalpindi, Pakistan: Khaksar Sher Zaman c/o Al-Tazkirah Publications.

Zaman, Sher. 1992. *Sir Syed, Jinnah, Mashriqi.* Rawalpindi, Pakistan: Khaksar Sher Zaman c/o Al-Tazkirah Publications.

India Office Records, British Library:

Abbreviations:
IOL – India Office Library, British Library (London)
IOR – India Office Records, British Library (London)

IOL L/I/1/629 (Microfilm Number: IOR NEG 13027)
IOL L/P&J/5/249
IOL L/P&J/5/250
IOL L/P&J/8/680
IOL MSS EUR F125/9 (Microfilm Number: IOR NEG 1196)
IOL MSS EUR F125/12
IOL MSS EUR F125/75 (Microfilm Number: IOR NEG 1262)
IOL MSS EUR F125/89 (Microfilm Number: IOR NEG 1276)
IOL MSS EUR F125/102 (Microfilm Number: IOR NEG 1289)
IOL MSS EUR F125/143 (Microfilm Number: IOR NEG 1330)

Newspapers:

Al-Islah, Lahore (1947)
Al-Islah weekly, 34 Zialdar Road Lahore, Pakistan (1997)
Dawn, Delhi (pre-partition) and Karachi (post partition)
Imroze, Lahore
Morning News, Dacca, East Pakistan (now Bangladesh)
Morning News, Karachi
The Bombay Chronicle, Bombay
The Civil & Military Gazette, Lahore
The Deccan Times, Madras
The Eastern Examiner, Chittagong
The Eastern Times, Lahore
The Free Press Journal, Bombay
The Hindustan Times, Delhi
The Leader, Allahabad
The Pakistan Times, Lahore
The Radiance, Aligarh (U.P.). (Published by M. Obaidur Rehman, Civil Lines, Aligarh. Printed by A.H. Rizvi at the National Ptg [Printing] Works, Aligarh. Editor Riaz Ahmed Khan)
The Sind Observer, Karachi
The Star of India, Calcutta
The Statesman, Calcutta
The Times, London
The Tribune, Lahore
Zamindar, Lahore

Glossary

Azad	Free
Belcha	Spade
Darbar	Court of the ruler
Goonda	Hooligan
Khaksar	Literal meaning, Humble
Lathi	Baton, stick (used by police)
Maulvi	Priest of the Muslims
Mohallah	Locality, a ward or a quarter
Quaid-e-Azam	The Great Leader
Raj	Kingdom, sovereignty, rule
Sardar	Leader/chief of the tribe
Zamindar	Landlord

Index

1

100,000 people, 219

2

2.5 million, 51, 69
24 principles, 41

3

300,000 Khaksars, 35, 242, 244,
    247, 263, 264
313 Khaksars, 51

4

4,000 Khaksars, 175, 177
40 lakh, 49, 116
40,000,000, 260
400 million, 25, 143, 157, 235,
    247, 253, 290, 394, 398

5

50,000 Khaksars, 71, 73, 111
50,000 people, 223, 247

6

60,000,000 Muslims, 260

7

70,000, 35, 263

8

80 days, 32, 109, 112
80,000, 35, 263

A

A.I.C.C., 135
Abbasi, Dr. Muzhar Ali, 209
Abdurrahman Sahib, 126
Abra, Dr. F.K., 238, 239

Addendum, 151
Adjournment motion, 92
Afridis, 261
Afzal, Khawaja Muhammad, 409
Ahmad, Saeed, 117
Ahmad, Shamsuddin, 219
Ahmed, Dr. Rafique, 174, 175
Ahmed, Lt.-Col. Dr. Sir Zia ud
    Din, 407
Ahmed, S. Shamim, 409
Ahmed, Saeed, 117, 118
Ahrars, 86, 217, 291, 381
AIML, 19, 20, 21, 23, 24, 25, 32,
    51, 57, 59, 60, 69, 71, 75, 76,
    95, 115, 116, 117, 118, 119,
    120, 122, 123, 124, 127, 128,
    130, 132, 133, 134, 135, 137,
    138, 139, 140, 142, 145, 146,
    147, 148, 150, 151, 152, 153,
    162, 163, 164, 167, 172, 180,
    181, 184, 187, 188, 191, 193,
    194, 195, 197, 199, 200, 201,
    205, 208, 209, 212, 213, 214,
    215, 216, 217, 218, 221, 222,
    223, 224, 227, 228, 229, 230,
    232, 233, 234, 235, 236, 238,
    244, 246, 247, 249, 251, 252,
    254, 256, 257, 258, 259, 260,
    263, 265, 267, 268, 269, 270,
    276, 278, 279, 280, 283, 284,
    285, 286, 287, 288, 294, 296,
    298, 299, 356, 357, 365
Akbar, 144
Akhtar, Syeda Sardar, 407
Alexander, A.V., 228
Ali, Nawabzada Mahmud, 374,
    375
Ali, Sir Raza, 59, 79
Aligarh Muslim University, 22,
    109, 174
Al-Islah, 47, 51, 69, 73, 217, 241,
    248, 264, 359, 362
Allahabad, 84, 124, 125, 126, 130,
    131, 133, 134, 135, 200, 375

Allama Inayatullah, 38
Allama Mashraqi, 5, 19, 25, 27,
31, 32, 35, 36, 50, 51, 60, 66,
75, 84, 88, 89, 92, 93, 106, 117,
121, 124, 126, 127, 130, 133,
137, 153, 156, 159, 166, 168,
175, 184, 185, 197, 204, 205,
213, 215, 219, 220, 221, 222,
224, 227, 228, 230, 231, 234,
241, 261, 264, 303, 304
Allama Mashriqi, 19, 30, 33, 37,
38, 51, 61, 80, 97, 98, 100, 112,
114, 119, 128, 133, 138, 139,
140, 153, 161, 166, 167, 187,
189, 205, 207, 218, 224, 264,
385, 386, 401, 402
Allama Mashriqi Zindabad, 80,
264
Allama Mashriqui, 149, 150, 165,
168, 210, 219, 239, 267, 358
Allama Saheb, 196
Allama Sahib, 45, 118, 119, 178,
206, 386
All-India Hindu Mahasabha, 229
All-India Jamiat Ulema, 213
All-India Liberal Federation, 229
All-India Muslim League, 8, 19,
20, 23, 24, 51, 57, 71, 72, 73,
76, 77, 79, 81, 82, 89, 90, 99,
115, 119, 120, 141, 146, 179,
190, 218, 255, 258, 272, 283,
284, 353, 367, 376, 377, 378,
382, 402, 409
All-India Muslim League
Propaganda Board, 167
All-India Muslim Majlis, 214, 229
Alva, Joachim, 410
Amalgamate, 93, 227, 228
Ambassador, 140
Ambassadorship, 29, 147
Ambedkar, Dr., 204
Amery, L.S., 95, 147, 158, 166,
185, 259, 260, 356, 381
Amir ud Din, Mian, 84
Amritsar, 27, 33, 75, 211, 218,
254, 380, 381
Anarkali, 84

Anderson, Sir George, 28
Anjuman Nasir- ul- Musalmin,
373
Ansari, Abdul Qaiyum, 290, 377
Ansari, Dr. M.S., 378
Ansari, Shaukatullah, 155
Anti-communalism, 116, 135, 177
Anwar, Ikramullah Khan, 409
Arbabs, 49
Army of Spades, 50
Arundale, Dr. George A., 407
Arya Smaj, 190, 192
Asar, Maulana Nazar, 227
Asghar, Inayatullah Khan, 266,
267
Ashraf, Dr. K.M., 375
Aslam, Ehsanullah Khan, 32, 52,
75
Associated Members, 408, 410
Ataturk, 293
Attlee, Lord Clement, 189, 227,
238, 241, 249, 297
Azad Hind Fauj Conference, 231,
237
Azad Muslim Conference, 87, 155
Azad, Maulana Abul Kalam, 28,
88, 112, 113, 115, 118, 120,
124, 125, 126, 127, 128, 129,
130, 137, 139, 153, 192, 204,
222, 380
Azhar, Maulana Mazhar Ali, 87,
215, 291, 374, 380, 381
Aziz, Professor Abdul, 408

B

Backward Hindu Classes, 190,
204
Backward Muslims, 190, 204, 405
Badshahi Mosque, 150, 151, 164,
190
Bahmany, S.S.M., 112, 114, 128
Baig, Mohammad Rashid Ali, 289
Ball, Professor U.N., 156, 286
Baluchis, 299
Ban(ned), 35, 51, 52, 72, 74, 75,
77, 78, 81, 84, 86, 89, 90, 91,
92, 93, 94, 95, 96, 98, 99, 100,

101, 102, 104, 105, 106, 111,
112, 151, 159, 160, 266, 285,
286, 287, 295, 364, 385
Bangladesh, 23, 295, 299
Bankipur, 223, 410
Baqi, Qazi [Kazi] Abdul, 32, 51,
409
Barty, D.V., 221
Batheja, H.R., 410
Beaty, 79, 92
Beautiful cars, 106
Begum Habibullah, 59
Behari, Maulana Nur-uddin, 380
Belcha(s), 46, 84, 97, 98, 159,
160, 238
Bengal, 35, 57, 74, 104, 120, 151,
176, 179, 190, 209, 216, 218,
236, 243, 244, 245, 246, 247,
248, 249, 250, 252, 253, 254,
255, 256, 258, 259, 261, 262,
269, 271, 272, 278, 279, 280,
371, 372, 373, 380, 381, 391,
407, 409, 410, 411
Berlin Wall, 301
Bhai Saheb, 199
Bharghava, Gopichand, 92
Bhoy, Mauhammad, 378
Bhurgaries, 49
Bhutto, Zulifiqar Ali, 304
Bible, 160
Blagden, 163, 359, 360, 362, 365
Bombay, 34, 73, 95, 98, 99, 101,
130, 131, 137, 138, 139, 150,
151, 157, 162, 163, 164, 165,
166, 167, 169, 172, 174, 175,
176, 177, 178, 181, 197, 211,
220, 231, 235, 238, 274, 275,
290, 353, 354, 356, 357, 359,
360, 363, 364, 371, 372, 378,
388, 393, 403, 408, 409, 410,
411
Bose, Subhas Chandra, 124, 242
Boundary Commissions, 271, 272
Brahmans, 277
Brahmin Raj, 396, 398
Brahmins, 397
Brahmo Smaj, 190

Brailsford, H.N., 291
Brij Lal, Barrister, 408
Britons, 300
Brotherhood, 39, 42, 43, 46, 48,
110, 125, 175, 224
Brown, Oscar, 357
Budhists, 205, 406
Bukhari, Syed Attaullah Shah,
291, 375
Bukhsh, Peer Ilahi, 410
Bukhsh, Professor Sultan, 408
Bukhsh, Syed Allah, 386, 408
Buksh, Khan Bahadur Allah, 147,
379
Bulundshahr, 67
Bustin, F.W., 410
Butt, Abdulla, 374
Bux (Baksh), K.B. Allah, 289
Bux, Khan Bahadur Allah, 284

C

C.R. formula, 117, 131, 132, 168,
169, 171, 172, 174, 179
Cabinet Mission, 228, 229, 232,
233, 241, 253, 257
Capital punishment, 97, 404
Caste, 27, 42, 49, 72, 116, 124,
125, 126, 133, 144, 192, 211,
236, 254, 293, 397, 399
Caste Hindus, 190, 207, 218, 393,
395, 398, 404
Central Legislative Assembly, 97,
98, 221, 237, 376, 410
Chairman of Senate, 304
Chairman of the National
Committee, 383
Character, 25, 33, 39, 41, 42, 46,
94, 150, 158, 176, 216, 221,
238, 276, 353, 368, 377, 386,
392
Chelmsford, Lord, 28
Chief Commissioner(s), 28, 29,
158, 164, 265
Chief Presidency Magistrate, 356,
357
Chief Secretary, 31, 103
Chishti, Dr. Hajee Aslam, 130

Chisti, Dr. Muhammad Aslam, 246
Chisti, Maulana, 374
Chopra, Amar Nath, 408
Christ's College, 28
Christians, 49, 190, 192, 204, 392, 402, 403, 405, 406, 408
Chundrigar, I. I., 236
Churchill, Sir Winston Leonard Spencer, 111, 147, 166, 187, 188, 189, 195, 206, 207, 385
City Magistrate, 84
Civil Disobedience, 60, 137, 139, 386
Civil Disobedience Movement, 60, 137, 139, 386
Co-exist, 144, 294
Commander-in-Chief, 95
Communal, 42, 72, 74, 114, 116, 122, 123, 126, 127, 133, 144, 149, 150, 152, 154, 155, 156, 166, 167, 178, 191, 205, 208, 235, 239, 242, 243, 251, 273, 276, 285, 286, 288, 289, 365, 373, 379, 398, 403
Communal Unity Committee, 112, 128
Communalism, 38, 42, 70, 72, 116, 119, 123, 144, 145, 146, 150, 151, 152, 177, 208, 209, 210, 218, 232, 233, 235, 237, 285, 287, 288, 294, 295, 303, 373
Communist Party, 229
Community service, 33, 39, 42, 46, 48, 126
Congress, 6, 49, 51, 55, 56, 57, 58, 60, 61, 64, 66, 67, 68, 69, 71, 84, 88, 96, 112, 113, 114, 115, 116, 117, 118, 119, 120, 121, 122, 125, 127, 128, 129, 130, 131, 133, 134, 135, 136, 137, 138, 139, 140, 142, 144, 147, 151, 152, 153, 155, 156, 157, 166, 168, 170, 174, 180, 185, 187, 188, 190, 191, 192, 193, 195, 197, 198, 199, 200, 201, 204, 205, 207, 208, 209, 217, 218, 221, 228, 229, 232, 233, 234, 235, 236, 238, 244, 245, 246, 249, 251, 253, 254, 260, 261, 262, 263, 269, 270, 274, 278, 280, 284, 285, 286, 287, 291, 363, 371, 372, 374, 376, 377, 379, 380, 382, 385, 386, 388, 394, 395, 397, 411
Congress Ministry, 55, 56, 58, 60, 61, 62, 66, 67, 71
Constituent Assembly, 256, 293
Constitutional, 35, 228, 230, 234, 239, 277, 280, 381, 397, 398
Convicted, 104
Corridor(s), 39, 103, 249
Council of the All-India Muslim League, 169, 257, 258, 375
Council of the Central Jamiat Ulema, 213
Cove, W.G., 181
Craik, Sir Henry Duffield, 64, 67, 82, 83, 85, 86, 87, 96
Creed, 27, 42, 44, 49, 72, 94, 116, 124, 125, 126, 133, 134, 144, 192, 211, 215, 289, 293, 381, 399
Criminal Investigation Department, 33, 151
Cripps, Sir Stafford, 111, 113, 114, 115, 185, 207, 228, 229, 232, 385, 395, 401
Cunningham, Sir George, 93

D

Dabbi Bazaar, 84
Dagger, 353, 392
Dastagir, Ahmed, 196, 386, 408
Day of Deliverance, 377, 378, 379
Decree, 41, 116, 124
Delhi is Ours, 264
Dev Smaj, 190, 192
Direct Action, 234, 235
Discipline, 33, 39, 41, 43, 45, 48, 50, 51, 52, 56, 67, 71, 84, 93, 126, 158, 159, 176
District Magistrate, 221

Dominion, 258
Dominion Status, 113, 255
Dravidians, 190, 192, 204, 405
Drill(s), 43, 46, 48, 159, 160
Durrani, Obaidullah, 407

E

East Pakistan, 121, 277, 299, 300
Eastern India, 253
Ebrahim, Sir Currimbhoy, 176,
    409
Editor of Paigham, 381
Education Department, 28
Egypt, 30, 296, 387
Einstein, Professor Albert, 30, 33
Elections, 34, 57, 144, 145, 147,
    189, 195, 208, 209, 210, 212,
    213, 214, 216, 217, 218, 221,
    222, 227, 284, 296, 299, 376,
    380, 398, 411
ex-Chief Minister, 35, 407
Executive, 185, 189, 190, 191,
    193, 207, 228, 235, 299, 404,
    409

F

Facts are Sacred, 103, 190, 297
Fakhri, Maulana Shahid, 84, 261,
    375
Faramarzi, 275
Farooqi, Maulana Mohammand
    Miyan, 375
Fasting, 32, 105, 110, 111, 187
Fatima Begum, 407
Fatima Jinnah, 92, 93
Fazl-ul-Haq, A.K., 74, 87, 89, 98,
    105, 120, 206, 227, 372, 380,
    407
Features of the Constitution, 8,
    402, 406
Federal Ministers, 304
Federal Secretary, 304
Ferozepur, 49, 254, 271
Feudal system, 298, 299
Fifth Columnists, 96, 98

First Legal Committee, 203, 206,
    406, 407
Fleming Road, 45
Foot's article, 195
Fortnightly report, 209, 283, 293
Four million, 38, 48, 49, 116, 127
Funeral, 32, 363, 365, 388

G

Gainsford, D., 79, 92
Galaxy, 70
Gallery, 92
Gandhi, M.K. (Mahatma), 7, 24,
    112, 113, 115, 117, 124, 127,
    128, 136, 137, 138, 139, 140,
    141, 148, 149, 153, 154, 155,
    156, 157, 158, 160, 161, 162,
    163, 164, 165, 166, 167, 168,
    169, 170, 171, 172, 173, 174,
    175, 176, 177, 178, 179, 180,
    181, 183, 184, 185, 186, 187,
    188, 189, 192, 195, 196, 197,
    198, 199, 200, 201, 204, 205,
    207, 217, 227, 228, 229, 234,
    235, 243, 244, 245, 249, 250,
    251, 252, 253, 260, 269, 280,
    286, 357, 358, 359, 361, 363,
    365, 374, 386, 387, 388, 391,
    392, 395, 396, 397, 401
Gandhi, Behind the Mask of
    Divinity, 250
Gandhiji, 140, 155, 161, 162, 165,
    167, 168, 178
Gauba, Barrister K.L., 75, 84, 92,
    209, 407
Geeta, 160
General Secretary of the Jammu
    and Kashmir National
    Conference, 288
Ghauri, Mohammad Rafiq, 355
Golbagh, 380
Golden Mosque, 84
Goonda(s), 162, 212, 218, 221,
    222, 269, 421
Goondaism, 220
Government High School, 28

Government of United Provinces, 31, 52, 55, 103

Governor General, 28, 37, 95, 102, 117, 263, 280, 297, 409

Governor General of Pakistan, 263, 280, 297

Governor of North West Frontier Province, 93

Governor of Punjab, 64, 67, 77, 82, 83, 85, 87, 96, 146, 262

Governor of the United Provinces (U.P.), 96

Governor of West Pakistan, 37

Grant, Sir Alfred Hamilton, 29

Granth, 160

Guard of Honor, 63, 74, 268

H

H. M-Government, 103

H.E.H. the Nizam, 204

H.H. the Jam of Nawanagar, 204

H.H. the Nawab of Bhopal, 204

H.M.G.'s plan, 253, 254, 258

Habibullah, Nawab Bahadur Sir, 410

Haig, Sir Harry Graham, 57, 59, 64, 67

Hallett, Sir Maurice Garnier, 96

Hamdani, Maulana Abdus Salam, 381

Hamid, Barrister K.A., 410

Handkerchiefs, 160

Harijan, 136, 200

Haroon, Sir Abdulla, 284

Hashim, Abdul, 258

Hassan, Dr. Syed Zafarul, 410

Hassan, Mufti Ziaul, 214

Hassan, Sahibzada Faizul, 379

Hassan, Sir Wazir, 204

Haye, Mian Abdul, 79

Head of the State, 42

Headquarters, 46, 47, 52, 75, 106, 209, 216, 231, 237, 238, 284

Health, 33, 35, 110, 117, 164, 165, 169, 175, 188, 189, 404

Heritage, 22, 23, 143, 272, 301

Hindu Mahasabha, 112, 114, 190, 192, 193, 204, 277, 402

Hindu Rajput princesses, 144

Hindu-Muslim, 133, 135, 136, 140, 150, 151, 152, 157, 161, 165, 167, 168, 175, 176, 177, 185, 193, 204, 205, 238, 239, 248, 260, 363, 366, 367, 368, 383, 385, 386, 388, 393

Hiralal, Professor, 205

Hissamuddin, Sheikh, 217

Historical, 19, 24, 79, 123, 142, 143, 146, 147, 232, 272, 278, 300

Historical maps, 300

Historiography, 303

Hitler, Adolph, 30, 33, 68, 97, 98, 385

HMG Plan, 252

Hockey sticks, 219

Holy Quran, 29, 97, 374

Home Department, 104, 153, 154, 161, 163

Home Member, 96

Husain, Dr. Zakir, 266

Husanain, Mazahar, 409

Hussain, Dr. Syed, 383

Hussain, Sayed Muzaffar, 375

Hyder, Barrister Wahidud Din, 408

I

Idara-i-Aliya, 62, 160, 231, 263, 391, 406

Illness, 32, 139

Imperial Hotel, 255, 256, 257, 261

INC, 24, 115

Indian Constituent Assembly, 267

Indian Independence Bill, 265, 297

Indian National Army, 237, 242

Indian National Congress, 23, 71, 115, 124, 189, 252, 402

Indian nationalism, 143

Inter-Cultural Association, 292, 383

Interview(ed), 61, 73, 111, 132,
133, 138, 161, 164, 170, 179,
196, 205, 214, 218, 235, 238,
249, 252, 274, 275, 285, 292,
375, 376
Iqbal, Barrister Aftab, 232, 291
Iranian Government, 275
Iranian Parliament, 275
Islamia College, 28, 38, 410
Ismay, General Lord, 249

J

Jagirs, 22
Jahangir, 144
Jail, 31, 32, 34, 36, 39, 56, 57, 58,
59, 60, 61, 62, 72, 84, 89, 92,
93, 99, 105, 106, 109, 110, 111,
116, 127, 145, 149, 153, 156,
169, 183, 194, 235, 263, 266,
269, 366, 381, 382
Jailal, Justice Sir, 407
Jain, Rajendra Kumar, 205
Jains, 205, 277, 392, 402, 403,
405, 406
Jairajpuri, Hafiz Aslam, 410
Jallianwala Bagh, 75
Jama'at-i-Islami, 37
James, Sir Frederick E., 409
Jamiat ul Ulema, 261
Jamiat Ulamah-e-Hind, 86
Jamiat-ul-ulema Hind, 217
Jan, Nawab Ali Ahmad, 209
Jang, Nawab Bahadur Yar, 51, 75,
84, 86, 92, 93, 102
Jehangir, Sir Cowasji, 205
Jenkins, Sir Evan, 293
Jews, 385, 402, 405, 406
Jhansi Railway, 149
Jinnah, Quaid-e-Azam
Muhammad Ali, 7, 19, 20, 32,
34, 57, 58, 60, 61, 62, 63, 64,
65, 66, 67, 69, 72, 73, 74, 75,
76, 78, 79, 80, 81, 82, 83, 84,
85, 87, 88, 90, 95, 99, 100, 101,
102, 103, 104, 105, 106, 112,
113, 114, 118, 119, 120, 121,
122, 123, 124, 125, 126, 127,
128, 129, 130, 131, 132, 133,
134, 135, 136, 138, 139, 140,
141, 142, 143, 144, 145, 146,
147, 148, 149, 153, 154, 155,
156, 157, 158, 159, 160, 161,
162, 163, 164, 165, 166, 167,
168, 169, 170, 171, 172, 173,
174, 175, 176, 177, 178, 179,
180, 181, 182, 183, 185, 186,
187, 188, 189, 191, 192, 193,
194, 195, 196, 197, 200, 201,
204, 205, 206, 209, 210, 214,
215, 216, 217, 221, 223, 224,
227, 228, 230, 231, 232, 233,
234, 235, 236, 244, 245, 246,
249, 250, 251, 252, 253, 254,
255, 256, 258, 259, 260, 261,
262, 263, 267, 268, 269, 274,
275, 284, 285, 286, 287, 288,
290, 291, 292, 293, 297, 299,
300, 353, 354, 355, 356, 357,
358, 359, 360, 361, 362, 363,
364, 365, 366, 367, 368, 371,
372, 373, 374, 375, 376, 377,
378, 379, 380, 381, 382, 383,
387, 388, 391, 392, 395, 396,
397, 407, 408
Jinnah-Gandhi meeting, 140, 156,
177
Jinnah-Sikander, 284
Judiciary, 299, 404
Jullundhar, 271

K

Kabir, Professor Humayun, 219,
227, 407
Kameez, 45
Karachi Municipal Corporation,
197, 221
Karol Bagh, 63, 65
Kashmir, 35, 36, 38, 166, 167,
277, 278, 279, 280, 281, 301
Kashmir ka kia banay ga, 36
Kazis, 49
Kazmi, Qazi Mohammad Ahmad,
105
Khaki, 43, 45, 46, 55, 276

Khaksar camp(s), 47, 48, 49, 63,
65, 175, 263, 280
Khaksar Constitution, 7, 8, 179,
184, 185, 187, 189, 190, 197,
198, 199, 203, 204, 205, 206,
207, 208, 209, 210, 211, 216,
217, 219, 220, 222, 224, 225,
227, 250, 401, 406
Khaksar flag, 46, 122
Khaksar Movement, 21, 25, 31,
33, 34, 35, 37, 38, 43, 45, 49,
55, 59, 72, 74, 77, 78, 81, 95,
96, 97, 98, 100, 105, 110, 117,
150, 151, 163, 212, 238, 264,
267, 269, 364, 365
Khaksar Resolution, 82, 83, 88,
89, 90, 91
Khaksar Shuhdha Zindabad, 80
Khaksar Tehreek, 7, 19, 21, 31,
32, 36, 41, 42, 43, 44, 46, 47,
48, 49, 50, 51, 52, 55, 57, 59,
60, 61, 64, 65, 67, 69, 70, 71,
72, 73, 74, 75, 77, 78, 84, 85,
86, 88, 89, 91, 92, 93, 95, 97,
98, 99, 101, 102, 104, 105, 106,
112, 114, 115, 116, 119, 120,
122, 123, 124, 127, 129, 134,
137, 142, 145, 147, 150, 151,
152, 158, 160, 162, 163, 172,
191, 194, 199, 203, 209, 211,
212, 213, 215, 216, 217, 219,
221, 222, 227, 229, 231, 236,
237, 251, 255, 259, 264, 265,
270, 278, 284, 285, 286, 287,
288, 303, 353, 354, 356, 364,
365, 376
Khaksar Tehreek Zindabad, 264
Khaksar-Congress Ministry, 57,
58, 59, 60, 61, 63, 66, 67
Khaksar-e-Azam Zindabad, 80,
264
Khaksars Zindabad, 88
Khan Bahadur Raj, 248, 398
Khan Bahadurs, 70, 196, 216, 372,
375, 376, 380, 397
Khan Saheb, Maulana Akram, 98
Khan Sahib, Dr., 35, 383

Khan, Barrister Nawabzada Allah
Nawaz, 410
Khan, Begum Liaquat Ali, 92, 93
Khan, Col. Nawab Mohammad
Akbar, 205
Khan, Col. Sir Hussamuddin, 205
Khan, Col. Sir Sher Mohammad,
205
Khan, Dr. Abdul Aziz, 373
Khan, Dr. Akhtar Hameed, 19,
409
Khan, Dr. Nawazish Ali, 408
Khan, Dr. Rafiq Ahmed, 109, 407
Khan, Faiz Muhammad, 409
Khan, Ghazanfar Ali, 222, 236
Khan, Habib ullah, 408
Khan, Ibrahim Ali, 408
Khan, Inayatullah, 27, 33, 62, 129,
131, 134, 136, 137, 172, 173,
186, 187, 266, 267, 366
Khan, Khan Abdul Ghaffar, 137,
196, 262, 383
Khan, Khan Abdul Qayyum, 377
Khan, Khan Abdul Wali, 103, 190,
297
Khan, Khan Akhbar, 87
Khan, Khan Ata Mohammed, 27
Khan, Khan Bahadur Saadullah,
410
Khan, Liaquat Ali, 63, 83, 93, 105,
165, 193, 204, 228, 236, 249,
251, 295, 359, 367, 382
Khan, Lt.-Col. Sir Muhammad
Nawaz, 410
Khan, Major General Dost
Mohammad, 244
Khan, Major General S.D., 237,
242
Khan, Malik Amir Muhammad, 37
Khan, Malik Khuda Bukhsh, 410
Khan, Maulana Zafar Ali, 204
Khan, Nawab Ismail, 59, 60, 61,
92, 367
Khan, Nawab Mohamed Ismail,
367
Khan, Nawab Salimullah, 23
Khan, Pir Bukhsh, 408

Khan, President Muhammad
Ayub, 36
Khan, Professor Abdul Majid,
253, 371, 372, 373, 376
Khan, Rai Faiz Muhammad, 408
Khan, Raja Sarfraz, 408
Khan, Sahibzada Khurshid
Ahmed, 265
Khan, Sir Muhammad Yamin, 98
Khan, Sir Sikandar Hayat, 51, 58,
71, 72, 73, 74, 75, 76, 77, 78,
79, 80, 81, 82, 83, 85, 86, 87,
88, 89, 90, 91, 92, 93, 95, 96,
97, 98, 100, 101, 102, 103, 104,
105, 106, 146, 284, 285, 363,
364, 365, 375, 380, 382, 388
Khan, Sir Syed Ahmed, 22
Khans, 49
Khilafat Movement, 24, 29, 106
Khitab-e-Lahore, 43
Khitab-e-Misr, 30
Kidwai, Mubashar Hussain, 60
Kidwai, Rafi Ahmed, 58, 60, 67
Killed, 51, 67, 75, 77, 92, 100,
234, 266, 272
Kitchlew, Dr. Saifuddin, 288, 289
Knife, 353, 355, 358, 361, 362
Knighthood, 22, 29, 147
Knights, 70, 372, 374, 375, 376,
381
Knives, 219
Kohistan, 37
Koran, 164
Kripalani, Acharya, 251
Krishak Proja Party, 219, 407
Kunjpura, 49, 408
Kusmandi, Nawab Abdullah
Khan, 102

L

Lahore Resolution, 180, 256, 286,
287, 289, 296
Lahori, Professor Inayatullah, 359
Laithwaite, Sir John Gilbert, 96
Lal Fort is Ours, 264
Landlords, 45, 49, 70, 291
Lari, Z.H., 59, 80, 256

Lathi(s), 62, 218, 219, 256, 257,
265
Latif, Dr. Syed Abdul, 214
League-Congress rapprochement,
167
League-Congress settlement, 127,
168
Legislative, 72, 73, 75, 84, 87, 97,
98, 179, 209, 221, 223, 237,
261, 289, 291, 371, 372, 373,
376, 377, 378, 380, 407, 408,
410
Legislative Assembly(ies), 49, 72,
73, 84, 87, 179, 209, 223, 261,
289, 291, 371, 372, 373, 377,
378, 380, 407, 408, 410
Letter(s), 24, 31, 32, 57, 58, 59,
61, 62, 64, 65, 66, 67, 68, 69,
78, 82, 83, 85, 86, 89, 93, 99,
101, 102, 103, 104, 105, 109,
110, 114, 117, 118, 126, 128,
129, 130, 131, 134, 135, 136,
137, 145, 151, 153, 154, 155,
156, 157, 158, 159, 161, 162,
164, 166, 168, 169, 171, 172,
173, 174, 175, 183, 184, 185,
186, 187, 188, 189, 192, 195,
196, 198, 199, 200, 201, 205,
206, 207, 210, 227, 231, 234,
235, 238, 242, 248, 260, 266,
280, 287, 291, 304, 356, 357,
358, 359, 360, 361, 363, 365,
366, 367, 368, 387, 388, 401
Linlithgow, Lord, 57, 58, 59, 67,
82, 85, 86, 99, 100, 101, 102,
103, 145, 158, 170, 259, 260,
285, 356
Lljee, Hussainbhai, 227
Loot, 243, 248, 269, 298, 395
Ludhianvi, Maulana Habibur
Rehman, 373, 377, 378
Luxury, 31, 63, 119, 276, 298

M

Madni, Hussain Muhammad, 227
Madni, Maulana Hussain Ahmed,
213

Madras, 32, 33, 50, 109, 110, 112, 117, 118, 120, 125, 126, 127, 128, 133, 134, 137, 139, 140, 149, 168, 172, 177, 211, 220, 227, 253, 403, 407, 411

Maharajah of Mysore, 204

Maharajkumar of Mahmudabad, 204

Mahasthavir, Bodhanand, 205

Mahmands, 261

Mahmud, Dr. Syed, 376, 379

Majeed, Professor Abdul, 374

Majid, Sheikh Abdul, 179, 292, 383

Maleecha Pakistan, 277

Malihabad Railway Station, 56

Maliks, 261

Mamdot, Sir Shah Nawaz, 78

Mandal, Jogandra Nath, 236

Manifesto, 144, 157, 290

Maraikayar, Mohi-ud Din, 371

Mashraqi Day, 104

Mashraqi's sons, 31

Mashraqi's sons and daughters, 304

Mashriqi's family, 31

Masina, Dr. Dinsnaw, 359

Massacre, 33, 34, 75, 77, 78, 81, 84, 88, 89, 91, 107, 194, 201, 205, 221, 239, 241, 243, 251, 363, 366, 388

Maududi, Maulana Syed Abul Ala, 37

Maulvi Ka Ghalat Mazhab, 29

Maxwell, Sir Reginald, 96

Mazangavi, Rafiq Sabir, 161, 353, 354, 356, 357, 359, 360, 362, 363, 368

Meerza, Sir Syed Wasif Ali, 410

Mehdi, Maulana Zafar, 253

Meherally, Yusuf, 380

Member of the Punjab Legislative Assembly, 75

Members of First Legal Committee, 407

Members of Second Legal Committee, 409

Mians, 49

Migration, 29, 272, 294

Military, 34, 36, 43, 46, 48, 50, 51, 55, 63, 65, 74, 85, 94, 126, 158, 160, 164, 221, 280, 293, 403

Minto Park, 79, 82, 121

Mitha, Abdur Rehman, 155

Mitha, Muhammad Suleman Cassum, 379

Mobilization, 237

Mobilized, 31, 33, 149, 365

Mohani, Maulana Hasrat, 258

Momin Conference, 217, 378

Momin(s), 147, 190, 192, 204, 217, 377, 378, 405

Moonje, Dr., 204

Mountbatten Plan, 252, 255, 257, 258, 259, 261, 262, 278

Mountbatten, Lord Louis, 117, 243, 245, 247, 248, 249, 250, 251, 252, 253, 254, 255, 257, 258, 259, 261, 262, 263, 267, 268, 278, 280, 297

Mozang Branch, 353

Mudie, Sir Francis, 31, 103

Mughal Empire, 21, 24, 144

Mukerjit, S.P., 204

Munshi, K.M., 176

Murdabad, 81, 121, 256

Musalmans, 62, 63, 119, 193, 196, 197, 224, 247, 248, 260, 362, 363, 374, 387, 388

Muslim League, 7, 8, 21, 34, 35, 37, 53, 55, 57, 59, 60, 61, 64, 66, 67, 68, 69, 70, 71, 72, 73, 76, 77, 78, 79, 80, 81, 82, 83, 84, 85, 86, 87, 88, 89, 90, 91, 92, 93, 94, 95, 98, 99, 101, 103, 104, 105, 106, 107, 112, 114, 116, 117, 118, 119, 120, 122, 123, 128, 129, 131, 135, 137, 140, 142, 143, 144, 145, 146, 147, 151, 152, 153, 154, 157, 159, 161, 163, 164, 165, 167, 168, 170, 171, 172, 174, 175, 179, 181, 182, 185, 189, 190, 191, 192, 193, 196, 197, 201,

204, 206, 207, 208, 209, 213,
214, 215, 216, 217, 218, 220,
221, 223, 224, 227, 228, 229,
230, 234, 238, 239, 245, 246,
247, 252, 254, 255, 256, 257,
258, 262, 264, 266, 270, 271,
272, 275, 276, 278, 279, 284,
285, 288, 289, 290, 291, 292,
293, 295, 298, 299, 353, 356,
359, 360, 363, 364, 365, 366,
367, 368, 371, 372, 373, 374,
375, 376, 377, 379, 380, 381,
387, 388, 394, 396, 397, 407,
411
Muslim League National Guards,
95, 255, 256
Muslim Majlis, 157, 217, 290
Muslim-Hindu unity, 123, 135,
150, 151, 152, 153, 157, 167,
199, 220, 250
Mussalman(s), 33, 76, 100, 106,
132, 147, 166, 213, 214, 215,
216, 220, 234, 253, 291, 292,
355, 366, 367, 368, 375, 376,
378, 382, 383

N

Naib Salar, 84
Nami, Dr. Muhammad Ismail, 99,
100, 101, 102, 103
National Government, 118, 120,
121, 122, 123, 124, 126, 142
National Guards, 82, 258
Nationalist Muslim Parliamentary
Board, 291
Nationalist(s), 20, 117, 122, 123,
124, 133, 134, 145, 146, 147,
148, 157, 178, 179, 181, 182,
194, 195, 200, 211, 213, 214,
217, 220, 222, 246, 247, 252,
259, 260, 269, 270, 273, 276,
277, 278, 279, 283, 285, 286,
288, 291, 293, 295, 297, 299,
300, 371, 382
Nawab Bahadur of Murshidabad,
151, 410

Nawabs, 45, 49, 120, 216, 291,
292, 372, 374, 375, 376, 380,
381
Nawabzadas, 70
Nawai-waqat, 37
Nazi(s), 73, 96, 97, 98, 176
Nazimuddin, Khawaja, 37, 98, 293
Nehru, Pandit Jawaharlal, 58, 98,
112, 115, 124, 125, 127, 128,
129, 130, 131, 134, 135, 137,
139, 144, 192, 204, 232, 235,
236, 249, 251, 252, 266, 267,
291, 406
News Week, 255
Nishtar, Sardar Abdur Rab, 236,
251, 272

O

Orient Press, 161, 162, 165, 168
Ottoman Empire, 19, 29, 30, 147,
201, 262
Oudh, 49, 408

P

Pakistan Resolution, 87, 89, 107,
120, 122, 142, 145, 146, 148,
235, 256, 269, 285, 286, 287,
288, 294, 296
Pal, G.S., 204
Pant, Pandit Govind Vallabh, 58,
67, 68
Parade(s), 38, 43, 45, 46, 48, 220,
238, 242
Parliamentary Board, 209, 213,
216
Parsee(s), 27, 175, 205, 229, 386,
392, 402, 403, 405, 406
Parsi, 42, 116
Partnership, 103, 145
Patel, Sardar Vallabhbhai, 137,
249, 251, 266
Pathanistan, 262
Pathans, 262, 299
Patna, 220, 223, 247, 250, 410
Peerbhoy, Barrister Akbar A., 353
Pethick-Lawrence, 228

Piracha, Khan Bahadur Shaikh
Fazl-i-Haq, 55
Pirs, 49, 209
Playboys of British Imperialism,
383
Plunder, 241, 243, 298
Prasad, Rajendra, 137, 245
Prasad, Ramchandra, 205
Prediction(s), 121, 141, 241, 300
Premier of Bengal, 87, 223
Premier of Punjab, 285
Premier of Sind, 147, 284, 289,
379
Premiership, 28
President, 36, 37, 57, 59, 73, 84,
88, 119, 129, 136, 146, 147,
151, 182, 196, 200, 211, 217,
233, 244, 245, 251, 254, 258,
266, 289, 290, 304, 360, 373,
377, 378, 382, 383, 402, 403,
407, 408, 409
President Bihar Provincial Jamiat-
ul-Momineen, 290, 377
President of Indian Progressive
Group, 289
President of the Majlis-i-Ahrar-
Hind, 373
Prime Minister, 37, 61, 63, 83,
111, 117, 147, 189, 227, 231,
235, 238, 239, 241, 295, 304
Prime Minister of Pakistan, 37, 83
Princely State of Alwar, 28
Principal, 28, 33, 38, 407, 410
Prison, 32, 35, 36, 109, 179, 266,
267, 269, 276
Propaganda Secretary, 161, 353,
360, 364
Property confiscated, 100
Prophet Muhammad, 43, 44
Provincial Propaganda Boards,
167
Public outcry, 88, 89, 91, 107
Punishment(s), 28, 152, 299, 404
Punjab, 33, 34, 35, 51, 52, 55, 57,
58, 71, 72, 73, 74, 76, 77, 78,
79, 81, 84, 85, 89, 90, 91, 92,
93, 94, 95, 96, 98, 99, 100, 101,

102, 103, 104, 106, 145, 150,
151, 179, 190, 209, 213, 217,
218, 221, 222, 243, 244, 245,
246, 247, 249, 250, 252, 253,
254, 255, 258, 259, 261, 262,
269, 271, 272, 273, 277, 278,
279, 280, 284, 285, 292, 293,
295, 364, 365, 371, 372, 373,
374, 382, 410, 411
Punjab Assembly, 72, 92
Punjab Governor, 76
Punjabis, 299
Pyjama, 45

Q

Qadir, Colonel Ihsan, 237, 242
Qadir, Colonel Khan, 244
Qadir, Ghulam, 168
Qadri, Ghulam Mohy-ud-Din, 209
Qamarud Din, S., 409
Qayyum, Mir Abdul, 372
Quaid-e-Azam, 5, 8, 19, 20, 34,
57, 58, 59, 60, 61, 63, 64, 65,
66, 67, 68, 69, 70, 73, 74, 75,
76, 78, 79, 80, 81, 82, 83, 84,
85, 86, 87, 88, 89, 90, 91, 92,
93, 94, 95, 98, 99, 100, 101,
102, 103, 104, 105, 106, 114,
115, 119, 120, 121, 122, 123,
124, 125, 126, 127, 128, 130,
131, 132, 133, 134, 135, 136,
137, 139, 140, 141, 142, 143,
144, 146, 148, 153, 155, 156,
157, 161, 163, 165, 166, 168,
169, 170, 171, 172, 173, 174,
175, 177, 179, 180, 181, 182,
183, 184, 186, 187, 189, 190,
193, 194, 195, 199, 200, 204,
209, 210, 215, 216, 217, 220,
223, 224, 227, 230, 234, 235,
237, 238, 244, 246, 247, 249,
251, 252, 255, 257, 259, 261,
263, 267, 268, 269, 273, 274,
275, 280, 286, 287, 293, 295,
297, 299, 300, 353, 354, 355,
356, 357, 358, 359, 362, 363,

364, 365, 366, 367, 368, 369, 374, 382, 387, 388, 421
Quit India, 111, 231, 238, 241
Quit India Movement, 112, 136, 137, 139, 140, 141, 153
Quraishi, Nawab Makhdum Sir Murid Hussain, 410
Quran, 29, 42, 123, 160, 163, 164, 223, 291
Quran-i-Awwal, 42, 123
Qureshi, Abdul Rashed, 209
Qureshi, Abdur Rashid, 178

R

Radcliffe Award, 271, 272
Radcliffe, Lord Cyril, 271, 272, 280
Radical Democratic Party, 229
Rafiq, Mohamed, 355
Rafique, Dr., 173
Rafique, Professor, 174
Rahim, Professor Abdur, 256
Raja, 92, 204, 222, 408
Raja of Mahmoodabad, 193
Rajagopalachariar, Chakravarti, 117, 118, 120, 121, 122, 131, 132, 134, 135, 136, 137, 138, 162, 168, 169, 170, 177, 179
Rajas, 381
Rallia Ram, B.L., 408
Ramasami, E. V., 204
Ranchi Momin Conference, 377
Rangoon, 111
Rani of Mandi, 92
Rasikh, Mahmood, 354
Reader Members, 408, 410
Reading, Lord, 24
Red Shirts, 86
Release(d), 32, 33, 34, 35, 56, 58, 60, 61, 62, 63, 67, 68, 77, 78, 81, 86, 88, 89, 91, 93, 95, 98, 99, 100, 101, 102, 104, 105, 106, 109, 110, 111, 112, 116, 140, 149, 150, 154, 164, 165, 169, 177, 183, 185, 213, 261, 266, 267
Resignation, 67, 68, 135, 377

Ross-Keppel, Sir George, 28
Rowjee, I. M., 378
Royalty, 106

S

Sachhutanand, Swami, 204
Sadhus, 277
Sadick, Dr. Muhammad, 408
Sadiq, Dr. Mohammad, 354
Sadiq, Khawaja Ghulam, 409
Saeed, Muhammad, 45
Sahibs, 298
Salar(s), 46, 49, 84
Sambamurty, Bulusu, 137, 138, 407
Sandilivi, Chaudhri Nurul Hassan, 381
Sangh, Rashtrya Sevak, 277
Sapru, Sir Tej Bahadur, 184, 186, 205
Sarkar, N.R., 220
Satyagraha, 84
Savarkar, Veer D., 112, 114, 115, 204
Sayeds, 49
Scheduled Castes, 190, 248, 398, 403, 405, 406
Scheduled Classes, 192, 204
Scholar of the East, 35, 46, 97
Second Legal Committee, 188, 203, 204, 206, 406, 409
Secretary of State, 24, 78, 95, 98, 104, 114, 147, 158, 181, 207, 228, 285, 356
Secretary of the U.P. Muslim League, 60
Secularism, 293
Self-styled Muslim leaders, 373
Shah, Agha Ghazanfar Ali, 140, 409
Shah, Barrister Mian Ahmed, 31, 63, 67, 93, 98, 102, 103, 104, 408
Shah, Mir Hazrat, 409
Shahab, Qudrat Ullah, 304
Shaikh Mohammad Jan, Khan Bahadur, 288

Sharar, Muhammad Ibrahim, 408
Shariat, 298, 405
Sheoraj, R. B., 204
Shiah Muslims, 190, 192
Shiahs, 196, 405
Shia-Sunni, 55, 56, 57, 67, 69,
    145, 285
Shirwani, 268
Shop(s), 45, 84, 141, 243
Shujabadi, Qazi Ehsan Ahmed,
    194, 381
Shujra, Allah Dad, 409
Siddiqi, Abdur Rehman, 377, 378
Siddiqi, Malih Ahmed, 410
Siddiqui, A.H., 407
Sikh(s), 42, 49, 72, 116, 150, 151,
    160, 190, 192, 204, 217, 245,
    252, 254, 275, 386, 392, 402,
    403, 404, 405, 406
Simla, 95, 99, 100, 104, 190, 191,
    194, 208, 381, 391, 393
Simla Conference, 191, 194, 208,
    393
Sindhi, Maulana Obaidullah, 379
Sindhis, 299
Singapore, 111
Singh, Justice Sir Dalip, 409
Singh, Master Tara, 204
Singh, Saint Nihal, 410
Singh, Sardar Baldev, 236, 251,
    252
Singh, Sardar Labh, 410
Singh, Sardar Ujjal, 204
Singh, Sir Jogendra, 204
Singh, Sir Maharaj, 204, 205
Sirajhuddin, Abdul Samad, 220
Sitaramiyya, Pattabhi, 115, 133,
    134, 137, 192
Slogan(s), 78, 79, 80, 81, 82, 88,
    91, 107, 122, 145, 208, 211,
    212, 219, 220, 221, 222, 256,
    264, 287, 300, 363, 380, 388,
    394
Social service, 43, 46, 48, 74, 85,
    94, 110, 125, 126, 142, 150,
    151, 159, 160, 176, 353
Soldiers, 48, 113, 190, 205, 404

Son(s), 31, 32, 35, 52, 75, 111,
    128, 232, 266, 267, 291, 353
South India Liberation Federation
    (Justice Party), 229
Speaker National Assembly, 304
Srinivasan, K., 118, 120
Stephenson, H.S., 96
Strike(rs), 44, 231, 358
Subjects Committee, 80, 82, 83,
    90
Suhrawardy, 250
Sunni Muslims, 190, 192, 204
Sunnis, 55, 405
Syed, G.M., 168
Syed, Maulana Moulvi
    Mohammad, 288

T

Talpurs, 49
Tameer, 37
Tazkirah, 29, 30, 38, 97
Tear-gas(ed), 32, 52, 75, 81, 84,
    257, 265
Telegram(s), 24, 62, 64, 65, 68,
    73, 74, 93, 95, 98, 99, 100, 104,
    110, 111, 112, 114, 115, 116,
    120, 121, 122, 123, 124, 125,
    126, 127, 128, 129, 130, 131,
    132, 134, 137, 138, 139, 147,
    151, 155, 156, 157, 164, 165,
    166, 172, 174, 175, 183, 184,
    185, 192, 193, 195, 230, 253,
    267, 356, 357, 365, 385, 386,
    387
Thanksgiving, 150
The Christian Science Monitor, 50
The Constitution of Free India,
    1946 A.C., 184, 185, 188, 190,
    203, 204, 205, 206, 207, 209,
    210, 211, 216, 218, 224, 250,
    391, 398, 406, 407, 409
The High Court of Judicature at
    Bombay, 357
The Radiance, 41, 109, 112, 114,
    115, 116, 118, 120, 121, 122,
    123, 124, 125, 126, 127, 128,
    130, 131, 132, 133, 134, 135,

136, 137, 138, 139, 152, 162,
164, 385, 386
The Scotsman of Edinburgh, 50,
51
Thomson, Edward, 292
Thousand Lights, Madras, 135
Title of Sir, 22, 147
Tiwana, Malik Khizar Hayat, 227
Tottenham, Sir Richard, 151, 158,
159, 163, 164
Traffic, 84
Transfer of power, 154, 155, 238,
239, 242, 247, 248, 254, 257,
258, 268
Truncated Pakistan, 232, 233, 246,
255, 256, 257, 260, 269, 273,
278
Two-Nation Theory, 144, 147,
151, 273, 279, 285, 286, 287,
288, 291, 293, 294, 295, 296,
297, 300, 382

U

U.P. Muslim League Council, 59
Under Secretary, 28, 38
Uniform(s), 43, 46, 48, 55, 74, 84,
97, 98, 151, 158, 160
Unionists, 86, 224, 372
University of Cambridge, 28
Untouchable, 42, 116, 398
Urdu, 23, 43, 197, 241, 276, 355,
359

V

Vakil, 27
Vellore Jail, 32, 109, 117, 177
Verma, Professor B.D., 408
Vice Chancellor of Aligarh, 219
Vice Principal, 28
Viceroy, 24, 57, 58, 59, 60, 65, 67,
68, 71, 73, 75, 78, 82, 85, 89,
93, 95, 96, 97, 98, 99, 100, 101,
102, 103, 104, 111, 112, 114,
145, 146, 147, 149, 155, 156,
157, 161, 162, 166, 174, 183,
185, 187, 189, 190, 192, 193,
194, 203, 206, 207, 209, 210,
235, 236, 243, 246, 249, 250,
251, 252, 254, 255, 257, 263,
268, 285, 286, 287, 293, 297,
356, 363, 365, 377, 387, 388
Viceroy of India, 24, 57, 59, 65,
67, 71, 73, 78, 82, 93, 95, 96,
100, 114, 174, 203, 206, 207,
268, 356
Volunteer Corps, 95

W

Wardha, 129, 133, 134, 138
Wavell, 166, 167, 168, 174, 180,
183, 185, 189, 190, 191, 193,
194, 195, 200, 203, 206, 207,
208, 209, 228, 229, 232, 233,
236, 243, 393, 401, 402
Wavell Plan, 189, 191, 194
Western India, 253
Western trade, 232
Where Leaders Fail, 8, 391
Working Committee, 51, 72, 73,
75, 88, 89, 98, 99, 119, 120,
131, 134, 136, 137, 141, 143,
145, 146, 169, 170, 179, 193,
196, 214, 272, 285, 291, 376,
377, 378
World War II, 52, 67, 71, 111,
116, 134, 139, 141, 145, 189,
278, 286
WWII, 295

Y

Yaqub, Syed Ahmed Syed, 357,
359
Yezdani, Dr. M.A. Latif, 222
Yogies, 277
Young, Sir Douglas, 87, 95

Z

Zaheer, Barrister Syed Ali, 146,
182, 382, 383
Zahir, Syed Sajjad, 375
Zahiruddin, Mauvli, 204

Zahir-ud-Din, Shiakh Mohammad, 147
Zauqi, 104
Zetland, Lord, 78, 145, 260, 287

Zia ud Din, Dr. Sir, 59, 61, 62, 63, 75, 97, 102, 237, 407
Zindabad, 80, 121, 255, 256
Zira, 271

God bless the people of
Pakistan